LLEWELLYN'S

2·0·2·2

ASTROLOGICAL

POCKET PLANNER

Daily Ephemeris & Aspectarian
2021–2023

Cover design by Shannon McKuhen
Edited by Hanna Grimson

A special thanks to Beth Rosato for astrological proofreading.

Astrological calculations compiled and programmed by Rique Pottenger based on
the earlier work of Neil F. Michelsen. Reuse is prohibited.

Published by
LLEWELLYN WORLDWIDE LTD.
2143 Wooddale Drive
Woodbury, MN 55125-2989
www.llewellyn.com

Printed in the United States of America

Table of Contents

Mercury Retrograde and Moon Void-of-Course / 3
How to Use the *Pocket Planner* / 5
Symbol Key / 6
World Map of Time Zones / 7
Time Zone Conversions / 8
Planetary Stations for 2022 / 9
2022 Week-at-a-Glance Calendar Pages / 10
2021–2023 Aspectarian and Ephemeris / 118

Mercury Retrograde 2022

	DATE	ET	PT			DATE	ET	PT
Mercury Retrograde	1/14	**6:41 am**	3:41 am	—	Mercury Direct	2/3	**11:13 pm**	8:13 pm
Mercury Retrograde	5/10	**7:47 am**	4:47 am	—	Mercury Direct	6/3	**4:00 am**	1:00 am
Mercury Retrograde	9/9	**11:38 pm**	8:38 pm	—	Mercury Direct	10/2	**5:07 am**	2:07 am
Mercury Retrograde	12/29	**4:32 am**	1:32 pm	—	Mercury Direct	1/18/23	**8:12 am**	5:12 am

Moon Void-of-Course 2022

Times are listed in Eastern Time in this table only. All other information in the *Pocket Planner* is listed in both Eastern time and Pacific time. Refer to "Time Zone Conversions" on page 8 for changing to other time zones. Note: All times are corrected for Daylight Saving Time.

Last Aspect		Moon Enters New Sign			Last Aspect		Moon Enters New Sign			Last Aspect		Moon Enters New Sign		
Date	Time	Date	Sign	Time	Date	Time	Date	Sign	Time	Date	Time	Date	Sign	Time
JANUARY					**FEBRUARY**					**MARCH**				
1	3:16 am	1	♑	6:02 pm	1	6:01 am	2	♓	6:00 am	2/28	9:01 pm	1	♓	3:53 pm
3	11:21 am	3	♒	5:44 pm	4	4:41 am	4	♈	9:57 am	3	4:45 pm	3	♈	7:52 pm
4	7:45 pm	5	♓	7:17 pm	6	12:21 pm	6	♉	5:52 pm	5	11:02 pm	6	♉	3:00 am
7	5:23 pm	8	♈	12:26 am	8	11:48 pm	9	♊	5:27 am	8	9:35 am	8	♊	1:40 pm
10	2:23 am	10	♉	9:47 am	11	3:23 am	11	♋	6:27 pm	10	11:43 am	11	♋	2:24 am
12	2:39 pm	12	♊	10:08 pm	14	5:27 am	14	♌	6:17 am	13	11:44 am	13	♌	3:32 pm
14	9:22 pm	15	♋	11:11 am	16	11:56 am	16	♍	3:42 pm	15	6:56 am	16	♍	12:59 am
17	6:48 pm	17	♌	11:03 pm	18	6:20 pm	18	♎	10:51 pm	18	4:11 am	18	♎	7:26 am
20	3:15 am	20	♍	9:02 am	21	12:02 am	21	♏	4:19 am	20	8:40 am	20	♏	11:45 am
22	2:46 pm	22	♎	5:03 pm	23	4:24 am	23	♐	8:29 am	22	12:01 pm	22	♐	2:59 pm
24	5:10 pm	24	♏	10:57 pm	25	10:24 pm	25	♑	11:27 am	24	8:59 am	24	♑	5:54 pm
27	12:28 am	27	♐	2:34 am	27	9:49 am	27	♒	1:36 am	26	7:51 pm	28	♒	8:55 pm
28	2:00 pm	29	♑	4:09 am	28	9:01 pm	3/1	♓	3:53 pm	28	10:11 am	29	♓	12:32 am
30	11:44 pm	31	♒	4:43 am						31	2:37 am	31	♈	5:30 am

Moon Void-of-Course 2022 (cont.)

APRIL

Last Aspect Date	Time	Moon Enters New Sign Date	Sign	Time
2	9:51 am	2	♉	12:50 pm
4	9:53 pm	4	♊	11:04 pm
6	11:15 pm	7	♋	11:30 am
9	9:01 pm	10	♌	12:00 am
12	6:16 am	12	♍	10:07 am
14	2:11 pm	14	♎	4:46 pm
16	5:57 pm	16	♏	8:23 pm
18	7:55 pm	18	♐	10:16 pm
20	4:56 pm	20	♑	11:52 pm
22	11:53 pm	23	♒	2:17 am
24	8:33 pm	25	♓	6:15 am
27	9:36 am	27	♈	12:10 pm
29	5:38 pm	29	♉	8:19 pm

MAY

Last Aspect Date	Time	Moon Enters New Sign Date	Sign	Time
2	6:13 am	2	♊	6:47 am
4	4:37 pm	4	♋	7:05 pm
7	6:26 am	7	♌	7:50 am
9	8:39 am	9	♍	6:53 pm
12	12:00 am	12	♎	2:34 am
14	4:07 am	14	♏	6:34 am
16	5:28 am	16	♐	7:50 am
17	11:59 pm	18	♑	8:02 am
20	8:00 am	20	♒	8:53 am
22	3:19 am	22	♓	11:49 am
24	5:33 pm	24	♈	5:39 pm
26	11:20 pm	27	♉	2:22 am
29	10:11 am	29	♊	1:23 pm
31	4:10 pm	6/1	♋	1:49 am

JUNE

Last Aspect Date	Time	Moon Enters New Sign Date	Sign	Time
5/31	4:10 pm	1	♋	1:49 am
3	11:15 am	3	♌	2:38 pm
5	7:12 pm	6	♍	2:22 am
8	8:09 am	8	♎	11:23 am
10	1:36 pm	10	♏	4:41 pm
12	5:40 pm	12	♐	6:31 pm
14	10:58 am	14	♑	6:14 pm
16	2:41 pm	16	♒	5:44 pm
18	2:50 pm	18	♓	7:01 pm
20	11:11 pm	20	♈	11:37 pm
23	4:02 am	23	♉	7:58 am
25	3:02 pm	25	♊	7:13 pm
27	10:38 pm	28	♋	7:53 am
30	4:14 pm	30	♌	8:40 pm

JULY

Last Aspect Date	Time	Moon Enters New Sign Date	Sign	Time
3	5:59 am	3	♍	8:31 am
5	2:04 pm	5	♎	6:25 pm
7	9:04 pm	8	♏	1:15 am
10	12:34 am	10	♐	4:34 am
11	9:42 pm	12	♑	5:01 am
14	12:17 am	14	♒	4:13 am
16	12:36 am	16	♓	4:18 am
18	2:43 am	18	♈	7:17 am
20	10:19 am	20	♉	2:23 pm
22	7:45 pm	23	♊	1:11 am
25	4:14 am	25	♋	1:54 pm
27	8:54 pm	28	♌	2:36 am
30	12:29 am	30	♍	2:11 pm

AUGUST

Last Aspect Date	Time	Moon Enters New Sign Date	Sign	Time
1	6:29 pm	2	♎	12:06 am
4	2:20 am	4	♏	7:47 am
6	7:24 am	6	♐	12:39 pm
8	6:30 am	8	♑	2:39 pm
10	12:39 pm	10	♒	2:45 pm
12	7:07 am	12	♓	2:44 pm
14	11:11 am	14	♈	4:43 pm
16	4:18 pm	16	♉	10:22 pm
19	7:06 am	19	♊	8:06 am
21	6:06 pm	21	♋	8:29 pm
24	5:40 am	24	♌	9:09 am
26	2:55 am	26	♍	8:25 pm
28	11:08 pm	29	♎	5:45 am
31	6:43 am	31	♏	1:11 pm

SEPTEMBER

Last Aspect Date	Time	Moon Enters New Sign Date	Sign	Time
2	1:22 pm	2	♐	6:39 pm
4	9:51 pm	4	♑	10:03 pm
6	5:43 pm	6	♒	11:41 pm
8	8:34 am	9	♓	12:42 am
10	8:29 pm	11	♈	2:47 am
12	12:53 am	13	♉	7:39 am
15	8:59 am	15	♊	4:16 pm
17	5:52 pm	18	♋	3:59 am
20	11:57 am	20	♌	4:38 pm
22	7:07 am	23	♍	3:53 am
25	8:49 am	25	♎	12:43 pm
27	12:21 pm	27	♏	7:15 pm
29	5:20 pm	30	♐	12:03 am

OCTOBER

Last Aspect Date	Time	Moon Enters New Sign Date	Sign	Time
1	5:46 pm	2	♑	3:38 am
3	11:49 pm	4	♒	6:20 am
6	6:46 pm	6	♓	8:47 am
8	7:10 am	8	♈	11:57 am
10	10:02 am	10	♉	5:04 pm
12	5:42 pm	13	♊	1:08 am
15	12:11 am	15	♋	12:11 pm
17	4:56 pm	18	♌	12:45 am
20	6:35 am	20	♍	12:25 pm
22	2:17 pm	22	♎	9:24 pm
24	8:36 pm	25	♏	3:18 am
27	12:27 am	27	♐	6:55 am
29	9:10 am	29	♑	9:21 am
31	11:14 am	31	♒	11:43 am

NOVEMBER

Last Aspect Date	Time	Moon Enters New Sign Date	Sign	Time
2	7:08 am	2	♓	2:46 am
4	6:05 pm	4	♈	7:07 pm
6	5:30 pm	7	♉	12:15 am
9	7:00 am	9	♊	8:37 am
11	5:28 pm	11	♋	7:22 pm
14	5:41 am	14	♌	7:48 am
16	6:55 pm	16	♍	8:04 pm
19	3:47 am	19	♎	5:58 am
21	6:14 am	21	♏	12:16 pm
23	1:16 pm	23	♐	3:16 pm
25	2:22 pm	25	♑	4:18 pm
27	3:11 pm	27	♒	5:07 pm
29	1:53 am	29	♓	7:15 pm

DECEMBER

Last Aspect Date	Time	Moon Enters New Sign Date	Sign	Time
1	9:44 am	1	♈	11:41 pm
4	12:46 am	4	♉	6:38 am
6	2:02 pm	6	♊	3:49 pm
9	1:13 am	9	♋	2:49 am
11	1:49 pm	11	♌	3:09 pm
13	10:52 am	14	♍	3:45 am
16	2:13 pm	16	♎	2:49 pm
18	5:35 pm	18	♏	10:31 pm
20	9:45 pm	21	♐	2:12 am
22	3:16 pm	23	♑	2:49 am
24	10:11 pm	25	♒	2:14 am
26	1:19 pm	27	♓	2:34 am
29	1:21 am	29	♈	5:36 am
31	7:44 am	31	♉	12:08 pm

How to Use the *Pocket Planner*

by Leslie Nielsen

This handy guide contains information that can be most valuable to you as you plan your daily activities. As you read through the first few pages, you can start to get a feel for how well organized this guide is.

Read the Symbol Key on the next page, which is rather like astrological shorthand. The characteristics of the planets can give you direction in planning your strategies. Much like traffic signs that signal "go," "stop," or even "caution," you can determine for yourself the most propitious time to get things done.

You'll find tables that show the dates when Mercury is retrograde (℞) or direct (D). Because Mercury deals with the exchange of information, a retrograde Mercury makes miscommunication more noticeable.

There's also a section dedicated to the times when the Moon is void-of-course (V/C). These are generally poor times to conduct business because activities begun during these times usually end badly or fail to get started. If you make an appointment during a void-of-course, you might save yourself a lot of aggravation by confirming the time and date later. The Moon is only void-of-course for 7 percent of the time when business is usually conducted during a normal workday (that is, 8:00 am to 5:00 pm). Sometimes, by waiting a matter of minutes or a few hours until the Moon has left the void-of-course phase, you have a much better chance to make action move more smoothly. Moon voids can also be used successfully to do routine activities or inner work, such as dream therapy or personal contemplation.

You'll find Moon phases, as well as each of the Moon's entries into a new sign. Times are expressed in Eastern time (in bold type) and Pacific time (in regular type). The New Moon time is generally best for beginning new activities, as the Moon is increasing in light and can offer the element of growth to our endeavors. When the Moon is Full, its illumination is greatest and we can see the results of our efforts. When it moves from the Full stage back to the New stage, it can best be used to reflect on our projects. If necessary, we can make corrections at the New Moon.

The section of "Planetary Stations" on page 9 will give you the times when the planets are changing signs or direction, thereby affording us opportunities for new starts.

The ephemeris in the back of your *Pocket Planner* can be very helpful to you. As you start to work with the ephemeris, you may notice that not all planets seem to be comfortable in every sign. Think of the planets as actors and the signs as the costumes they wear. Sometimes, costumes just itch. If you find this to be so for a certain time period, you may choose to delay your plans for a time or be more creative with the energies at hand.

As you turn to the daily pages, you'll find information about the Moon's sign, phase, and the time it changes phase. You'll find icons indicating the best days to plant and fish. Also, you will find times and dates when the planets and asteroids change signs and go either retrograde or direct, major holidays, a three-month calendar, and room to record your appointments.

This guide is a powerful tool. Make the most of it!

Symbol Key

Planets:	☉ Sun	⚳ Ceres	♄ Saturn
	☽ Moon	⚴ Pallas	⚷ Chiron
	☿ Mercury	⚵ Juno	♅ Uranus
	♀ Venus	⚶ Vesta	♆ Neptune
	♂ Mars	♃ Jupiter	♇ Pluto
Signs:	♈ Aries	♌ Leo	♐ Sagittarius
	♉ Taurus	♍ Virgo	♑ Capricorn
	♊ Gemini	♎ Libra	♒ Aquarius
	♋ Cancer	♏ Scorpio	♓ Pisces
Aspects:	♂ Conjunction (0°)	⚺ Semisextile (30°)	✶ Sextile (60°)
	☐ Square (90°)	△ Trine (120°)	
	⚻ Quincunx (150°)	☍ Opposition (180°)	
Motion:	℞ Retrograde	D Direct	

Best Days for Planting: 🌱   Best Days for Fishing: 🐟

World Map of Time Zones

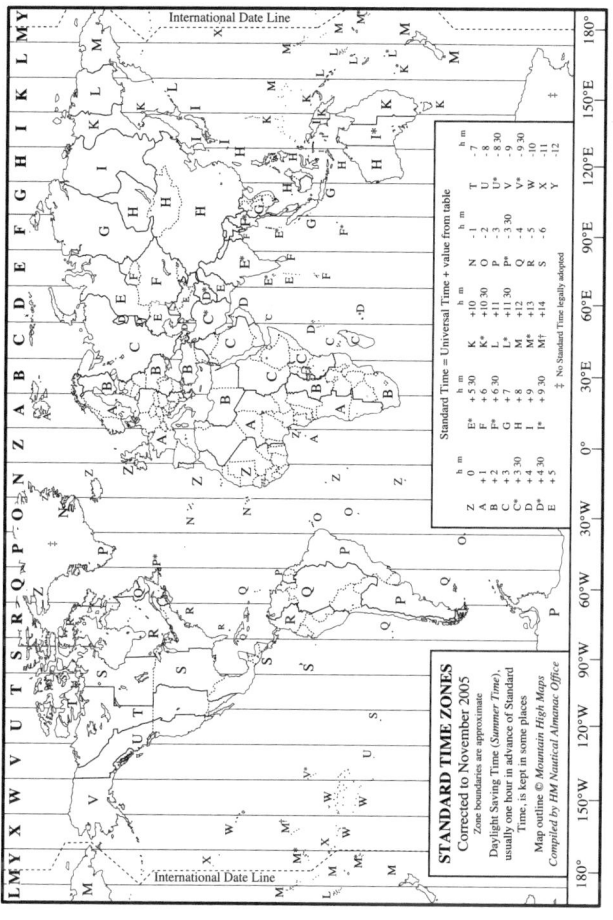

International Date Line

Standard Time = Universal Time + value from table

	h m			h m
Z	0		K	+10
A	+1		K*	+10.30
B	+2		L	+11
C	+3		L*	+11.30
C*	+3.30		M	+12
D	+4		M*	+13
D*	+4.30		M‡	+14
E	+5			
E*	+5.30		N	−1
F	+6		O	−2
F*	+6.30		P	−3
G	+7		P*	−3.30
H	+8		Q	−4
I	+9		R	−5
I*	+9.30		S	−6
			T	−7
			U	−8
			U*	−8.30
			V	−9
			V*	−9.30
			W	−10
			X	−11
			Y	−12

‡ No Standard Time legally adopted

STANDARD TIME ZONES
Corrected to November 2005
Zone boundaries are approximate
Daylight Saving Time (*Summer Time*),
usually one hour in advance of Standard
Time, is kept in some places
Map outline © Mountain High Maps
Compiled by HM Nautical Almanac Office

Time Zone Conversions

World Time Zones
Compared to Eastern Standard Time

( ) From Map	(Y) Subtract 7 hours	(C*) Add 8.5 hours
(S) CST/Subtract 1 hour	(A) Add 6 hours	(D*) Add 9.5 hours
(R) EST	(B) Add 7 hours	(E*) Add 10.5 hours
(Q) Add 1 hour	(C) Add 8 hours	(F*) Add 11.5 hours
(P) Add 2 hours	(D) Add 9 hours	(I*) Add 14.5 hours
(O) Add 3 hours	(E) Add 10 hours	(K*) Add 15.5 hours
(N) Add 4 hours	(F) Add 11 hours	(L*) Add 16.5 hours
(Z) Add 5 hours	(G) Add 12 hours	(M*) Add 18 hours
(T) MST/Subtract 2 hours	(H) Add 13 hours	(P*) Add 2.5 hours
(U) PST/Subtract 3 hours	(I) Add 14 hours	(U*) Subtract 3.5 hours
(V) Subtract 4 hours	(K) Add 15 hours	(V*) Subtract 4.5 hours
(W) Subtract 5 hours	(L) Add 16 hours	
(X) Subtract 6 hours	(M) Add 17 hours	

World Map of Time Zones is supplied by HM Nautical Almanac Office © Center for the Central Laboratory of the Research Councils. Note: This is not an official map. Countries change their time zones as they wish.

Planetary Stations for 2022

	JAN	FEB	MAR	APR	MAY	JUN	JUL	AUG	SEP	OCT	NOV	DEC
☿	1/14–2/3				5/10–6/3				9/9–10/2			12/29–
♀	–1/29											
♂										10/30–1/12/23		
♃								7/28–11/23				
♄	–1/18						6/4–10/23					
♅								8/19–1/18/22				
♆						6/28–12/3						
♇						4/29–10/8						
⚷							7/19–12/19					
♈	–1/14											
◇								11/30–2/16				
✳							7/25–10/23					
⟫						7/7–10/5						

9

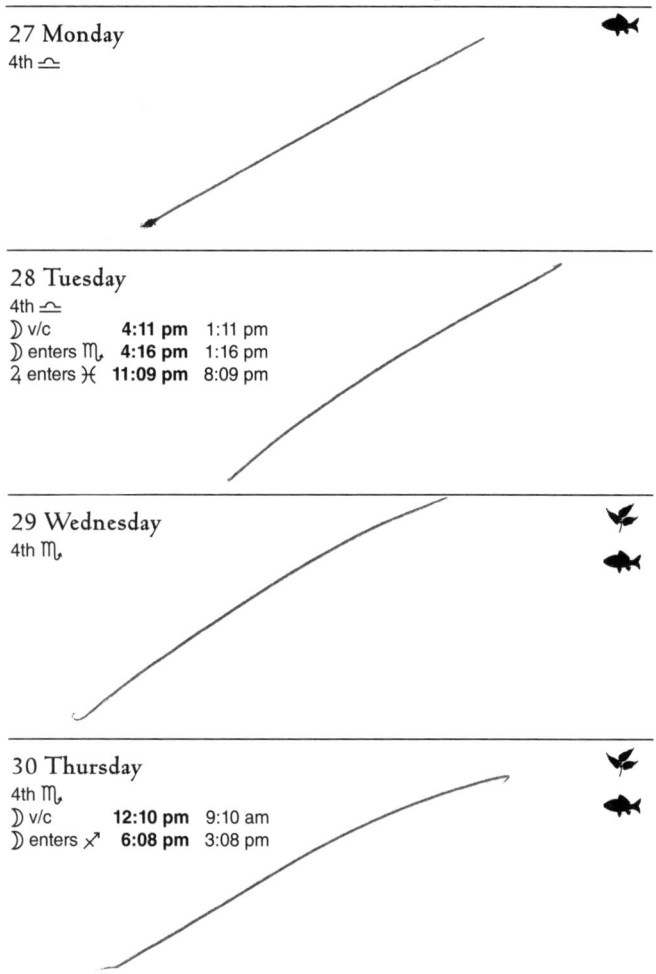

27 Monday
4th ♎

28 Tuesday
4th ♎
☽ v/c   **4:11 pm**   1:11 pm
☽ enters ♏   **4:16 pm**   1:16 pm
♃ enters ♓   **11:09 pm**   8:09 pm

29 Wednesday
4th ♏

30 Thursday
4th ♏
☽ v/c   **12:10 pm**   9:10 am
☽ enters ♐   **6:08 pm**   3:08 pm

31 Friday
4th ♐

New Year's Eve

1 Saturday
4th ♐

☽ v/c	**3:16 am**	12:16 am
☽ enters ♑	**6:02 pm**	3:02 pm
☿ enters ♒		11:10 pm

New Year's Day • Kwanzaa ends

2 Sunday
4th ♑

| ☿ enters ♒ | **2:10 am** | |
| New Moon | **1:33 pm** | 10:33 am |

December 2021							January 2022							February 2022						
S	M	T	W	T	F	S	S	M	T	W	T	F	S	S	M	T	W	T	F	S
			1	2	3	4							1			1	2	3	4	5
5	6	7	8	9	10	11	2	3	4	5	6	7	8	6	7	8	9	10	11	12
12	13	14	15	16	17	18	9	10	11	12	13	14	15	13	14	15	16	17	18	19
19	20	21	22	23	24	25	16	17	18	19	20	21	22	20	21	22	23	24	25	26
26	27	28	29	30	31		23	24	25	26	27	28	29	27	28					
							30	31												

Eastern time in bold type
Pacific time in medium type

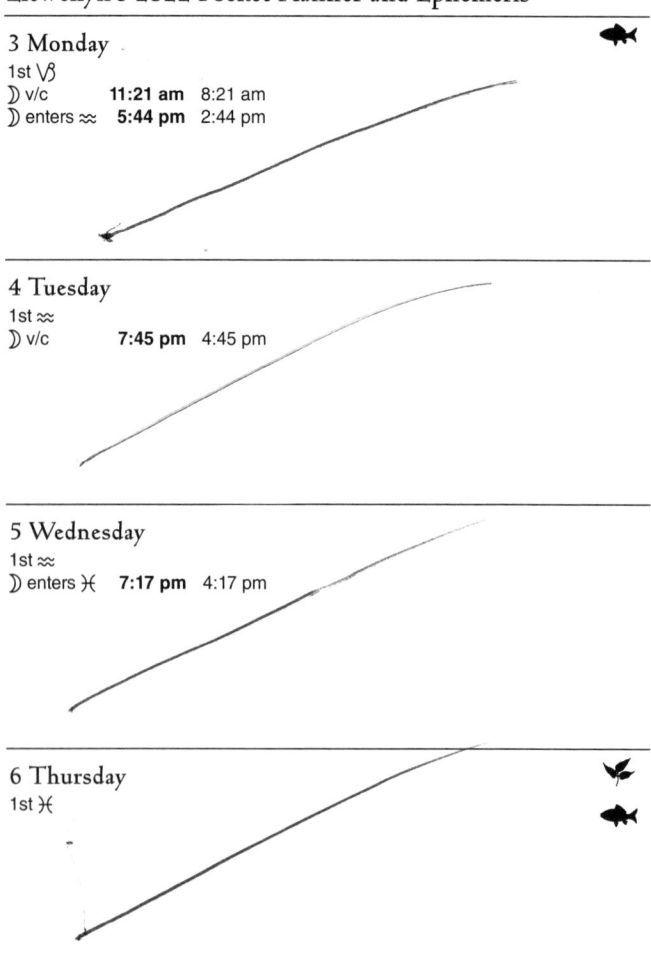

3 Monday

1st ♑
☽ v/c   **11:21 am**   8:21 am
☽ enters ♒   **5:44 pm**   2:44 pm

4 Tuesday

1st ♒
☽ v/c   **7:45 pm**   4:45 pm

5 Wednesday

1st ♒
☽ enters ♓   **7:17 pm**   4:17 pm

6 Thursday

1st ♓

Eastern time in bold type
Pacific time in medium type

7 Friday

1st ♓
☽ v/c   **5:23 pm**   2:23 pm
☽ enters ♈   9:26 pm

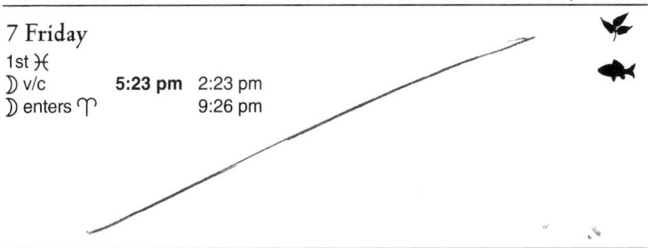

8 Saturday

1st ♓
☽ enters ♈ **12:26 am**

9 Sunday

1st ♈
2nd Quarter **1:11 pm** 10:11 am
☽ v/c   11:23 pm

December 2021						
S	M	T	W	T	F	S
			1	2	3	4
5	6	7	8	9	10	11
12	13	14	15	16	17	18
19	20	21	22	23	24	25
26	27	28	29	30	31	

January 2022						
S	M	T	W	T	F	S
						1
2	3	4	5	6	7	8
9	10	11	12	13	14	15
16	17	18	19	20	21	22
23	24	25	26	27	28	29
30	31					

February 2022						
S	M	T	W	T	F	S
		1	2	3	4	5
6	7	8	9	10	11	12
13	14	15	16	17	18	19
20	21	22	23	24	25	26
27	28					

Eastern time in bold type
Pacific time in medium type

10 Monday

2nd ♈
☽ v/c   **2:23 am**
☽ enters ♉   **9:47 am**   6:47 am
⚷ enters ♑   9:19 pm

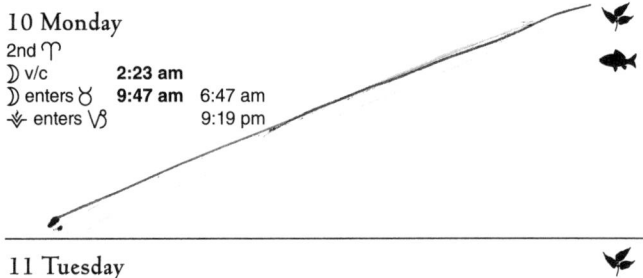

11 Tuesday

2nd ♉
⚷ enters ♑ **12:19 am**

12 Wednesday

2nd ♉
☽ v/c   **2:39 pm**   11:39 am
☽ enters ♊ **10:08 pm**   7:08 pm

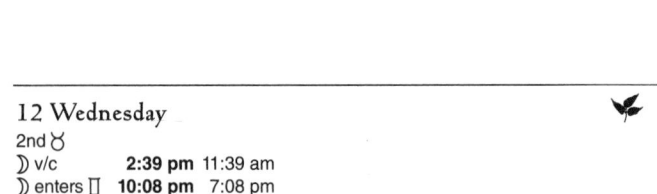

13 Thursday

2nd ♊

Eastern time in bold type
Pacific time in medium type

14 Friday

2nd ♊
☿ Rx **6:41 am** 3:41 am
♃ D **4:20 pm** 1:20 pm
☽ v/c **9:22 pm** 6:22 pm

Mercury retrograde until 2/3

15 Saturday

2nd ♊
☽ enters ♋ **11:11 am** 8:11 am

12:30 MST
Tarot 101: WTF is Tarot

16 Sunday

2nd ♋

December 2021						
S	M	T	W	T	F	S
			1	2	3	4
5	6	7	8	9	10	11
12	13	14	15	16	17	18
19	20	21	22	23	24	25
26	27	28	29	30	31	

January 2022						
S	M	T	W	T	F	S
						1
2	3	4	5	6	7	8
9	10	11	12	13	14	15
16	17	18	19	20	21	22
23	24	25	26	27	28	29
30	31					

February 2022						
S	M	T	W	T	F	S
		1	2	3	4	5
6	7	8	9	10	11	12
13	14	15	16	17	18	19
20	21	22	23	24	25	26
27	28					

Eastern time in bold type
Pacific time in medium type

17 Monday

2nd ♋

☽ v/c	**6:48 pm**	3:48 pm
Full Moon	**6:48 pm**	3:48 pm
☽ enters ♌	**11:03 pm**	8:03 pm

Martin Luther King Jr. Day

18 Tuesday

3rd ♌

♅ D	**10:27 am**	7:27 am

19 Wednesday

3rd ♌

☉ enters ≈	**9:39 pm**	6:39 pm

Sun enters Aquarius

20 Thursday

3rd ♌

☽ v/c	**3:15 am**	12:15 am
☽ enters ♍	**9:02 am**	6:02 am

Eastern time in bold type
Pacific time in medium type

21 Friday
3rd ♍

22 Saturday
3rd ♍
☽ v/c   **2:46 pm** 11:46 am
☽ enters ♎   **5:03 pm** 2:03 pm

23 Sunday
3rd ♎

December 2021						
S	M	T	W	T	F	S
			1	2	3	4
5	6	7	8	9	10	11
12	13	14	15	16	17	18
19	20	21	22	23	24	25
26	27	28	29	30	31	

January 2022						
S	M	T	W	T	F	S
						1
2	3	4	5	6	7	8
9	10	11	12	13	14	15
16	17	18	19	20	21	22
23	24	25	26	27	28	29
30	31					

February 2022						
S	M	T	W	T	F	S
		1	2	3	4	5
6	7	8	9	10	11	12
13	14	15	16	17	18	19
20	21	22	23	24	25	26
27	28					

Eastern time in bold type
Pacific time in medium type

24 Monday

3rd ♎︎
♂ enters ♑ **7:53 am** 4:53 am
☽ v/c   **5:10 pm** 2:10 pm
☽ enters ♏︎ **10:57 pm** 7:57 pm

25 Tuesday

3rd ♏︎
4th Quarter **8:41 am** 5:41 am
☿ enters ♑ **10:05 pm** 7:05 pm

26 Wednesday

4th ♏︎
☽ v/c   9:28 pm
☽ enters ♐   11:34 pm

27 Thursday

4th ♏︎
☽ v/c   **12:28 am**
☽ enters ♐   **2:34 am**

28 Friday
4th ♐
☽ v/c   **2:00 pm** 11:00 am

29 Saturday

4th ♐
♀ D   **3:46 am** 12:46 am
☽ enters ♑   **4:09 am** 1:09 am

30 Sunday
4th ♑
☽ v/c   **11:44 pm** 8:44 pm

December 2021						
S	M	T	W	T	F	S
			1	2	3	4
5	6	7	8	9	10	11
12	13	14	15	16	17	18
19	20	21	22	23	24	25
26	27	28	29	30	31	

January 2022						
S	M	T	W	T	F	S
						1
2	3	4	5	6	7	8
9	10	11	12	13	14	15
16	17	18	19	20	21	22
23	24	25	26	27	28	29
30	31					

February 2022						
S	M	T	W	T	F	S
		1	2	3	4	5
6	7	8	9	10	11	12
13	14	15	16	17	18	19
20	21	22	23	24	25	26
27	28					

Eastern time in bold type
Pacific time in medium type

31 Monday

4th ♑
☽ enters ≈ **4:43 am** 1:43 am
New Moon 9:46 pm

1 Tuesday

4th ≈
New Moon **12:46 am**
☽ v/c **6:01 am** 3:01 am
☿ enters ≈ **6:04 pm** 3:04 pm

Lunar New Year (Tiger)

2 Wednesday

1st ≈
☽ enters ♓ **6:00 am** 3:00 am

Imbolc • Groundhog Day

3 Thursday

1st ♓
☿ D **11:13 pm** 8:13 pm

Eastern time in bold type
Pacific time in medium type

4 Friday

1st ♓

☽ v/c	**4:41 am**	1:41 am
☽ enters ♈	**9:57 am**	6:57 am

5 Saturday

1st ♈

6 Sunday

1st ♈

☽ v/c	**12:21 pm**	9:21 am
☽ enters ♉	**5:52 pm**	2:52 pm

January 2022						
S	M	T	W	T	F	S
						1
2	3	4	5	6	7	8
9	10	11	12	13	14	15
16	17	18	19	20	21	22
23	24	25	26	27	28	29
30	31					

February 2022						
S	M	T	W	T	F	S
		1	2	3	4	5
6	7	8	9	10	11	12
13	14	15	16	17	18	19
20	21	22	23	24	25	26
27	28					

March 2022						
S	M	T	W	T	F	S
		1	2	3	4	5
6	7	8	9	10	11	12
13	14	15	16	17	18	19
20	21	22	23	24	25	26
27	28	29	30	31		

Eastern time in bold type
Pacific time in medium type

7 Monday

1st ♉

8 Tuesday

1st ♉
2nd Quarter **8:50 am** 5:50 am
♃ enters ♊ **9:13 pm** 6:13 pm
☽ v/c **11:48 pm** 8:48 pm

9 Wednesday

2nd ♉
☽ enters ♊ **5:27 am** 2:27 am

10 Thursday

2nd ♊

Eastern time in bold type
Pacific time in medium type

11 Friday

2nd ♊
☽ v/c   **3:23 am** 12:23 am
☽ enters ♋   **6:27 pm** 3:27 pm

12 Saturday

2nd ♋

13 Sunday

2nd ♋
♀ enters ♈   9:53 pm

January 2022						
S	M	T	W	T	F	S
						1
2	3	4	5	6	7	8
9	10	11	12	13	14	15
16	17	18	19	20	21	22
23	24	25	26	27	28	29
30	31					

February 2022						
S	M	T	W	T	F	S
		1	2	3	4	5
6	7	8	9	10	11	12
13	14	15	16	17	18	19
20	21	22	23	24	25	26
27	28					

March 2022						
S	M	T	W	T	F	S
		1	2	3	4	5
6	7	8	9	10	11	12
13	14	15	16	17	18	19
20	21	22	23	24	25	26
27	28	29	30	31		

14 Monday

2nd ♋
♀ enters ♈ **12:53 am**
☽ v/c   **5:27 am**   2:27 am
☽ enters ♌ **6:17 am**   3:17 am
☿ enters ♒ **4:54 pm**   1:54 pm

Valentine's Day

15 Tuesday

2nd ♌

16 Wednesday

2nd ♌
☽ v/c   **11:56 am**   8:56 am
Full Moon   **11:56 am**   8:56 am
☽ enters ♍ **3:42 pm**   12:42 pm

17 Thursday

3rd ♍

Eastern time in bold type
Pacific time in medium type

18 Friday
3rd ♏

☉ enters ♓	**11:43 am**	8:43 am
☽ v/c	**6:20 pm**	3:20 pm
☽ enters ♎	**10:51 pm**	7:51 pm

Sun enters Pisces

19 Saturday
3rd ♎

20 Sunday
3rd ♎

| ☽ v/c | | 9:02 pm |

January 2022							February 2022							March 2022					
S	M	T	W	T	F	S	S	M	T	W	T	F	S	S	M	T	W	T	F	S
						1			1	2	3	4	5			1	2	3	4	5
2	3	4	5	6	7	8	6	7	8	9	10	11	12	6	7	8	9	10	11	12
9	10	11	12	13	14	15	13	14	15	16	17	18	19	13	14	15	16	17	18	19
16	17	18	19	20	21	22	20	21	22	23	24	25	26	20	21	22	23	24	25	26
23	24	25	26	27	28	29	27	28						27	28	29	30	31		
30	31																			

21 Monday

3rd ♎

☽ v/c   **12:02 am**

☽ enters ♏   **4:19 am**   1:19 am

Presidents' Day

22 Tuesday

3rd ♏

23 Wednesday

3rd ♏

☽ v/c   **4:24 am**   1:24 am
☽ enters ♐   **8:29 am**   5:29 am
4th Quarter **5:32 pm**   2:32 pm

24 Thursday

4th ♐

☽ v/c   **10:24 pm** 7:24 pm

Eastern time in bold type
Pacific time in medium type

25 Friday

4th ♐
☽ enters ♑ **11:27 am** 8:27 am

26 Saturday

4th ♑

27 Sunday

4th ♑
☽ v/c **9:49 am** 6:49 am
☽ enters ♒ **1:36 pm** 10:36 am

January 2022						
S	M	T	W	T	F	S
						1
2	3	4	5	6	7	8
9	10	11	12	13	14	15
16	17	18	19	20	21	22
23	24	25	26	27	28	29
30	31					

February 2022						
S	M	T	W	T	F	S
		1	2	3	4	5
6	7	8	9	10	11	12
13	14	15	16	17	18	19
20	21	22	23	24	25	26
27	28					

March 2022						
S	M	T	W	T	F	S
		1	2	3	4	5
6	7	8	9	10	11	12
13	14	15	16	17	18	19
20	21	22	23	24	25	26
27	28	29	30	31		

28 Monday

4th ≈
☽ v/c   **9:01 pm**   6:01 pm

1 Tuesday

4th ≈
☽ enters ♓   **3:53 pm** 12:53 pm

Mardi Gras (Fat Tuesday)

2 Wednesday

4th ♓
New Moon   **12:35 pm**   9:35 am

Ash Wednesday

3 Thursday

1st ♓
☽ v/c   **4:45 pm**   1:45 pm
☽ enters ♈   **7:52 pm**   4:52 pm

Eastern time in bold type
Pacific time in medium type

4 Friday
1st ♈

5 Saturday
1st ♈
☽ v/c	**11:02 pm**	8:02 pm
☌ enters ♒		10:23 pm
♀ enters ♒		10:30 pm

6 Sunday
1st ♈

☌ enters ♒	**1:23 am**	
♀ enters ♒	**1:30 am**	
☽ enters ♉	**3:00 am**	12:00 am

February 2022								March 2022								April 2022					
S	M	T	W	T	F	S		S	M	T	W	T	F	S		S	M	T	W	T	F	S
		1	2	3	4	5				1	2	3	4	5							1	2
6	7	8	9	10	11	12		6	7	8	9	10	11	12		3	4	5	6	7	8	9
13	14	15	16	17	18	19		13	14	15	16	17	18	19		10	11	12	13	14	15	16
20	21	22	23	24	25	26		20	21	22	23	24	25	26		17	18	19	20	21	22	23
27	28							27	28	29	30	31				24	25	26	27	28	29	30

Eastern time in bold type
Pacific time in medium type

7 Monday

1st ♉

8 Tuesday

1st ♉
☽ v/c   **9:35 am** 6:35 am
☽ enters ♊ **1:40 pm** 10:40 am

9 Wednesday

1st ♊
☿ enters ♓   **8:32 pm** 5:32 pm

10 Thursday

1st ♊
2nd Quarter **5:45 am** 2:45 am
☽ v/c   **11:43 am** 8:43 am
⚸ enters ≈ **1:22 pm** 10:22 am
☽ enters ♋   11:24 pm

11 Friday

2nd ♊

☽ enters ♋ **2:24 am**

12 Saturday

2nd ♋

13 Sunday

2nd ♋

☽ v/c **11:44 am** 8:44 am

☽ enters ♌ **3:32 pm** 12:32 pm

Daylight Saving Time begins at 2 am

February 2022						
S	M	T	W	T	F	S
		1	2	3	4	5
6	7	8	9	10	11	12
13	14	15	16	17	18	19
20	21	22	23	24	25	26
27	28					

March 2022						
S	M	T	W	T	F	S
		1	2	3	4	5
6	7	8	9	10	11	12
13	14	15	16	17	18	19
20	21	22	23	24	25	26
27	28	29	30	31		

April 2022						
S	M	T	W	T	F	S
					1	2
3	4	5	6	7	8	9
10	11	12	13	14	15	16
17	18	19	20	21	22	23
24	25	26	27	28	29	30

14 Monday
2nd ♌

15 Tuesday
2nd ♌
☽ v/c   **6:56 am**   3:56 am
☽ enters ♍   9:59 pm

16 Wednesday
2nd ♌
☽ enters ♍ **12:59 am**

Purim begins at sundown

17 Thursday
2nd ♍

St. Patrick's Day

Eastern time in bold type
Pacific time in medium type

18 Friday

2nd ♍

Full Moon	**3:18 am**	12:18 am
☽ v/c	**4:11 am**	1:11 am
☽ enters ♎	**7:26 am**	4:26 am

19 Saturday

3rd ♎

20 Sunday

3rd ♎

☽ v/c	**8:40 am**	5:40 am
☉ enters ♈	**11:33 am**	8:33 am
☽ enters ♏	**11:45 am**	8:45 am

Int'l Astrology Day

Sun enters Aries • Ostara • Spring Equinox • 11:33 am EDT/8:33 am PDT

February 2022						
S	M	T	W	T	F	S
		1	2	3	4	5
6	7	8	9	10	11	12
13	14	15	16	17	18	19
20	21	22	23	24	25	26
27	28					

March 2022						
S	M	T	W	T	F	S
		1	2	3	4	5
6	7	8	9	10	11	12
13	14	15	16	17	18	19
20	21	22	23	24	25	26
27	28	29	30	31		

April 2022						
S	M	T	W	T	F	S
					1	2
3	4	5	6	7	8	9
10	11	12	13	14	15	16
17	18	19	20	21	22	23
24	25	26	27	28	29	30

21 Monday
3rd ♏

22 Tuesday
3rd ♏
☽ v/c   **12:01 pm**   9:01 am
☽ enters ♐   **2:59 pm**   11:59 am

23 Wednesday
3rd ♐

24 Thursday
3rd ♐
☽ v/c   **8:59 am**   5:59 am
☽ enters ♑   **5:54 pm**   2:54 pm
4th Quarter   10:37 pm

25 Friday
3rd ♐
4th Quarter **1:37 am**

26 Saturday
4th ♐
☽ v/c **7:51 pm** 4:51 pm
☽ enters ≈ **8:55 pm** 5:55 pm

27 Sunday
4th ≈
☿ enters ♈ **3:44 am** 12:44 am

February 2022						
S	M	T	W	T	F	S
		1	2	3	4	5
6	7	8	9	10	11	12
13	14	15	16	17	18	19
20	21	22	23	24	25	26
27	28					

March 2022						
S	M	T	W	T	F	S
		1	2	3	4	5
6	7	8	9	10	11	12
13	14	15	16	17	18	19
20	21	22	23	24	25	26
27	28	29	30	31		

April 2022						
S	M	T	W	T	F	S
					1	2
3	4	5	6	7	8	9
10	11	12	13	14	15	16
17	18	19	20	21	22	23
24	25	26	27	28	29	30

28 Monday

4th ≈
D v/c   **10:11 am**   7:11 am
D enters ♓   9:32 pm

29 Tuesday

4th ≈
D enters ♓ **12:32 am**

30 Wednesday

4th ♓
D v/c   11:37 pm

31 Thursday

4th ♓
D v/c   **2:37 am**
D enters ♈   **5:30 am**   2:30 am
New Moon   11:24 pm

1 Friday

4th ♈
New Moon   **2:24 am**

April Fools' Day (All Fools' Day—Pagan)

2 Saturday

1st ♈
☽ v/c   **9:51 am**   6:51 am
☽ enters ♉   **12:50 pm**   9:50 am

Ramadan begins at sundown

3 Sunday

1st ♉

March 2022						
S	M	T	W	T	F	S
		1	2	3	4	5
6	7	8	9	10	11	12
13	14	15	16	17	18	19
20	21	22	23	24	25	26
27	28	29	30	31		

April 2022						
S	M	T	W	T	F	S
					1	2
3	4	5	6	7	8	9
10	11	12	13	14	15	16
17	18	19	20	21	22	23
24	25	26	27	28	29	30

May 2022						
S	M	T	W	T	F	S
1	2	3	4	5	6	7
8	9	10	11	12	13	14
15	16	17	18	19	20	21
22	23	24	25	26	27	28
29	30	31				

Eastern time in bold type
Pacific time in medium type

4 Monday

1st ♉
☽ v/c   **9:53 pm**   6:53 pm
☽ enters ♊   **11:04 pm**   8:04 pm

5 Tuesday

1st ♊
♀ enters ♓   **11:18 am**   8:18 am

6 Wednesday

1st ♊
☽ v/c   **11:15 pm**   8:15 pm

7 Thursday

1st ♊
☽ enters ♋   **11:30 am**   8:30 am

8 Friday

1st ♋
2nd Quarter 11:48 pm

9 Saturday

1st ♋
2nd Quarter **2:48 am**
☽ v/c **9:01 pm** 6:01 pm
☽ enters ♌ 9:00 pm

10 Sunday

2nd ♌
☽ enters ♌ **12:00 am**
☿ enters ♉ **10:09 pm** 7:09 pm

Palm Sunday

	March 2022					
S	M	T	W	T	F	S
		1	2	3	4	5
6	7	8	9	10	11	12
13	14	15	16	17	18	19
20	21	22	23	24	25	26
27	28	29	30	31		

	April 2022					
S	M	T	W	T	F	S
					1	2
3	4	5	6	7	8	9
10	11	12	13	14	15	16
17	18	19	20	21	22	23
24	25	26	27	28	29	30

	May 2022					
S	M	T	W	T	F	S
1	2	3	4	5	6	7
8	9	10	11	12	13	14
15	16	17	18	19	20	21
22	23	24	25	26	27	28
29	30	31				

11 Monday
2nd ♌

12 Tuesday
2nd ♌
☽ v/c   **6:16 am**   3:16 am
☽ enters ♍ **10:07 am**   7:07 am

13 Wednesday
2nd ♍

14 Thursday
2nd ♍
☽ v/c   **2:11 pm**   11:11 am
☽ enters ♎ **4:46 pm**   1:46 pm
♂ enters ♓ **11:06 pm**   8:06 pm

15 Friday

2nd ♎︎

Good Friday • Passover begins at sundown

16 Saturday

2nd ♎︎
Full Moon	**2:55 pm**	11:55 am
☽ v/c	**5:57 pm**	2:57 pm
☽ enters ♏︎	**8:23 pm**	5:23 pm

17 Sunday

3rd ♏︎

Easter

	March 2022								April 2022								May 2022					
S	M	T	W	T	F	S		S	M	T	W	T	F	S		S	M	T	W	T	F	S
		1	2	3	4	5							1	2		1	2	3	4	5	6	7
6	7	8	9	10	11	12		3	4	5	6	7	8	9		8	9	10	11	12	13	14
13	14	15	16	17	18	19		10	11	12	13	14	15	16		15	16	17	18	19	20	21
20	21	22	23	24	25	26		17	18	19	20	21	22	23		22	23	24	25	26	27	28
27	28	29	30	31				24	25	26	27	28	29	30		29	30	31				

18 Monday

3rd ♏

| ☽ v/c | **7:55 pm** | 4:55 pm |
| ☽ enters ♐ | **10:16 pm** | 7:16 pm |

19 Tuesday

3rd ♐

| ☉ enters ♉ | **10:24 pm** | 7:24 pm |

Sun enters Taurus

20 Wednesday

3rd ♐

☿ enters ♓	**11:51 am**	8:51 am
☽ v/c	**4:56 pm**	1:56 pm
☽ enters ♑	**11:52 pm**	8:52 pm

21 Thursday

3rd ♑

22 Friday

3rd ♑
☽ v/c   **11:53 pm**   8:53 pm
☽ enters ♒   11:17 pm

Earth Day • Orthodox Good Friday

23 Saturday

3rd ♑
☽ enters ♒   **2:17 am**
4th Quarter   **7:56 am**   4:56 am

Passover ends

24 Sunday

4th ♒
☽ v/c   **8:33 pm**   5:33 pm

Orthodox Easter

March 2022						
S	M	T	W	T	F	S
		1	2	3	4	5
6	7	8	9	10	11	12
13	14	15	16	17	18	19
20	21	22	23	24	25	26
27	28	29	30	31		

April 2022						
S	M	T	W	T	F	S
					1	2
3	4	5	6	7	8	9
10	11	12	13	14	15	16
17	18	19	20	21	22	23
24	25	26	27	28	29	30

May 2022						
S	M	T	W	T	F	S
1	2	3	4	5	6	7
8	9	10	11	12	13	14
15	16	17	18	19	20	21
22	23	24	25	26	27	28
29	30	31				

25 Monday

4th ≈
☽ enters ♓ **6:15 am** 3:15 am

26 Tuesday

4th ♓

27 Wednesday

4th ♓
☽ v/c **9:36 am** 6:36 am
☽ enters ♈ **12:10 pm** 9:10 am

28 Thursday

4th ♈

Eastern time in bold type
Pacific time in medium type

29 Friday

4th ♈

♀ ℞	**2:38 pm**	11:38 am
☽ v/c	**5:38 pm**	2:38 pm
☿ enters ♊	**6:23 pm**	3:23 pm
☽ enters ♉	**8:19 pm**	5:19 pm

30 Saturday

4th ♉

♀ enters ♉	**4:50 am**	1:50 am
New Moon	**4:28 pm**	1:28 pm

Solar Eclipse 10° ♉ 28'

1 Sunday

1st ♉

Beltane • Ramadan ends

April 2022						
S	M	T	W	T	F	S
					1	2
3	4	5	6	7	8	9
10	11	12	13	14	15	16
17	18	19	20	21	22	23
24	25	26	27	28	29	30

May 2022						
S	M	T	W	T	F	S
1	2	3	4	5	6	7
8	9	10	11	12	13	14
15	16	17	18	19	20	21
22	23	24	25	26	27	28
29	30	31				

June 2022						
S	M	T	W	T	F	S
			1	2	3	4
5	6	7	8	9	10	11
12	13	14	15	16	17	18
19	20	21	22	23	2	25
26	27	28	29	30		

2 Monday

1st ♉
☽ v/c   **6:13 am**   3:13 am
☽ enters ♊   **6:47 am**   3:47 am
♀ enters ♈   **12:10 pm** 9:10 am

3 Tuesday

1st ♊

4 Wednesday

1st ♊
☽ v/c   **4:37 pm**   1:37 pm
☽ enters ♋   **7:05 pm**   4:05 pm

5 Thursday

1st ♋

Cinco de Mayo

Eastern time in bold type
Pacific time in medium type

6 Friday
1st ♋

7 Saturday
1st ♋
☽ v/c   **6:26 am**   3:26 am
☽ enters ♌   **7:50 am**   4:50 am

8 Sunday
1st ♌
2nd Quarter   **8:21 pm**   5:21 pm

Mother's Day

April 2022						
S	M	T	W	T	F	S
					1	2
3	4	5	6	7	8	9
10	11	12	13	14	15	16
17	18	19	20	21	22	23
24	25	26	27	28	29	30

May 2022						
S	M	T	W	T	F	S
1	2	3	4	5	6	7
8	9	10	11	12	13	14
15	16	17	18	19	20	21
22	23	24	25	26	27	28
29	30	31				

June 2022						
S	M	T	W	T	F	S
			1	2	3	4
5	6	7	8	9	10	11
12	13	14	15	16	17	18
19	20	21	22	23	2	25
26	27	28	29	30		

Eastern time in bold type
Pacific time in medium type

9 Monday

2nd ♌
☽ v/c   **8:39 am**   5:39 am
☽ enters ♍   **6:53 pm**   3:53 pm

10 Tuesday

2nd ♍
☿ ℞   **7:47 am**   4:47 am
♃ enters ♈   **7:22 pm**   4:22 pm

Mercury retrograde until 6/3

11 Wednesday

2nd ♍
☽ v/c   9:00 pm
☽ enters ♎   11:34 pm

12 Thursday

2nd ♍
☽ v/c   **12:00 am**
☽ enters ♎   **2:34 am**

13 Friday

2nd ♎

14 Saturday

2nd ♎
| ☽ v/c | **4:07 am** | 1:07 am |
| ☽ enters ♏ | **6:34 am** | 3:34 am |

15 Sunday

2nd ♏
| ♀ enters ♋ | **3:11 am** | 12:11 am |
| Full Moon | | 9:14 pm |

April 2022						
S	M	T	W	T	F	S
					1	2
3	4	5	6	7	8	9
10	11	12	13	14	15	16
17	18	19	20	21	22	23
24	25	26	27	28	29	30

May 2022						
S	M	T	W	T	F	S
1	2	3	4	5	6	7
8	9	10	11	12	13	14
15	16	17	18	19	20	21
22	23	24	25	26	27	28
29	30	31				

June 2022						
S	M	T	W	T	F	S
			1	2	3	4
5	6	7	8	9	10	11
12	13	14	15	16	17	18
19	20	21	22	23	2	25
26	27	28	29	30		

Eastern time in bold type
Pacific time in medium type

16 Monday

2nd ♏
Full Moon **12:14 am**
☽ v/c **5:28 am** 2:28 am
☽ enters ♐ **7:50 am** 4:50 am

Lunar Eclipse 25° ♏ 18'

17 Tuesday

3rd ♐
☽ v/c **11:59 pm** 8:59 pm

18 Wednesday

3rd ♐
☽ enters ♑ **8:02 am** 5:02 am

19 Thursday

3rd ♑

20 Friday

3rd ♑

☽ v/c	**8:00 am**	5:00 am
☽ enters ♒	**8:53 am**	5:53 am
☉ enters ♊	**9:23 pm**	6:23 pm

Sun enters Gemini

21 Saturday

3rd ♒

22 Sunday

3rd ♒

☽ v/c	**3:19 am**	12:19 am
☽ enters ♓	**11:49 am**	8:49 am
4th Quarter	**2:43 pm**	11:43 am
☿ enters ♉	**9:15 pm**	6:15 pm

April 2022								May 2022								June 2022					
S	M	T	W	T	F	S		S	M	T	W	T	F	S		S	M	T	W	T	F	S
					1	2		1	2	3	4	5	6	7					1	2	3	4
3	4	5	6	7	8	9		8	9	10	11	12	13	14		5	6	7	8	9	10	11
10	11	12	13	14	15	16		15	16	17	18	19	20	21		12	13	14	15	16	17	18
17	18	19	20	21	22	23		22	23	24	25	26	27	28		19	20	21	22	23	2	25
24	25	26	27	28	29	30		29	30	31						26	27	28	29	30		

23 Monday
4th ♓

24 Tuesday
4th ♓

⚸ enters ♓	**5:46 am**	2:46 am
☽ v/c	**5:33 pm**	2:33 pm
☽ enters ♈	**5:39 pm**	2:39 pm
♂ enters ♈	**7:17 pm**	4:17 pm

25 Wednesday
4th ♈

26 Thursday
4th ♈

☽ v/c	**11:20 pm**	8:20 pm
☽ enters ♉		11:22 pm

Eastern time in bold type
Pacific time in medium type

27 Friday

4th ♈
☽ enters ♉ **2:22 am**

28 Saturday

4th ♉
♀ enters ♉ **10:46 am** 7:46 am

29 Sunday

4th ♉
☽ v/c **10:11 am** 7:11 am
☽ enters ♊ **1:23 pm** 10:23 am

April 2022						
S	M	T	W	T	F	S
					1	2
3	4	5	6	7	8	9
10	11	12	13	14	15	16
17	18	19	20	21	22	23
24	25	26	27	28	29	30

May 2022						
S	M	T	W	T	F	S
1	2	3	4	5	6	7
8	9	10	11	12	13	14
15	16	17	18	19	20	21
22	23	24	25	26	27	28
29	30	31				

June 2022						
S	M	T	W	T	F	S
			1	2	3	4
5	6	7	8	9	10	11
12	13	14	15	16	17	18
19	20	21	22	23	2	25
26	27	28	29	30		

Eastern time in bold type
Pacific time in medium type

30 Monday
4th ♊
New Moon **7:30 am** 4:30 am

Memorial Day

31 Tuesday
1st ♊
☽ v/c **4:10 pm** 1:10 pm
☽ enters ♋ 10:49 pm

1 Wednesday
1st ♊
☽ enters ♋ **1:49 am**

2 Thursday
1st ♋

3 Friday

1st ♋
☿ D	**4:00 am**	1:00 am
☽ v/c	**11:15 am**	8:15 am
☽ enters ♌	**2:38 pm**	11:38 am

4 Saturday

1st ♌
| ♄ ℞ | **5:47 pm** | 2:47 pm |

Shavuot begins at sundown

5 Sunday

1st ♌
| ☽ v/c | **7:12 pm** | 4:12 pm |
| ☽ enters ♍ | | 11:22 pm |

	May 2022							June 2022							July 2022					
S	M	T	W	T	F	S	S	M	T	W	T	F	S	S	M	T	W	T	F	S
1	2	3	4	5	6	7				1	2	3	4						1	2
8	9	10	11	12	13	14	5	6	7	8	9	10	11	3	4	5	6	7	8	9
15	16	17	18	19	20	21	12	13	14	15	16	17	18	10	11	12	13	14	15	16
22	23	24	25	26	27	28	19	20	21	22	23	2	25	17	18	19	20	21	22	23
29	30	31					26	27	28	29	30			24	25	26	27	28	29	30
														31						

6 Monday

1st ♌
☽ enters ♍ **2:22 am**

7 Tuesday

1st ♍
2nd Quarter **10:48 am** 7:48 am

8 Wednesday

2nd ♍
☽ v/c **8:09 am** 5:09 am
☽ enters ♎ **11:23 am** 8:23 am

9 Thursday

2nd ♎

Eastern time in bold type
Pacific time in medium type

10 Friday

2nd ♎︎
☽ v/c   **1:36 pm** 10:36 am
☽ enters ♏︎ **4:41 pm** 1:41 pm

11 Saturday

2nd ♏︎

12 Sunday

2nd ♏︎
☽ v/c   **5:40 pm** 2:40 pm
☽ enters ♐︎ **6:31 pm** 3:31 pm

		May 2022				
S	M	T	W	T	F	S
1	2	3	4	5	6	7
8	9	10	11	12	13	14
15	16	17	18	19	20	21
22	23	24	25	26	27	28
29	30	31				

		June 2022				
S	M	T	W	T	F	S
			1	2	3	4
5	6	7	8	9	10	11
12	13	14	15	16	17	18
19	20	21	22	23	2	25
26	27	28	29	30		

		July 2022				
S	M	T	W	T	F	S
					1	2
3	4	5	6	7	8	9
10	11	12	13	14	15	16
17	18	19	20	21	22	23
24	25	26	27	28	29	30
31						

Eastern time in bold type
Pacific time in medium type

13 Monday

2nd ✗
☿ enters ♊   **11:27 am**   8:27 am

14 Tuesday

2nd ✗
Full Moon   **7:52 am**   4:52 am
☽ v/c   **10:58 am**   7:58 am
☽ enters ♑   **6:14 pm**   3:14 pm

Flag Day

15 Wednesday

3rd ♑

16 Thursday

3rd ♑
☽ v/c   **2:41 pm**   11:41 am
☽ enters ♒   **5:44 pm**   2:44 pm

Eastern time in bold type
Pacific time in medium type

17 Friday
3rd ≈≈

18 Saturday
3rd ≈≈
☽ v/c   **2:50 pm** 11:50 am
☽ enters ♓   **7:01 pm**   4:01 pm

19 Sunday
3rd ♓

Father's Day • Juneteenth

	May 2022					
S	M	T	W	T	F	S
1	2	3	4	5	6	7
8	9	10	11	12	13	14
15	16	17	18	19	20	21
22	23	24	25	26	27	28
29	30	31				

	June 2022					
S	M	T	W	T	F	S
			1	2	3	4
5	6	7	8	9	10	11
12	13	14	15	16	17	18
19	20	21	22	23	2	25
26	27	28	29	30		

	July 2022					
S	M	T	W	T	F	S
					1	2
3	4	5	6	7	8	9
10	11	12	13	14	15	16
17	18	19	20	21	22	23
24	25	26	27	28	29	30
31						

20 Monday

3rd ♓
☽ v/c   **11:11 pm**   8:11 pm
4th Quarter **11:11 pm**   8:11 pm
☽ enters ♈   **11:37 pm**   8:37 pm

21 Tuesday

4th ♈
☉ enters ♋   **5:14 am**   2:14 am

Sun enters Cancer • Litha • Summer Solstice • 5:14 am EDT/2:14 am PDT

22 Wednesday

4th ♈
♀ enters ♊   **8:34 pm**   5:34 pm

23 Thursday

4th ♈
☽ v/c   **4:02 am**   1:02 am
☽ enters ♉   **7:58 am**   4:58 am

Eastern time in bold type
Pacific time in medium type

24 Friday
4th ♉

25 Saturday
4th ♉
☽ v/c   **3:02 pm** 12:02 pm
☽ enters ♊   **7:13 pm** 4:13 pm

26 Sunday
4th ♊

			May 2022			
S	M	T	W	T	F	S
1	2	3	4	5	6	7
8	9	10	11	12	13	14
15	16	17	18	19	20	21
22	23	24	25	26	27	28
29	30	31				

			June 2022			
S	M	T	W	T	F	S
			1	2	3	4
5	6	7	8	9	10	11
12	13	14	15	16	17	18
19	20	21	22	23	2	25
26	27	28	29	30		

			July 2022			
S	M	T	W	T	F	S
					1	2
3	4	5	6	7	8	9
10	11	12	13	14	15	16
17	18	19	20	21	22	23
24	25	26	27	28	29	30
31						

Eastern time in bold type
Pacific time in medium type

27 Monday

4th ♊
☽ v/c   **10:38 pm**   7:38 pm

28 Tuesday

4th ♊
♆ ℞   **3:55 am**   12:55 am
☽ enters ♋   **7:53 am**   4:53 am
New Moon   **10:52 pm**   7:52 pm

29 Wednesday

1st ♋

30 Thursday

1st ♋
☽ v/c   **4:14 pm**   1:14 pm
☽ enters ♌   **8:40 pm**   5:40 pm

1 Friday
1st ♌

2 Saturday
1st ♌

3 Sunday
1st ♌
☽ v/c   **5:59 am**   2:59 am
☽ enters ♍ **8:31 am**   5:31 am

June 2022						
S	M	T	W	T	F	S
			1	2	3	4
5	6	7	8	9	10	11
12	13	14	15	16	17	18
19	20	21	22	23	2	25
26	27	28	29	30		

July 2022						
S	M	T	W	T	F	S
					1	2
3	4	5	6	7	8	9
10	11	12	13	14	15	16
17	18	19	20	21	22	23
24	25	26	27	28	29	30
31						

August 2022						
S	M	T	W	T	F	S
	1	2	3	4	5	6
7	8	9	10	11	12	13
14	15	16	17	18	19	20
21	22	23	24	25	26	27
28	29	30	31			

Eastern time in bold type
Pacific time in medium type

4 Monday

1st ♍
♀ enters ♊ **11:16 pm** 8:16 pm
♂ enters ♉   11:04 pm
☿ enters ♋   11:25 pm

Independence Day

5 Tuesday

Atlin's birthday
Drive to Edson

1st ♍
♂ enters ♉ **2:04 am**
☿ enters ♋ **2:25 am**
☽ v/c   **2:04 pm** 11:04 am
☽ enters ♎ **6:25 pm** 3:25 pm

6 Wednesday

1st ♎
2nd Quarter **10:14 pm** 7:14 pm

7 Thursday

2nd ♎
♆ R℞   **5:30 pm** 2:30 pm
☽ v/c   **9:04 pm** 6:04 pm
☽ enters ♏   10:15 pm

8 Friday

2nd ♎︎
☽ enters ♏︎ **1:15 am**

9 Saturday

2nd ♏︎
☽ v/c   9:34 pm

10 Sunday

2nd ♏︎
☽ v/c   **12:34 am**
☽ enters ♐︎ **4:34 am**   1:34 am

June 2022						
S	M	T	W	T	F	S
			1	2	3	4
5	6	7	8	9	10	11
12	13	14	15	16	17	18
19	20	21	22	23	2	25
26	27	28	29	30		

July 2022						
S	M	T	W	T	F	S
					1	2
3	4	5	6	7	8	9
10	11	12	13	14	15	16
17	18	19	20	21	22	23
24	25	26	27	28	29	30
31						

August 2022						
S	M	T	W	T	F	S
	1	2	3	4	5	6
7	8	9	10	11	12	13
14	15	16	17	18	19	20
21	22	23	24	25	26	27
28	29	30	31			

Eastern time in bold type
Pacific time in medium type

11 Monday

2nd ♐

☽ v/c   **9:42 pm** 6:42 pm

12 Tuesday

2nd ♐

☽ enters ♑   **5:01 am** 2:01 am

13 Wednesday

2nd ♑

Full Moon   **2:38 pm** 11:38 am

☽ v/c   9:17 pm

14 Thursday

3rd ♑

☽ v/c   **12:17 am**

☽ enters ≈   **4:13 am** 1:13 am

15 Friday

3rd ≈
☽ v/c   9:36 pm

16 Saturday

3rd ≈
☽ v/c   **12:36 am**
☽ enters ♓   **4:18 am**   1:18 am

17 Sunday

3rd ♓
♀ enters ⊙   **9:32 pm**   6:32 pm
☽ v/c   11:43 pm

June 2022							July 2022							August 2022					
S	M	T	W	T	F	S	S	M	T	W	T	F	S	S	M	T	W	T	F	S
			1	2	3	4						1	2		1	2	3	4	5	6
5	6	7	8	9	10	11	3	4	5	6	7	8	9	7	8	9	10	11	12	13
12	13	14	15	16	17	18	10	11	12	13	14	15	16	14	15	16	17	18	19	20
19	20	21	22	23	2	25	17	18	19	20	21	22	23	21	22	23	24	25	26	27
26	27	28	29	30			24	25	26	27	28	29	30	28	29	30	31			
							31													

Eastern time in bold type
Pacific time in medium type

18 Monday

3rd ♓
☽ v/c   **2:43 am**
☽ enters ♈   **7:17 am**   4:17 am

19 Tuesday

3rd ♈
☿ enters ♌   **8:35 am**   5:35 am
⚷ Rℝ   **11:21 am** 8:21 am

20 Wednesday

3rd ♈
☽ v/c   **10:19 am** 7:19 am
4th Quarter   **10:19 am** 7:19 am
☽ enters ♉   **2:23 pm** 11:23 am

21 Thursday

4th ♉

22 Friday
4th ♉
⊙ enters ♌ **4:07 pm** 1:07 pm
☽ v/c   **7:45 pm** 4:45 pm
☽ enters ♊   10:11 pm

Sun enters Leo

23 Saturday
4th ♉
☽ enters ♊ **1:11 am**
♀ enters ♌ **1:29 pm** 10:29 am

24 Sunday
4th ♊
⚹ ℞   11:48 pm

June 2022						
S	M	T	W	T	F	S
			1	2	3	4
5	6	7	8	9	10	11
12	13	14	15	16	17	18
19	20	21	22	23	2	25
26	27	28	29	30		

July 2022						
S	M	T	W	T	F	S
					1	2
3	4	5	6	7	8	9
10	11	12	13	14	15	16
17	18	19	20	21	22	23
24	25	26	27	28	29	30
31						

August 2022						
S	M	T	W	T	F	S
	1	2	3	4	5	6
7	8	9	10	11	12	13
14	15	16	17	18	19	20
21	22	23	24	25	26	27
28	29	30	31			

25 Monday

4th ♊
☀ ℞   **2:48 am**
☽ v/c   **4:14 am**   1:14 am
☽ enters ♋   **1:54 pm**   10:54 am

26 Tuesday

4th ♋

27 Wednesday

4th ♋
☽ v/c   **8:54 pm**   5:54 pm
☽ enters ♌   11:36 pm

28 Thursday

4th ♋
☽ enters ♌   **2:36 am**
New Moon   **1:55 pm**   10:55 am
♃ ℞   **4:37 pm**   1:37 pm

29 Friday

1st ♌
☽ v/c   9:29 pm

Islamic New Year begins at sundown

30 Saturday

1st ♌
☽ v/c   **12:29 am**
☽ enters ♍   **2:11 pm** 11:11 am

31 Sunday

1st ♍

June 2022						
S	M	T	W	T	F	S
			1	2	3	4
5	6	7	8	9	10	11
12	13	14	15	16	17	18
19	20	21	22	23	2	25
26	27	28	29	30		

July 2022						
S	M	T	W	T	F	S
					1	2
3	4	5	6	7	8	9
10	11	12	13	14	15	16
17	18	19	20	21	22	23
24	25	26	27	28	29	30
31						

August 2022						
S	M	T	W	T	F	S
	1	2	3	4	5	6
7	8	9	10	11	12	13
14	15	16	17	18	19	20
21	22	23	24	25	26	27
28	29	30	31			

Eastern time in bold type
Pacific time in medium type

1 Monday

1st ♍
☽ v/c   **6:29 pm**   3:29 pm
☽ enters ♎   9:06 pm

Lammas

2 Tuesday

1st ♍
☽ enters ♎ **12:06 am**

3 Wednesday

1st ♎
☽ v/c   11:20 pm
☿ enters ♍   11:58 pm

4 Thursday

1st ♎
☽ v/c   **2:20 am**
☿ enters ♍ **2:58 am**
☽ enters ♏ **7:47 am**   4:47 am

5 Friday

1st ♏
2nd Quarter   **7:07 am**   4:07 am

6 Saturday

2nd ♏
☽ v/c   **7:24 am**   4:24 am
☽ enters ♐   **12:39 pm**   9:39 am

7 Sunday

2nd ♐

July 2022						
S	M	T	W	T	F	S
					1	2
3	4	5	6	7	8	9
10	11	12	13	14	15	16
17	18	19	20	21	22	23
24	25	26	27	28	29	30
31						

August 2022						
S	M	T	W	T	F	S
	1	2	3	4	5	6
7	8	9	10	11	12	13
14	15	16	17	18	19	20
21	22	23	24	25	26	27
28	29	30	31			

September 2022						
S	M	T	W	T	F	S
				1	2	3
4	5	6	7	8	9	10
11	12	13	14	15	16	17
18	19	20	21	22	23	24
25	26	27	28	29	30	

Eastern time in bold type
Pacific time in medium type

8 Monday

2nd ♐
☽ v/c   **6:30 am**   3:30 am
☽ enters ♑ **2:39 pm** 11:39 am

9 Tuesday

2nd ♑

10 Wednesday

2nd ♑
☽ v/c   **12:39 pm** 9:39 am
☽ enters ≈ **2:45 pm** 11:45 am

11 Thursday

2nd ≈
♀ enters ♌ **2:30 pm** 11:30 am
Full Moon   **9:36 pm** 6:36 pm

12 Friday

3rd ≈
☽ v/c   **7:07 am**   4:07 am
☽ enters ⟓   **2:44 pm** 11:44 am

13 Saturday

3rd ⟓

14 Sunday

3rd ⟓
☽ v/c   **11:11 am**   8:11 am
☽ enters ♈   **4:43 pm**   1:43 pm

July 2022						
S	M	T	W	T	F	S
					1	2
3	4	5	6	7	8	9
10	11	12	13	14	15	16
17	18	19	20	21	22	23
24	25	26	27	28	29	30
31						

August 2022						
S	M	T	W	T	F	S
	1	2	3	4	5	6
7	8	9	10	11	12	13
14	15	16	17	18	19	20
21	22	23	24	25	26	27
28	29	30	31			

September 2022						
S	M	T	W	T	F	S
				1	2	3
4	5	6	7	8	9	10
11	12	13	14	15	16	17
18	19	20	21	22	23	24
25	26	27	28	29	30	

Eastern time in bold type
Pacific time in medium type

15 Monday
3rd ♈

16 Tuesday
3rd ♈
☽ v/c   **4:18 pm** 1:18 pm
☽ enters ♉ **10:22 pm** 7:22 pm

17 Wednesday
3rd ♉

18 Thursday
3rd ♉
4th Quarter   9:36 pm

Eastern time in bold type
Pacific time in medium type

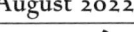

19 Friday

3rd ♉
4th Quarter **12:36 am**
☽ v/c   **7:06 am**   4:06 am
☽ enters ♊   **8:06 am**   5:06 am

20 Saturday

4th ♊
♂ enters ♊   **3:56 am** 12:56 am

21 Sunday

4th ♊
⛢ enters ♒   **6:33 am**   3:33 am
☽ v/c   **6:06 pm**   3:06 pm
☽ enters ♋   **8:29 pm**   5:29 pm

July 2022						
S	M	T	W	T	F	S
					1	2
3	4	5	6	7	8	9
10	11	12	13	14	15	16
17	18	19	20	21	22	23
24	25	26	27	28	29	30
31						

August 2022						
S	M	T	W	T	F	S
	1	2	3	4	5	6
7	8	9	10	11	12	13
14	15	16	17	18	19	20
21	22	23	24	25	26	27
28	29	30	31			

September 2022						
S	M	T	W	T	F	S
				1	2	3
4	5	6	7	8	9	10
11	12	13	14	15	16	17
18	19	20	21	22	23	24
25	26	27	28	29	30	

Eastern time in bold type
Pacific time in medium type

22 Monday

4th ♋
☉ enters ♍ **11:16 pm** 8:16 pm

Sun enters Virgo

23 Tuesday

4th ♋

24 Wednesday

4th ♋
☽ v/c   **5:40 am** 2:40 am
☽ enters ♌ **9:09 am** 6:09 am
♅ R℟   **9:54 am** 6:54 am

25 Thursday

4th ♌
☿ enters ♎ **9:03 pm** 6:03 pm
☽ v/c   11:55 pm

26 Friday
4th ♌
☽ v/c   **2:55 am**
☽ enters ♍   **8:25 pm**   5:25 pm

27 Saturday
4th ♍
New Moon   **4:17 am**   1:17 am

28 Sunday
1st ♍
☽ v/c   **11:08 pm**   8:08 pm

	July 2022					
S	M	T	W	T	F	S
					1	2
3	4	5	6	7	8	9
10	11	12	13	14	15	16
17	18	19	20	21	22	23
24	25	26	27	28	29	30
31						

	August 2022					
S	M	T	W	T	F	S
	1	2	3	4	5	6
7	8	9	10	11	12	13
14	15	16	17	18	19	20
21	22	23	24	25	26	27
28	29	30	31			

	September 2022					
S	M	T	W	T	F	S
				1	2	3
4	5	6	7	8	9	10
11	12	13	14	15	16	17
18	19	20	21	22	23	24
25	26	27	28	29	30	

Eastern time in bold type
Pacific time in medium type

29 Monday
1st ♍
☽ enters ♎ **5:45 am** 2:45 am

30 Tuesday
1st ♎

31 Wednesday
1st ♎
☽ v/c **6:43 am** 3:43 am
☽ enters ♏ **1:11 pm** 10:11 am

1 Thursday
1st ♏

Eastern time in bold type
Pacific time in medium type

2 Friday
1st ♏

☽ v/c   **1:22 pm** 10:22 am
☽ enters ♐   **6:39 pm** 3:39 pm

3 Saturday
1st ♐

2nd Quarter   **2:08 pm** 11:08 am

4 Sunday
2nd ♐

☽ v/c   **9:51 pm** 6:51 pm
☽ enters ♑   **10:03 pm** 7:03 pm
♀ enters ♍   9:05 pm

August 2022	September 2022	October 2022
S M T W T F S	S M T W T F S	S M T W T F S
1 2 3 4 5 6	1 2 3	1
7 8 9 10 11 12 13	4 5 6 7 8 9 10	2 3 4 5 6 7 8
14 15 16 17 18 19 20	11 12 13 14 15 16 17	9 10 11 12 13 14 15
21 22 23 24 25 26 27	18 19 20 21 22 23 24	16 17 18 19 20 21 22
28 29 30 31	25 26 27 28 29 30	23 24 25 26 27 28 29
		30 31

Eastern time in bold type
Pacific time in medium type

5 Monday

2nd ♑
♀ enters ♍ **12:05 am**
♀ enters ♋   10:04 pm

Labor Day

6 Tuesday

2nd ♑
♀ enters ♋ **1:04 am**
☽ v/c   **5:43 pm** 2:43 pm
☽ enters ♒ **11:41 pm** 8:41 pm

7 Wednesday

2nd ♒

8 Thursday

2nd ♒
☽ v/c   **8:34 am** 5:34 am
☽ enters ♓   9:42 pm

Eastern time in bold type
Pacific time in medium type

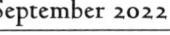

9 Friday

2nd ≈
☽ enters ♓ **12:42 am**
☿ ℞   **11:38 pm** 8:38 pm

Mercury retrograde until 10/2

10 Saturday

2nd ♓
Full Moon   **5:59 am** 2:59 am
☽ v/c   **8:29 pm** 5:29 pm
☽ enters ♈   11:47 pm

11 Sunday

3rd ♓
☽ enters ♈ **2:47 am**

August 2022						
S	M	T	W	T	F	S
	1	2	3	4	5	6
7	8	9	10	11	12	13
14	15	16	17	18	19	20
21	22	23	24	25	26	27
28	29	30	31			

September 2022						
S	M	T	W	T	F	S
				1	2	3
4	5	6	7	8	9	10
11	12	13	14	15	16	17
18	19	20	21	22	23	24
25	26	27	28	29	30	

October 2022						
S	M	T	W	T	F	S
						1
2	3	4	5	6	7	8
9	10	11	12	13	14	15
16	17	18	19	20	21	22
23	24	25	26	27	28	29
30	31					

Eastern time in bold type
Pacific time in medium type

12 Monday

3rd ♈
☽ v/c   9:53 pm

13 Tuesday

3rd ♈
☽ v/c   **12:53 am**
☽ enters ♉   **7:39 am**   4:39 am

14 Wednesday

3rd ♉

15 Thursday

3rd ♉
☽ v/c   **8:59 am**   5:59 am
☽ enters ♊   **4:16 pm**   1:16 pm

Eastern time in bold type
Pacific time in medium type

16 Friday
3rd ♊

17 Saturday
3rd ♊
☽ v/c   **5:52 pm**   2:52 pm
4th Quarter   **5:52 pm**   2:52 pm

18 Sunday
4th ♊
☽ enters ♋   **3:59 am**   12:59 am

August 2022						
S	M	T	W	T	F	S
	1	2	3	4	5	6
7	8	9	10	11	12	13
14	15	16	17	18	19	20
21	22	23	24	25	26	27
28	29	30	31			

September 2022						
S	M	T	W	T	F	S
				1	2	3
4	5	6	7	8	9	10
11	12	13	14	15	16	17
18	19	20	21	22	23	24
25	26	27	28	29	30	

October 2022						
S	M	T	W	T	F	S
						1
2	3	4	5	6	7	8
9	10	11	12	13	14	15
16	17	18	19	20	21	22
23	24	25	26	27	28	29
30	31					

Eastern time in bold type
Pacific time in medium type

19 Monday
4th ♋

20 Tuesday
4th ♋
☽ v/c   **11:57 am** 8:57 am
☽ enters ♌   **4:38 pm** 1:38 pm

21 Wednesday
4th ♌

UN International Day of Peace

22 Thursday
4th ♌
☽ v/c   **7:07 am** 4:07 am
☉ enters ♎ **9:04 pm** 6:04 pm

Sun enters Libra • Mabon • Fall Equinox • 9:04 pm EDT/6:04 pm PDT

Eastern time in bold type
Pacific time in medium type

23 Friday

4th ♌

☽ enters ♍	**3:53 am**	12:53 am
☿ enters ♍	**8:04 am**	5:04 am

24 Saturday

4th ♍

25 Sunday

4th ♍

☽ v/c	**8:49 am**	5:49 am
☽ enters ♎	**12:43 pm**	9:43 am
New Moon	**5:55 pm**	2:55 pm

Rosh Hashanah begins at sundown

August 2022						
S	M	T	W	T	F	S
	1	2	3	4	5	6
7	8	9	10	11	12	13
14	15	16	17	18	19	20
21	22	23	24	25	26	27
28	29	30	31			

September 2022						
S	M	T	W	T	F	S
				1	2	3
4	5	6	7	8	9	10
11	12	13	14	15	16	17
18	19	20	21	22	23	24
25	26	27	28	29	30	

October 2022						
S	M	T	W	T	F	S
						1
2	3	4	5	6	7	8
9	10	11	12	13	14	15
16	17	18	19	20	21	22
23	24	25	26	27	28	29
30	31					

26 Monday
1st ♎

27 Tuesday
1st ♎
☽ v/c   **12:21 pm**   9:21 am
☽ enters ♏ **7:15 pm**   4:15 pm

28 Wednesday
1st ♏

29 Thursday
1st ♏
♀ enters ♎ **3:49 am** 12:49 am
♃ enters ♍ **4:59 am**   1:59 am
☽ v/c   **5:20 pm**   2:20 pm
☽ enters ♐   9:03 pm

Eastern time in bold type
Pacific time in medium type

30 Friday

1st ♏
☽ enters ♐ **12:03 am**

1 Saturday

1st ♐
☽ v/c   **5:46 pm**   2:46 pm

2 Sunday

1st ♐
☽ enters ♑ **3:38 am** 12:38 am
☿ D   **5:07 am** 2:07 am
2nd Quarter **8:14 pm** 5:14 pm

September 2022						
S	M	T	W	T	F	S
				1	2	3
4	5	6	7	8	9	10
11	12	13	14	15	16	17
18	19	20	21	22	23	24
25	26	27	28	29	30	

October 2022						
S	M	T	W	T	F	S
						1
2	3	4	5	6	7	8
9	10	11	12	13	14	15
16	17	18	19	20	21	22
23	24	25	26	27	28	29
30	31					

November 2022						
S	M	T	W	T	F	S
		1	2	3	4	5
6	7	8	9	10	11	12
13	14	15	16	17	18	19
20	21	22	23	24	25	26
27	28	29	30			

Eastern time in bold type
Pacific time in medium type

3 Monday

2nd \Vs

D v/c **11:49 pm** 8:49 pm

4 Tuesday

2nd \Vs
D enters ≈ **6:20 am** 3:20 am

Yom Kippur begins at sundown

5 Wednesday

2nd ≈
⚹ D **2:10 pm** 11:10 am
D v/c **6:46 pm** 3:46 pm

6 Thursday

2nd ≈

D enters)(**8:47 am** 5:47 am

7 Friday

2nd ♓

8 Saturday

2nd ♓

☽ v/c	**7:10 am**	4:10 am
☽ enters ♈	**11:57 am**	8:57 am
♇ D	**5:56 pm**	2:56 pm

9 Sunday

2nd ♈

Full Moon   **4:55 pm**   1:55 pm

Sukkot begins at sundown

September 2022						
S	M	T	W	T	F	S
				1	2	3
4	5	6	7	8	9	10
11	12	13	14	15	16	17
18	19	20	21	22	23	24
25	26	27	28	29	30	

October 2022						
S	M	T	W	T	F	S
						1
2	3	4	5	6	7	8
9	10	11	12	13	14	15
16	17	18	19	20	21	22
23	24	25	26	27	28	29
30	31					

November 2022						
S	M	T	W	T	F	S
		1	2	3	4	5
6	7	8	9	10	11	12
13	14	15	16	17	18	19
20	21	22	23	24	25	26
27	28	29	30			

10 Monday

3rd ♈

☽ v/c	10:02 am	7:02 am
☽ enters ♉	5:04 pm	2:04 pm
☿ enters ♎	7:51 pm	4:51 pm

Indigenous Peoples' Day

11 Tuesday

3rd ♉

12 Wednesday

3rd ♉

| ☽ v/c | 5:42 pm | 2:42 pm |
| ☽ enters ♊ | | 10:08 pm |

13 Thursday

3rd ♉

| ☽ enters ♊ | 1:08 am |

Eastern time in bold type
Pacific time in medium type

14 Friday

3rd ♊
☽ v/c   9:11 pm

15 Saturday

3rd ♊
☽ v/c   **12:11 am**
☽ enters ♋   **12:11 pm**   9:11 am

16 Sunday

3rd ♋

Sukkot ends

September 2022						
S	M	T	W	T	F	S
				1	2	3
4	5	6	7	8	9	10
11	12	13	14	15	16	17
18	19	20	21	22	23	24
25	26	27	28	29	30	

October 2022						
S	M	T	W	T	F	S
						1
2	3	4	5	6	7	8
9	10	11	12	13	14	15
16	17	18	19	20	21	22
23	24	25	26	27	28	29
30	31					

November 2022						
S	M	T	W	T	F	S
		1	2	3	4	5
6	7	8	9	10	11	12
13	14	15	16	17	18	19
20	21	22	23	24	25	26
27	28	29	30			

Eastern time in bold type
Pacific time in medium type

17 Monday

3rd ♋
4th Quarter **1:15 pm** 10:15 am
☽ v/c **4:56 pm** 1:56 pm
☽ enters ♌ 9:45 pm

18 Tuesday

4th ♋
☽ enters ♌ **12:45 am**

19 Wednesday

4th ♌

20 Thursday

4th ♌
☽ v/c **6:35 am** 3:35 am
☽ enters ♍ **12:25 pm** 9:25 am

Eastern time in bold type
Pacific time in medium type

21 Friday
4th ♍

22 Saturday
4th ♍

☽ v/c	**2:17 pm**	11:17 am
☽ enters ♎	**9:24 pm**	6:24 pm
♄ D		9:07 pm

23 Sunday
4th ♎

♄ D	**12:07 am**	
♀ enters ♏	**3:52 am**	12:52 am
☉ enters ♏	**6:36 am**	3:36 am
✷ D	**9:05 am**	6:05 am

Sun enters Scorpio

September 2022						
S	M	T	W	T	F	S
				1	2	3
4	5	6	7	8	9	10
11	12	13	14	15	16	17
18	19	20	21	22	23	24
25	26	27	28	29	30	

October 2022						
S	M	T	W	T	F	S
						1
2	3	4	5	6	7	8
9	10	11	12	13	14	15
16	17	18	19	20	21	22
23	24	25	26	27	28	29
30	31					

November 2022						
S	M	T	W	T	F	S
		1	2	3	4	5
6	7	8	9	10	11	12
13	14	15	16	17	18	19
20	21	22	23	24	25	26
27	28	29	30			

Eastern time in bold type
Pacific time in medium type

24 Monday

4th ♎
☽ v/c   **8:36 pm**   5:36 pm

25 Tuesday

4th ♎
☽ enters ♏   **3:18 am** 12:18 am
New Moon   **6:49 am**   3:49 am

Solar Eclipse 2° ♏ oo'

26 Wednesday

1st ♏
☽ v/c   9:27 pm

27 Thursday

1st ♏
☽ v/c   **12:27 am**
☽ enters ♐   **6:55 am**   3:55 am
♃ enters ♓   10:10 pm

28 Friday

1st ♐
♃ enters ♓ **1:10 am**

29 Saturday

1st ♐
☽ v/c   **9:10 am**   6:10 am
☽ enters ♑   **9:21 am**   6:21 am
☿ enters ♏,   **3:22 pm** 12:22 pm

30 Sunday

1st ♑
♂ ℞   **9:26 am**   6:26 am

Mars retrograde until 1/12/23

| September 2022 |
S M T W T F S
1 2 3
4 5 6 7 8 9 10
11 12 13 14 15 16 17
18 19 20 21 22 23 24
25 26 27 28 29 30

| October 2022 |
S M T W T F S
1
2 3 4 5 6 7 8
9 10 11 12 13 14 15
16 17 18 19 20 21 22
23 24 25 26 27 28 29
30 31

| November 2022 |
S M T W T F S
1 2 3 4 5
6 7 8 9 10 11 12
13 14 15 16 17 18 19
20 21 22 23 24 25 26
27 28 29 30

31 Monday
1st ♑
☽ v/c	**11:14 am**	8:14 am
☽ enters ♒	**11:43 am**	8:43 am
2nd Quarter		11:37 pm

Halloween • Samhain

1 Tuesday
1st ♒
2nd Quarter **2:37 am**

All Saints' Day

2 Wednesday
2nd ♒
| ☽ v/c | **7:08 am** | 4:08 am |
| ☽ enters ♓ | **2:46 pm** | 11:46 am |

3 Thursday
2nd ♓

4 Friday
2nd ♓

☽ v/c	**6:05 pm**	3:05 pm
☽ enters ♈	**7:07 pm**	4:07 pm

5 Saturday
2nd ♈

6 Sunday
2nd ♈

☽ v/c	**5:30 pm**	2:30 pm
☽ enters ♉		9:15 pm

Daylight Saving Time ends at 2 am

October 2022						
S	M	T	W	T	F	S
						1
2	3	4	5	6	7	8
9	10	11	12	13	14	15
16	17	18	19	20	21	22
23	24	25	26	27	28	29
30	31					

November 2022						
S	M	T	W	T	F	S
		1	2	3	4	5
6	7	8	9	10	11	12
13	14	15	16	17	18	19
20	21	22	23	24	25	26
27	28	29	30			

December 2022						
S	M	T	W	T	F	S
				1	2	3
4	5	6	7	8	9	10
11	12	13	14	15	16	17
18	19	20	21	22	23	24
25	26	27	28	29	30	31

Eastern time in bold type
Pacific time in medium type

7 Monday

2nd ♈
☽ enters ♉ **12:15 am**

8 Tuesday

2nd ♉
Full Moon **6:02 am** 3:02 am

Election Day (general) • Lunar Eclipse 16° ♉ 01'

9 Wednesday

3rd ♉
☽ v/c **7:00 am** 4:00 am
☽ enters ♊ **8:37 am** 5:37 am

10 Thursday

3rd ♊

11 Friday

3rd ♊

☽ v/c   **5:28 pm**   2:28 pm
☽ enters ♋   **7:22 pm**   4:22 pm

Veterans Day

12 Saturday

3rd ♋

13 Sunday

3rd ♋

October 2022						
S	M	T	W	T	F	S
						1
2	3	4	5	6	7	8
9	10	11	12	13	14	15
16	17	18	19	20	21	22
23	24	25	26	27	28	29
30	31					

November 2022						
S	M	T	W	T	F	S
		1	2	3	4	5
6	7	8	9	10	11	12
13	14	15	16	17	18	19
20	21	22	23	24	25	26
27	28	29	30			

December 2022						
S	M	T	W	T	F	S
				1	2	3
4	5	6	7	8	9	10
11	12	13	14	15	16	17
18	19	20	21	22	23	24
25	26	27	28	29	30	31

Eastern time in bold type
Pacific time in medium type

14 Monday

3rd ♋
☽ v/c   **5:41 am** 2:41 am
☽ enters ♌ **7:48 am** 4:48 am

15 Tuesday

3rd ♌
♀ enters ♐   10:09 pm

16 Wednesday

3rd ♌
♀ enters ♐ **1:09 am**
4th Quarter **8:27 am** 5:27 am
☽ v/c   **6:55 pm** 3:55 pm
☽ enters ♍ **8:04 pm** 5:04 pm

17 Thursday

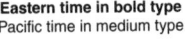

4th ♍
☿ enters ♐ **3:42 am** 12:42 am

Eastern time in bold type
Pacific time in medium type

18 Friday
4th ♍

19 Saturday
4th ♍
☽ v/c   **3:47 am** 12:47 am
☽ enters ♎   **5:58 am** 2:58 am

20 Sunday
4th ♎
⚥ enters ♓ **4:25 pm** 1:25 pm

October 2022						
S	M	T	W	T	F	S
						1
2	3	4	5	6	7	8
9	10	11	12	13	14	15
16	17	18	19	20	21	22
23	24	25	26	27	28	29
30	31					

November 2022						
S	M	T	W	T	F	S
		1	2	3	4	5
6	7	8	9	10	11	12
13	14	15	16	17	18	19
20	21	22	23	24	25	26
27	28	29	30			

December 2022						
S	M	T	W	T	F	S
				1	2	3
4	5	6	7	8	9	10
11	12	13	14	15	16	17
18	19	20	21	22	23	24
25	26	27	28	29	30	31

21 Monday

4th ♎︎
D v/c   **6:14 am**   3:14 am
D enters ♏︎ **12:16 pm**   9:16 am

22 Tuesday

4th ♏︎
☉ enters ♐︎ **3:20 am** 12:20 am

Sun enters Sagittarius

23 Wednesday

4th ♏︎
D v/c   **1:16 pm** 10:16 am
D enters ♐︎ **3:16 pm** 12:16 pm
New Moon   **5:57 pm**   2:57 pm
♃ D   **6:02 pm**   3:02 pm

24 Thursday

1st ♐︎

Thanksgiving Day

Eastern time in bold type
Pacific time in medium type

25 Friday

1st ♐
☽ v/c   **2:22 pm** 11:22 am
☽ enters ♑ **4:18 pm** 1:18 pm

26 Saturday

1st ♑

27 Sunday

1st ♑
☽ v/c   **3:11 pm** 12:11 pm
☽ enters ♒ **5:07 pm** 2:07 pm

October 2022						
S	M	T	W	T	F	S
						1
2	3	4	5	6	7	8
9	10	11	12	13	14	15
16	17	18	19	20	21	22
23	24	25	26	27	28	29
30	31					

November 2022						
S	M	T	W	T	F	S
		1	2	3	4	5
6	7	8	9	10	11	12
13	14	15	16	17	18	19
20	21	22	23	24	25	26
27	28	29	30			

December 2022						
S	M	T	W	T	F	S
				1	2	3
4	5	6	7	8	9	10
11	12	13	14	15	16	17
18	19	20	21	22	23	24
25	26	27	28	29	30	31

28 Monday

1st ≈
☽ v/c   10:53 pm

29 Tuesday

1st ≈
☽ v/c   **1:53 am**
☽ enters ♓   **7:15 pm**   4:15 pm

30 Wednesday

1st ♓
♀ Rx   **3:33 am** 12:33 am
2nd Quarter   **9:37 am**   6:37 am

1 Thursday

2nd ♓
☽ v/c   **9:44 pm**   6:44 pm
☽ enters ♈   **11:41 pm**   8:41 pm

Eastern time in bold type
Pacific time in medium type

2 Friday
2nd ♈

3 Saturday
2nd ♈
Ψ D   **7:15 pm**   4:15 pm
☽ v/c   9:46 pm

4 Sunday
2nd ♈
☽ v/c   **12:46 am**
☽ enters ♉   **6:38 am**   3:38 am

November 2022						
S	M	T	W	T	F	S
		1	2	3	4	5
6	7	8	9	10	11	12
13	14	15	16	17	18	19
20	21	22	23	24	25	26
27	28	29	30			

December 2022						
S	M	T	W	T	F	S
				1	2	3
4	5	6	7	8	9	10
11	12	13	14	15	16	17
18	19	20	21	22	23	24
25	26	27	28	29	30	31

January 2023						
S	M	T	W	T	F	S
1	2	3	4	5	6	7
8	9	10	11	12	13	14
15	16	17	18	19	20	21
22	23	24	25	26	27	28
29	30	31				

Eastern time in bold type
Pacific time in medium type

5 Monday

2nd ♉

6 Tuesday

2nd ♉
☽ v/c   **2:02 pm** 11:02 am
☽ enters ♊ **3:49 pm** 12:49 pm
☿ enters ♑ **5:08 pm** 2:08 pm

7 Wednesday

2nd ♊
Full Moon   **11:08 pm** 8:08 pm

8 Thursday

3rd ♊
☽ v/c   10:13 pm
☽ enters ♋   11:49 pm

9 Friday

3rd ♊

☽ v/c   **1:13 am**
☽ enters ♋   **2:49 am**
♀ enters ♑ **10:54 pm** 7:54 pm

10 Saturday

3rd ♋

11 Sunday

3rd ♋

☽ v/c   **1:49 pm** 10:49 am
☽ enters ♌ **3:09 pm** 12:09 pm

November 2022						
S	M	T	W	T	F	S
		1	2	3	4	5
6	7	8	9	10	11	12
13	14	15	16	17	18	19
20	21	22	23	24	25	26
27	28	29	30			

December 2022						
S	M	T	W	T	F	S
				1	2	3
4	5	6	7	8	9	10
11	12	13	14	15	16	17
18	19	20	21	22	23	24
25	26	27	28	29	30	31

January 2023						
S	M	T	W	T	F	S
1	2	3	4	5	6	7
8	9	10	11	12	13	14
15	16	17	18	19	20	21
22	23	24	25	26	27	28
29	30	31				

12 Monday
3rd ♌

13 Tuesday
3rd ♌
☽ v/c   **10:52 am**   7:52 am

14 Wednesday
3rd ♌
☽ enters ♍   **3:45 am**   12:45 am

15 Thursday
3rd ♍

16 Friday

3rd ♍
4th Quarter   **3:56 am**   12:56 am
☽ v/c   **2:13 pm**   11:13 am
☽ enters ♎   **2:49 pm**   11:49 am

17 Saturday

4th ♎

18 Sunday

4th ♎
☽ v/c   **5:35 pm**   2:35 pm
♀ enters ♎   **6:34 pm**   3:34 pm
☽ enters ♏   **10:31 pm**   7:31 pm

Hanukkah begins at sundown

November 2022						
S	M	T	W	T	F	S
		1	2	3	4	5
6	7	8	9	10	11	12
13	14	15	16	17	18	19
20	21	22	23	24	25	26
27	28	29	30			

December 2022						
S	M	T	W	T	F	S
				1	2	3
4	5	6	7	8	9	10
11	12	13	14	15	16	17
18	19	20	21	22	23	24
25	26	27	28	29	30	31

January 2023						
S	M	T	W	T	F	S
1	2	3	4	5	6	7
8	9	10	11	12	13	14
15	16	17	18	19	20	21
22	23	24	25	26	27	28
29	30	31				

19 Monday

4th ♏

20 Tuesday

4th ♏
♃ enters ♈ **9:32 am** 6:32 am
☽ v/c **9:45 pm** 6:45 pm
☽ enters ♐ 11:12 pm

21 Wednesday

4th ♏
☽ enters ♐ **2:12 am**
☉ enters ♑ **4:48 pm** 1:48 pm

Sun enters Capricorn • Yule • Winter Solstice • 4:48 pm EDT/1:48 pm PDT

22 Thursday

4th ♐
☽ v/c **3:16 pm** 12:16 pm
☽ enters ♑ 11:49 pm

Eastern time in bold type
Pacific time in medium type

23 Friday
4th ♐

☽ enters ♑	**2:49 am**	
☿ D	**4:31 am**	1:31 am
New Moon	**5:17 am**	2:17 am

24 Saturday
1st ♑

☽ v/c	**10:11 pm**	7:11 pm
☽ enters ≈		11:14 pm

Christmas Eve

25 Sunday
1st ♑

☽ enters ≈	**2:14 am**	

Christmas Day

November 2022	December 2022	January 2023
S M T W T F S	S M T W T F S	S M T W T F S
1 2 3 4 5	1 2 3	1 2 3 4 5 6 7
6 7 8 9 10 11 12	4 5 6 7 8 9 10	8 9 10 11 12 13 14
13 14 15 16 17 18 19	11 12 13 14 15 16 17	15 16 17 18 19 20 21
20 21 22 23 24 25 26	18 19 20 21 22 23 24	22 23 24 25 26 27 28
27 28 29 30	25 26 27 28 29 30 31	29 30 31

26 Monday

1st ≈
)) v/c   **1:19 pm** 10:19 am
)) enters ⓧ   11:34 pm

Kwanzaa begins

27 Tuesday

1st ≈
)) enters ⓧ   **2:34 am**

28 Wednesday

1st ⓧ
)) v/c   10:21 pm

29 Thursday

1st ⓧ
)) v/c   **1:21 am**
☿ ℞   **4:32 am**   1:32 am
)) enters ♈   **5:36 am**   2:36 am
2nd Quarter   **8:21 pm**   5:21 pm

Eastern time in bold type
Pacific time in medium type

30 Friday
2nd ♈

31 Saturday
2nd ♈
☽ v/c   **7:44 am**   4:44 am
☽ enters ♉   **12:08 pm**   9:08 am

New Year's Eve

1 Sunday
2nd ♉

Kwanzaa ends • New Year's Day

November 2022						
S	M	T	W	T	F	S
		1	2	3	4	5
6	7	8	9	10	11	12
13	14	15	16	17	18	19
20	21	22	23	24	25	26
27	28	29	30			

December 2022						
S	M	T	W	T	F	S
				1	2	3
4	5	6	7	8	9	10
11	12	13	14	15	16	17
18	19	20	21	22	23	24
25	26	27	28	29	30	31

January 2023						
S	M	T	W	T	F	S
1	2	3	4	5	6	7
8	9	10	11	12	13	14
15	16	17	18	19	20	21
22	23	24	25	26	27	28
29	30	31				

The Year 2022

January

S	M	T	W	T	F	S
						1
2	3	4	5	6	7	8
9	10	11	12	13	14	15
16	17	18	19	20	21	22
23	24	25	26	27	28	29
30	31					

February

S	M	T	W	T	F	S
		1	2	3	4	5
6	7	8	9	10	11	12
13	14	15	16	17	18	19
20	21	22	23	24	25	26
27	28					

March

S	M	T	W	T	F	S
		1	2	3	4	5
6	7	8	9	10	11	12
13	14	15	16	17	18	19
20	21	22	23	24	25	26
27	28	29	30	31		

April

S	M	T	W	T	F	S
					1	2
3	4	5	6	7	8	9
10	11	12	13	14	15	16
17	18	19	20	21	22	23
24	25	26	27	28	29	30

May

S	M	T	W	T	F	S
1	2	3	4	5	6	7
8	9	10	11	12	13	14
15	16	17	18	19	20	21
22	23	24	25	26	27	28
29	30	31				

June

S	M	T	W	T	F	S
			1	2	3	4
5	6	7	8	9	10	11
12	13	14	15	16	17	18
19	20	21	22	23	24	25
26	27	28	29	30		

July

S	M	T	W	T	F	S
					1	2
3	4	5	6	7	8	9
10	11	12	13	14	15	16
17	18	19	20	21	22	23
24	25	26	27	28	29	30
31						

August

S	M	T	W	T	F	S
	1	2	3	4	5	6
7	8	9	10	11	12	13
14	15	16	17	18	19	20
21	22	23	24	25	26	27
28	29	30	31			

September

S	M	T	W	T	F	S
				1	2	3
4	5	6	7	8	9	10
11	12	13	14	15	16	17
18	19	20	21	22	23	24
25	26	27	28	29	30	

October

S	M	T	W	T	F	S
						1
2	3	4	5	6	7	8
9	10	11	12	13	14	15
16	17	18	19	20	21	22
23	24	25	26	27	28	29
30	31					

November

S	M	T	W	T	F	S
		1	2	3	4	5
6	7	8	9	10	11	12
13	14	15	16	17	18	19
20	21	22	23	24	25	26
27	28	29	30			

December

S	M	T	W	T	F	S
				1	2	3
4	5	6	7	8	9	10
11	12	13	14	15	16	17
18	19	20	21	22	23	24
25	26	27	28	29	30	31

The Year 2023

January
S	M	T	W	T	F	S
1	2	3	4	5	6	7
8	9	10	11	12	13	14
15	16	17	18	19	20	21
22	23	24	25	26	27	28
29	30	31				

February
S	M	T	W	T	F	S
			1	2	3	4
5	6	7	8	9	10	11
12	13	14	15	16	17	18
19	20	21	22	23	24	25
26	27	28				

March
S	M	T	W	T	F	S
			1	2	3	4
5	6	7	8	9	10	11
12	13	14	15	16	17	18
19	20	21	22	23	24	25
26	27	28	29	30	31	

April
S	M	T	W	T	F	S
						1
2	3	4	5	6	7	8
9	10	11	12	13	14	15
16	17	18	19	20	21	22
23	24	25	26	27	28	29
30						

May
S	M	T	W	T	F	S
	1	2	3	4	5	6
7	8	9	10	11	12	13
14	15	16	17	18	19	20
21	22	23	24	25	26	27
28	29	30	31			

June
S	M	T	W	T	F	S
				1	2	3
4	5	6	7	8	9	10
11	12	13	14	15	16	17
18	19	20	21	22	23	24
25	26	27	28	29	30	

July
S	M	T	W	T	F	S
						1
2	3	4	5	6	7	8
9	10	11	12	13	14	15
16	17	18	19	20	21	22
23	24	25	26	27	28	29
30	31					

August
S	M	T	W	T	F	S
		1	2	3	4	5
6	7	8	9	10	11	12
13	14	15	16	17	18	19
20	21	22	23	24	25	26
27	28	29	30	31		

September
S	M	T	W	T	F	S
					1	2
3	4	5	6	7	8	9
10	11	12	13	14	15	16
17	18	19	20	21	22	23
24	25	26	27	28	29	30

October
S	M	T	W	T	F	S
1	2	3	4	5	6	7
8	9	10	11	12	13	14
15	16	17	18	19	20	21
22	23	24	25	26	27	28
29	30	31				

November
S	M	T	W	T	F	S
			1	2	3	4
5	6	7	8	9	10	11
12	13	14	15	16	17	18
19	20	21	22	23	24	25
26	27	28	29	30		

December
S	M	T	W	T	F	S
					1	2
3	4	5	6	7	8	9
10	11	12	13	14	15	16
17	18	19	20	21	22	23
24	25	26	27	28	29	30
31						

JANUARY 2021

D Last Aspect / D Ingress

D Last Aspect day ET / hr:mn / PT	D Ingress sign day ET / hr:mn / PT
17 10:44 pm 7:44 pm	17 11:07 pm
17 10:44 pm 7:44 pm	18 2:07 am 9:00 pm
20 3:29 am 12:29 am	20 1:56 pm 10:56 am
	11:43 pm
22 4:28 am 1:28 am	22 2:43 am
22 4:28 am 1:28 am	23 1:52 am 10:52 am
24 11:17	25 1:52 am 10:52 am
25 2:17 am	9:54 pm 6:54 pm
27 12:55 am	27 3:02 pm 12:02 am
29 8:53 am 5:53 pm	30

D Phases & Eclipses

phase day	ET / hr:mn / PT
4th Quarter 6	4:37 am 1:37 am
New Moon 12	9:00 pm
New Moon 13	12:00 am
2nd Quarter 20	4:02 pm 1:02 pm
Full Moon 28	2:16 pm 11:16 am

Planet Ingress

day	ET / hr:mn / PT
♂ ♒ 6	5:27 pm 2:27 pm
☿ ♒ 8	7:00 am 4:00 am
♀ ♑ 8	10:41 am 7:41 am
⊙ ♒ 19	3:40 pm 12:40 pm

Planetary Motion

day	ET / hr:mn / PT
♇ R, 14	3:36 am 12:36 am
♀ R, 19	3:54 am 12:54 am
☿ R, 30	10:52 am 7:52 am

1 FRIDAY
ET / hr:mn / PT	
2:26 am	
6:18 am 3:18 am	
10:55 am 7:55 am	
11:39 pm 8:39 pm	
11:02 pm	

2 SATURDAY
2:02 am	
6:24 am 3:24 am	
9:57 am 6:57 am	
11:32 pm 8:32 pm	
11:05 pm	

3 SUNDAY
2:05 am	
8:12 am 5:12 am	
9:19 am 6:19 am	

4 MONDAY
4:50 am 1:50 am	
4:11 am 1:11 am	
4:34 am 1:34 am	
7:58 am 4:58 am	
11:19 pm 8:19 pm	

5 TUESDAY
4:22 am 1:22 am	
7:17 am 4:17 am	
12:19 pm 9:19 am	

6 WEDNESDAY
4:37 am 1:37 am	
8:32 am 5:32 am	
6:23 pm 3:23 pm	
9:21 pm	
9:55 pm	

7 THURSDAY
12:21 am	
12:55 am	
4:14 am 1:14 am	
7:54 am 4:54 am	
11:11 am 8:11 am	
3:16 pm 12:16 pm	
7:04 pm 4:04 pm	

8 FRIDAY
11:11 am 8:11 am	
11:54 am 8:54 am	
11:53 pm 8:53 pm	
8:59 pm	
9:44 pm	

9 SATURDAY
8:07 am 5:07 am	
8:17 am 5:17 am	
9:15 am 6:15 am	
10:38 am 7:38 am	
10:53 am 7:53 am	
2:18 pm 11:18 am	
5:30 pm 2:30 pm	
10:17 pm 7:17 pm	

10 SUNDAY
1:29 am 10:29 pm	
3:39 am 12:39 am	
5:12 am 2:12 am	
11:17 8:17 pm	

11 MONDAY
12:16 am 9:16 am	
12:19 am 9:19 am	
1:20 am 10:20 am	
3:14 am 12:14 am	
5:28 am 2:28 am	
6:02 am 3:02 am	
7:51 am 4:51 am	

12 TUESDAY
10:00 am 7:00 am	
4:17 pm 1:17 pm	
9:40 pm 6:40 pm	
11:22 pm	

13 WEDNESDAY
12:00 am	
6:02 am 3:02 am	
5:11 am 2:11 am	
5:30 am 2:30 am	
7:22 am 4:22 am	
9:55 am 6:55 am	
11:29 pm 8:29 pm	
11:54 pm 8:54 pm	

14 THURSDAY
4:26 am 1:26 am	
9:19 am 6:19 am	
8:55 pm 5:55 pm	

15 FRIDAY
7:33 am 4:33 am	
9:21 am 6:21 am	
11:33 pm 8:33 pm	
10:29 pm	

16 SATURDAY
1:29 am	
5:03 am 2:03 am	
5:43 am 2:43 am	
12:02 pm 9:02 am	
6:33 pm 3:33 pm	

17 SUNDAY
4:35 am 1:35 am	
3:55 pm 12:55 pm	
5:50 pm 2:50 pm	
10:44 pm 7:44 pm	

18 MONDAY
9:20 am 6:20 am	
10:16 am 7:16 am	
3:20 pm 12:20 pm	
3:45 pm 12:45 pm	

19 TUESDAY
4:43 am 1:43 am	
12:54 pm 9:54 am	
3:34 pm 12:34 pm	

20 WEDNESDAY
3:29 am 12:29 am	
1:04 am 10:04 am	
3:38 pm 12:38 pm	
4:02 pm 1:02 pm	
10:00 pm 7:00 pm	

21 THURSDAY
3:37 am 12:37 am	
4:08 am 1:08 am	
5:15 am 2:15 am	

22 FRIDAY
12:28 am	
4:27 am 1:27 am	
8:59 am 5:59 am	
4:28 am 1:28 am	
11:49 pm	

23 SATURDAY
2:49 am	
10:27 am 7:27 am	
11:19 am 8:19 am	
2:49 pm 11:16 am	
7:04 am 4:04 am	
7:27 am 4:27 am	

24 SUNDAY
10:01 am 7:01 am	

25 MONDAY
2:17 am	
4:12 am 1:12 am	
10:38 pm 7:38 pm	
11:23 pm	
11:49 pm	

26 TUESDAY
2:23 am	
2:49 am	
6:32 am 3:32 am	
7:38 am 4:38 am	
8:17 am 5:17 am	
9:35 am 6:35 am	
10:57	

27 WEDNESDAY
1:57 am	
10:37 am 7:37 am	
12:55 pm 9:55 am	
2:09 pm 11:09 am	

28 THURSDAY
6:41 am 3:41 am	
10:11 am 7:11 am	
11:18 am 8:18 am	
2:16 pm 11:16 am	
2:39 pm 11:39 am	
5:32 pm 2:32 pm	
8:40 pm 5:40 pm	

29 FRIDAY
4:36 am 1:36 am	
7:28 am 4:28 am	
11:17	
8:10 am 5:10 am	
12:19 pm 9:19 am	

30 SATURDAY
6:36 am 3:36 pm	
8:53 am 5:53 pm	
9:39 am 6:39 pm	
11:54 am 8:54 am	
2:52 pm 11:52 am	
8:01 pm 5:01 pm	
10:51 pm 7:51 pm	
11:57 pm 8:57 pm	

31 SUNDAY
12:09 pm 9:09 am	
10:17 pm 7:17 pm	
9:05 pm	

Eastern time in bold type
Pacific time in medium type

JANUARY 2021

DATE	SID.TIME	SUN	MOON	NODE	MERCURY	VENUS	MARS	JUPITER	SATURN	URANUS	NEPTUNE	PLUTO	CERES	PALLAS	JUNO	VESTA	CHIRON
1 F	6 47 27	10♑46 47	2♋44	19♊53R	17♑43	20♐25	27♈21	2≈47	1≈33	6♉48R	18♓28	24♑11	12♏00	7≈55	4♈15	20♍09	5♈04
2 Sa	6 47 24	11 47 56	15 55	19 49	19 21	21 40	27 48	3 01	1 44	6 47	18 30	24 13	12 18	8 11	4 34	20 16	5 04
3 Su	6 51 21	12 49 04	29 19	19 46	20 59	22 55	28 14	3 14	1 51	6 47	18 31	24 15	12 37	8 31	4 52	20 24	5 05
4 M	6 55 17	13 50 13	12♍55	19 43	22 37	24 10	28 40	3 28	1 58	6 46	18 32	24 17	12 56	8 51	5 11	20 30	5 06
5 T	6 59 14	14 51 22	26 42	19 40	24 15	25 25	29 07	3 42	2 05	6 46	18 33	24 19	13 15	9 11	5 30	20 37	5 08
6 W	7 3 10	15 52 31	10♎55	19 39D	25 54	26 40	29 34	3 56	2 12	6 45	18 34	24 21	13 34	9 31	5 48	20 43	5 09
7 Th	7 7 7	16 53 40	24 45	19 40	27 32	27 56	0♉02	4 10	2 19	6 45	18 36	24 23	13 53	9 51	6 07	20 49	5 10
8 F	7 11 3	17 54 50	8♏58	19 40	29 11	29 11	0 29	4 24	2 26	6 44	18 37	24 25	14 13	10 11	6 25	20 54	5 11
9 Sa	7 15 0	18 56 00	23 16	19 42	0≈49	0♑26	0 57	4 38	2 33	6 44	18 38	24 27	14 32	10 31	6 43	20 59	5 12
10 Su	7 18 56	19 57 09	7♐38	19 43R	2 27	1 41	1 25	4 52	2 40	6 44	18 40	24 29	14 52	10 51	7 01	21 04	5 14
11 M	7 22 53	20 58 19	21 58	19 44	4 05	2 56	1 54	5 06	2 47	6 44	18 41	24 31	15 11	11 11	7 19	21 08	5 15
12 T	7 26 50	21 59 29	6♑13	19 43	5 43	4 12	2 22	5 20	2 54	6 43	18 42	24 33	15 31	11 31	7 37	21 11	5 16
13 W	7 30 46	23 00 39	20 19	19 40	7 20	5 27	2 51	5 34	3 01	6 43	18 44	24 35	15 51	11 51	7 55	21 14	5 18
14 Th	7 34 43	24 01 48	4≈10	19 35	8 56	6 42	3 20	5 48	3 08	6 43D	18 45	24 37	16 11	12 12	8 13	21 17	5 19
15 F	7 38 39	25 02 57	17 43	19 30	10 30	7 57	3 49	6 02	3 15	6 43	18 47	24 39	16 31	12 32	8 31	21 19	5 21
16 Sa	7 42 36	26 04 05	0♓56	19 23	12 04	9 13	4 19	6 16	3 22	6 43	18 48	24 41	16 52	12 52	8 49	21 21	5 23
17 Su	7 46 32	27 05 12	13 48	19 17	13 35	10 28	4 48	6 30	3 30	6 43	18 50	24 43	17 12	13 12	9 06	21 22	5 24
18 M	7 50 29	28 06 19	26 20	19 11	15 05	11 43	5 18	6 44	3 37	6 44	18 52	24 45	17 32	13 33	9 24	21 23	5 26
19 T	7 54 25	29 07 24	8♈35	19 07	16 32	12 58	5 48	6 59	3 44	6 44	18 53	24 47	17 53	13 53	9 41	21 24R	5 28
20 W	7 58 22	0≈08 29	20 37	19 05D	17 55	14 13	6 18	7 13	3 51	6 44	18 55	24 49	18 13	14 13	9 58	21 23	5 30
21 Th	8 2 19	1 09 34	2♉30	19 04	19 15	15 29	6 49	7 27	3 58	6 44	18 56	24 51	18 34	14 34	10 15	21 22	5 31
22 F	8 6 15	2 10 37	14 19	19 05	20 31	16 44	7 19	7 41	4 05	6 45	18 58	24 53	18 55	14 54	10 32	21 21	5 33
23 Sa	8 10 12	3 11 39	26 10	19 07	21 42	17 59	7 50	7 55	4 12	6 45	19 00	24 55	19 16	15 14	10 49	21 19	5 35
24 Su	8 14 8	4 12 40	8♊08	19 08R	22 47	19 14	8 21	8 10	4 19	6 46	19 01	24 57	19 37	15 34	11 06	21 16	5 37
25 M	8 18 5	5 13 41	20 17	19 09	23 45	20 30	8 52	8 24	4 27	6 46	19 03	24 59	19 58	15 55	11 23	21 13	5 39
26 T	8 22 1	6 14 40	2♋41	19 07	24 35	21 45	9 23	8 38	4 34	6 47	19 05	25 01	20 19	16 15	11 39	21 10	5 41
27 W	8 25 58	7 15 39	15 23	19 04	25 18	23 00	9 54	8 52	4 41	6 48	19 07	25 03	20 41	16 36	11 56	21 06	5 44
28 Th	8 29 54	8 16 36	28 24	18 59	25 51	24 15	10 26	9 07	4 48	6 48	19 09	25 05	21 02	16 56	12 12	21 02	5 46
29 F	8 33 51	9 17 33	11♌45	18 51	26 14	25 30	10 57	9 21	4 55	6 49	19 10	25 07	21 23	17 16	12 29	20 57	5 48
30 Sa	8 37 48	10 18 28	25 23	18 42	26 27R	26 45	11 29	9 35	5 02	6 50	19 12	25 09	21 45	17 37	12 45	20 52	5 50
31 Su	8 41 44	11 19 23	9♍15	18 33	26 29	28 01	12 01	9 49	5 09	6 51	19 14	25 11	22 07	17 57	13 01	20 52	5 53

EPHEMERIS CALCULATED FOR 12 MIDNIGHT GREENWICH MEAN TIME. ALL OTHER DATA AND FACING ASPECTARIAN PAGE IN **EASTERN TIME (BOLD)** AND PACIFIC TIME (REGULAR).

FEBRUARY 2021

☽ Last Aspect day	ET / hr:mn / PT	asp	☽ Ingress sign day	ET / hr:mn / PT
1	**6:10 am** 3:10 am	△♀	♎ 1	**6:25 am** 3:25 am
2	10:15 pm	△☿	♏ 3	**9:15 am** 6:15 am
3	**1:15 am**	△☿	♏ 3	**9:15 am** 6:15 am
5	**4:20 am** 1:20 am	⚹♇	♐ 5	**12:16 pm** 9:16 am
6	10:16 pm	⚹☿	♑ 7	**3:52 pm** 12:52 pm
7	**1:16 am**	⚹☿	♑ 7	**3:52 pm** 12:52 pm
9	**12:22 pm** 9:22 am	☌♇	♒ 9	**8:20 pm** 5:20 pm
11	**2:06 pm** 11:06 am	☌☉	♓ 11	11:23 pm
11	**2:06 pm** 11:06 am	☌☉	♓ 12	**2:23 am**
13	11:29 pm	⚹♇	♈ 14	**10:54 am** 7:54 am
14	**2:29 am**	⚹♇	♈ 14	**10:54 am** 7:54 am
16	**7:17 pm** 4:17 pm	⚹☉	♉ 16	**10:12 pm** 7:12 pm
18	11:28 pm	△♇	♊ 19	**11:04 am** 8:04 am
19	**2:28 am**	△♇	♊ 19	**11:04 am** 8:04 am
21	**1:39 pm** 10:39 am	△♀	♋ 21	**10:53 pm** 7:53 pm
23	**11:54 pm** 8:54 pm	☍♇	♌ 24	**7:23 am** 4:23 am
26	**6:32 am** 3:32 am	□♂	♍ 26	**12:07 pm** 9:07 am
28	**10:58 am** 7:58 am	△♂	♎ 28	**2:17 pm** 11:17 am

☽ Phases & Eclipses

phase	day	ET / hr:mn / PT
4th Quarter	4	**12:37 pm** 9:37 am
New Moon	11	**2:06 pm** 11:06 am
2nd Quarter	19	**1:47 pm** 10:47 am
Full Moon	27	**3:17 am** 12:17 am

Planet Ingress

	day	ET / hr:mn / PT
♀ ♒	1	**9:05 am** 6:05 am
☉ ♓	18	**5:44 am** 2:44 am
⚳ ♈	20	9:23 pm
⚳ ♈	21	**12:23 am**
♀ ♓	25	**8:11 am** 5:11 am

Planetary Motion

		day	ET / hr:mn / PT
☿	D	20	**7:52 pm** 4:52 pm

1 MONDAY
☽ ⚻ ☿ **12:05 am**
☉ □ ♂ **5:34 am** 2:34 am
☽ △ ♀ **6:10 am** 3:10 am
☽ △ ♄ **3:32 pm** 12:32 pm
☽ ⚻ ♅ **6:05 pm** 3:05 pm
☽ △ ♃ **11:58 pm** 8:58 pm

2 TUESDAY
☽ ⚻ ♂ **4:59 am** 1:59 am
☽ △ ☉ **5:50 am** 2:50 am
☽ ⚻ ♆ **3:10 pm** 12:10 pm
☽ □ ♇ 10:15 pm
☽ △ ☿ 10:15 pm
☿ ⚺ ♇ 10:22 pm

3 WEDNESDAY
☽ □ ♇ **1:15 am**
☽ △ ☿ **1:15 am**
☿ ⚺ ♇ **1:22 am**
☽ □ ♀ **1:55 pm** 10:55 am
☽ □ ♄ **6:47 pm** 3:47 pm
☽ ☍ ♅ **8:57 pm** 5:57 pm

4 THURSDAY
☽ □ ♃ **3:40 am** 12:40 am
☽ ☍ ♂ **9:51 am** 6:51 am
☽ □ ☉ **12:37 pm** 9:37 am
☽ △ ♆ **6:11 pm** 3:11 pm
☽ □ ☿ 10:27 pm

5 FRIDAY
☽ □ ☿ **1:27 am**
☽ ⚹ ♇ **4:20 am** 1:20 am
☽ ⚹ ♀ **10:00 pm** 7:00 pm
☽ ⚹ ♄ **10:20 pm** 7:20 pm
☽ ⚻ ♅ 9:10 pm
♀ ☌ ♄ 11:07 pm

6 SATURDAY
☽ ⚻ ♅ **12:10 am**
♀ ☌ ♄ **2:07 am**
☽ ⚹ ♃ **7:45 am** 4:45 am
☽ ⚻ ♂ **3:12 pm** 12:12 pm
☽ ⚹ ☉ **7:56 pm** 4:56 pm
☽ □ ♆ **9:40 pm** 6:40 pm
♀ □ ♅ **10:33 pm** 7:33 pm
☽ ⚹ ☿ 10:16 pm

7 SUNDAY
☽ ⚹ ☿ **1:16 am**
☽ ⚺ ♇ **7:56 am** 4:56 am
☉ ⚺ ♆ **8:32 pm** 5:32 pm
☽ ⚺ ♄ 11:31 pm

8 MONDAY
☽ ⚺ ♄ **2:31 am**
☽ △ ♅ **4:00 am** 1:00 am
☽ ⚺ ♀ **6:53 am** 3:53 am
☉ ☌ ☿ **8:48 am** 5:48 am
☽ ⚺ ♃ **12:32 pm** 9:32 am
☿ ⚺ ♆ **6:35 pm** 3:35 pm
☽ △ ♂ **9:21 pm** 6:21 pm
☽ ⚺ ☿ 10:18 pm
☽ ⚹ ♆ 10:55 pm

9 TUESDAY
☽ ⚺ ☿ **1:18 am**
☽ ⚹ ♆ **1:55 am**
☽ ⚺ ☉ **4:11 am** 1:11 am
☽ ☌ ♇ **12:22 pm** 9:22 am

10 WEDNESDAY
☿ □ ♂ **7:16 am** 4:16 am
☽ ☌ ♄ **7:42 am** 4:42 am
☽ □ ♅ **8:51 am** 5:51 am
☽ ☌ ♀ **5:11 pm** 2:11 pm
☽ ☌ ♃ **6:29 pm** 3:29 pm
☽ ☌ ☿ 11:22 pm

11 THURSDAY
☽ ☌ ☿ **2:22 am**
☽ □ ♂ **4:55 am** 1:55 am
☽ ⚺ ♆ **7:27 am** 4:27 am
♀ ☌ ♃ **10:00 am** 7:00 am
☽ ☌ ☉ **2:06 pm** 11:06 am
☽ ⚺ ♇ **6:14 pm** 3:14 pm

12 FRIDAY
☽ ⚺ ♄ **2:42 pm** 11:42 am
☽ ⚹ ♅ **3:30 pm** 12:30 pm
☽ ⚺ ♃ 11:29 pm
☿ ☌ ♀ 11:48 pm

13 SATURDAY
☽ ⚺ ♃ **2:29 am**
☿ ☌ ♀ **2:48 am**
☽ ⚺ ☿ **5:32 am** 2:32 am
☽ ⚺ ♀ **6:03 am** 3:03 am
☽ ⚹ ♂ **2:55 pm** 11:55 am
☽ ☌ ♆ **3:11 pm** 12:11 pm
♂ ⚹ ♆ **9:13 pm** 6:13 pm
☉ ⚺ ♇ **9:34 pm** 6:34 pm
☽ ⚹ ♇ 11:29 pm
☽ ⚺ ☉ 11:54 pm

14 SUNDAY
☽ ⚹ ♇ **2:29 am**
☽ ⚺ ☉ **2:54 am**
☿ ☌ ♃ **4:40 pm** 1:40 pm
☽ ⚹ ♄ 9:23 pm
☽ ⚺ ♅ 9:49 pm

15 MONDAY
☽ ⚹ ♄ **12:23 am**
☽ ⚺ ♅ **12:49 am**
☽ ⚹ ☿ **11:50 am** 8:50 am
☽ ⚹ ♃ **1:22 pm** 10:22 am
☽ ⚹ ♀ **10:40 pm** 7:40 pm
☽ ⚺ ♆ 10:44 pm

16 TUESDAY
☽ ⚺ ♆ **1:44 am**
☽ ⚺ ♂ **4:08 am** 1:08 am
☽ □ ♇ **1:32 pm** 10:32 am
☽ ⚹ ☉ **7:17 pm** 4:17 pm

17 WEDNESDAY
♀ ⚺ ♆ **5:00 am** 2:00 am
☽ □ ♄ **12:48 pm** 9:48 am
☽ ☌ ♅ **12:48 pm** 9:48 am
♄ □ ♅ **2:08 pm** 11:08 am
☽ □ ☿ **9:32 pm** 6:32 pm
☽ □ ♃ 11:51 pm

18 THURSDAY
☽ □ ♃ **2:51 am**
☽ ⚹ ♆ **2:30 pm** 11:30 am
☽ □ ♀ **6:21 pm** 3:21 pm
☽ ☌ ♂ **7:48 pm** 4:48 pm
☽ △ ♇ 11:28 pm

19 FRIDAY
☽ △ ♇ **2:28 am**
☽ □ ☉ **1:47 pm** 10:47 am
♀ □ ♂ **6:04 pm** 3:04 pm
☽ ⚺ ♅ 10:50 pm
☽ △ ♄ 11:15 pm

20 SATURDAY
☽ ⚺ ♅ **1:50 am**
☽ △ ♄ **2:15 am**
☽ △ ☿ **9:20 am** 6:20 am
☽ △ ♃ **4:46 pm** 1:46 pm

21 SUNDAY
☽ □ ♆ **3:10 am** 12:10 am
☽ ⚺ ♂ **11:06 am** 8:06 am
☽ △ ♀ **1:39 pm** 10:39 am
☽ ⚻ ♇ **2:45 pm** 11:45 am
♀ ⚺ ♇ 9:31 pm

22 MONDAY
♀ ⚺ ♇ **12:31 am**
☽ △ ☉ **6:47 am** 3:47 am
☽ ⚹ ♅ **1:09 pm** 10:09 am
☽ ⚻ ♄ **1:55 pm** 10:55 am
☽ ⚻ ☿ **8:31 pm** 5:31 pm

23 TUESDAY
☽ ⚻ ♃ **4:14 am** 1:14 am
☽ △ ♆ **1:06 pm** 10:06 am
☽ ⚹ ♂ **10:59 pm** 7:59 pm
☽ ☍ ♇ **11:54 pm** 8:54 pm

24 WEDNESDAY
☽ ⚻ ♀ **4:47 am** 1:47 am
☽ ⚻ ☉ **7:18 pm** 4:18 pm
☽ □ ♅ **8:49 pm** 5:49 pm
♂ △ ♇ **8:52 pm** 5:52 pm
☽ ☍ ♄ **9:52 pm** 6:52 pm

25 THURSDAY
☽ ☍ ☿ **4:56 am** 1:56 am
☽ ☍ ♃ **11:40 am** 8:40 am
☉ ⚹ ♅ **4:13 pm** 1:13 pm
☽ ⚻ ♆ **7:09 pm** 4:09 pm

26 FRIDAY
☽ ⚻ ♇ **5:12 am** 2:12 am
☽ □ ♂ **6:32 am** 3:32 am
☉ ⚺ ♄ **9:25 am** 6:25 am
☽ ☍ ♀ **2:50 pm** 11:50 am
☽ △ ♅ 9:54 pm
☽ ⚻ ♄ 11:09 pm

27 SATURDAY
☽ △ ♅ **12:54 am**
☽ ⚻ ♄ **2:09 am**
☽ ☍ ☉ **3:17 am** 12:17 am
☽ ⚻ ☿ **10:25 am** 7:25 am
☽ ⚻ ♃ **3:40 pm** 12:40 pm
☽ ☍ ♆ **10:06 pm** 7:06 pm

28 SUNDAY
☽ △ ♇ **7:42 am** 4:42 am
☽ △ ♂ **10:58 am** 7:58 am
☽ ⚻ ♀ **9:36 pm** 6:36 pm
☽ ⚻ ♅ 11:49 pm

Eastern time in bold type
Pacific time in medium type

FEBRUARY 2021

DATE	SID.TIME	SUN	MOON	NODE	MERCURY	VENUS	MARS	JUPITER	SATURN	URANUS	NEPTUNE	PLUTO	CERES	PALLAS	JUNO	VESTA	CHIRON
1 M	8 45 41	12≈20 16	23♏17	18Ⅱ25R	26≈19R	29♑16	22♉33	10≈04	5≈17	6♉51	19ℋ16	25♑13	22♈28	18≈17	13♈17	20♍46R	5♈55
2 T	8 49 37	13 21 09	7✗25	18 18	25 59	0≈31	23 05	10 18	5 24	6 52	19 18	25 15	22 50	18 38	13 33	20 40	5 57
3 W	8 53 34	14 22 01	21 36	18 13	25 27	1 46	23 37	10 32	5 31	6 53	19 20	25 16	23 12	18 58	13 48	20 33	6 00
4 Th	8 57 30	15 22 52	5♑45	18 11D	24 45	3 01	24 10	10 46	5 38	6 54	19 22	25 18	23 34	19 19	14 04	20 26	6 02
5 F	9 1 27	16 23 43	19 52	18 11	23 54	4 17	24 42	11 00	5 45	6 56	19 24	25 20	23 56	19 39	14 19	20 18	6 05
6 Sa	9 5 23	17 24 32	3✗56	18 11	22 56	5 32	25 15	11 15	5 52	6 57	19 26	25 22	24 18	19 59	14 34	20 10	6 07
7 Su	9 9 20	18 25 21	17 55	18 12R	21 51	6 47	25 47	11 29	5 59	6 58	19 28	25 24	24 40	20 20	14 50	20 02	6 10
8 M	9 13 17	19 26 09	1♒49	18 11	20 42	8 02	26 20	11 43	6 06	6 59	19 30	25 26	25 02	20 40	15 05	19 53	6 12
9 T	9 17 13	20 26 56	15 36	18 08	19 31	9 17	26 53	11 57	6 13	7 00	19 32	25 28	25 24	21 00	15 19	19 43	6 15
10 W	9 21 10	21 27 42	29 15	18 02	18 19	10 32	27 26	12 12	6 20	7 02	19 34	25 30	25 46	21 21	15 34	19 33	6 18
11 Th	9 25 6	22 28 26	12ℋ43	17 53	17 09	11 48	27 59	12 26	6 27	7 03	19 36	25 31	26 09	21 41	15 49	19 23	6 20
12 F	9 29 3	23 29 09	25 58	17 42	16 03	13 03	28 33	12 40	6 34	7 05	19 38	25 33	26 31	22 01	16 03	19 12	6 23
13 Sa	9 32 59	24 29 51	8♈58	17 30	15 01	14 18	29 06	12 54	6 41	7 06	19 40	25 35	26 53	22 22	16 17	19 01	6 26
14 Su	9 36 56	25 30 31	21 43	17 18	14 05	15 33	29 39	13 08	6 48	7 08	19 42	25 37	27 16	22 42	16 31	18 50	6 29
15 M	9 40 52	26 31 10	4♉11	17 06	13 16	16 48	0≈13	13 22	6 55	7 09	19 44	25 39	27 38	23 02	16 45	18 38	6 32
16 T	9 44 49	27 31 47	16 24	16 57	12 35	18 03	0 47	13 36	7 02	7 11	19 47	25 40	28 01	23 22	16 59	18 26	6 35
17 W	9 48 46	28 32 22	28 25	16 50	12 01	19 18	1 20	13 50	7 08	7 13	19 49	25 42	28 24	23 43	17 13	18 13	6 37
18 Th	9 52 42	29 32 56	10Ⅱ17	16 46	11 35	20 33	1 54	14 04	7 15	7 14	19 51	25 44	28 46	24 03	17 26	18 00	6 40
19 F	9 56 39	0ℋ33 28	22 06	16 44D	11 16	21 49	2 28	14 18	7 22	7 16	19 53	25 46	29 09	24 23	17 39	17 47	6 43
20 Sa	10 0 35	1 33 58	3♋55	16 44	11 16	23 04	3 02	14 32	7 29	7 18	19 55	25 47	29 32	24 43	17 52	17 34	6 46
21 Su	10 4 32	2 34 26	15 52	16 44R	11 01	24 19	3 36	14 46	7 36	7 20	19 57	25 49	29 55	25 03	18 05	17 20	6 49
22 M	10 8 28	3 34 52	28 01	16 44	11 05	25 34	4 10	15 00	7 42	7 22	20 00	25 51	0♉18	25 24	18 18	17 06	6 52
23 T	10 12 25	4 35 17	10♋27	16 41	11 14	26 49	4 44	15 14	7 49	7 23	20 02	25 52	0 41	25 44	18 31	16 52	6 55
24 W	10 16 21	5 35 40	23 15	16 35	11 30	28 04	5 19	15 28	7 55	7 25	20 04	25 54	1 04	26 04	18 43	16 37	6 59
25 Th	10 20 18	6 36 00	6♍27	16 29	11 51	29 19	5 53	15 42	8 02	7 27	20 06	25 55	1 27	26 24	18 55	16 22	7 02
26 F	10 24 15	7 36 19	20 03	16 20	12 18	0ℋ34	6 27	15 56	8 09	7 30	20 09	25 57	1 50	26 44	19 07	16 07	7 05
27 Sa	10 28 11	8 36 36	4♍03	16 08	12 50	1 49	7 02	16 09	8 15	7 32	20 11	25 59	2 13	27 04	19 19	15 52	7 08
28 Su	10 32 8	9 36 52	18 21	15 56	13 26	3 04	7 36	16 23	8 22	7 34	20 13	26 00	2 36	27 24	19 31	15 37	7 11

EPHEMERIS CALCULATED FOR 12 MIDNIGHT GREENWICH MEAN TIME. ALL OTHER DATA AND FACING ASPECTARIAN PAGE IN **EASTERN TIME (BOLD)** AND PACIFIC TIME (REGULAR).

MARCH 2021

☽ Last Aspect day	ET / hr:mn / PT	asp	☽ Ingress sign	day	ET / hr:mn / PT
2	**9:09 am** 6:09 am	□♇	♏	2	**3:38 pm** 12:38 pm
4	**11:10 am** 8:10 am	⚹♇	♐	4	**5:43 pm** 2:43 pm
6	**4:44 am** 1:44 am	□♆	♑	6	**9:20 pm** 6:20 pm
8	**7:52 pm** 4:52 pm	☌♇	♒	8	11:41 pm
8	**7:52 pm** 4:52 pm	☌♇	♒	9	**2:41 am**
10	**10:32 pm** 7:32 pm	☌☿	♓	11	**9:44 am** 6:44 am
13	**11:38 am** 8:38 am	⚹♇	♈	13	**6:44 pm** 3:44 pm
15	**11:40 pm** 8:40 pm	□♇	♉	16	**6:56 am** 3:56 am
18	**4:40 pm** 1:40 pm	⚹☉	♊	18	**7:47 pm** 4:47 pm
21	**8:04 am** 5:04 am	□♀	♋	21	**8:18 am** 5:18 am
23	**11:26 am** 8:26 am	☍♇	♌	23	**5:56 pm** 2:56 pm
25	**9:27 am** 6:27 am	☍♃	♍	25	**11:25 pm** 8:25 pm
27	**7:48 pm** 4:48 pm	△♇	♎	27	10:22 pm
27	**7:48 pm** 4:48 pm	△♇	♎	28	**1:22 am**
29	**8:08 pm** 5:08 pm	□♇	♏	29	10:33 pm
29	**8:08 pm** 5:08 pm	□♇	♏	30	**1:33 am**
31	**8:29 pm** 5:29 pm	⚹♇	♐	31	10:59 pm
31	**8:29 pm** 5:29 pm	⚹♇	♐	4/1	**1:59 am**

☽ Phases & Eclipses phase	day	ET / hr:mn / PT
4th Quarter	5	**8:30 pm** 5:30 pm
New Moon	13	**5:21 am** 2:21 am
2nd Quarter	21	**10:40 am** 7:40 am
Full Moon	28	**2:48 pm** 11:48 am

Planet Ingress	day	ET / hr:mn / PT
♂ ♊	3	**10:30 pm** 7:30 pm
♀ ♓	7	**4:06 pm** 1:06 pm
☿ ♓	15	**6:26 pm** 3:26 pm
☉ ♈	20	**5:37 am** 2:37 am
♀ ♈	21	**10:16 am** 7:16 am

Planetary Motion	day	ET / hr:mn / PT

1 MONDAY
☽ ⚻ ♅ **2:49 am**
☽ △ ♄ **4:17 am** 1:17 am
☽ ⚻ ☉ **8:42 am** 5:42 am
☽ △ ☿ **2:27 pm** 11:27 am
☽ △ ♃ **5:57 pm** 2:57 pm
☽ ⚻ ♆ **11:40 pm** 8:40 pm

2 TUESDAY
☽ □ ♇ **9:09 am** 6:09 am
☽ ⚻ ♂ **2:22 pm** 11:22 am

3 WEDNESDAY
☽ △ ♀ **3:39 am** 12:39 am
☽ ☍ ♅ **4:22 am** 1:22 am
☽ □ ♄ **6:05 am** 3:05 am
♀ ⚹ ♅ **12:09 pm** 9:09 am
☽ △ ☉ **1:52 pm** 10:52 am
☽ □ ☿ **7:01 pm** 4:01 pm
☽ □ ♃ **8:22 pm** 5:22 pm
☽ △ ♆ 10:30 pm

4 THURSDAY
☽ △ ♆ **1:30 am**
♀ ⚺ ♄ **10:14 am** 7:14 am
☽ ⚹ ♇ **11:10 am** 8:10 am
☽ ☍ ♂ **6:32 pm** 3:32 pm
☿ ☌ ♃ **10:27 pm** 7:27 pm

5 FRIDAY
☽ ⚻ ♅ **6:55 am** 3:55 am
☽ ⚹ ♄ **8:56 am** 5:56 am
☽ □ ♀ **10:58 am** 7:58 am
☽ □ ☉ **8:30 pm** 5:30 pm
☽ ⚹ ♃ 9:07 pm
☽ ⚹ ☿ 10:36 pm

6 SATURDAY
☽ ⚹ ♃ **12:07 am**
☽ ⚹ ☿ **1:36 am**
☽ □ ♆ **4:44 am** 1:44 am
☽ ⚺ ♇ **2:39 pm** 11:39 am
☽ ⚻ ♂ 9:29 pm

7 SUNDAY
☽ ⚻ ♂ **12:29 am**
☽ △ ♅ **11:09 am** 8:09 am
☽ ⚺ ♄ **1:28 pm** 10:28 am
☽ ⚹ ♀ **8:29 pm** 5:29 pm
☿ ⚺ ♆ **9:12 pm** 6:12 pm

8 MONDAY
☽ ⚹ ☉ **5:15 am** 2:15 am
☽ ⚺ ♃ **5:39 am** 2:39 am
☽ ⚹ ♆ **9:41 am** 6:41 am
☽ ⚺ ☿ **10:44 am** 7:44 am
☉ ⚺ ♃ **12:04 pm** 9:04 am
☽ ☌ ♇ **7:52 pm** 4:52 pm

9 TUESDAY
☽ △ ♂ **8:23 am** 5:23 am
☽ □ ♅ **5:06 pm** 2:06 pm
☽ ☌ ♄ **7:45 pm** 4:45 pm

10 WEDNESDAY
☽ ⚺ ♀ **8:16 am** 5:16 am
☽ ☌ ♃ **12:58 pm** 9:58 am
☽ ⚺ ☉ **4:08 pm** 1:08 pm
☽ ⚺ ♆ **4:21 pm** 1:21 pm
☉ ☌ ♆ **7:01 pm** 4:01 pm
☽ ☌ ☿ **10:32 pm** 7:32 pm
☽ ⚺ ♇ 11:48 pm

11 THURSDAY
☽ ⚺ ♇ **2:48 am**
☽ □ ♂ **6:16 pm** 3:16 pm
☽ ⚹ ♅ 9:50 pm

12 FRIDAY
☽ ⚹ ♅ **12:50 am**
☽ ⚺ ♄ **3:49 am** 12:49 am
♀ ⚺ ♃ **6:53 pm** 3:53 pm
☿ ⚺ ♇ **8:41 pm** 5:41 pm
☽ ⚺ ♃ **10:11 pm** 7:11 pm
☽ ☌ ♀ **10:29 pm** 7:29 pm
☽ ☌ ♆ 9:52 pm

13 SATURDAY
☽ ☌ ♆ **12:52 am**
☽ ☌ ☉ **5:21 am** 2:21 am
☽ ⚹ ♇ **11:38 am** 8:38 am
☽ ⚺ ☿ **1:17 pm** 10:17 am
♀ ☌ ♆ **11:08 pm** 8:08 pm

14 SUNDAY
☽ ⚹ ♂ **7:28 am** 4:28 am
☽ ⚺ ♅ **11:37 am** 8:37 am
☽ ⚹ ♄ **2:58 pm** 11:58 am

15 MONDAY
☽ ⚹ ♃ **10:40 am** 7:40 am
☽ ⚺ ♆ **12:35 pm** 9:35 am
☽ ⚺ ♀ **4:39 pm** 1:39 pm
☽ ⚺ ☉ **10:22 pm** 7:22 pm
☽ □ ♇ **11:40 pm** 8:40 pm

16 TUESDAY
☽ ⚹ ☿ **8:31 am** 5:31 am
☉ ⚹ ♇ **2:26 pm** 11:26 am
☽ ⚺ ♂ **10:12 pm** 7:12 pm
☽ ☌ ♅ **11:37 pm** 8:37 pm

17 WEDNESDAY
☽ □ ♄ **3:20 am** 12:20 am
☽ □ ♃ 9:14 pm
☽ ⚹ ♆ 10:16 pm

18 THURSDAY
☽ □ ♃ **12:14 am**
☽ ⚹ ♆ **1:16 am**
♂ ⚺ ♅ **4:48 am** 1:48 am
☽ ⚹ ♀ **12:24 pm** 9:24 am
☽ △ ♇ **12:30 pm** 9:30 am
♀ ⚹ ♇ **1:20 pm** 10:20 am
☽ ⚹ ☉ **4:40 pm** 1:40 pm

19 FRIDAY
☽ □ ☿ **5:28 am** 2:28 am
☽ ⚺ ♅ **12:52 pm** 9:52 am
☽ ☌ ♂ **2:25 pm** 11:25 am
☽ △ ♄ **4:50 pm** 1:50 pm

20 SATURDAY
☽ △ ♃ **2:14 pm** 11:14 am
☽ □ ♆ **2:20 pm** 11:20 am
♃ ⚺ ♆ **9:51 pm** 6:51 pm
☽ ⚻ ♇ 10:17 pm

21 SUNDAY
☽ ⚻ ♇ **1:17 am**
☽ □ ♀ **8:04 am** 5:04 am
☽ □ ☉ **10:40 am** 7:40 am
☿ ⚹ ♅ **7:35 pm** 4:35 pm
♂ △ ♄ **10:35 pm** 7:35 pm
☽ ⚹ ♅ 10:02 pm
☽ △ ☿ 10:46 pm

22 MONDAY
☽ ⚹ ♅ **1:02 am**
☽ △ ☿ **1:46 am**
☽ ⚻ ♄ **5:02 am** 2:02 am
☽ ⚺ ♂ **5:19 am** 2:19 am
☽ △ ♆ 10:14 pm
☽ ⚻ ♃ 10:56 pm

23 TUESDAY
☽ △ ♆ **1:14 am**
☽ ⚻ ♃ **1:56 am**
☿ ⚺ ♄ **6:12 am** 3:12 am
☽ ☍ ♇ **11:26 am** 8:26 am
☿ □ ♂ **11:26 pm** 8:26 pm
☽ △ ♀ **11:50 pm** 8:50 pm
☽ △ ☉ 9:54 pm

24 WEDNESDAY
☽ △ ☉ **12:54 am**
☽ □ ♅ **9:45 am** 6:45 am
☽ ☍ ♄ **1:38 pm** 10:38 am
☽ ⚹ ♂ **4:08 pm** 1:08 pm
☽ ⚻ ☿ **5:28 pm** 2:28 pm

25 THURSDAY
☽ ⚻ ♆ **8:07 am** 5:07 am
☽ ☍ ♃ **9:27 am** 6:27 am
☽ ⚻ ♇ **5:28 pm** 2:28 pm
☉ ☌ ♀ 11:58 pm

26 FRIDAY
☉ ☌ ♀ **2:58 am**
☽ ⚻ ☉ **9:52 am** 6:52 am
☽ ⚻ ♀ **10:00 am** 7:00 am
☽ △ ♅ **2:17 pm** 11:17 am
☽ ⚻ ♄ **6:00 pm** 3:00 pm
☽ □ ♂ **10:16 pm** 7:16 pm

27 SATURDAY
☽ ☍ ☿ **3:37 am** 12:37 am
☽ ☍ ♆ **11:05 am** 8:05 am
☽ ⚻ ♃ **12:55 pm** 9:55 am
☽ △ ♇ **7:48 pm** 4:48 pm

28 SUNDAY
♀ ⚺ ♅ **12:53 pm** 9:53 am
☽ ☍ ☉ **2:48 pm** 11:48 am
☽ ⚻ ♅ **3:40 pm** 12:40 pm
☽ ☍ ♀ **3:55 pm** 12:55 pm
☽ △ ♄ **7:21 pm** 4:21 pm
☽ △ ♂ 10:12 pm

29 MONDAY
☽ △ ♂ **1:12 am**
☉ ⚺ ♅ **4:34 am** 1:34 am
☽ ⚻ ☿ **10:16 am** 7:16 am
☽ ⚻ ♆ **11:42 am** 8:42 am
☽ △ ♃ **2:01 pm** 11:01 am
☽ □ ♇ **8:08 pm** 5:08 pm
☿ ☌ ♆ **11:24 pm** 8:24 pm

30 TUESDAY
♀ ⚹ ♄ **11:47 am** 8:47 am
☽ ☍ ♅ **3:54 pm** 12:54 pm
☽ ⚻ ☉ **6:16 pm** 3:16 pm
☽ □ ♄ **7:39 pm** 4:39 pm
☽ ⚻ ♀ **8:20 pm** 5:20 pm
☿ ⚺ ♃ **11:54 pm** 8:54 pm

31 WEDNESDAY
☽ ⚻ ♂ **3:17 am** 12:17 am
☽ △ ♆ **11:59 am** 8:59 am
☽ □ ♃ **2:52 pm** 11:52 am
☽ △ ☿ **4:35 pm** 1:35 pm
☉ ⚹ ♄ **5:04 pm** 2:04 pm
☽ ⚹ ♇ **8:29 pm** 5:29 pm

Eastern time in bold type
Pacific time in medium type

MARCH 2021

DATE	SID. TIME	SUN	MOON	NODE	MERCURY	VENUS	MARS	JUPITER	SATURN	URANUS	NEPTUNE	PLUTO	CERES	PALLAS	JUNO	VESTA	CHIRON
1 M	10 36 4	10✶37 05	2≏52	15Ⅱ44℞	14≈06	4✶19	28ŏ11	16≈37	8≈28	7♈36	20✶15	26\β02	2♍59	27✿44	19✗42	15♍29℞	7♈14
2 T	10 40 1	11 37 17	17 28	15 34	14 51	5 34	28 46	16 50	8 34	7 38	20 17	26 03	3 22	28 04	19 53	15 06	7 18
3 W	10 43 57	12 37 27	2♏22	15 27	15 39	6 49	29 20	17 04	8 41	7 41	20 20	26 05	3 46	28 23	20 04	14 50	7 21
4 Th	10 47 54	13 37 36	16 29	15 23	16 30	8 04	29 55	17 17	8 47	7 43	20 22	26 06	4 09	28 43	20 15	14 35	7 24
5 F	10 51 50	14 37 44	0✗46	15 22	17 24	9 18	0Ⅱ30	17 31	8 53	7 45	20 24	26 08	4 32	29 03	20 26	14 19	7 27
6 Sa	10 55 47	15 37 49	14 49	15 21	18 22	10 33	1 05	17 44	9 00	7 48	20 27	26 09	4 56	29 23	20 38	14 03	7 31
7 Su	10 59 44	16 37 54	28 40	15 21	19 23	11 48	1 40	17 58	9 06	7 50	20 29	26 11	5 19	29 43	20 46	13 48	7 34
8 M	11 3 40	17 37 57	12✓18	15 20	20 25	13 03	2 14	18 11	9 12	7 52	20 31	26 12	5 42	0♈02	20 56	13 32	7 37
9 T	11 7 37	18 37 58	25 44	15 20	21 31	14 18	2 50	18 24	9 18	7 55	20 33	26 13	6 06	0 22	21 06	13 16	7 41
10 W	11 11 33	19 37 57	9≈00	15 09	22 38	15 33	3 25	18 38	9 24	7 57	20 36	26 15	6 29	0 42	21 16	13 00	7 44
11 Th	11 15 30	20 37 55	22 04	14 59	23 48	16 48	4 00	18 51	9 30	8 00	20 38	26 16	6 53	1 01	21 25	12 45	7 48
12 F	11 19 26	21 37 51	4✶57	14 47	25 00	18 03	4 35	19 04	9 36	8 03	20 40	26 17	7 16	1 21	21 34	12 29	7 51
13 Sa	11 23 23	22 37 45	17 39	14 33	26 13	19 17	5 10	19 17	9 42	8 05	20 43	26 19	7 40	1 40	21 43	12 14	7 54
14 Su	11 27 19	23 37 37	0♈08	14 19	27 29	20 32	5 45	19 30	9 48	8 08	20 45	26 20	8 04	2 00	21 51	11 59	7 58
15 M	11 31 16	24 37 27	12 26	14 08	28 46	21 47	6 21	19 43	9 53	8 11	20 47	26 21	8 27	2 19	22 00	11 44	8 01
16 T	11 35 13	25 37 15	24 32	13 56	0✶05	23 02	6 56	19 56	9 59	8 13	20 49	26 22	8 51	2 39	22 08	11 29	8 05
17 W	11 39 9	26 37 01	6♈29	13 47	1 26	24 17	7 31	20 09	10 05	8 16	20 52	26 23	9 14	2 58	22 16	11 14	8 08
18 Th	11 43 6	27 36 44	18 19	13 42	2 48	25 31	8 07	20 22	10 10	8 19	20 54	26 25	9 38	3 17	22 23	11 00	8 12
19 F	11 47 2	28 36 26	0ŏ06	13 39	4 12	26 46	8 42	20 35	10 16	8 22	20 56	26 26	10 02	3 36	22 30	10 46	8 15
20 Sa	11 50 59	29 36 05	11 55	13 38D	5 37	28 01	9 18	20 47	10 21	8 25	20 58	26 27	10 25	3 56	22 38	10 32	8 19
21 Su	11 54 55	0♈35 42	23 50	13 39℞	7 04	29 16	9 53	21 00	10 27	8 27	21 01	26 28	10 49	4 15	22 44	10 18	8 22
22 M	11 58 52	1 35 17	5♊56	13 39	8 32	0♈30	10 29	21 12	10 32	8 30	21 03	26 29	11 13	4 34	22 51	10 05	8 26
23 T	12 2 48	2 34 50	18 20	13 37	10 01	1 45	11 05	21 25	10 38	8 33	21 05	26 30	11 37	4 53	22 57	9 52	8 29
24 W	12 6 45	3 34 20	1♋07	13 34	11 32	3 00	11 40	21 37	10 43	8 36	21 07	26 31	12 00	5 12	23 03	9 40	8 33
25 Th	12 10 42	4 33 48	14 20	13 29	13 05	4 14	12 16	21 50	10 48	8 39	21 10	26 32	12 24	5 31	23 09	9 27	8 36
26 F	12 14 38	5 33 14	28 01	13 23	14 38	5 29	12 52	22 02	10 53	8 42	21 12	26 33	12 48	5 49	23 14	9 16	8 40
27 Sa	12 18 35	6 32 37	12♍09	13 11	16 13	6 43	13 27	22 14	10 58	8 45	21 14	26 34	13 12	6 08	23 20	9 04	8 43
28 Su	12 22 31	7 31 58	26 42	13 01	17 50	7 58	14 03	22 26	11 03	8 48	21 16	26 35	13 36	6 27	23 24	8 53	8 47
29 M	12 26 28	8 31 17	11≏32	12 51	19 28	9 13	14 39	22 38	11 08	8 51	21 18	26 36	13 59	6 45	23 29	8 42	8 50
30 T	12 30 24	9 30 34	26 32	12 43	21 07	10 27	15 15	22 50	11 13	8 54	21 21	26 36	14 23	7 04	23 33	8 32	8 54
31 W	12 34 21	10 29 50	11♏30	12 37	22 47	11 42	15 51	23 02	11 18	8 58	21 23	26 37	14 47	7 23	23 37	8 22	8 57

EPHEMERIS CALCULATED FOR 12 MIDNIGHT GREENWICH MEAN TIME. ALL OTHER DATA AND FACING ASPECTARIAN PAGE IN **EASTERN TIME (BOLD)** AND PACIFIC TIME (REGULAR).

APRIL 2021

☽ Last Aspect day	ET / hr:mn / PT		asp	☽ Ingress sign	day	ET / hr:mn / PT	
3/31	**8:29 pm**	5:29 pm	⚹♇	♐	1	**1:59 am**	
2		10:24 pm	□☿	♑	3	**4:13 am**	1:13 am
3	**1:24 am**		□☿	♑	3	**4:13 am**	1:13 am
5	**3:05 am**	12:05 am	☌♇	♒	5	**9:04 am**	6:04 am
7	**6:05 am**	3:05 am	☌♃	♓	7	**4:30 pm**	1:30 pm
9	**7:48 pm**	4:48 pm	⚹♇	♈	9		11:11 pm
9	**7:48 pm**	4:48 pm	⚹♇	♈	10	**2:11 am**	
12	**8:06 am**	5:06 am	☌♀	♉	12	**1:44 pm**	10:44 am
14	**8:00 pm**	5:00 pm	△♇	♊	14		11:35 pm
14	**8:00 pm**	5:00 pm	△♇	♊	15	**2:35 am**	

☽ Last Aspect day	ET / hr:mn / PT		asp	☽ Ingress sign	day	ET / hr:mn / PT	
17	**11:03 am**	8:03 am	⚹☉	♋	17	**3:25 pm**	12:25 pm
19	**8:03 pm**	5:03 pm	☍♇	♌	19		11:11 pm
19	**8:03 pm**	5:03 pm	☍♇	♌	20	**2:11 am**	
22	**8:05 am**	5:05 am	⚹♂	♍	22	**9:08 am**	6:08 am
24	**6:50 am**	3:50 am	△♇	♎	24	**12:06 pm**	9:06 am
26	**8:40 am**	5:40 am	△♃	♏	26	**12:18 pm**	9:18 am
28	**8:31 am**	5:31 am	□♃	♐	28	**11:42 am**	8:42 am
30	**9:27 am**	6:27 am	⚹♃	♑	30	**12:16 pm**	9:16 am

☽ Phases & Eclipses phase	day	ET / hr:mn / PT	
4th Quarter	4	**6:02 am**	3:02 am
New Moon	11	**10:31 pm**	7:31 pm
2nd Quarter	19		11:59 pm
2nd Quarter	20	**2:59 pm**	
Full Moon	26	**11:32 pm**	8:32 pm

Planet Ingress		day	ET / hr:mn / PT	
☿	♈	3	**11:41 pm**	8:41 pm
♀	♉	14	**2:22 pm**	11:22 am
☿	♉	19	**6:29 am**	3:29 am
☉	♉	19	**4:33 pm**	1:33 pm
♂	♋	23	**7:49 am**	4:49 am

Planetary Motion		day	ET / hr:mn / PT	
⚵	R	12	**6:13 am**	3:13 am
⚶	D	20	**3:06 am**	12:06 am
♇	R	27	**4:04 pm**	1:04 pm

1 THURSDAY
☽ ⚻ ♅ **4:54 pm** 1:54 pm
☽ ⚹ ♄ **8:53 pm** 5:53 pm
☽ △ ☉ **10:46 pm** 7:46 pm
☽ △ ♀ 10:56 pm
☿ ⚹ ♇ 11:04 pm

2 FRIDAY
☽ △ ♀ **1:56 am**
☿ ⚹ ♇ **2:04 am**
☽ ☍ ♂ **6:40 am** 3:40 am
☽ □ ♆ **1:42 pm** 10:42 am
☽ ⚹ ♃ **5:17 pm** 2:17 pm
☽ ⚺ ♇ **10:30 pm** 7:30 pm
☽ □ ☿ 10:24 pm

3 SATURDAY
☽ □ ☿ **1:24 am**
☽ △ ♅ **8:05 pm** 5:05 pm
☽ ⚺ ♄ 9:21 pm

4 SUNDAY
☽ ⚺ ♄ **12:21 am**
☽ □ ☉ **6:02 am** 3:02 am
☽ □ ♀ **10:33 am** 7:33 am
☽ ⚻ ♂ **12:46 pm** 9:46 am
☽ ⚹ ♆ **5:55 pm** 2:55 pm
☽ ⚺ ♃ **10:18 pm** 7:18 pm

5 MONDAY
☽ ☌ ♇ **3:05 am** 12:05 am
☽ ⚹ ☿ **2:19 pm** 11:19 am
☽ □ ♅ 10:58 pm

6 TUESDAY
☽ □ ♅ **1:58 am**
☽ ☌ ♄ **6:32 am** 3:32 am
♀ ⚹ ♂ **7:18 am** 4:18 am
☽ ⚹ ☉ **4:40 pm** 1:40 pm
☽ △ ♂ **9:55 pm** 6:55 pm
☽ ⚹ ♀ **10:44 pm** 7:44 pm
☽ ⚺ ♆ 9:49 pm

7 WEDNESDAY
☽ ⚺ ♆ **12:49 am**
☽ ☌ ♃ **6:05 am** 3:05 am
☽ ⚺ ♇ **10:18 am** 7:18 am
♀ ⚺ ♆ **8:55 pm** 5:55 pm

8 THURSDAY
☽ ⚺ ☿ **7:36 am** 4:36 am
☽ ⚹ ♅ **10:24 am** 7:24 am
☽ ⚺ ♄ **3:13 pm** 12:13 pm
☿ ⚺ ♅ 11:37 pm

9 FRIDAY
☿ ⚺ ♅ **2:37 am**
☽ ⚺ ☉ **6:19 am** 3:19 am
☽ □ ♂ **9:49 am** 6:49 am
☽ ☌ ♆ **10:04 am** 7:04 am
☽ ⚺ ♀ **2:05 pm** 11:05 am
♂ □ ♆ **3:18 pm** 12:18 pm
☽ ⚺ ♃ **4:15 pm** 1:15 pm
☽ ⚹ ♇ **7:48 pm** 4:48 pm

10 SATURDAY
☿ ⚹ ♄ **11:09 am** 8:09 am
♀ ⚹ ♃ **2:53 pm** 11:53 am
☽ ⚺ ♅ **8:58 pm** 5:58 pm
☽ ⚹ ♄ 11:01 pm

11 SUNDAY
☽ ⚹ ♄ **2:01 am**
☽ ☌ ☿ **4:46 am** 1:46 am
☉ ⚺ ♆ **7:10 am** 4:10 am
☽ ⚺ ♆ **9:18 pm** 6:18 pm
☽ ☌ ☉ **10:31 pm** 7:31 pm
♀ □ ♇ **11:20 pm** 8:20 pm
☽ ⚹ ♂ 9:00 pm

12 MONDAY
☽ ⚹ ♂ **12:00 am**
☽ ⚹ ♃ **4:24 am** 1:24 am
☽ □ ♇ **7:12 am** 4:12 am
☽ ☌ ♀ **8:06 am** 5:06 am

13 TUESDAY
☽ ☌ ♅ **9:18 am** 6:18 am
☽ □ ♄ **2:30 pm** 11:30 am
☉ ⚹ ♂ **7:09 pm** 4:09 pm

14 WEDNESDAY
☽ ⚺ ☿ **5:14 am** 2:14 am
☽ ⚹ ♆ **10:03 am** 7:03 am
☽ ⚺ ♂ **3:54 pm** 12:54 pm
☽ ⚺ ☉ **4:37 pm** 1:37 pm
☽ □ ♃ **6:02 pm** 3:02 pm
☽ △ ♇ **8:00 pm** 5:00 pm

15 THURSDAY
☽ ⚺ ♀ **4:01 am** 1:01 am
☿ ⚺ ♆ **9:32 am** 6:32 am
☉ ⚹ ♃ **12:59 pm** 9:59 am
☽ ⚺ ♅ **10:38 pm** 7:38 pm

16 FRIDAY
☽ △ ♄ **3:53 am** 12:53 am
☉ □ ♇ **9:27 am** 6:27 am
☽ □ ♆ **11:15 pm** 8:15 pm
♂ △ ♃ 10:14 pm

17 SATURDAY
♂ △ ♃ **1:14 am**
☽ ⚹ ☿ **7:05 am** 4:05 am
☽ △ ♃ **7:53 am** 4:53 am
☽ ☌ ♂ **8:08 am** 5:08 am
☽ ⚻ ♇ **8:58 am** 5:58 am
☽ ⚹ ☉ **11:03 am** 8:03 am
☿ ⚹ ♃ **12:00 pm** 9:00 am
☿ ⚹ ♂ **3:09 pm** 12:09 pm
☿ □ ♇ **5:49 pm** 2:49 pm
☽ ⚹ ♀ **11:49 pm** 8:49 pm
♂ ⚻ ♇ 9:26 pm

18 SUNDAY
♂ ⚻ ♇ **12:26 am**
☽ ⚹ ♅ **11:19 am** 8:19 am
☽ ⚻ ♄ **4:24 pm** 1:24 pm
☉ ☌ ☿ **9:50 pm** 6:50 pm

19 MONDAY
☽ △ ♆ **10:56 am** 7:56 am
☽ ⚻ ♃ **7:49 pm** 4:49 pm
☽ ☍ ♇ **8:03 pm** 5:03 pm
☽ ⚺ ♂ **10:15 pm** 7:15 pm
☽ □ ☉ 11:59 pm

20 TUESDAY
☽ □ ☉ **2:59 am**
☽ □ ☿ **6:08 am** 3:08 am
♃ ⚺ ♇ **3:09 pm** 12:09 pm
☽ □ ♀ **4:21 pm** 1:21 pm
☽ □ ♅ **9:11 pm** 6:11 pm
☽ ☍ ♄ 10:56 pm

21 WEDNESDAY
☽ ☍ ♄ **1:56 am**
☽ ⚻ ♆ **7:07 pm** 4:07 pm

22 THURSDAY
☽ ⚻ ♇ **3:29 am** 12:29 am
☽ ☍ ♃ **3:54 am** 12:54 am
☽ ⚹ ♂ **8:05 am** 5:05 am
☽ △ ☉ **2:06 pm** 11:06 am
♀ ☌ ♅ **9:01 pm** 6:01 pm
☽ △ ☿ **10:47 pm** 7:47 pm
☽ △ ♅ 11:57 pm

23 FRIDAY
☽ △ ♅ **2:57 am**
☽ △ ♀ **3:30 am** 12:30 am
☽ ⚻ ♄ **7:19 am** 4:19 am
☽ ☍ ♆ **11:10 pm** 8:10 pm
☿ ☌ ♅ 11:42 pm

24 SATURDAY
☿ ☌ ♅ **2:42 am**
☽ △ ♇ **6:50 am** 3:50 am
☽ ⚻ ♃ **7:47 am** 4:47 am
☽ □ ♂ **1:19 pm** 10:19 am
☽ ⚻ ☉ **8:19 pm** 5:19 pm
♀ □ ♄ 9:22 pm

25 SUNDAY
♀ □ ♄ **12:22 am**
☽ ⚻ ♅ **4:58 am** 1:58 am
☿ □ ♄ **7:58 am** 4:58 am
☽ △ ♄ **9:02 am** 6:02 am
☽ ⚻ ☿ **9:13 am** 6:13 am
☽ ⚻ ♀ **9:48 am** 6:48 am
☿ ☌ ♀ **6:19 pm** 3:19 pm
☽ ⚻ ♆ 9:01 pm

26 MONDAY
☽ ⚻ ♆ **12:01 am**
☽ □ ♇ **7:15 am** 4:15 am
☽ △ ♃ **8:40 am** 5:40 am
☽ △ ♂ **3:29 pm** 12:29 pm
☽ ☍ ☉ **11:32 pm** 8:32 pm

27 TUESDAY
☽ ☍ ♅ **4:51 am** 1:51 am
☽ □ ♄ **8:47 am** 5:47 am
☽ ☍ ♀ **1:35 pm** 10:35 am
☽ ☍ ☿ **4:24 pm** 1:24 pm
☽ △ ♆ **11:31 pm** 8:31 pm

28 WEDNESDAY
☽ ⚹ ♇ **6:38 am** 3:38 am
☽ □ ♃ **8:31 am** 5:31 am
☽ ⚻ ♂ **4:54 pm** 1:54 pm
☽ ⚻ ☉ 11:20 pm

29 THURSDAY
☽ ⚻ ☉ **2:20 am**
☽ ⚻ ♅ **4:38 am** 1:38 am
☽ ⚹ ♄ **8:36 am** 5:36 am
☽ ⚻ ♀ **5:44 pm** 2:44 pm
☿ ⚹ ♆ **10:27 pm** 7:27 pm
☽ □ ♆ **11:42 pm** 8:42 pm
☽ ⚻ ☿ **11:54 pm** 8:54 pm

30 FRIDAY
☽ ⚺ ♇ **7:00 am** 4:00 am
☽ ⚹ ♃ **9:27 am** 6:27 am
☉ ☌ ♅ **3:54 pm** 12:54 pm
☽ ☍ ♂ **7:51 pm** 4:51 pm

Eastern time in bold type
Pacific time in medium type

APRIL 2021

DATE	SID. TIME	SUN	MOON	NODE	MERCURY	VENUS	MARS	JUPITER	SATURN	URANUS	NEPTUNE	PLUTO	CERES	PALLAS	JUNO	VESTA	CHIRON
1 Th	12 38 17	11♈29 03	26♏20	12♊33R	24♓09	12♈56	16♊27	23≈14	11≈22	9♉01	21♓25	26♑38	15♑11	7♓41	23♐41	8♍12R	9♈01
2 F	12 42 14	12 28 14	10♐55	12 32D	26 13	14 11	17 03	23 25	11 27	9 04	21 27	26 39	15 35	7 59	23 45	8 03	9 04
3 Sa	12 46 10	13 27 24	25 12	12 33	27 57	15 25	17 38	23 37	11 32	9 07	21 29	26 40	15 59	8 18	23 48	7 55	9 08
4 Su	12 50 7	14 26 32	9♑07	12 33R	29 44	16 40	18 14	23 49	11 36	9 10	21 31	26 40	16 22	8 36	23 51	7 47	9 11
5 M	12 54 4	15 25 39	22 44	12 33	1♈31	17 54	18 50	24 00	11 41	9 13	21 34	26 41	16 46	8 54	23 53	7 39	9 15
6 T	12 58 0	16 24 43	6≈02	12 27	3 20	19 08	19 26	24 11	11 45	9 17	21 36	26 42	17 10	9 12	23 55	7 32	9 18
7 W	13 1 57	17 23 46	19 03	12 21	5 11	20 23	20 02	24 23	11 49	9 20	21 38	26 42	17 34	9 30	23 57	7 25	9 22
8 Th	13 5 53	18 22 47	1♓51	12 21	7 03	21 37	20 39	24 34	11 53	9 23	21 40	26 43	17 58	9 48	23 59	7 19	9 25
9 F	13 9 50	19 21 46	14 26	12 26	8 56	22 52	21 15	24 45	11 57	9 27	21 42	26 43	18 22	10 06	24 00	7 13	9 29
10 Sa	13 13 46	20 20 43	26 50	12 03	10 51	24 06	21 51	24 56	12 01	9 30	21 44	26 44	18 46	10 24	24 01	7 08	9 32
11 Su	13 17 43	21 19 39	9♈04	11 53	12 47	25 20	22 27	25 07	12 05	9 33	21 46	26 44	19 10	10 42	24 02	7 03	9 36
12 M	13 21 39	22 18 32	21 09	11 44	14 45	26 35	23 03	25 17	12 09	9 36	21 48	26 45	19 34	10 59	24 02R	6 58	9 39
13 T	13 25 36	23 17 23	3♉07	11 36	16 44	27 49	23 39	25 28	12 13	9 40	21 50	26 45	19 57	11 17	24 02	6 55	9 43
14 W	13 29 33	24 16 13	14 58	11 31	18 44	29 03	24 15	25 39	12 17	9 43	21 52	26 46	20 21	11 34	24 01	6 51	9 46
15 Th	13 33 29	25 15 00	26 46	11 27	20 46	0♉17	24 52	25 49	12 20	9 47	21 54	26 46	20 45	11 52	24 00	6 48	9 50
16 F	13 37 26	26 13 45	8♊33	11 26D	22 49	1 32	25 28	26 00	12 24	9 50	21 56	26 46	21 09	12 09	23 59	6 46	9 53
17 Sa	13 41 22	27 12 28	20 22	11 26	24 53	2 46	26 04	26 10	12 27	9 53	21 58	26 47	21 33	12 26	23 57	6 44	9 56
18 Su	13 45 19	28 11 09	2♋17	11 28	26 58	4 00	26 40	26 20	12 31	9 57	22 00	26 47	21 57	12 43	23 55	6 43	10 00
19 M	13 49 15	29 09 48	14 24	11 29	29 05	5 14	27 17	26 30	12 34	10 00	22 02	26 47	22 21	13 00	23 53	6 42	10 03
20 T	13 53 12	0♉08 24	26 46	11 30R	1♉12	6 28	27 53	26 40	12 37	10 04	22 04	26 48	22 44	13 17	23 50	6 42D	10 07
21 W	13 57 8	1 06 59	9♌29	11 30	3 19	7 43	28 29	26 50	12 40	10 07	22 06	26 48	23 08	13 34	23 47	6 42	10 10
22 Th	14 1 5	2 05 31	22 37	11 28	5 27	8 57	29 06	26 59	12 43	10 10	22 08	26 48	23 32	13 51	23 44	6 42	10 13
23 F	14 5 2	3 04 01	6♍13	11 24	7 35	10 11	29 42	27 09	12 46	10 14	22 09	26 48	23 56	14 07	23 40	6 43	10 16
24 Sa	14 8 58	4 02 28	20 18	11 19	9 43	11 25	0♋18	27 18	12 49	10 17	22 11	26 48R	24 20	14 24	23 36	6 45	10 20
25 Su	14 12 55	5 00 54	4♎50	11 14	11 50	12 39	0 55	27 28	12 52	10 21	22 13	26 48	24 43	14 40	23 32	6 47	10 23
26 M	14 16 51	5 59 17	19 44	11 09	13 57	13 53	1 31	27 37	12 55	10 24	22 15	26 48	25 07	14 57	23 27	6 49	10 26
27 T	14 20 48	6 57 39	4♏52	11 02	16 02	15 07	2 08	27 46	12 57	10 28	22 17	26 48	25 31	15 13	23 22	6 52	10 30
28 W	14 24 44	7 55 59	20 05	11 00D	18 06	16 21	2 44	27 55	13 00	10 31	22 18	26 48	25 55	15 29	23 17	6 56	10 33
29 Th	14 28 41	8 54 17	5♐12	11 00	20 09	17 35	3 21	28 04	13 02	10 35	22 20	26 48	26 18	15 45	23 17	7 00	10 36
30 F	14 32 37	9 52 34	20 06	11 00	22 10	18 49	3 57	28 13	13 04	10 38	22 22	26 48	26 42	16 01	23 11	7 04	10 39

EPHEMERIS CALCULATED FOR 12 MIDNIGHT GREENWICH MEAN TIME. ALL OTHER DATA AND FACING ASPECTARIAN PAGE IN EASTERN TIME (BOLD) AND PACIFIC TIME (REGULAR).

MAY 2021

☽ Last Aspect day	ET / hr:mn / PT		asp	☽ Ingress sign	day	ET / hr:mn / PT	
2	**10:38 am**	7:38 am	△ ☿	♒	2	**3:31 pm**	12:31 pm
4	**8:05 pm**	5:05 pm	☌ ♃	♓	4	**10:09 pm**	7:09 pm
7	**3:36 am**	12:36 am	⚹ ♀	♈	7	**7:52 am**	4:52 am
9	**6:50 pm**	3:50 pm	⚹ ♃	♉	9	**7:46 pm**	4:46 pm
12	**8:23 am**	5:23 am	□ ♃	♊	12	**8:43 am**	5:43 am
14	**6:51 am**	3:51 am	□ ♆	♋	14	**9:30 pm**	6:30 pm
16		11:23 pm	☍ ♇	♌	17	**8:44 am**	5:44 am
17	**2:23 am**		☍ ♇	♌	17	**8:44 am**	5:44 am
19	**3:13 pm**	12:13 pm	□ ☉	♍	19	**4:59 pm**	1:59 pm
21	**3:56 pm**	12:56 pm	△ ♇	♎	21	**9:35 pm**	6:35 pm

☽ Last Aspect day	ET / hr:mn / PT		asp	☽ Ingress sign	day	ET / hr:mn / PT	
23	**5:36 pm**	2:36 pm	□ ♇	♏	23	**11:00 pm**	8:00 pm
25	**5:20 pm**	2:20 pm	⚹ ♇	♐	25	**10:39 pm**	7:39 pm
27	**1:35 pm**	10:35 am	☍ ☿	♑	27	**10:23 pm**	7:23 pm
29	**6:15 pm**	3:15 pm	☌ ♇	♒	29		9:04 pm
29	**6:15 pm**	3:15 pm	☌ ♇	♒	30	**12:04 am**	
31		11:14 pm	△ ♀	♓	6/1	**5:07 am**	2:07 am
6/1	**2:14 am**		△ ♀	♓	6/1	**5:07 am**	2:07 am

☽ Phases & Eclipses phase	day	ET / hr:mn / PT	
4th Quarter	3	**3:50 pm**	12:50 pm
New Moon	11	**3:00 pm**	12:00 pm
2nd Quarter	19	**3:13 pm**	12:13 pm
Full Moon	26	**7:14 am**	4:14 am
☍ (eclipse)	26	5° ♐ 26'	

Planet Ingress		day	ET / hr:mn / PT	
☿	♊	3	**10:49 pm**	7:49 pm
⚳	♉	8	**4:54 am**	1:54 am
♀	♊	8	**10:01 pm**	7:01 pm
♃	♓	13	**6:36 pm**	3:36 pm
☉	♊	20	**3:37 pm**	12:37 pm

Planetary Motion		day	ET / hr:mn / PT	
♄	℞	23	**5:21 am**	2:21 am
☿	℞	29	**6:34 pm**	3:34 pm

1 SATURDAY
- ☽ △ ♅ **6:13 am** 3:13 am
- ☽ △ ☉ **7:12 am** 4:12 am
- ☽ ⚺ ♄ **10:18 am** 7:18 am
- ☽ △ ♀ 9:42 pm
- ☽ ⚹ ♆ 11:16 pm

2 SUNDAY
- ☽ △ ♀ **12:42 am**
- ☽ ⚹ ♆ **2:16 am**
- ☿ △ ♇ **5:19 am** 2:19 am
- ☽ ☌ ♇ **9:54 am** 6:54 am
- ☽ △ ☿ **10:38 am** 7:38 am
- ☽ ⚺ ♃ **1:02 pm** 10:02 am
- ♀ ⚹ ♆ **6:38 pm** 3:38 pm
- ☽ ⚻ ♂ 11:02 pm

3 MONDAY
- ☽ ⚻ ♂ **2:02 am**
- ☿ □ ♃ **5:33 am** 2:33 am
- ☉ □ ♄ **6:02 am** 3:02 am
- ☽ □ ♅ **10:52 am** 7:52 am
- ☽ ☌ ♄ **3:08 pm** 12:08 pm
- ☽ □ ☉ **3:50 pm** 12:50 pm

4 TUESDAY
- ☽ ⚺ ♆ **8:08 am** 5:08 am
- ☽ □ ♀ **12:00 pm** 9:00 am
- ☽ ⚺ ♇ **4:09 pm** 1:09 pm
- ☽ ☌ ♃ **8:05 pm** 5:05 pm
- ☽ □ ☿ 10:54 pm

5 WEDNESDAY
- ☽ □ ☿ **1:54 am**
- ☽ △ ♂ **12:07 pm** 9:07 am
- ☽ ⚹ ♅ **6:57 pm** 3:57 pm
- ☽ ⚺ ♄ **11:21 pm** 8:21 pm

6 THURSDAY
- ☽ ⚹ ☉ **4:41 am** 1:41 am
- ♀ △ ♇ **7:25 am** 4:25 am
- ☽ ☌ ♆ **5:17 pm** 2:17 pm
- ☽ ⚹ ♇ 10:34 pm

7 FRIDAY
- ☽ ⚹ ♇ **1:34 am**
- ☽ ⚹ ♀ **3:36 am** 12:36 am
- ☽ ⚺ ♃ **6:21 am** 3:21 am
- ☽ ⚹ ☿ **9:01 pm** 6:01 pm
- ☽ □ ♂ 10:35 pm

8 SATURDAY
- ☽ □ ♂ **1:35 am**
- ☽ ⚺ ♅ **5:53 am** 2:53 am
- ♀ □ ♃ **9:38 am** 6:38 am
- ☽ ⚹ ♄ **10:18 am** 7:18 am
- ☽ ⚺ ☉ **8:54 pm** 5:54 pm

9 SUNDAY
- ☽ ⚺ ♆ **4:52 am** 1:52 am
- ☽ □ ♇ **1:16 pm** 10:16 am
- ☽ ⚹ ♃ **6:50 pm** 3:50 pm
- ☽ ⚺ ♀ **10:17 pm** 7:17 pm

10 MONDAY
- ☿ ⚺ ♂ **7:48 am** 4:48 am
- ☽ ⚹ ♂ **5:12 pm** 2:12 pm
- ☽ ⚺ ☿ **5:55 pm** 2:55 pm
- ☽ ☌ ♅ **6:35 pm** 3:35 pm
- ☽ □ ♄ **10:55 pm** 7:55 pm
- ☿ ⚺ ♅ **11:48 pm** 8:48 pm

11 TUESDAY
- ☽ ☌ ☉ **3:00 pm** 12:00 pm
- ☽ ⚹ ♆ **5:47 pm** 2:47 pm
- ♂ ⚹ ♅ **10:48 pm** 7:48 pm
- ☽ △ ♇ 11:07 pm

12 WEDNESDAY
- ☽ △ ♇ **2:07 am**
- ☽ □ ♃ **8:23 am** 5:23 am
- ☿ △ ♄ **2:34 pm** 11:34 am
- ☽ ☌ ♀ **6:20 pm** 3:20 pm
- ☉ ⚹ ♆ 10:45 pm

13 THURSDAY
- ☉ ⚹ ♆ **1:45 am**
- ☽ ⚺ ♅ **7:55 am** 4:55 am
- ☽ ⚺ ♂ **9:33 am** 6:33 am
- ☽ △ ♄ **12:03 pm** 9:03 am
- ☽ ☌ ☿ **2:32 pm** 11:32 am

14 FRIDAY
- ☽ □ ♆ **6:51 am** 3:51 am
- ☽ ⚺ ☉ **9:22 am** 6:22 am
- ☽ ⚻ ♇ **2:57 pm** 11:57 am
- ☽ △ ♃ **9:45 pm** 6:45 pm

15 SATURDAY
- ♂ ⚻ ♄ **10:49 am** 7:49 am
- ☽ ⚺ ♀ **1:53 pm** 10:53 am
- ☽ ⚹ ♅ **8:35 pm** 5:35 pm
- ☽ ⚻ ♄ 9:24 pm
- ☽ ☌ ♂ 10:06 pm

16 SUNDAY
- ☽ ⚻ ♄ **12:24 am**
- ☽ ☌ ♂ **1:06 am**
- ☽ ⚺ ☿ **8:51 am** 5:51 am
- ☽ △ ♆ **6:42 pm** 3:42 pm
- ☽ ⚹ ☉ 11:05 pm
- ☽ ☍ ♇ 11:23 pm

17 MONDAY
- ☽ ⚹ ☉ **2:05 am**
- ☽ ☍ ♇ **2:23 am**
- ☉ △ ♇ **5:49 am** 2:49 am
- ☽ ⚻ ♃ **9:29 am** 6:29 am

18 TUESDAY
- ☽ ⚹ ♀ **6:43 am** 3:43 am
- ☽ □ ♅ **7:04 am** 4:04 am
- ☽ ☍ ♄ **10:29 am** 7:29 am
- ♀ ⚺ ♅ **10:31 am** 7:31 am
- ☽ ⚺ ♂ **2:01 pm** 11:01 am
- ☽ ⚹ ☿ **10:55 pm** 7:55 pm

19 WEDNESDAY
- ☽ ⚻ ♆ **3:51 am** 12:51 am
- ☽ ⚻ ♇ **10:58 am** 7:58 am
- ☽ □ ☉ **3:13 pm** 12:13 pm
- ☽ ☍ ♃ **6:07 pm** 3:07 pm
- ♀ △ ♄ **9:58 pm** 6:58 pm

20 THURSDAY
- ☽ △ ♅ **2:09 pm** 11:09 am
- ☽ ⚻ ♄ **5:08 pm** 2:08 pm
- ☽ □ ♀ **7:01 pm** 4:01 pm
- ☽ ⚹ ♂ **10:57 pm** 7:57 pm

21 FRIDAY
- ☽ □ ☿ **7:47 am** 4:47 am
- ☽ ☍ ♆ **9:24 am** 6:24 am
- ☉ □ ♃ **11:03 am** 8:03 am
- ☽ △ ♇ **3:56 pm** 12:56 pm
- ☽ ⚻ ♃ **10:59 pm** 7:59 pm
- ☽ △ ☉ **11:46 pm** 8:46 pm

22 SATURDAY
- ☽ ⚻ ♅ **5:34 pm** 2:34 pm
- ☽ △ ♄ **8:11 pm** 5:11 pm
- ☿ □ ♆ **10:43 pm** 7:43 pm
- ☽ △ ♀ 11:36 pm

23 SUNDAY
- ☽ △ ♀ **2:36 am**
- ☽ □ ♂ **3:51 am** 12:51 am
- ☽ ⚻ ♆ **11:33 am** 8:33 am
- ☽ △ ☿ **11:59 am** 8:59 am
- ☽ □ ♇ **5:36 pm** 2:36 pm
- ☽ △ ♃ 9:37 pm

24 MONDAY
- ☽ △ ♃ **12:37 am**
- ☽ ⚻ ☉ **4:28 am** 1:28 am
- ♀ ⚺ ♂ **7:15 am** 4:15 am
- ☽ ☍ ♅ **6:15 pm** 3:15 pm
- ☽ □ ♄ **8:35 pm** 5:35 pm

25 TUESDAY
- ☽ △ ♂ **6:01 am** 3:01 am
- ☽ ⚻ ♀ **7:01 am** 4:01 am
- ☽ △ ♆ **11:30 am** 8:30 am
- ☽ ⚻ ☿ **1:13 pm** 10:13 am
- ☽ ⚹ ♇ **5:20 pm** 2:20 pm
- ☽ □ ♃ 9:30 pm

26 WEDNESDAY
- ☽ □ ♃ **12:30 am**
- ☽ ☍ ☉ **7:14 am** 4:14 am
- ☽ ⚻ ♅ **5:52 pm** 2:52 pm
- ☽ ⚹ ♄ **8:01 pm** 5:01 pm

27 THURSDAY
- ☽ ⚻ ♂ **7:31 am** 4:31 am
- ☽ ☍ ♀ **10:43 am** 7:43 am
- ☽ □ ♆ **11:06 am** 8:06 am
- ☽ ☍ ☿ **1:35 pm** 10:35 am
- ♀ □ ♆ **3:25 pm** 12:25 pm
- ☽ ⚺ ♇ **4:55 pm** 1:55 pm
- ☽ ⚹ ♃ 9:31 pm

28 FRIDAY
- ☽ ⚹ ♃ **12:31 am**
- ☽ ⚻ ☉ **10:32 am** 7:32 am
- ☽ △ ♅ **6:22 pm** 3:22 pm
- ☽ ⚺ ♄ **8:23 pm** 5:23 pm
- ☿ ☌ ♀ 10:13 pm

29 SATURDAY
- ☿ ☌ ♀ **1:13 am**
- ☽ ☍ ♂ **10:36 am** 7:36 am
- ☽ ⚹ ♆ **12:13 pm** 9:13 am
- ☽ ⚻ ☿ **3:07 pm** 12:07 pm
- ☽ ⚻ ♀ **4:23 pm** 1:23 pm
- ☽ ☌ ♇ **6:15 pm** 3:15 pm
- ☽ ⚺ ♃ 11:34 pm

30 SUNDAY
- ☽ ⚺ ♃ **2:34 am**
- ♀ ⚻ ♇ **1:47 pm** 10:47 am
- ☽ △ ☉ **4:43 pm** 1:43 pm
- ☽ □ ♅ **9:30 pm** 6:30 pm
- ☽ ☌ ♄ **11:25 pm** 8:25 pm
- ♂ △ ♆ 10:15 pm

31 MONDAY
- ♂ △ ♆ **1:15 am**
- ☽ ⚺ ♆ **4:27 pm** 1:27 pm
- ☽ ⚻ ♂ **5:11 pm** 2:11 pm
- ☽ △ ☿ **7:13 pm** 4:13 pm
- ☽ ⚺ ♇ **10:48 pm** 7:48 pm
- ☽ △ ♀ 11:14 pm

Eastern time in bold type
Pacific time in medium type

MAY 2021

DATE	SID. TIME	SUN	MOON	NODE	MERCURY	VENUS	MARS	JUPITER	SATURN	URANUS	NEPTUNE	PLUTO	CERES	PALLAS	JUNO	VESTA	CHIRON
1 Sa	14 36 34	10♉50 49	4♈39	11♊01	24♊08	20♉03	4♋33	28♒21	13♒07	10♉41	22♓23	26♑48℞	27♈06	16♓17	23♑06℞	7♓09	10♈42
2 Su	14 40 31	11 49 02	18 48	11 03	26 04	21 17	5 10	28 30	13 09	10 45	22 25	26 48	27 30	16 32	22 59	7 14	10 45
3 M	14 44 27	12 47 14	2♉32	11 04℞	27 57	22 31	5 46	28 38	13 11	10 48	22 27	26 48	27 53	16 48	22 52	7 19	10 49
4 T	14 48 24	13 45 25	15 53	11 04	29 47	23 45	6 23	28 46	13 13	10 52	22 28	26 48	28 17	17 03	22 45	7 25	10 52
5 W	14 52 20	14 43 34	28 51	11 04	1♊34	24 58	6 59	28 54	13 14	10 55	22 30	26 48	28 40	17 17	22 38	7 32	10 55
6 Th	14 56 17	15 41 41	11♊32	11 02	3 18	26 12	7 36	29 02	13 16	10 59	22 31	26 48	29 04	17 34	22 30	7 39	10 58
7 F	15 0 13	16 39 47	23 56	10 59	4 58	27 26	8 13	29 10	13 18	11 02	22 33	26 47	29 28	17 49	22 22	7 46	11 01
8 Sa	15 4 10	17 37 52	6♋09	10 55	6 35	28 40	8 49	29 18	13 19	11 06	22 34	26 47	29 51	18 04	22 14	7 54	11 04
9 Su	15 8 6	18 35 55	18 11	10 51	8 08	29 54	9 26	29 25	13 21	11 09	22 36	26 47	0♉15	18 19	22 06	8 02	11 07
10 M	15 12 3	19 33 57	0♌07	10 48	9 38	1♊08	10 02	29 32	13 22	11 13	22 37	26 46	0 38	18 34	21 57	8 10	11 10
11 T	15 16 0	20 31 57	11 57	10 45	11 03	2 21	10 39	29 40	13 24	11 16	22 39	26 46	1 02	18 48	21 48	8 19	11 12
12 W	15 19 56	21 29 56	23 45	10 43	12 25	3 35	11 15	29 47	13 25	11 19	22 40	26 46	1 25	19 03	21 38	8 29	11 15
13 Th	15 23 53	22 27 53	5♍33	10 42D	13 43	4 49	11 52	29 54	13 26	11 23	22 41	26 45	1 49	19 17	21 29	8 38	11 18
14 F	15 27 49	23 25 49	17 22	10 42	14 57	6 03	12 29	0♓00	13 27	11 26	22 43	26 45	2 12	19 31	21 19	8 49	11 21
15 Sa	15 31 46	24 23 43	29 15	10 43	16 06	7 16	13 05	0 07	13 28	11 30	22 44	26 44	2 36	19 45	21 09	8 59	11 24
16 Su	15 35 42	25 21 35	11♎16	10 44	17 12	8 30	13 42	0 13	13 28	11 33	22 45	26 44	2 59	19 59	20 58	9 10	11 27
17 M	15 39 39	26 19 26	23 27	10 46	18 17	9 44	14 19	0 20	13 29	11 36	22 47	26 43	3 22	20 13	20 48	9 21	11 29
18 T	15 43 35	27 17 15	5♏52	10 47	19 10	10 57	14 55	0 26	13 30	11 40	22 48	26 43	3 46	20 26	20 37	9 33	11 32
19 W	15 47 32	28 15 03	18 35	10 47℞	19 51	12 11	15 32	0 32	13 30	11 43	22 49	26 42	4 09	20 40	20 25	9 44	11 35
20 Th	15 51 29	29 12 48	1♐40	10 48	20 29	13 24	16 09	0 38	13 30	11 46	22 50	26 41	4 32	20 53	20 14	9 57	11 37
21 F	15 55 25	0♊10 32	15 09	10 47	21 00	14 38	16 46	0 43	13 31	11 50	22 51	26 41	4 55	21 06	20 02	10 09	11 40
22 Sa	15 59 22	1 08 15	29 04	10 47	21 35	15 52	17 22	0 49	13 31	11 53	22 53	26 40	5 18	21 19	19 51	10 22	11 42
23 Su	16 3 18	2 05 55	13♑24	10 46	22 50	17 05	17 59	0 54	13 31℞	11 56	22 54	26 40	5 42	21 32	19 39	10 36	11 45
24 M	16 7 15	3 03 35	28 08	10 46	23 20	18 19	18 36	0 59	13 31	12 00	22 55	26 39	6 05	21 44	19 27	10 49	11 47
25 T	16 11 11	4 01 12	13♒09	10 45	23 46	19 32	19 13	1 04	13 31	12 03	22 56	26 38	6 28	21 57	19 14	11 03	11 50
26 W	16 15 8	4 58 49	28 19	10 44D	24 07	20 46	19 49	1 09	13 31	12 06	22 57	26 37	6 51	22 09	19 02	11 17	11 52
27 Th	16 19 4	5 56 24	13♓30	10 43	24 23	21 59	20 26	1 14	13 30	12 09	22 58	26 37	7 14	22 21	18 49	11 32	11 54
28 F	16 23 1	6 53 58	28 31	10 44	24 34	23 12	21 03	1 18	13 30	12 13	22 59	26 36	7 37	22 33	18 36	11 47	11 57
29 Sa	16 26 58	7 51 31	13♈15	10 44	24 41℞	24 26	21 40	1 22	13 30	12 16	23 00	26 35	8 00	22 45	18 23	12 02	11 59
30 Su	16 30 54	8 49 04	27 36	10 44	24 43	25 39	22 17	1 27	13 29	12 19	23 00	26 34	8 23	22 57	18 10	12 17	12 01
31 M	16 34 51	9 46 35	11♉31	10 44	24 40	26 53	22 53	1 31	13 28	12 22	23 01	26 33	8 45	23 08	17 57	12 33	12 04

EPHEMERIS CALCULATED FOR 12 MIDNIGHT GREENWICH MEAN TIME. ALL OTHER DATA AND FACING ASPECTARIAN PAGE IN **EASTERN TIME (BOLD)** AND PACIFIC TIME (REGULAR).

☽ Last Aspect day	ET / hr:mn / PT	asp	☽ Ingress sign	day	ET / hr:mn / PT
1	**2:14 am**	△♀	♓	1	**5:07 am** 2:07 am
3	**7:10 am** 4:10 am	⚹♇	♈	3	**1:59 pm** 10:59 am
5	**6:47 pm** 3:47 pm	□♂	♉	5	10:46 pm
5	**6:47 pm** 3:47 pm	□♂	♉	6	**1:46 am**
8	**11:07 am** 8:07 am	⚹♂	♊	8	**2:47 pm** 11:47 am
10	**1:38 pm** 10:38 am	□♆	♋	11	**3:23 am** 12:23 am
13	**7:16 am** 4:16 am	☍♇	♌	13	**2:22 pm** 11:22 am
15	**1:27 pm** 10:27 am	⚹☉	♍	15	**11:02 pm** 8:02 pm
17	**11:54 pm** 8:54 pm	□☉	♎	18	**4:54 am** 1:54 am
20	**6:52 am** 3:52 am	△☉	♏	20	**7:58 am** 4:58 am
21	11:43 pm	⚹♇	♐	22	**8:55 am** 5:55 am
22	**2:43 am**	⚹♇	♐	22	**8:55 am** 5:55 am
23	**10:09 pm** 7:09 pm	□♆	♑	24	**9:05 am** 6:05 am
26	**8:49 am** 5:49 am	☍♀	♒	26	**10:09 am** 7:09 am
27	**3:08 pm** 12:08 pm	△☿	♓	28	**1:51 pm** 10:51 am
30	**1:40 pm** 10:40 am	⚹♇	♈	30	**9:21 pm** 6:21 pm

☽ Phases & Eclipses phase	day	ET / hr:mn / PT
4th Quarter	2	**3:24 am** 12:24 am
New Moon	10	**6:53 am** 3:53 am
●	10	19° ♊ 47'
2nd Quarter	17	**11:54 pm** 8:54 pm
Full Moon	24	**2:40 pm** 11:40 am

Planet Ingress		day	ET / hr:mn / PT
♀	♋	2	**9:19 am** 6:19 am
♂	♌	11	**9:34 am** 6:34 am
☉	♋	20	**11:32 pm** 8:32 pm
♀	♌	26	9:27 pm
♀	♌	27	**12:27 am**

Planetary Motion		day	ET / hr:mn / PT
♃	℞	20	**11:06 am** 8:06 am
☿	D	22	**6:00 pm** 3:00 pm
♆	℞	25	**3:21 pm** 12:21 pm

1 TUESDAY
☽ △ ♀ **2:14 am**
☽ ☌ ♃ **8:04 am** 5:04 am

2 WEDNESDAY
☿ ⚺ ♂ **3:14 am** 12:14 am
☽ □ ☉ **3:24 am** 12:24 am
☽ ⚹ ♅ **4:22 am** 1:22 am
☽ ⚺ ♄ **6:08 am** 3:08 am
☉ ⚺ ♅ **4:43 pm** 1:43 pm
☽ ☌ ♆ 9:31 pm
☽ □ ☿ 11:24 pm

3 THURSDAY
☽ ☌ ♆ **12:31 am**
☽ □ ☿ **2:24 am**
☽ △ ♂ **4:08 am** 1:08 am
☽ ⚹ ♇ **7:10 am** 4:10 am
☉ △ ♄ **3:05 pm** 12:05 pm
☽ □ ♀ **5:09 pm** 2:09 pm
☽ ⚺ ♃ **5:23 pm** 2:23 pm
♀ △ ♃ **7:33 pm** 4:33 pm

4 FRIDAY
☽ ⚺ ♅ **2:52 pm** 11:52 am
☽ ⚹ ♄ **4:24 pm** 1:24 pm
☽ ⚹ ☉ **6:38 pm** 3:38 pm

5 SATURDAY
☽ ⚺ ♆ **11:49 am** 8:49 am
☽ ⚹ ☿ **11:56 am** 8:56 am
☿ □ ♆ **3:05 pm** 12:05 pm
♂ ☍ ♇ **3:45 pm** 12:45 pm
☽ □ ♇ **6:37 pm** 3:37 pm
☽ □ ♂ **6:47 pm** 3:47 pm

6 SUNDAY
☽ ⚹ ♃ **5:32 am** 2:32 am
☽ ⚹ ♀ **11:57 am** 8:57 am

7 MONDAY
☽ ☌ ♅ **3:39 am** 12:39 am
☽ □ ♄ **4:51 am** 1:51 am
☽ ⚺ ☉ **12:36 pm** 9:36 am
☽ ⚺ ☿ **10:27 pm** 7:27 pm
☽ ⚹ ♆ 9:47 pm

8 TUESDAY
☽ ⚹ ♆ **12:47 am**
☽ △ ♇ **7:30 am** 4:30 am
☽ ⚹ ♂ **11:07 am** 8:07 am
☽ □ ♃ **6:47 pm** 3:47 pm

9 WEDNESDAY
☽ ⚺ ♀ **8:01 am** 5:01 am
☽ ⚺ ♅ **4:55 pm** 1:55 pm
☽ △ ♄ **5:44 pm** 2:44 pm

10 THURSDAY
☽ ☌ ☉ **6:53 am** 3:53 am
☽ ☌ ☿ **8:37 am** 5:37 am
☽ □ ♆ **1:38 pm** 10:38 am
☽ ⚻ ♇ **8:07 pm** 5:07 pm
☉ ☌ ☿ **9:13 pm** 6:13 pm

11 FRIDAY
☽ ⚺ ♂ **3:02 am** 12:02 am
☽ △ ♃ **7:28 am** 4:28 am
☽ ☌ ♀ 11:59 pm

12 SATURDAY
☽ ☌ ♀ **2:59 am**
☽ ⚹ ♅ **5:11 am** 2:11 am
☽ ⚻ ♄ **5:35 am** 2:35 am
☽ ⚺ ☿ **5:38 pm** 2:38 pm
☽ ⚺ ☉ **11:33 pm** 8:33 pm
☽ △ ♆ 10:06 pm
♀ ⚹ ♅ 10:38 pm

13 SUNDAY
☽ △ ♆ **1:06 am**
♀ ⚹ ♅ **1:38 am**
♀ ⚻ ♄ **4:15 am** 1:15 am
☽ ☍ ♇ **7:16 am** 4:16 am
☽ ☌ ♂ **5:08 pm** 2:08 pm
☽ ⚻ ♃ **6:27 pm** 3:27 pm
☉ □ ♆ **7:40 pm** 4:40 pm

14 MONDAY
☽ □ ♅ **3:27 pm** 12:27 pm
☽ ☍ ♄ **3:28 pm** 12:28 pm
♄ □ ♅ **6:01 pm** 3:01 pm
☽ ⚺ ♀ **7:19 pm** 4:19 pm
♂ ⚻ ♃ **8:39 pm** 5:39 pm
☽ ⚹ ☿ 9:58 pm

15 TUESDAY
☽ ⚹ ☿ **12:58 am**
☽ ⚻ ♆ **10:22 am** 7:22 am
☽ ⚹ ☉ **1:27 pm** 10:27 am
☽ ⚻ ♇ **4:10 pm** 1:10 pm

16 WEDNESDAY
☽ ☍ ♃ **3:00 am** 12:00 am
☽ ⚺ ♂ **4:28 am** 1:28 am
☿ ⚺ ♀ **4:11 pm** 1:11 pm
☽ ⚻ ♄ **10:47 pm** 7:47 pm
☽ △ ♅ **11:07 pm** 8:07 pm
☉ ⚻ ♇ 10:24 pm

17 THURSDAY
☉ ⚻ ♇ **1:24 am**
☽ □ ☿ **6:16 am** 3:16 am
☽ ⚹ ♀ **8:07 am** 5:07 am
☽ ☍ ♆ **4:55 pm** 1:55 pm
☽ △ ♇ **10:18 pm** 7:18 pm
☽ □ ☉ **11:54 pm** 8:54 pm

18 FRIDAY
☽ ⚻ ♃ **8:41 am** 5:41 am
☽ ⚹ ♂ **12:32 pm** 9:32 am

19 SATURDAY
☽ △ ♄ **3:15 am** 12:15 am
☽ ⚻ ♅ **3:53 am** 12:53 am
☽ △ ☿ **9:22 am** 6:22 am
☽ □ ♀ **5:07 pm** 2:07 pm
☽ ⚻ ♆ **8:36 pm** 5:36 pm
☽ □ ♇ 10:37 pm

20 SUNDAY
☽ □ ♇ **1:37 am**
☽ △ ☉ **6:52 am** 3:52 am
☽ △ ♃ **11:35 am** 8:35 am
☽ □ ♂ **5:29 pm** 2:29 pm

21 MONDAY
☽ □ ♄ **5:09 am** 2:09 am
☽ ☍ ♅ **6:02 am** 3:02 am
♀ △ ♆ **9:57 am** 6:57 am
☽ ⚻ ☿ **10:35 am** 7:35 am
☽ △ ♆ **9:57 pm** 6:57 pm
☽ △ ♀ **11:01 pm** 8:01 pm
☽ ⚹ ♇ 11:43 pm

22 TUESDAY
☽ ⚹ ♇ **2:43 am**
☽ ⚻ ☉ **11:12 am** 8:12 am
☽ □ ♃ **12:26 pm** 9:26 am
☽ △ ♂ **8:17 pm** 5:17 pm

23 WEDNESDAY
☽ ⚹ ♄ **5:25 am** 2:25 am
☉ △ ♃ **6:11 am** 3:11 am
☽ ⚻ ♅ **6:35 am** 3:35 am
☽ ☍ ☿ **10:50 am** 7:50 am
♀ ☍ ♇ **7:39 pm** 4:39 pm
☽ □ ♆ **10:09 pm** 7:09 pm
☽ ⚺ ♇ 11:49 pm

24 THURSDAY
☽ ⚺ ♇ **2:49 am**
☽ ⚻ ♀ **3:28 am** 12:28 am
☽ ⚹ ♃ **12:33 pm** 9:33 am
☽ ☍ ☉ **2:40 pm** 11:40 am
☽ ⚻ ♂ **10:35 pm** 7:35 pm

25 FRIDAY
☽ ⚺ ♄ **5:35 am** 2:35 am
☽ △ ♅ **7:04 am** 4:04 am
☽ ⚻ ☿ **11:42 am** 8:42 am
☽ ⚹ ♆ **10:51 pm** 7:51 pm

26 SATURDAY
☽ ☌ ♇ **3:36 am** 12:36 am
☽ ☍ ♀ **8:49 am** 5:49 am
☽ ⚺ ♃ **1:42 pm** 10:42 am
☽ ⚻ ☉ **7:29 pm** 4:29 pm
☽ ☍ ♂ 11:30 pm

27 SUNDAY
☽ ☍ ♂ **2:30 am**
☽ ☌ ♄ **7:23 am** 4:23 am
☽ □ ♅ **9:16 am** 6:16 am
☽ △ ☿ **3:08 pm** 12:08 pm
☽ ⚺ ♆ 10:49 pm

28 MONDAY
☽ ⚺ ♆ **1:49 am**
☽ ⚺ ♇ **6:47 am** 3:47 am
♀ ⚻ ♃ **5:31 pm** 2:31 pm
☽ ☌ ♃ **5:33 pm** 2:33 pm
☽ ⚻ ♀ **5:34 pm** 2:34 pm

29 TUESDAY
☽ △ ☉ **3:54 am** 12:54 am
☽ ⚻ ♂ **9:58 am** 6:58 am
☽ ⚺ ♄ **12:24 pm** 9:24 am
☽ ⚹ ♅ **2:47 pm** 11:47 am
☽ □ ☿ **11:00 pm** 8:00 pm

30 WEDNESDAY
☽ ☌ ♆ **8:25 am** 5:25 am
☽ ⚹ ♇ **1:40 pm** 10:40 am
☽ ⚺ ♃ 10:12 pm

Eastern time in bold type
Pacific time in medium type

JUNE 2021

DATE	SID.TIME	SUN	MOON	NODE	MERCURY	VENUS	MARS	JUPITER	SATURN	URANUS	NEPTUNE	PLUTO	CERES	PALLAS	JUNO	VESTA	CHIRON
1 T	16 38 47	10♊44 05	25≈00	10♉44℞	24♊34℞	28♉06	23♊30	1♓34	13≈27℞	12♉25	23♓02	26♑39℞	9♋08	23♈19	17♐44℞	12♉49	12♈06
2 W	16 42 44	11 41 35	8♓02	10 44D	24 22	29 19	24 07	1 38	13 27	12 29	23 03	26 32	9 31	23 30	17 30	13 05	12 08
3 Th	16 46 40	12 39 04	20 43	10 44	24 07	0♊33	24 44	1 41	13 25	12 32	23 04	26 31	9 54	23 41	17 17	13 22	12 10
4 F	16 50 37	13 36 32	3♈05	10 44	23 48	1 46	25 21	1 45	13 23	12 35	23 04	26 30	10 16	23 52	17 03	13 38	12 12
5 Sa	16 54 33	14 33 59	15 12	10 45	23 26	2 59	25 58	1 48	13 23	12 38	23 05	26 29	10 39	24 02	16 50	13 55	12 14
6 Su	16 58 30	15 31 26	27 09	10 45	23 00	4 13	26 34	1 51	13 22	12 41	23 06	26 28	11 02	24 13	16 36	14 13	12 16
7 M	17 2 27	16 28 52	8♉59	10 46	22 32	5 26	27 11	1 53	13 21	12 44	23 06	26 27	11 24	24 23	16 23	14 30	12 18
8 T	17 6 23	17 26 17	20 46	10 46	22 02	6 39	27 48	1 56	13 19	12 47	23 07	26 25	11 47	24 33	16 09	14 48	12 20
9 W	17 10 20	18 23 42	2♊34	10 47℞	21 30	7 52	28 25	1 58	13 18	12 50	23 07	26 24	12 09	24 42	15 55	15 06	12 22
10 Th	17 14 16	19 21 06	14 24	10 47	20 57	9 05	29 02	2 00	13 16	12 53	23 08	26 23	12 31	24 52	15 42	15 25	12 23
11 F	17 18 13	20 18 29	26 19	10 46	20 23	10 19	29 39	2 02	13 14	12 56	23 08	26 22	12 54	25 01	15 28	15 43	12 25
12 Sa	17 22 9	21 15 51	8♋21	10 46	19 50	11 32	0♋16	2 04	13 13	12 59	23 09	26 21	13 16	25 10	15 15	16 02	12 27
13 Su	17 26 6	22 13 13	20 33	10 44	19 17	12 45	0 53	2 05	13 11	13 01	23 09	26 20	13 38	25 19	15 01	16 21	12 28
14 M	17 30 2	23 10 33	2♌55	10 43	18 45	13 58	1 30	2 07	13 09	13 04	23 10	26 19	14 00	25 27	14 48	16 40	12 30
15 T	17 33 59	24 07 53	15 31	10 41	18 15	15 11	2 07	2 08	13 07	13 07	23 10	26 18	14 22	25 36	14 34	17 00	12 32
16 W	17 37 56	25 05 12	28 21	10 39	17 47	16 24	2 44	2 09	13 05	13 10	23 10	26 17	14 44	25 44	14 21	17 20	12 33
17 Th	17 41 52	26 02 30	11♍29	10 38	17 22	17 37	3 21	2 10	13 02	13 13	23 11	26 16	15 06	25 52	14 08	17 40	12 35
18 F	17 45 49	26 59 47	24 56	10 38D	17 00	18 50	3 58	2 10	13 00	13 15	23 11	26 15	15 28	25 59	13 55	18 00	12 36
19 Sa	17 49 45	27 57 04	8♎43	10 38	16 41	20 03	4 35	2 11	12 58	13 18	23 11	26 14	15 50	26 07	13 42	18 20	12 37
20 Su	17 53 42	28 54 19	22 50	10 39	16 27	21 16	5 12	2 11℞	12 55	13 21	23 11	26 12	16 12	26 14	13 29	18 41	12 39
21 M	17 57 38	29 51 34	7♏17	10 40	16 16	22 29	5 49	2 11	12 53	13 23	23 12	26 11	16 34	26 21	13 16	19 01	12 40
22 T	18 1 35	0♋48 48	22 00	10 42℞	16 10D	23 42	6 26	2 11	12 50	13 26	23 12	26 09	16 55	26 27	13 04	19 22	12 41
23 W	18 5 32	1 46 02	6♐53	10 41	16 08	24 55	7 03	2 11	12 47	13 29	23 12	26 08	17 17	26 34	12 52	19 44	12 42
24 Th	18 9 28	2 43 15	21 52	10 41	16 10D	26 08	7 40	2 10	12 44	13 31	23 12	26 07	17 38	26 40	12 39	20 05	12 44
25 F	18 13 25	3 40 28	6♑46	10 40	16 18	27 21	8 18	2 10	12 41	13 34	23 12℞	26 06	18 00	26 46	12 28	20 26	12 45
26 Sa	18 17 21	4 37 40	21 28	10 38	16 30	28 34	8 55	2 09	12 39	13 36	23 12	26 04	18 21	26 52	12 16	20 48	12 46
27 Su	18 21 18	5 34 52	5≈52	10 34	16 47	29 47	9 32	2 07	12 35	13 38	23 12	26 03	18 43	26 57	12 04	21 10	12 47
28 M	18 25 14	6 32 04	19 52	10 31	17 09	0♋59	10 09	2 06	12 32	13 41	23 12	26 02	19 04	27 02	11 53	21 32	12 48
29 T	18 29 11	7 29 16	3♓26	10 27	17 35	2 12	10 46	2 04	12 29	13 43	23 12	26 00	19 25	27 07	11 42	21 54	12 49
30 W	18 33 7	8 26 28	16 34	10 25	18 06	3 25	11 23	2 03	12 26	13 46	23 12	25 59	19 46	27 11	11 31	22 17	12 49

JULY 2021

☽ Last Aspect / ☽ Ingress

day	ET / hr:mn / PT		asp	sign	day	ET / hr:mn / PT	
2		9:15 pm	□ ♀	⊀	19	5:08 pm	2:08 pm
	12:15 am	9:30 am	△ ♂	✓	21	6:36 pm	3:36 pm
5	12:57 pm	9:57 am	♂ ♄	♈	23	8:12 pm	5:12 pm
		9:20 pm	⚹ ♀	≈	23	11:30 am	8:30 pm
8	12:20 am		♂ ♃	⊬	25	11:37 am	8:30 pm
10	12:10 pm	9:10 am	□ ♂	♈	28	2:13 am	6:13 pm
	8:29 am	5:29 am	△ ♀	⧫	28	5:58 am	2:58 am
14		11:46 am	△ ♃	≏	30	4:06 pm	1:06 am
15	2:46 pm		⚹ ♄				
17	7:03 am	4:03 am					

☽ Ingress

day	ET / hr:mn / PT		sign	day
♈	3	8:28 am	5:28 am
♉	5	9:24 am	6:24 am
♊	7	9:51 am	6:51 am
♋	9	9:51 am	6:51 am
♌	12	8:21 pm	5:21 pm
♍	13	4:30 pm	1:30 pm
♎	15	10:32 pm	7:32 pm
♏	17	2:38 am	11:38 am

☽ Phases & Eclipses

phase	day	ET / hr:mn / PT	
4th Quarter	1	5:11 am	2:11 am
New Moon	9	9:17 pm	6:17 pm
2nd Quarter	17	6:11 am	3:11 am
Full Moon	23	10:37 pm	7:37 pm
4th Quarter	31	9:16 am	6:16 am

Planet Ingress

day	ET / hr:mn / PT	
☿ ♋	11	4:35 pm	1:35 pm
♀ ♌	21	11:37 pm	11:31 pm
☉ ♌	22	2:31 am	
☿ ♌	27	8:37 pm	5:37 pm
	26	10:26 am	7:26 am
	27	9:12 pm	6:12 pm
	28	8:43 am	5:43 am
	29	4:32 pm	1:32 pm
	31	4:13 am	1:13 am

Planetary Motion

day	ET / hr:mn / PT	
♀ R	14	3:40 pm	12:40 am
♃ R	15	12:41 pm	9:41 am

Eastern time in **bold type**
Pacific time in medium type

JULY 2021

DATE	SID. TIME	SUN	MOON	NODE	MERCURY	VENUS	MARS	JUPITER	SATURN	URANUS	NEPTUNE	PLUTO	CERES	PALLAS	JUNO	VESTA	CHIRON
1 Th	18 37 4	9♋23 40	29♏18	10♊23	18♊42	4♌37	12♋00	2♓01R	12≈29R	13♉48	23♓12R	25♑58R	20♌07	27♓16	11♐20R	22♍40	12♈50
2 F	18 41 1	10 20 52	11♐41	10 23	19 23	5 50	12 38	1 59	12 22	13 50	23 11	25 57	20 28	27 20	11 10	23 02	12 51
3 Sa	18 44 57	11 18 05	23 47	10 23	20 08	7 03	13 15	1 56	12 16	13 52	23 11	25 56	20 49	27 23	11 00	23 25	12 52
4 Su	18 48 54	12 15 17	5♑43	10 25	20 58	8 15	13 52	1 54	12 12	13 55	23 11	25 55	21 10	27 27	10 50	23 48	12 52
5 M	18 52 50	13 12 30	17 32	10 26	21 52	9 28	14 29	1 51	12 09	13 57	23 11	25 53	21 30	27 30	10 40	24 12	12 53
6 T	18 56 47	14 09 43	29 19	10 28R	22 51	10 41	15 07	1 48	12 05	13 59	23 11	25 52	21 51	27 33	10 31	24 35	12 53
7 W	19 0 43	15 06 56	11≈08	10 28	23 54	11 53	15 44	1 45	12 02	14 01	23 10	25 51	22 12	27 35	10 22	24 59	12 54
8 Th	19 4 40	16 04 10	23 04	10 28	25 01	13 06	16 21	1 42	11 58	14 03	23 10	25 49	22 32	27 37	10 13	25 22	12 54
9 F	19 8 36	17 01 23	5♓07	10 25	26 12	14 18	16 58	1 39	11 54	14 05	23 10	25 48	22 52	27 39	10 05	25 46	12 54
10 Sa	19 12 33	17 58 37	17 22	10 21	27 28	15 31	17 36	1 35	11 50	14 07	23 09	25 46	23 13	27 41	9 57	26 10	12 55
11 Su	19 16 30	18 55 52	29 49	10 15	28 48	16 43	18 13	1 32	11 46	14 09	23 08	25 45	23 33	27 42	9 49	26 35	12 55
12 M	19 20 26	19 53 06	12♈29	10 09	0♋12	17 56	18 50	1 28	11 42	14 11	23 08	25 44	23 53	27 43	9 42	26 59	12 55
13 T	19 24 23	20 50 20	25 23	10 02	1 40	19 08	19 28	1 24	11 38	14 12	23 07	25 42	24 13	27 43	9 34	27 23	12 56
14 W	19 28 19	21 47 34	8♉29	9 56	3 12	20 20	20 05	1 19	11 34	14 14	23 07	25 41	24 33	27 44R	9 28	27 48	12 56
15 Th	19 32 16	22 44 49	21 49	9 50	4 48	21 33	20 43	1 15	11 30	14 16	23 06	25 39	24 53	27 44	9 21	28 13	12 56
16 F	19 36 12	23 42 03	5♊25	9 47	6 27	22 45	21 20	1 11	11 26	14 18	23 06	25 38	25 12	27 44	9 15	28 38	12 56R
17 Sa	19 40 9	24 39 18	19 09	9 46D	8 10	23 57	21 57	1 06	11 22	14 19	23 05	25 36	25 32	27 43	9 09	29 03	12 56
18 Su	19 44 5	25 36 32	3♋09	9 46	9 56	25 10	22 35	1 01	11 18	14 21	23 04	25 35	25 51	27 41	9 03	29 28	12 56
19 M	19 48 2	26 33 47	17 21	9 47	11 46	26 22	23 12	0 56	11 14	14 22	23 03	25 34	26 11	27 40	8 58	29 53	12 56
20 T	19 51 59	27 31 02	1♌44	9 48R	13 39	27 34	23 50	0 50	11 09	14 24	23 03	25 32	26 30	27 38	8 53	0♎19	12 55
21 W	19 55 55	28 28 17	16 15	9 48	15 34	28 46	24 27	0 45	11 05	14 25	23 02	25 31	26 49	27 36	8 49	0 44	12 55
22 Th	19 59 52	29 25 33	0♍51	9 46	17 32	29 58	25 05	0 39	11 01	14 27	23 01	25 29	27 08	27 34	8 45	1 10	12 55
23 F	20 3 48	0♌22 49	15 25	9 42	19 32	1♍10	25 42	0 34	10 56	14 28	23 00	25 28	27 27	27 31	8 41	1 35	12 54
24 Sa	20 7 45	1 20 05	29 53	9 36	21 34	2 22	26 20	0 28	10 52	14 30	22 59	25 26	27 46	27 28	8 37	2 01	12 54
25 Su	20 11 41	2 17 22	14♎06	9 30	23 37	3 34	26 57	0 22	10 48	14 31	22 59	25 25	28 04	27 25	8 34	2 27	12 54
26 M	20 15 38	3 14 40	28 00	9 20	25 47	4 46	27 35	0 16	10 43	14 33	22 58	25 23	28 23	27 21	8 31	2 54	12 53
27 T	20 19 34	4 11 58	11♏32	9 11	27 47	5 58	28 13	0 10	10 39	14 34	22 57	25 22	28 41	27 17	8 29	3 20	12 53
28 W	20 23 31	5 09 17	24 40	9 04	29 54	7 10	28 50	0 03	10 34	14 36	22 56	25 21	29 00	27 12	8 26	3 46	12 52
29 Th	20 27 28	6 06 37	7♐25	8 58	2♌00	8 22	29 28	29≈57	10 30	14 36	22 55	25 19	29 18	27 07	8 25	4 13	12 52
30 F	20 31 24	7 03 58	19 49	8 55	4 07	9 33	0♌05	29 50	10 26	14 37	22 54	25 18	29 36	27 02	8 23	4 39	12 51
31 Sa	20 35 21	8 01 21	1♑56	8 53D	6 13	10 45	0 43	29 44	10 21	14 38	22 54	25 15	29 54	26 57	8 22	5 06	12 50

EPHEMERIS CALCULATED FOR 12 MIDNIGHT GREENWICH MEAN TIME. ALL OTHER DATA AND FACING ASPECTARIAN PAGE IN EASTERN TIME (BOLD) AND PACIFIC TIME (REGULAR).

AUGUST 2021

☽ Last Aspect day	ET / hr:mn	PT	asp	☽ Ingress sign	day	ET / hr:mn	PT
2	**3:41 am**	12:41 am	□ ♃	♊	2	**4:46 am**	1:46 am
4	**3:38 pm**	12:38 pm	△ ♃	♋	4	**5:17 pm**	2:17 pm
6	**6:12 pm**	3:12 pm	☍ ♇	♌	7	**3:31 am**	12:31 am
9	**8:23 am**	5:23 am	☍ ♃	♍	9	**10:56 am**	7:56 am
11	**7:22 am**	4:22 am	△ ♇	♎	11	**4:08 pm**	1:08 pm
13	**4:39 pm**	1:39 pm	△ ♃	♏	13	**8:01 pm**	5:01 pm
15	**11:05 pm**	8:05 pm	⚹ ♀	♐	15	**11:12 pm**	8:12 pm
17	**9:43 pm**	6:43 pm	⚹ ♃	♑	17		10:58 pm
17	**9:43 pm**	6:43 pm	⚹ ♃	♑	18	**1:58 am**	
19	**7:59 pm**	4:59 pm	☌ ♇	♒	20	**4:49 am**	1:49 am
22	**8:02 am**	5:02 am	☍ ☉	♓	22	**8:43 am**	5:43 am
24	**5:12 am**	2:12 am	⚹ ♇	♈	24	**2:57 pm**	11:57 am
26	**5:14 pm**	2:14 pm	⚹ ♃	♉	26		9:27 pm
26	**5:14 pm**	2:14 pm	⚹ ♃	♉	27	**12:27 am**	
29	**10:59 am**	7:59 am	△ ☿	♊	29	**12:42 pm**	9:42 am
31	**4:48 pm**	1:48 pm	△ ♃	♋	31		10:26 pm

☽ Phases & Eclipses phase	day	ET / hr:mn	PT
New Moon	8	**9:50 am**	6:50 am
2nd Quarter	15	**11:20 am**	8:20 am
Full Moon	22	**8:02 am**	5:02 am
4th Quarter	30	**3:13 am**	12:13 am

Planet Ingress	day	ET / hr:mn	PT
☿ ♍	11	**5:57 pm**	2:57 pm
♀ ♎	15		9:27 pm
♀ ♎	16	**12:27 am**	
☉ ♍	22	**5:35 pm**	2:35 pm
☿ ♎	29		10:10 pm
☿ ♎	30	1:10 am	

Planetary Motion	day	ET / hr:mn	PT
⚵ D	2	**7:43 pm**	4:43 pm
♅ ℞	19	**9:40 pm**	6:40 pm

1 SUNDAY
☉ ☌ ☿ **10:08 am** 7:08 am
☽ ⚹ ♆ **2:13 pm** 11:13 am
☿ ☍ ♄ **5:50 pm** 2:50 pm
☽ △ ♇ **7:01 pm** 4:01 pm
☉ ☍ ♄ 11:14 pm

2 MONDAY
☉ ☍ ♄ **2:14 am**
☽ □ ♃ **3:41 am** 12:41 am
☽ □ ♂ **9:30 am** 6:30 am
☽ △ ♄ 10:19 pm
♀ △ ♅ 11:53 pm

3 TUESDAY
☽ △ ♄ **1:19 am**
♀ △ ♅ **2:53 am**
☽ ⚹ ☉ **3:30 am** 12:30 am
☽ ⚹ ☿ **8:12 am** 5:12 am
☽ ⚺ ♅ **10:34 am** 7:34 am
☽ □ ♀ **11:25 am** 8:25 am
☿ □ ♅ **9:57 pm** 6:57 pm
☽ □ ♆ 11:55 pm

4 WEDNESDAY
☽ □ ♆ **2:55 am**
☽ ⚻ ♇ **7:37 am** 4:37 am
☽ △ ♃ **3:38 pm** 12:38 pm
☿ ⚺ ♀ 9:43 pm
☽ ⚹ ♂ 10:12 pm

5 THURSDAY
☿ ⚺ ♀ **12:43 am**
☽ ⚹ ♂ **1:12 am**
☽ ⚻ ♄ **12:52 pm** 9:52 am
☽ ⚺ ☉ **8:24 pm** 5:24 pm
☽ ⚹ ♅ **10:12 pm** 7:12 pm

6 FRIDAY
☽ ⚹ ♀ **5:17 am** 2:17 am
☽ ⚺ ☿ **7:31 am** 4:31 am
☽ △ ♆ **1:43 pm** 10:43 am
☽ ☍ ♇ **6:12 pm** 3:12 pm
☉ □ ♅ **7:57 pm** 4:57 pm
☽ ⚻ ♃ 10:23 pm

7 SATURDAY
☽ ⚻ ♃ **1:23 am**
☽ ⚺ ♂ **2:04 pm** 11:04 am
☽ ☍ ♄ **9:50 pm** 6:50 pm
☿ ⚻ ♆ **10:24 pm** 7:24 pm

8 SUNDAY
☽ □ ♅ **7:04 am** 4:04 am
☽ ☌ ☉ **9:50 am** 6:50 am
☽ ⚺ ♀ **7:24 pm** 4:24 pm
☽ ⚻ ♆ **9:42 pm** 6:42 pm
☽ ☌ ☿ 10:45 pm
☽ ⚻ ♇ 10:57 pm

9 MONDAY
☽ ☌ ☿ **1:45 am**
☽ ⚻ ♇ **1:57 am**
☿ ⚻ ♇ **3:03 am** 12:03 am

☽ ☍ ♃ **8:23 am** 5:23 am
♀ ☍ ♆ **8:20 pm** 5:20 pm
☽ ☌ ♂ **11:42 pm** 8:42 pm

10 TUESDAY
☽ ⚻ ♄ **4:07 am** 1:07 am
☽ △ ♅ **1:19 pm** 10:19 am
☽ ⚺ ☉ **8:03 pm** 5:03 pm
☿ ☍ ♃ **9:20 pm** 6:20 pm

11 WEDNESDAY
☽ ☍ ♆ **3:16 am** 12:16 am
☽ ☌ ♀ **6:15 am** 3:15 am
☽ △ ♇ **7:22 am** 4:22 am
☽ ⚻ ♃ **1:10 pm** 10:10 am
☽ ⚺ ☿ **3:51 pm** 12:51 pm
♀ △ ♇ **6:46 pm** 3:46 pm

12 THURSDAY
☽ ⚺ ♂ **7:03 am** 4:03 am
☽ △ ♄ **8:32 am** 5:32 am
☽ ⚻ ♅ **5:48 pm** 2:48 pm

13 FRIDAY
☽ ⚹ ☉ **4:13 am** 1:13 am
☽ ⚻ ♆ **7:19 am** 4:19 am
☽ □ ♇ **11:20 am** 8:20 am
♂ ⚻ ♄ **12:27 pm** 9:27 am
☽ ⚺ ♀ **3:10 pm** 12:10 pm
☽ △ ♃ **4:39 pm** 1:39 pm

14 SATURDAY
☽ ⚹ ☿ **3:33 am** 12:33 am
♀ ⚻ ♃ **6:58 am** 3:58 am
☽ □ ♄ **11:54 am** 8:54 am

☽ ⚹ ♂ **1:08 pm** 10:08 am
☽ ☍ ♅ **9:18 pm** 6:18 pm
☉ ⚻ ♆ 9:14 pm

15 SUNDAY
☉ ⚻ ♆ **12:14 am**
☽ △ ♆ **10:33 am** 7:33 am
☽ □ ☉ **11:20 am** 8:20 am
☽ ⚹ ♇ **2:32 pm** 11:32 am
☽ □ ♃ **7:23 pm** 4:23 pm
☽ ⚹ ♀ **11:05 pm** 8:05 pm

16 MONDAY
☽ □ ☿ **1:57 pm** 10:57 am
☽ ⚹ ♄ **2:40 pm** 11:40 am
☽ □ ♂ **6:31 pm** 3:31 pm
☿ ⚻ ♄ **7:35 pm** 4:35 pm
☽ ⚻ ♅ 9:15 pm

17 TUESDAY
☽ ⚻ ♅ **12:15 am**
☉ ⚻ ♇ **9:31 am** 6:31 am
☽ □ ♆ **1:19 pm** 10:19 am
☽ ⚺ ♇ **5:17 pm** 2:17 pm
☽ △ ☉ **5:51 pm** 2:51 pm
☽ ⚹ ♃ **9:43 pm** 6:43 pm

18 WEDNESDAY
☽ □ ♀ **6:27 am** 3:27 am
☽ ⚺ ♄ **5:08 pm** 2:08 pm
☿ ☌ ♂ **11:28 pm** 8:28 pm
☽ △ ♂ **11:37 pm** 8:37 pm
☽ △ ☿ **11:38 pm** 8:38 pm
☽ △ ♅ 11:59 pm

19 THURSDAY
☽ △ ♅ **2:59 am**
☽ ⚹ ♆ **3:59 pm** 12:59 pm
☽ ☌ ♇ **7:59 pm** 4:59 pm
☉ ☍ ♃ **8:29 pm** 5:29 pm
☽ ⚺ ♃ 9:03 pm
☽ ⚻ ☉ 9:21 pm

20 FRIDAY
☽ ⚺ ♃ **12:03 am**
☽ ⚻ ☉ **12:21 am**
☿ △ ♅ **4:06 am** 1:06 am
☽ △ ♀ **2:01 pm** 11:01 am
☽ ☌ ♄ **7:55 pm** 4:55 pm

21 SATURDAY
☽ ⚻ ♂ **5:13 am** 2:13 am
☽ □ ♅ **6:12 am** 3:12 am
☽ ⚻ ☿ **9:41 am** 6:41 am
☽ ⚺ ♆ **7:24 pm** 4:24 pm
☽ ⚺ ♇ **11:32 pm** 8:32 pm
♂ △ ♅ 11:38 pm

22 SUNDAY
♂ △ ♅ **2:38 am**
☽ ☌ ♃ **3:19 am** 12:19 am
☽ ☍ ☉ **8:02 am** 5:02 am
☽ ⚻ ♀ **11:14 pm** 8:14 pm
☽ ⚺ ♄ 9:07 pm

23 MONDAY
☽ ⚺ ♄ **12:07 am**
♀ △ ♄ **8:48 am** 5:48 am
☽ ⚹ ♅ **11:04 am** 8:04 am
☽ ☍ ♂ **12:43 pm** 9:43 am

☽ ☍ ☿ **10:03 pm** 7:03 pm
☽ ☌ ♆ 9:50 pm

24 TUESDAY
☽ ☌ ♆ **12:50 am**
☽ ⚹ ♇ **5:12 am** 2:12 am
☽ ⚺ ♃ **8:43 am** 5:43 am
☽ ⚻ ☉ **6:37 pm** 3:37 pm
☿ ☍ ♆ **9:14 pm** 6:14 pm

25 WEDNESDAY
☽ ⚹ ♄ **6:58 am** 3:58 am
☽ ☍ ♀ **11:57 am** 8:57 am
☽ ⚺ ♅ **6:51 pm** 3:51 pm
☽ ⚻ ♂ **11:37 pm** 8:37 pm

26 THURSDAY
☽ ⚺ ♆ **9:22 am** 6:22 am
☿ △ ♇ **10:23 am** 7:23 am
☽ □ ♇ **2:02 pm** 11:02 am
☽ ⚻ ☿ **2:33 pm** 11:33 am
☽ ⚹ ♃ **5:14 pm** 2:14 pm

27 FRIDAY
☽ △ ☉ **9:19 am** 6:19 am
☿ ⚻ ♃ **11:05 am** 8:05 am
☽ □ ♄ **5:04 pm** 2:04 pm

28 SATURDAY
☽ ⚻ ♀ **5:00 am** 2:00 am
☽ ☌ ♅ **5:52 am** 2:52 am
♀ ⚻ ♅ **1:43 pm** 10:43 am
☽ △ ♂ **2:14 pm** 11:14 am
☽ ⚹ ♆ **8:56 pm** 5:56 pm
☽ △ ♇ 10:50 pm

29 SUNDAY
☽ △ ♇ **1:50 am**
☽ □ ♃ **4:36 am** 1:36 am
☽ △ ☿ **10:59 am** 7:59 am

30 MONDAY
☽ □ ☉ **3:13 am** 12:13 am
☽ △ ♄ **5:26 am** 2:26 am
☽ ⚺ ♅ **6:40 pm** 3:40 pm
☽ △ ♀ 9:30 pm

31 TUESDAY
☽ △ ♀ **12:30 am**
☉ ⚻ ♄ **4:46 am** 1:46 am
☽ □ ♂ **6:36 am** 3:36 am
☽ □ ♆ **9:41 am** 6:41 am
☽ ⚻ ♇ **2:37 pm** 11:37 am
☽ △ ♃ **4:48 pm** 1:48 pm

Eastern time in bold type
Pacific time in medium type

AUGUST 2021

DATE	SID.TIME	SUN	MOON	NODE	MERCURY	VENUS	MARS	JUPITER	SATURN	URANUS	NEPTUNE	PLUTO	CERES	PALLAS	JUNO	VESTA	CHIRON
1 Su	20 39 17	8♌58 44	13♎52	8♊53	8♌19	11♍57	1♍21	29♒37℞	10♒17℞	14♉39	22♓52℞	25♑14℞	0♊12	26♈51℞	8♐21℞	5♎33	12♈49℞
2 M	20 43 14	9 56 08	25 41	8 54	10 24	13 08	1 58	29 30	10 12	14 40	22 51	25 11	0 29	26 44	8 21D	5 59	12 48
3 T	20 47 10	10 53 34	7♏29	8 54℞	12 28	14 20	2 36	29 23	10 08	14 40	22 49	25 11	0 47	26 38	8 20	6 26	12 47
4 W	20 51 7	11 51 01	19 22	8 53	14 31	15 32	3 14	29 16	10 03	14 41	22 48	25 08	1 04	26 31	8 21	6 54	12 46
5 Th	20 55 3	12 48 29	1♐22	8 51	16 33	16 43	3 52	29 09	9 59	14 42	22 47	25 08	1 21	26 24	8 21	7 21	12 45
6 F	20 59 0	13 45 58	13 35	8 46	18 34	17 55	4 29	29 01	9 54	14 42	22 46	25 05	1 39	26 16	8 22	7 48	12 44
7 Sa	21 2 57	14 43 28	26 02	8 39	20 34	19 06	5 07	28 54	9 50	14 43	22 45	25 05	1 55	26 08	8 23	8 15	12 43
8 Su	21 6 53	15 40 59	8♑46	8 29	22 32	20 17	5 45	28 47	9 46	14 44	22 44	25 04	2 12	25 59	8 25	8 43	12 42
9 M	21 10 50	16 38 32	21 47	8 18	24 28	21 29	6 23	28 39	9 41	14 45	22 42	25 03	2 29	25 51	8 26	9 10	12 41
10 T	21 14 46	17 36 05	5♒03	8 07	26 24	22 40	7 01	28 32	9 37	14 45	22 41	25 01	2 45	25 42	8 29	9 38	12 40
11 W	21 18 43	18 33 39	18 32	7 56	28 17	23 51	7 39	28 24	9 32	14 46	22 40	25 00	3 02	25 32	8 31	10 06	12 38
12 Th	21 22 39	19 31 15	2♓13	7 47	0♍10	25 03	8 17	28 16	9 28	14 46	22 39	24 59	3 18	25 23	8 34	10 34	12 37
13 F	21 26 36	20 28 51	16 03	7 41	2 00	26 14	8 55	28 09	9 24	14 46	22 38	24 58	3 34	25 13	8 37	11 02	12 36
14 Sa	21 30 32	21 26 28	29 59	7 37	3 50	27 25	9 33	28 01	9 19	14 47	22 36	24 56	3 49	25 02	8 40	11 30	12 34
15 Su	21 34 29	22 24 06	14♈01	7 36D	5 37	28 36	10 11	27 53	9 15	14 47	22 34	24 55	4 05	24 52	8 44	11 58	12 33
16 M	21 38 26	23 21 45	28 07	7 35℞	7 24	29 47	10 49	27 45	9 11	14 47	22 33	24 54	4 20	24 41	8 48	12 26	12 31
17 T	21 42 22	24 19 25	12♉17	7 35	9 08	0≏58	11 27	27 37	9 06	14 47	22 32	24 53	4 36	24 29	8 52	12 54	12 30
18 W	21 46 19	25 17 07	26 28	7 34	10 52	2 09	12 05	27 30	9 02	14 47	22 30	24 51	4 51	24 18	8 57	13 23	12 28
19 Th	21 50 15	26 14 49	10♊40	7 31	12 34	3 19	12 43	27 22	8 58	14 48℞	22 29	24 50	5 06	24 06	9 02	13 51	12 26
20 F	21 54 12	27 12 32	24 49	7 25	14 14	4 30	13 21	27 14	8 54	14 48	22 27	24 49	5 20	23 54	9 07	14 20	12 25
21 Sa	21 58 8	28 10 17	8♋53	7 17	15 53	5 41	13 59	27 06	8 50	14 48	22 26	24 48	5 35	23 41	9 13	14 48	12 23
22 Su	22 2 5	29 08 02	22 45	7 06	17 31	6 52	14 37	26 58	8 46	14 47	22 25	24 47	5 49	23 29	9 18	15 17	12 21
23 M	22 6 1	0♍05 49	6♌23	6 54	19 07	8 02	15 15	26 50	8 42	14 47	22 23	24 46	6 03	23 16	9 24	15 46	12 19
24 T	22 9 58	1 03 38	19 43	6 42	20 42	9 13	15 53	26 42	8 38	14 47	22 22	24 45	6 17	23 03	9 31	16 15	12 18
25 W	22 13 55	2 01 28	2♍43	6 31	22 15	10 23	16 31	26 35	8 34	14 47	22 20	24 43	6 31	22 49	9 37	16 44	12 16
26 Th	22 17 51	2 59 19	15 23	6 22	23 47	11 33	17 10	26 27	8 30	14 47	22 18	24 42	6 44	22 36	9 44	17 13	12 14
27 F	22 21 48	3 57 13	27 44	6 15	25 18	12 44	17 48	26 19	8 26	14 46	22 17	24 41	6 58	22 22	9 51	17 42	12 12
28 Sa	22 25 44	4 55 08	9♎51	6 11	26 47	13 54	18 26	26 11	8 23	14 46	22 15	24 40	7 11	22 08	9 59	18 11	12 10
29 Su	22 29 41	5 53 05	21 46	6 10	28 15	15 04	19 04	26 04	8 19	14 46	22 14	24 39	7 23	21 53	10 07	18 40	12 08
30 M	22 33 37	6 51 03	3♏36	6 09	29 42	16 14	19 43	25 56	8 15	14 45	22 12	24 38	7 36	21 39	10 15	19 09	12 06
31 T	22 37 34	7 49 04	15 24	6 09	1≏07	17 24	20 21	25 48	8 12	14 45	22 11	24 37	7 48	21 24	10 23	19 38	12 04

EPHEMERIS CALCULATED FOR 12 MIDNIGHT GREENWICH MEAN TIME. ALL OTHER DATA AND FACING ASPECTARIAN PAGE IN EASTERN TIME (**BOLD**) AND PACIFIC TIME (REGULAR).

SEPTEMBER 2021

☽ Last Aspect day	ET / hr:mn	PT	asp	☽ Ingress sign	day	ET / hr:mn	PT
8/31	**4:48 pm**	1:48 pm	△♃	♋	1	**1:26 am**	
2		10:37 pm	☍♇	♌	3	**11:58 am**	8:58 am
3	**1:37 am**		☍♇	♌	3	**11:58 am**	8:58 am
5	**10:22 am**	7:22 am	☍♃	♍	5	**7:06 pm**	4:06 pm
7	**3:24 pm**	12:24 pm	☌♂	♎	7	**11:20 pm**	8:20 pm
9		9:48 pm	☌♀	♏	9		11:05 pm
10	**12:48 am**		☌♀	♏	10	**2:05 am**	
11		10:33 pm	⚹♂	♐	12	**4:34 am**	1:34 am
12	**1:33 am**		⚹♂	♐	12	**4:34 am**	1:34 am
14	**6:57 am**	3:57 am	□♂	♑	14	**7:34 am**	4:34 am
15		10:40 pm	☌♇	♒	16	**11:23 am**	8:23 am
16	**1:40 am**		☌♇	♒	16	**11:23 am**	8:23 am
18	**5:14 am**	2:14 am	☌♃	♓	18	**4:22 pm**	1:22 pm
20	**7:55 pm**	4:55 pm	☍☉	♈	20	**11:13 pm**	8:13 pm
22	**10:05 pm**	7:05 pm	☍☿	♉	23	**8:38 am**	5:38 am
25	**9:09 am**	6:09 am	△♇	♊	25	**8:36 pm**	5:36 pm
27		9:18 pm	△☿	♋	28	**9:34 am**	6:34 am
28	**12:18 pm**		△☿	♋	28	**9:34 am**	6:34 am
30	**10:49 am**	7:49 am	□☿	♌	30	**8:53 pm**	5:53 pm

☽ Phases & Eclipses phase	day	ET / hr:mn	PT
New Moon	6	**8:52 pm**	5:52 pm
2nd Quarter	13	**4:39 pm**	1:39 pm
Full Moon	20	**7:55 pm**	4:55 pm
4th Quarter	28	**9:57 pm**	6:57 pm

Planet Ingress	day	ET / hr:mn	PT
♀ ♏	10	**4:39 pm**	1:39 pm
♂ ♎	14	**8:14 pm**	5:14 pm
⚵ ♏	20	**12:57 pm**	9:57 am
☉ ♎	22	**3:21 pm**	12:21 pm

Planetary Motion	day	ET / hr:mn	PT
☿ ℞	26		10:10 pm
☿ ℞	27	**1:10 am**	

1 WEDNESDAY
☽ □ ☿ **7:46 am** 4:46 am
☽ ⊼ ♄ **5:30 pm** 2:30 pm
☽ ⚹ ☉ **8:52 pm** 5:52 pm

2 THURSDAY
☽ ⚹ ♅ **6:33 am** 3:33 am
♂ ☍ ♆ **1:43 pm** 10:43 am
☽ □ ♀ **6:24 pm** 3:24 pm
☽ △ ♆ **8:52 pm** 5:52 pm
☽ ⚹ ♂ **9:16 pm** 6:16 pm
☽ ☍ ♇ 10:37 pm

3 FRIDAY
☽ ☍ ♇ **1:37 am**
☽ ⊼ ♃ **3:12 am** 12:12 am
♀ ⊼ ♆ **8:13 pm** 5:13 pm
☽ ⚹ ☿ 9:45 pm
☽ ☍ ♄ 11:55 pm

4 SATURDAY
☽ ⚹ ☿ **12:45 am**
☽ ☍ ♄ **2:55 am**
☽ ⊻ ☉ **10:58 am** 7:58 am
☽ □ ♅ **3:23 pm** 12:23 pm
☿ △ ♄ **9:30 pm** 6:30 pm

5 SUNDAY
☽ ⊼ ♆ **4:47 am** 1:47 am
☽ ⚹ ♀ **7:58 am** 4:58 am
☽ ⊻ ♂ **8:07 am** 5:07 am
☽ ⊼ ♇ **9:18 am** 6:18 am
☽ ☍ ♃ **10:22 am** 7:22 am

♀ ⊻ ♂ **11:26 am** 8:26 am
♀ □ ♇ **11:07 pm** 8:07 pm

6 MONDAY
♂ △ ♇ **8:20 am** 5:20 am
☽ ⊼ ♄ **8:57 am** 5:57 am
♀ △ ♃ **9:05 am** 6:05 am
☽ ⊻ ☿ **12:41 pm** 9:41 am
☽ ☌ ☉ **8:52 pm** 5:52 pm
☽ △ ♅ **8:54 pm** 5:54 pm
☉ △ ♅ **9:29 pm** 6:29 pm
♂ ⊼ ♃ **11:50 pm** 8:50 pm

7 TUESDAY
☽ ☍ ♆ **9:34 am** 6:34 am
☽ △ ♇ **1:56 pm** 10:56 am
☽ ⊼ ♃ **2:33 pm** 11:33 am
☽ ☌ ♂ **3:24 pm** 12:24 pm
☽ ⊻ ♀ **5:29 pm** 2:29 pm

8 WEDNESDAY
☽ △ ♄ **12:29 pm** 9:29 am
☽ ☌ ☿ **9:01 pm** 6:01 pm
☽ ⊼ ♅ 9:11 pm

9 THURSDAY
☽ ⊼ ♅ **12:11 am**
☽ ⊻ ☉ **3:58 am** 12:58 am
☽ ⊼ ♆ **12:28 pm** 9:28 am
☽ □ ♇ **4:48 pm** 1:48 pm
☽ △ ♃ **5:03 pm** 2:03 pm
☽ ⊻ ♂ **8:40 pm** 5:40 pm
☽ ☌ ♀ 9:48 pm

10 FRIDAY
☽ ☌ ♀ **12:48 am**
☿ ⊼ ♅ **12:17 pm** 9:17 am
☽ □ ♄ **2:53 pm** 11:53 am
☽ ☍ ♅ 11:37 pm

11 SATURDAY
☽ ☍ ♅ **2:37 am**
☽ ⊻ ☿ **3:49 am** 12:49 am
♃ ⊻ ♇ **6:06 am** 3:06 am
☽ ⚹ ☉ **10:08 am** 7:08 am
☽ △ ♆ **2:50 pm** 11:50 am
☽ □ ♃ **7:08 pm** 4:08 pm
☽ ⚹ ♇ **7:13 pm** 4:13 pm
☽ ⚹ ♂ 10:33 pm

12 SUNDAY
☽ ⚹ ♂ **1:33 am**
☽ ⊻ ♀ **7:45 am** 4:45 am
☽ ⚹ ♄ **5:18 pm** 2:18 pm

13 MONDAY
☽ ⊼ ♅ **5:13 am** 2:13 am
☽ ⚹ ☿ **10:31 am** 7:31 am
☽ □ ☉ **4:39 pm** 1:39 pm
☽ □ ♆ **5:33 pm** 2:33 pm
☽ ⚹ ♃ **9:38 pm** 6:38 pm
☽ ⊻ ♇ **10:03 pm** 7:03 pm

14 TUESDAY
☉ ☍ ♆ **5:21 am** 2:21 am
☽ □ ♂ **6:57 am** 3:57 am
☽ ⚹ ♀ **3:21 pm** 12:21 pm
☽ ⊻ ♄ **8:19 pm** 5:19 pm

15 WEDNESDAY
☽ △ ♅ **8:31 am** 5:31 am
☽ □ ☿ **5:41 pm** 2:41 pm
☽ ⚹ ♆ **9:01 pm** 6:01 pm
☽ △ ☉ 9:07 pm
☽ ⊻ ♃ 9:54 pm
☽ ☌ ♇ 10:40 pm

16 THURSDAY
☽ △ ☉ **12:07 am**
☽ ⊻ ♃ **12:54 am**
☽ ☌ ♇ **1:40 am**
☉ ⊼ ♃ **10:18 am** 7:18 am
☽ △ ♂ **1:19 pm** 10:19 am
☉ △ ♇ **9:53 pm** 6:53 pm
☽ □ ♀ 9:03 pm
☽ ☌ ♄ 9:14 pm
♀ □ ♄ 11:15 pm

17 FRIDAY
☽ □ ♀ **12:03 am**
☽ ☌ ♄ **12:14 am**
♀ □ ♄ **2:15 am**
☽ □ ♅ **12:45 pm** 9:45 am
☿ ⊼ ♆ 9:18 pm
☽ ⊻ ♆ 10:32 pm
☽ △ ☿ 10:36 pm

18 SATURDAY
☿ ⊼ ♆ **12:18 am**
☽ ⊻ ♆ **1:32 am**
☽ △ ☿ **1:36 am**
☽ ☌ ♃ **5:14 am** 2:14 am
☽ ⊻ ♇ **6:21 am** 3:21 am

☽ ⊼ ☉ **8:55 am** 5:55 am
☽ ⊼ ♂ **9:04 pm** 6:04 pm

19 SUNDAY
☽ ⊻ ♄ **5:27 am** 2:27 am
☽ △ ♀ **10:26 am** 7:26 am
☽ ⚹ ♅ **6:26 pm** 3:26 pm

20 MONDAY
☽ ☌ ♆ **7:39 am** 4:39 am
☽ ⊼ ☿ **10:50 am** 7:50 am
☽ ⊻ ♃ **11:15 am** 8:15 am
☽ ⚹ ♇ **12:45 pm** 9:45 am
☿ △ ♃ **6:53 pm** 3:53 pm
☽ ☍ ☉ **7:55 pm** 4:55 pm

21 TUESDAY
☽ ☍ ♂ **7:03 am** 4:03 am
☽ ⚹ ♄ **12:43 pm** 9:43 am
☽ ⊼ ♀ **11:34 pm** 8:34 pm
☽ ⊻ ♅ 11:20 pm

22 WEDNESDAY
☽ ⊻ ♅ **2:20 am**
☿ □ ♇ **9:12 am** 6:12 am
☽ ⊻ ♆ **4:11 pm** 1:11 pm
☽ ⚹ ♃ **7:42 pm** 4:42 pm
☽ □ ♇ **9:37 pm** 6:37 pm
☽ ☍ ☿ **10:05 pm** 7:05 pm

23 THURSDAY
♀ ☍ ♅ **5:41 am** 2:41 am
☽ ⊼ ☉ **10:08 am** 7:08 am
☽ ⊼ ♂ **8:07 pm** 5:07 pm
☽ □ ♄ **10:40 pm** 7:40 pm

24 FRIDAY
☽ ☌ ♅ **12:56 pm** 9:56 am
☽ ☍ ♀ **4:16 pm** 1:16 pm

25 SATURDAY
☽ ⚹ ♆ **3:23 am** 12:23 am
☽ □ ♃ **6:49 am** 3:49 am
☽ △ ♇ **9:09 am** 6:09 am
☽ ⊼ ☿ **11:10 am** 8:10 am
♂ △ ♄ **5:50 pm** 2:50 pm

26 SUNDAY
☽ △ ☉ **3:35 am** 12:35 am
☽ △ ♄ **10:57 am** 7:57 am
☽ △ ♂ **11:59 am** 8:59 am
☽ ⊻ ♅ 10:32 pm

27 MONDAY
☽ ⊻ ♅ **1:32 am**
☽ ⊼ ♀ **11:28 am** 8:28 am
☽ □ ♆ **4:11 pm** 1:11 pm
☽ △ ♃ **7:25 pm** 4:25 pm
☽ ⊼ ♇ **10:06 pm** 7:06 pm
☽ △ ☿ 9:18 pm

28 TUESDAY
☽ △ ☿ **12:18 am**
☽ □ ☉ **9:57 pm** 6:57 pm
☽ ⊼ ♄ **11:39 pm** 8:39 pm

29 WEDNESDAY
☽ □ ♂ **4:17 am** 1:17 am
♀ △ ♆ **12:14 pm** 9:14 am
☽ ⚹ ♅ **1:54 pm** 10:54 am
☉ △ ♄ **6:19 pm** 3:19 pm

30 THURSDAY
☽ △ ♆ **4:06 am** 1:06 am
☽ △ ♀ **5:44 am** 2:44 am
☽ ⊼ ♃ **7:02 am** 4:02 am
☽ ☍ ♇ **9:54 am** 6:54 am
☽ □ ☿ **10:49 am** 7:49 am
♀ □ ♃ **7:31 pm** 4:31 pm

Eastern time in bold type
Pacific time in medium type

SEPTEMBER 2021

DATE	SID.TIME	SUN	MOON	NODE	MERCURY	VENUS	MARS	JUPITER	SATURN	URANUS	NEPTUNE	PLUTO	CERES	PALLAS	JUNO	VESTA	CHIRON
1 W	22 41 30	8♍47 07	27♊17	6♊08R	2♎30	18♎34	20♍59	25♒41R	8♒08R	14♉44R	22♓09R	24♑36R	8♊01	21♋09R	10♌31	20♎08	12♈01R
2 T	22 45 27	9 45 11	9♋21	6 06	3 52	19 44	21 38	25 36	8 05	14 43	22 07	24 35	8 12	20 54	10 40	20 37	11 59
3 F	22 49 24	10 43 17	21 39	6 01	5 13	20 54	22 16	25 28	8 01	14 42	22 06	24 34	8 24	20 39	10 49	21 07	11 57
4 Sa	22 53 20	11 41 26	4♌15	5 53	6 32	22 04	22 55	25 19	7 58	14 42	22 04	24 34	8 36	20 24	10 58	21 37	11 55
5 Su	22 57 17	12 39 36	17 12	5 43	7 50	23 13	23 33	25 12	7 55	14 41	22 03	24 33	8 47	20 09	11 08	22 06	11 53
6 M	23 1 13	13 37 47	0♍31	5 34	9 05	24 23	24 12	25 05	7 51	14 41	22 01	24 32	8 58	19 53	11 18	22 36	11 50
7 T	23 5 10	14 36 01	14 08	5 19	10 20	25 32	24 50	24 58	7 48	14 40	21 59	24 31	9 08	19 38	11 27	23 06	11 48
8 W	23 9 6	15 34 16	28 03	5 07	11 32	26 42	25 29	24 51	7 45	14 39	21 58	24 30	9 19	19 22	11 38	23 36	11 46
9 Th	23 13 3	16 32 33	12♎09	4 58	12 42	27 51	26 07	24 44	7 42	14 38	21 56	24 30	9 29	19 06	11 48	24 06	11 43
10 F	23 16 59	17 30 52	26 23	4 50	13 51	29 00	26 46	24 37	7 39	14 37	21 54	24 29	9 39	18 51	11 59	24 35	11 41
11 Sa	23 20 56	18 29 12	10♏40	4 46	14 57	0♏10	27 25	24 31	7 36	14 36	21 53	24 28	9 48	18 35	12 10	25 06	11 38
12 Su	23 24 53	19 27 34	24 55	4 44D	16 02	1 19	28 03	24 24	7 34	14 35	21 51	24 27	9 58	18 19	12 21	25 36	11 36
13 M	23 28 49	20 25 58	9♐07	4♊44R	17 03	2 28	28 42	24 18	7 31	14 34	21 49	24 27	10 07	18 03	12 32	26 06	11 34
14 T	23 32 46	21 24 23	23 14	4 44	18 00	3 37	29 21	24 12	7 28	14 32	21 48	24 26	10 15	17 47	12 44	26 36	11 31
15 W	23 36 42	22 22 49	7♑15	4 43	19 00	4 45	0♎00	24 06	7 26	14 31	21 46	24 26	10 24	17 32	12 56	27 06	11 29
16 Th	23 40 39	23 21 17	21 09	4 41	19 54	5 54	0 38	24 00	7 24	14 30	21 44	24 25	10 32	17 16	13 08	27 37	11 26
17 F	23 44 35	24 19 47	4♒56	4 35	20 45	7 03	1 17	23 54	7 21	14 29	21 43	24 24	10 40	17 00	13 20	28 07	11 23
18 Sa	23 48 32	25 18 19	18 34	4 27	21 33	8 11	1 56	23 48	7 19	14 27	21 41	24 24	10 47	16 45	13 32	28 37	11 21
19 Su	23 52 28	26 16 52	2♓01	4 17	22 17	9 20	2 35	23 43	7 17	14 26	21 40	24 23	10 55	16 29	13 45	29 08	11 18
20 M	23 56 25	27 15 26	15 16	4 06	22 58	10 28	3 14	23 37	7 15	14 25	21 38	24 23	11 01	16 14	13 58	29 38	11 16
21 T	0 0 22	28 14 03	28 17	3 55	23 34	11 36	3 53	23 32	7 13	14 23	21 36	24 22	11 08	15 58	14 11	0♏09	11 13
22 W	0 4 18	29 12 42	11♈02	3 44	24 06	12 44	4 32	23 27	7 11	14 22	21 35	24 22	11 14	15 43	14 24	0 40	11 10
23 Th	0 8 15	0♎11 22	23 31	3 36	24 33	13 52	5 11	23 22	7 09	14 20	21 33	24 22	11 20	15 28	14 37	1 10	11 08
24 F	0 12 11	1 10 05	5♉46	3 30	24 56	15 00	5 50	23 18	7 07	14 18	21 31	24 21	11 26	15 13	14 51	1 41	11 05
25 Sa	0 16 8	2 08 50	17 49	3 26	25 13	16 07	6 29	23 13	7 06	14 17	21 30	24 21	11 31	14 59	15 05	2 12	11 03
26 Su	0 20 4	3 07 37	29 42	3 25D	25 24	17 15	7 08	23 09	7 04	14 15	21 28	24 21	11 36	14 44	15 19	2 43	11 00
27 M	0 24 1	4 06 26	11♊30	3 25	25 28R	18 22	7 47	23 04	7 03	14 13	21 26	24 20	11 41	14 30	15 33	3 13	10 57
28 T	0 27 57	5 05 18	23 18	3 26	25 26	19 30	8 26	23 00	7 01	14 12	21 25	24 20	11 45	14 16	15 47	3 44	10 54
29 W	0 31 54	6 04 11	5♋11	3♊26R	25 17	20 37	9 05	22 57	7 00	14 10	21 23	24 20	11 49	14 02	16 01	4 15	10 52
30 Th	0 35 51	7 03 07	17 14	3 26	25 01	21 44	9 44	22 53	6 59	14 08	21 22	24 20	11 53	13 48	16 16	4 46	10 49

EPHEMERIS CALCULATED FOR 12 MIDNIGHT GREENWICH MEAN TIME. ALL OTHER DATA AND FACING ASPECTARIAN PAGE IN **EASTERN TIME (BOLD)** AND PACIFIC TIME (REGULAR).

OCTOBER 2021

☽ Last Aspect day	ET / hr:mn / PT	asp	☽ Ingress sign	day	ET / hr:mn / PT
2	**7:43 pm** 4:43 pm	□♀	♍	3	**4:38 am** 1:38 am
5	**4:46 am** 1:46 am	⚹♀	♎	5	**8:41 am** 5:41 am
6	10:03 pm	□♇	♏	7	**10:22 am** 7:22 am
7	**1:03 am**	□♇	♏	7	**10:22 am** 7:22 am
8	11:05 pm	⚹♇	♐	9	**11:24 am** 8:24 am
9	**2:05 am**	⚹♇	♐	9	**11:24 am** 8:24 am
10	9:30 pm	⚹♃	♑	11	**1:15 pm** 10:15 am
11	**12:30 am**	⚹♃	♑	11	**1:15 pm** 10:15 am
13	**6:53 am** 3:53 am	☌♇	♒	13	**4:47 pm** 1:47 pm
15	**8:33 am** 5:33 am	△☉	♓	15	**10:22 pm** 7:22 pm
17	**7:24 pm** 4:24 pm	⚹♇	♈	18	**6:04 am** 3:04 am
20	**10:57 am** 7:57 am	☍☉	♉	20	**3:59 pm** 12:59 pm
22	**4:35 pm** 1:35 pm	△♇	♊	23	**3:57 am** 12:57 am
25	**10:11 am** 7:11 am	△♂	♋	25	**5:00 pm** 2:00 pm
27	11:02 pm	□♂	♌	28	**5:07 am** 2:07 am
28	**2:02 am**	□♂	♌	28	**5:07 am** 2:07 am
30	**3:05 am** 12:05 am	△♀	♍	30	**2:09 pm** 11:09 am

☽ Phases & Eclipses phase	day	ET / hr:mn / PT
New Moon	6	**7:05 am** 4:05 am
2nd Quarter	12	**11:25 pm** 8:25 pm
Full Moon	20	**10:57 am** 7:57 am
4th Quarter	28	**4:05 pm** 1:05 pm

Planet Ingress	day	ET / hr:mn / PT
♀ ♐	7	**7:21 am** 4:21 am
☉ ♏	22	9:51 pm
☉ ♏	23	**12:51 am**
♂ ♏	30	**10:21 am** 7:21 am

Planetary Motion		day	ET / hr:mn / PT
♇	D	6	**2:29 pm** 11:29 am
⚷	R	8	**9:31 pm** 6:31 pm
♄	D	10	**10:17 pm** 7:17 pm
♃	D	17	10:30 pm
♃	D	18	**1:30 am**
☿	D	18	**11:17 am** 8:17 am

1 FRIDAY
☽ ☍ ♄ **10:10 am** 7:10 am
☿ □ ♇ **10:26 am** 7:26 am
☽ ⚹ ☉ **1:34 pm** 10:34 am
☽ ⚹ ♂ **5:46 pm** 2:46 pm
☿ ⚺ ♀ **9:56 pm** 6:56 pm
☽ □ ♅ **11:32 pm** 8:32 pm

2 SATURDAY
♀ ⚹ ♇ **3:48 am** 12:48 am
☽ ⚻ ♆ **12:51 pm** 9:51 am
☽ ☍ ♃ **3:29 pm** 12:29 pm
☽ ⚹ ☿ **4:57 pm** 1:57 pm
☽ ⚻ ♇ **6:22 pm** 3:22 pm
☽ □ ♀ **7:43 pm** 4:43 pm

3 SUNDAY
☽ ⚻ ♄ **4:56 pm** 1:56 pm
☿ △ ♃ **8:05 pm** 5:05 pm
☽ ⚺ ☉ 9:23 pm
☽ ⚺ ♂ 11:47 pm

4 MONDAY
☽ ⚺ ☉ **12:23 am**
☽ ⚺ ♂ **2:47 am**
☽ △ ♅ **5:19 am** 2:19 am
☽ ☍ ♆ **5:48 pm** 2:48 pm
☽ ⚺ ☿ **6:48 pm** 3:48 pm
☽ ⚻ ♃ **8:10 pm** 5:10 pm
☽ △ ♇ **11:03 pm** 8:03 pm

5 TUESDAY
☽ ⚹ ♀ **4:46 am** 1:46 am
☿ ⚻ ♆ **9:53 am** 6:53 am
☽ △ ♄ **8:16 pm** 5:16 pm

6 WEDNESDAY
♂ ⚻ ♅ **5:27 am** 2:27 am
☽ ☌ ☉ **7:05 am** 4:05 am
☽ ⚻ ♅ **7:56 am** 4:56 am
☽ ☌ ♂ **8:04 am** 5:04 am
☽ ☌ ☿ **5:40 pm** 2:40 pm
☉ ⚻ ♅ **7:11 pm** 4:11 pm
☽ ⚻ ♆ **7:54 pm** 4:54 pm
☽ △ ♃ **10:08 pm** 7:08 pm
☽ □ ♇ 10:03 pm

7 THURSDAY
☽ □ ♇ **1:03 am**
☽ ⚺ ♀ **10:37 am** 7:37 am
☽ □ ♄ **9:37 pm** 6:37 pm
☉ ☌ ♂ 9:01 pm

8 FRIDAY
☉ ☌ ♂ **12:01 am**
☽ ☍ ♅ **9:00 am** 6:00 am
☽ ⚺ ♂ **11:32 am** 8:32 am
☽ ⚺ ☉ **11:49 am** 8:49 am
☽ ⚺ ☿ **3:10 pm** 12:10 pm
☽ △ ♆ **8:53 pm** 5:53 pm
☽ □ ♃ **11:04 pm** 8:04 pm
☽ ⚹ ♇ 11:05 pm

9 SATURDAY
☽ ⚹ ♇ **2:05 am**
☉ ☌ ☿ **12:18 pm** 9:18 am
☽ ☌ ♀ **3:37 pm** 12:37 pm
☿ ☌ ♂ **6:48 pm** 3:48 pm
☽ ⚹ ♄ **10:43 pm** 7:43 pm

10 SUNDAY
☽ ⚻ ♅ **10:08 am** 7:08 am
☽ ⚹ ☿ **12:49 pm** 9:49 am
☽ ⚹ ♂ **3:12 pm** 12:12 pm
☽ ⚹ ☉ **4:45 pm** 1:45 pm
☽ □ ♆ **10:17 pm** 7:17 pm
☽ ⚹ ♃ 9:30 pm

11 MONDAY
☽ ⚹ ♃ **12:30 am**
☽ ⚺ ♇ **3:42 am** 12:42 am
☽ ⚺ ♀ **9:43 pm** 6:43 pm
☽ ⚺ ♄ 9:54 pm
☿ ⚻ ♅ 10:29 pm

12 TUESDAY
☽ ⚺ ♄ **12:54 am**
☿ ⚻ ♅ **1:29 am**
☽ □ ☿ **11:51 am** 8:51 am
☽ △ ♅ **12:34 pm** 9:34 am
☽ □ ♂ **8:27 pm** 5:27 pm
☽ □ ☉ **11:25 pm** 8:25 pm
☽ ⚹ ♆ 10:11 pm

13 WEDNESDAY
☽ ⚹ ♆ **1:11 am**
☽ ⚺ ♃ **3:30 am** 12:30 am
☽ ☌ ♇ **6:53 am** 3:53 am
♀ ⚹ ♄ **3:26 pm** 12:26 pm
☉ ⚻ ♆ **11:32 pm** 8:32 pm

14 THURSDAY
☽ ☌ ♄ **4:54 am** 1:54 am
☽ ⚹ ♀ **6:03 am** 3:03 am
☽ △ ☿ **1:09 pm** 10:09 am
☽ □ ♅ **4:52 pm** 1:52 pm

15 FRIDAY
☽ △ ♂ **3:58 am** 12:58 am
☽ ⚺ ♆ **6:02 am** 3:02 am
☉ △ ♃ **7:46 am** 4:46 am
☽ ☌ ♃ **8:29 am** 5:29 am
☽ △ ☉ **8:33 am** 5:33 am
☽ ⚺ ♇ **12:05 pm** 9:05 am

16 SATURDAY
☽ ⚺ ♄ **10:59 am** 7:59 am
☽ □ ♀ **4:59 pm** 1:59 pm
☽ ⚻ ☿ **5:27 pm** 2:27 pm
♂ ⚻ ♆ **8:32 pm** 5:32 pm
☿ ⚹ ♀ **9:24 pm** 6:24 pm
☽ ⚹ ♅ **11:14 pm** 8:14 pm

17 SUNDAY
☉ □ ♇ **8:12 am** 5:12 am
☽ ☌ ♆ **1:00 pm** 10:00 am
☽ ⚻ ♂ **1:56 pm** 10:56 am
☽ ⚺ ♃ **3:37 pm** 12:37 pm
☽ ⚹ ♇ **7:24 pm** 4:24 pm
☽ ⚻ ☉ **8:20 pm** 5:20 pm

18 MONDAY
☽ ⚹ ♄ **7:15 pm** 4:15 pm
♂ △ ♃ **10:36 pm** 7:36 pm
☽ ☍ ☿ 10:26 pm

19 TUESDAY
☽ ☍ ☿ **1:26 am**
☽ △ ♀ **6:40 am** 3:40 am
☽ ⚺ ♅ **7:46 am** 4:46 am
♀ ⚻ ♅ **7:15 pm** 4:15 pm
☽ ⚺ ♆ **10:09 pm** 7:09 pm
☽ ⚹ ♃ 9:59 pm
☽ ☍ ♂ 11:28 pm

20 WEDNESDAY
☽ ⚹ ♃ **12:59 am**
☽ ☍ ♂ **2:28 am**
☽ □ ♇ **4:56 am** 1:56 am
☽ ☍ ☉ **10:57 am** 7:57 am

21 THURSDAY
☽ □ ♄ **5:45 am** 2:45 am
☽ ⚻ ☿ **1:44 pm** 10:44 am
☽ ☌ ♅ **6:28 pm** 3:28 pm
☽ ⚻ ♀ **11:08 pm** 8:08 pm
♂ □ ♇ 9:20 pm

22 FRIDAY
♂ □ ♇ **12:20 am**
☽ ⚹ ♆ **9:26 am** 6:26 am
☽ □ ♃ **12:32 pm** 9:32 am
☽ △ ♇ **4:35 pm** 1:35 pm
☽ ⚻ ♂ **5:33 pm** 2:33 pm

23 SATURDAY
☽ ⚻ ☉ **4:14 am** 1:14 am
☽ △ ♄ **6:12 pm** 3:12 pm

24 SUNDAY
☽ △ ☿ **6:17 am** 3:17 am
☽ ⚺ ♅ **6:54 am** 3:54 am
☿ ⚻ ♅ **1:45 pm** 10:45 am
☽ ☍ ♀ **5:42 pm** 2:42 pm
☽ □ ♆ **10:14 pm** 7:14 pm
☽ △ ♃ 10:33 pm

25 MONDAY
☽ △ ♃ **1:33 am**
☽ ⚻ ♇ **5:36 am** 2:36 am
☽ △ ♂ **10:11 am** 7:11 am
☽ △ ☉ **10:54 pm** 7:54 pm

26 TUESDAY
☽ ⚻ ♄ **7:21 am** 4:21 am
☽ ⚹ ♅ **7:37 pm** 4:37 pm
♀ □ ♆ **9:06 pm** 6:06 pm
☽ □ ☿ 10:10 pm

27 WEDNESDAY
☽ □ ☿ **1:10 am**
☽ △ ♆ **10:48 am** 7:48 am
☽ ⚻ ♀ **12:04 pm** 9:04 am
☽ ⚻ ♃ **2:16 pm** 11:16 am
☽ ☍ ♇ **6:08 pm** 3:08 pm
☽ □ ♂ 11:02 pm

28 THURSDAY
☽ □ ♂ **2:02 am**
♀ ⚹ ♃ **3:15 pm** 12:15 pm
☽ □ ☉ **4:05 pm** 1:05 pm
☽ ☍ ♄ **7:03 pm** 4:03 pm

29 FRIDAY
☽ □ ♅ **6:25 am** 3:25 am
☽ ⚹ ☿ **6:32 pm** 3:32 pm
☽ ⚻ ♆ **8:53 pm** 5:53 pm
☽ ☍ ♃ 9:24 pm

30 SATURDAY
☽ ☍ ♃ **12:24 am**
☽ △ ♀ **3:05 am** 12:05 am
☽ ⚻ ♇ **3:54 am** 12:54 am
☉ □ ♄ **5:53 am** 2:53 am
♀ ⚺ ♇ **1:54 pm** 10:54 am
☽ ⚹ ♂ **2:22 pm** 11:22 am
☿ ⚻ ♆ **3:40 pm** 12:40 pm

31 SUNDAY
☽ ⚻ ♄ **3:17 am** 12:17 am
☽ ⚹ ☉ **4:58 am** 1:58 am
☽ △ ♅ **1:33 pm** 10:33 am
☿ △ ♃ 9:18 pm

Eastern time in bold type
Pacific time in medium type

OCTOBER 2021

DATE	SID.TIME	SUN	MOON	NODE	MERCURY	VENUS	MARS	JUPITER	SATURN	URANUS	NEPTUNE	PLUTO	CERES	PALLAS	JUNO	VESTA	CHIRON
1 F	0 39 47	8≏02 06	29♍32	3Ⅱ29R	24≏37R	22♏51	10≏24	22≈49R	6≈58R	14♉06R	21♓20R	24♑19R	11Ⅱ56	13♋34R	16♈31	5♍17	10♈46R
2 Sa	0 43 44	9 01 06	12≏11	3 19	24 06	23 58	11 03	22 46	6 57	14 04	21 19	24 19	11 59	13 21	16 46	5 48	10 44
3 Su	0 47 40	10 00 09	25 13	3 12	23 27	25 04	11 42	22 43	6 56	14 03	21 17	24 19	12 01	13 08	17 01	6 20	10 41
4 M	0 51 37	10 59 14	8♏44	3 04	22 40	26 11	12 22	22 40	6 55	14 01	21 15	24 19	12 03	12 55	17 17	6 51	10 38
5 T	0 55 33	11 58 22	22 32	2 55	21 47	27 17	13 01	22 37	6 55	13 59	21 14	24 19	12 05	12 43	17 32	7 22	10 36
6 W	0 59 30	12 57 31	6♐45	2 47	20 47	28 23	13 40	22 35	6 54	13 57	21 12	24 19D	12 06	12 31	17 48	7 53	10 33
7 Th	1 3 26	13 56 42	21 14	2 40	19 43	29 29	14 20	22 32	6 54	13 56	21 11	24 19	12 07	12 19	18 04	8 25	10 30
8 F	1 7 23	14 55 56	5♑54	2 35	18 34	0♐35	14 59	22 30	6 53	13 54	21 09	24 19	12 08	12 07	18 20	8 56	10 27
9 Sa	1 11 19	15 55 11	20 36	2 33D	17 24	1 40	15 39	22 28	6 53	13 53	21 08	24 19	12 08R	11 56	18 36	9 27	10 25
10 Su	1 15 16	16 54 28	5♒14	2 32	16 13	2 46	16 18	22 27	6 53	13 48	21 07	24 19	12 08	11 45	18 52	9 59	10 22
11 M	1 19 13	17 53 48	19 43	2 33	15 04	3 51	16 58	22 25	6 53D	13 46	21 05	24 19	12 08	11 34	19 08	10 30	10 19
12 T	1 23 9	18 53 08	4♓00	2 34	13 58	4 56	17 37	22 23	6 53	13 44	21 04	24 19	12 07	11 24	19 25	11 02	10 17
13 W	1 27 6	19 52 31	18 02	2 35R	12 58	6 01	18 17	22 23	6 53	13 42	21 02	24 19	12 05	11 14	19 42	11 33	10 14
14 Th	1 31 2	20 51 56	1♈50	2 35	12 05	7 05	18 57	22 22	6 53	13 40	21 01	24 20	12 04	11 04	19 59	12 05	10 11
15 F	1 34 59	21 51 22	15 23	2 32	11 21	8 10	19 36	22 21	6 53	13 37	20 59	24 20	12 01	10 55	20 16	12 36	10 09
16 Sa	1 38 55	22 50 49	28 42	2 28	10 46	9 14	20 16	22 20	6 54	13 35	20 58	24 20	11 59	10 46	20 33	13 08	10 06
17 Su	1 42 52	23 50 19	11♉48	2 22	10 23	10 18	20 56	22 20	6 54	13 33	20 57	24 20	11 56	10 38	20 50	13 40	10 03
18 M	1 46 48	24 49 50	24 40	2 16	10 10D	11 21	21 36	22 20D	6 55	13 31	20 55	24 21	11 53	10 29	21 08	14 11	10 01
19 T	1 50 45	25 49 23	7Ⅱ19	2 09	10 08	12 25	22 16	22 20	6 56	13 28	20 54	24 21	11 49	10 22	21 25	14 43	9 58
20 W	1 54 42	26 48 58	19 47	2 03	10 08	13 28	22 55	22 20	6 57	13 26	20 53	24 22	11 46	10 14	21 43	15 15	9 56
21 Th	1 58 38	27 48 35	2♋02	1 58	10 18	14 31	23 35	22 21	6 58	13 24	20 52	24 22	11 45	10 07	22 01	15 46	9 53
22 F	2 2 35	28 48 14	14 08	1 55	10 38	15 33	24 15	22 21	6 59	13 21	20 50	24 22	11 40	10 00	22 19	16 18	9 51
23 Sa	2 6 31	29 47 56	26 04	1 54D	11 08	16 36	24 55	22 22	7 00	13 19	20 49	24 23	11 36	9 54	22 37	16 50	9 48
24 Su	2 10 28	0♏47 39	7♌54	1 54	11 47	17 38	25 35	22 23	7 01	13 16	20 48	24 23	11 25	9 48	22 55	17 22	9 46
25 M	2 14 24	1 47 25	19 41	1 55	13 30	18 39	26 15	22 24	7 02	13 14	20 47	24 24	11 19	9 42	23 13	17 54	9 43
26 T	2 18 21	2 47 12	1♍29	1 57	14 32	19 41	26 55	22 26	7 04	13 11	20 46	24 24	11 12	9 37	23 32	18 26	9 41
27 W	2 22 17	3 47 02	13 21	1 58	15 40	20 42	27 35	22 27	7 05	13 09	20 45	24 25	11 05	9 32	23 50	18 58	9 38
28 Th	2 26 14	4 46 54	25 22	2 00R	16 53	21 43	28 16	22 29	7 07	13 07	20 44	24 26	10 58	9 28	24 09	19 30	9 36
29 F	2 30 11	5 46 48	7♎38	2 00	18 10	22 43	28 56	22 31	7 09	13 04	20 43	24 26	10 51	9 24	24 28	20 02	9 33
30 Sa	2 34 7	6 46 45	20 13	1 59	19 32	23 43	29 36	22 34	7 11	13 02	20 41	24 27	10 43	9 20	24 47	20 34	9 31
31 Su	2 38 4	7 46 43	3♏12	1 57	20 56	24 42	0♏16	22 36	7 13	12 59	20 40	24 28	10 35	9 17	25 06	21 06	9 29

EPHEMERIS CALCULATED FOR 12 MIDNIGHT GREENWICH MEAN TIME. ALL OTHER DATA AND FACING ASPECTARIAN PAGE IN **EASTERN TIME (BOLD)** AND PACIFIC TIME (REGULAR).

NOVEMBER 2021

☽ Last Aspect day	ET	PT	asp	☽ Ingress sign day	ET	PT
1	**1:00 pm**	10:00 am	□ ♀	♎ 1	**7:11 pm**	4:11 pm
3	**6:32 pm**	3:32 pm	⚹ ♀	♏ 3	**8:52 pm**	5:52 pm
5	**12:10 pm**	9:10 am	⚹ ♇	♐ 5	**8:52 pm**	5:52 pm
7	**8:44 am**	5:44 am	⚹ ♃	♑ 7	**8:03 pm**	5:03 pm
9	**12:51 pm**	9:51 am	☌ ♇	♒ 9	**10:03 pm**	7:03 pm
11	**2:52 pm**	11:52 am	☌ ♃	♓ 11		11:54 pm
11	**2:52 pm**	11:52 am	☌ ♃	♓ 12	**2:54 am**	
13		9:40 pm	⚹ ♇	♈ 14	**10:48 am**	7:48 am
14	**12:40 am**		⚹ ♇	♈ 14	**10:48 am**	7:48 am
16	**10:51 am**	7:51 am	□ ♇	♉ 16	**9:18 pm**	6:18 pm
19	**3:57 am**	12:57 am	☍ ☉	♊ 19	**9:33 am**	6:33 am
21	**10:52 am**	7:52 am	△ ♃	♋ 21	**10:33 pm**	7:33 pm
23		9:46 pm	☍ ♇	♌ 24	**10:59 am**	7:59 am
24	**12:46 am**		☍ ♇	♌ 24	**10:59 am**	7:59 am
26	**11:24 am**	8:24 am	☍ ♃	♍ 26	**9:12 pm**	6:12 pm
28	**7:02 pm**	4:02 pm	△ ♇	♎ 29	**3:55 am**	12:55 am
30	**11:20 pm**	8:20 pm	△ ♃	♏ 12/1	**6:55 am**	3:55 am

☽ Phases & Eclipses phase	day	ET	PT
New Moon	4	**5:15 pm**	2:15 pm
2nd Quarter	11	**7:46 am**	4:46 am
Full Moon	19	**3:57 am**	12:57 am
●	19	27° ♉ 14'	
4th Quarter	27	**7:28 am**	4:28 am

Planet Ingress	day	ET	PT
♀ ♑	5	**6:44 am**	3:44 am
⚵ ♑	14	**3:23 pm**	12:23 pm
⚶ ♐	16	**9:07 am**	6:07 am
☉ ♐	21	**9:34 pm**	6:34 pm
☿ ♐	24	**10:36 am**	7:36 am

Planetary Motion		day	ET	PT
⚴	D	8	**4:23 am**	1:23 am

1 MONDAY
☿ △ ♃ **12:18 am**
☽ ☍ ♆ **3:05 am** 12:05 am
☽ ⚻ ♃ **6:35 am** 3:35 am
☽ ⚺ ☿ **7:18 am** 4:18 am
☽ △ ♇ **9:43 am** 6:43 am
☽ □ ♀ **1:00 pm** 10:00 am
☽ ⚺ ♂ **10:01 pm** 7:01 pm

2 TUESDAY
☿ □ ♇ **5:39 am** 2:39 am
☽ △ ♄ **7:31 am** 4:31 am
☽ ⚺ ☉ **12:51 pm** 9:51 am
☽ ⚻ ♅ **4:50 pm** 1:50 pm

3 WEDNESDAY
☽ ⚻ ♆ **5:36 am** 2:36 am
☽ △ ♃ **9:08 am** 6:08 am
☽ □ ♇ **11:57 am** 8:57 am
☽ ☌ ☿ **3:27 pm** 12:27 pm
☽ ⚹ ♀ **6:32 pm** 3:32 pm
☽ ☌ ♂ 10:55 pm

4 THURSDAY
☽ ☌ ♂ **1:55 am**
☽ □ ♄ **8:46 am** 5:46 am
☽ ☌ ☉ **5:15 pm** 2:15 pm
☽ ☍ ♅ **5:26 pm** 2:26 pm
☉ ☍ ♅ **7:58 pm** 4:58 pm

5 FRIDAY
☽ △ ♆ **5:53 am** 2:53 am
☽ □ ♃ **9:33 am** 6:33 am
☽ ⚹ ♇ **12:10 pm** 9:10 am
☽ ⚺ ☿ **9:09 pm** 6:09 pm
☽ ⚺ ♀ **9:49 pm** 6:49 pm

6 SATURDAY
☽ ⚺ ♂ **4:06 am** 1:06 am
☽ ⚹ ♄ **8:46 am** 5:46 am
☿ ⚹ ♀ **11:59 am** 8:59 am
☽ ⚻ ♅ **5:09 pm** 2:09 pm
☽ ⚺ ☉ **8:32 pm** 5:32 pm

7 SUNDAY
☽ □ ♆ **4:47 am** 1:47 am
☽ ⚹ ♃ **8:44 am** 5:44 am
☽ ⚺ ♇ **11:14 am** 8:14 am
☽ ☌ ♀ 9:19 pm
☽ ⚹ ☿ 11:13 pm

8 MONDAY
☽ ☌ ♀ **12:19 am**
☽ ⚹ ☿ **2:13 am**
☽ ⚹ ♂ **5:49 am** 2:49 am
☽ ⚺ ♄ **8:25 am** 5:25 am
☽ △ ♅ **4:48 pm** 1:48 pm
☽ ⚹ ☉ 9:06 pm

9 TUESDAY
☽ ⚹ ☉ **12:06 am**
☽ ⚹ ♆ **6:01 am** 3:01 am
☽ ⚺ ♃ **10:26 am** 7:26 am
☽ ☌ ♇ **12:51 pm** 9:51 am

10 WEDNESDAY
☽ ⚺ ♀ **6:04 am** 3:04 am
☿ ☌ ♂ **7:57 am** 4:57 am
☽ □ ♂ **10:55 am** 7:55 am
☽ □ ☿ **11:08 am** 8:08 am
☽ ☌ ♄ **11:15 am** 8:15 am
☿ □ ♄ **12:04 pm** 9:04 am
♂ □ ♄ **6:14 pm** 3:14 pm
☽ □ ♅ **7:45 pm** 4:45 pm

11 THURSDAY
☽ □ ☉ **7:46 am** 4:46 am
☽ ⚺ ♆ **9:51 am** 6:51 am
☽ ☌ ♃ **2:52 pm** 11:52 am
☽ ⚺ ♇ **5:13 pm** 2:13 pm

12 FRIDAY
☉ △ ♆ **11:24 am** 8:24 am
☽ ⚹ ♀ **3:18 pm** 12:18 pm
☽ ⚺ ♄ **5:05 pm** 2:05 pm
☽ △ ♂ **7:28 pm** 4:28 pm
☽ △ ☿ 9:23 pm
☽ ⚹ ♅ 10:44 pm

13 SATURDAY
☽ △ ☿ **12:23 am**
☽ ⚹ ♅ **1:44 am**
☿ ☍ ♅ **10:57 am** 7:57 am
☽ ☌ ♆ **4:46 pm** 1:46 pm
☽ △ ☉ **7:19 pm** 4:19 pm
♀ ⚺ ♄ **7:43 pm** 4:43 pm
☽ ⚺ ♃ **10:29 pm** 7:29 pm
☽ ⚹ ♇ 9:40 pm

14 SUNDAY
☽ ⚹ ♇ **12:40 am**
☽ ⚹ ♄ 10:59 pm

15 MONDAY
☽ ⚹ ♄ **1:59 am**
☽ □ ♀ **4:06 am** 1:06 am
☽ ⚻ ♂ **7:32 am** 4:32 am
☽ ⚺ ♅ **10:36 am** 7:36 am
☉ □ ♃ **2:58 pm** 11:58 am
☽ ⚻ ☿ **5:58 pm** 2:58 pm
☽ ⚺ ♆ 11:29 pm

16 TUESDAY
☽ ⚺ ♆ **2:29 am**
☽ ⚹ ♃ **8:55 am** 5:55 am
☽ ⚻ ☉ **10:23 am** 7:23 am
☽ □ ♇ **10:51 am** 7:51 am
☉ ⚹ ♇ **4:01 pm** 1:01 pm

17 WEDNESDAY
♂ ☍ ♅ **12:23 pm** 9:23 am
☽ □ ♄ **1:19 pm** 10:19 am
☽ △ ♀ **7:39 pm** 4:39 pm
☽ ☌ ♅ **9:44 pm** 6:44 pm
☽ ☍ ♂ **10:20 pm** 7:20 pm

18 THURSDAY
☿ △ ♆ **10:38 am** 7:38 am
☽ ⚹ ♆ **2:14 pm** 11:14 am
☽ ☍ ☿ **2:48 pm** 11:48 am
☽ □ ♃ **9:23 pm** 6:23 pm
☽ △ ♇ **10:57 pm** 7:57 pm
♀ △ ♅ 10:08 pm

19 FRIDAY
♀ △ ♅ **1:08 am**
☽ ☍ ☉ **3:57 am** 12:57 am
☽ △ ♄ 11:12 pm

20 SATURDAY
☽ △ ♄ **2:12 am**
☽ ⚺ ♅ **10:14 am** 7:14 am
☽ ⚻ ♀ **12:43 pm** 9:43 am
☽ ⚻ ♂ **2:46 pm** 11:46 am
☿ □ ♃ **6:43 pm** 3:43 pm

21 SUNDAY
☽ □ ♆ **3:05 am** 12:05 am
☿ ⚹ ♇ **4:14 am** 1:14 am
☽ △ ♃ **10:52 am** 7:52 am
☽ ⚻ ♇ **12:01 pm** 9:01 am
☽ ⚻ ☿ **1:13 pm** 10:13 am
☽ ⚻ ☉ **10:38 pm** 7:38 pm

22 MONDAY
☽ ⚻ ♄ **3:32 pm** 12:32 pm
☽ ⚹ ♅ **10:59 pm** 7:59 pm

23 TUESDAY
☽ ☍ ♀ **5:49 am** 2:49 am
☽ △ ♂ **7:24 am** 4:24 am
☽ △ ♆ **3:50 pm** 12:50 pm
☽ ⚻ ♃ 9:06 pm
☽ ☍ ♇ 9:46 pm

24 WEDNESDAY
☽ ⚻ ♃ **12:06 am**
☽ ☍ ♇ **12:46 am**
☽ △ ☿ **11:02 am** 8:02 am
☽ △ ☉ **4:34 pm** 1:34 pm

25 THURSDAY
☽ ☍ ♄ **3:52 am** 12:52 am
☽ □ ♅ **10:32 am** 7:32 am
☽ ⚻ ♀ **8:57 pm** 5:57 pm
☽ □ ♂ **10:19 pm** 7:19 pm
☽ ⚻ ♆ 11:55 pm

26 FRIDAY
☽ ⚻ ♆ **2:55 am**
☽ ☍ ♃ **11:24 am** 8:24 am
☽ ⚻ ♇ **11:35 am** 8:35 am

27 SATURDAY
☽ □ ☿ **5:27 am** 2:27 am
☽ □ ☉ **7:28 am** 4:28 am
♃ ⚺ ♇ **11:16 am** 8:16 am
☽ ⚻ ♄ **1:30 pm** 10:30 am
☽ △ ♅ **7:18 pm** 4:18 pm

28 SUNDAY
☽ △ ♀ **8:15 am** 5:15 am
☽ ⚹ ♂ **9:37 am** 6:37 am
☽ ☍ ♆ **10:50 am** 7:50 am
☽ △ ♇ **7:02 pm** 4:02 pm
☽ ⚻ ♃ **7:17 pm** 4:17 pm
☉ ☌ ☿ **11:39 pm** 8:39 pm

29 MONDAY
♂ △ ♆ **9:10 am** 6:10 am
☽ ⚹ ☉ **5:44 pm** 2:44 pm
☽ ⚹ ☿ **6:33 pm** 3:33 pm
☽ △ ♄ **7:24 pm** 4:24 pm
☽ ⚻ ♅ 9:22 pm
☿ ⚹ ♄ 11:19 pm

30 TUESDAY
☽ ⚻ ♅ **12:22 am**
☿ ⚹ ♄ **2:19 am**
☽ □ ♀ **2:56 pm** 11:56 am
☽ ⚻ ♆ **2:58 pm** 11:58 am
♀ ⚹ ♆ **3:46 pm** 12:46 pm
☽ ⚺ ♂ **4:29 pm** 1:29 pm
☉ ⚹ ♄ **6:14 pm** 3:14 pm
☽ □ ♇ **10:43 pm** 7:43 pm
☽ △ ♃ **11:20 pm** 8:20 pm

Eastern time in bold type
Pacific time in medium type

NOVEMBER 2021

DATE	SID.TIME	SUN	MOON	NODE	MERCURY	VENUS	MARS	JUPITER	SATURN	URANUS	NEPTUNE	PLUTO	CERES	PALLAS	JUNO	VESTA	CHIRON
1 M	2 42 0	8♏46 44	16♍37	1♊56℞	22♎23	25♐42	0♏56	22♒39	7♒15	12♉57℞	20♓39℞	24♑28	10♏26℞	9♓11℞	25♐25	21♏38	9♈27℞
2 T	2 45 57	9 46 47	0♎29	1 51	23 53	26 41	1 37	22 42	7 17	12 54	20 39	24 29	10 17	9 11	25 44	22 10	9 24
3 W	2 49 53	10 46 52	14 47	1 48	25 24	27 39	2 17	22 45	7 19	12 52	20 38	24 30	10 08	9 09	26 03	22 42	9 22
4 Th	2 53 50	11 46 58	29 28	1 46	26 57	28 37	2 58	22 48	7 21	12 50	20 37	24 31	9 58	9 07	26 23	23 14	9 20
5 F	2 57 46	12 47 07	14♏24	1 44	28 31	29 34	3 38	22 51	7 24	12 47	20 36	24 31	9 48	9 06	26 42	23 46	9 18
6 Sa	3 1 43	13 47 18	29 27	1 43D	0♏06	0♑31	4 19	22 55	7 26	12 45	20 35	24 32	9 38	9 04	27 02	24 18	9 16
7 Su	3 5 40	14 47 30	14♐29	1 44	1 41	1 28	4 59	22 59	7 29	12 42	20 34	24 33	9 27	9 04	27 22	24 51	9 13
8 M	3 9 36	15 47 45	29 21	1 45	3 17	2 24	5 40	23 03	7 32	12 40	20 33	24 34	9 16	9 03D	27 41	25 23	9 11
9 T	3 13 33	16 48 00	13♑57	1 46	4 54	3 20	6 20	23 07	7 34	12 37	20 33	24 35	9 05	9 03	28 01	25 55	9 09
10 W	3 17 29	17 48 17	28 13	1 47	6 31	4 15	7 01	23 11	7 37	12 35	20 32	24 36	8 53	9 04	28 21	26 27	9 07
11 Th	3 21 26	18 48 36	12♒06	1 48℞	8 07	5 09	7 42	23 16	7 40	12 32	20 31	24 37	8 42	9 05	28 42	26 59	9 05
12 F	3 25 22	19 48 56	25 38	1 47	9 44	6 03	8 22	23 20	7 43	12 30	20 31	24 38	8 30	9 06	29 02	27 32	9 04
13 Sa	3 29 19	20 49 17	8♓48	1 46	11 21	6 56	9 03	23 25	7 47	12 27	20 30	24 39	8 17	9 07	29 22	28 04	9 02
14 Su	3 33 15	21 49 39	21 41	1 46	12 58	7 48	9 44	23 31	7 50	12 25	20 29	24 40	8 05	9 09	29 43	28 36	9 00
15 M	3 37 12	22 50 03	4♈17	1 45	14 35	8 40	10 25	23 36	7 53	12 22	20 29	24 41	7 52	9 11	0♑03	29 09	8 58
16 T	3 41 8	23 50 28	16 39	1 44	16 12	9 31	11 05	23 41	7 57	12 20	20 28	24 42	7 39	9 14	0 24	29 41	8 56
17 W	3 45 5	24 50 55	28 51	1 43	17 48	10 22	11 46	23 47	8 00	12 18	20 28	24 44	7 26	9 17	0 44	0♐13	8 55
18 Th	3 49 2	25 51 23	10♉53	1 42	19 24	11 11	12 27	23 53	8 04	12 15	20 27	24 45	7 13	9 20	1 05	0 46	8 53
19 F	3 52 58	26 51 53	22 49	1 42D	21 00	12 00	13 08	23 59	8 07	12 13	20 27	24 46	7 00	9 24	1 26	1 18	8 51
20 Sa	3 56 55	27 52 25	4♊40	1 41	22 36	12 48	13 49	24 05	8 11	12 10	20 26	24 47	6 46	9 27	1 47	1 50	8 50
21 Su	4 0 51	28 52 57	16 28	1 42	24 12	13 35	14 30	24 11	8 15	12 08	20 26	24 48	6 32	9 32	2 08	2 23	8 48
22 M	4 4 48	29 53 32	28 15	1 42	25 48	14 22	15 11	24 18	8 19	12 06	20 26	24 50	6 19	9 36	2 29	2 55	8 47
23 T	4 8 44	0♐54 08	10♋05	1 42℞	27 23	15 06	15 52	24 24	8 23	12 03	20 25	24 51	6 05	9 41	2 50	3 28	8 45
24 W	4 12 41	1 54 46	22 00	1 42	28 58	15 50	16 33	24 31	8 27	12 01	20 25	24 52	5 51	9 46	3 11	4 00	8 44
25 Th	4 16 38	2 55 25	4♌03	1 42	0♐33	16 34	17 15	24 38	8 31	11 59	20 25	24 54	5 37	9 52	3 33	4 32	8 43
26 F	4 20 34	3 56 06	16 19	1 42D	2 08	17 16	17 56	24 45	8 36	11 57	20 25	24 55	5 23	9 58	3 54	5 05	8 41
27 Sa	4 24 31	4 56 48	28 50	1 42	3 43	17 57	18 37	24 52	8 40	11 54	20 24	24 56	5 09	10 04	4 15	5 37	8 40
28 Su	4 28 27	5 57 32	11♍42	1 42	5 17	18 37	19 18	25 00	8 44	11 52	20 24	24 58	4 55	10 10	4 37	6 10	8 39
29 M	4 32 24	6 58 18	24 58	1 42	6 52	19 15	20 00	25 07	8 49	11 50	20 24	24 59	4 40	10 17	4 58	6 42	8 38
30 T	4 36 20	7 59 05	8♎40	1 42	8 26	19 53	20 41	25 15	8 53	11 48	20 24	25 01	4 26	10 24	5 20	7 15	8 37

EPHEMERIS CALCULATED FOR 12 MIDNIGHT GREENWICH MEAN TIME. ALL OTHER DATA AND FACING ASPECTARIAN PAGE IN EASTERN TIME (**BOLD**) AND PACIFIC TIME (REGULAR).

DECEMBER 2021

☽ Last Aspect day	ET / hr:mn / PT	asp	☽ Ingress sign	day	ET / hr:mn / PT
11/30	**11:20 pm** 8:20 pm	△♃	♏	1	**6:55 am** 3:55 am
2	9:22 pm	□♃	♐	3	**7:13 am** 4:13 am
3	**12:22 am**	□♃	♐	3	**7:13 am** 4:13 am
4	9:08 pm	⚹♃	♑	5	**6:31 am** 3:31 am
5	**12:08 am**	⚹♃	♑	5	**6:31 am** 3:31 am
6	**11:42 pm** 8:42 pm	⚹♂	♒	7	**6:49 am** 3:49 am
9	**5:00 am** 2:00 am	□♂	♓	9	**9:53 am** 6:53 am
11	**2:40 pm** 11:40 am	△♂	♈	11	**4:46 pm** 1:46 pm
13	**9:52 pm** 6:52 pm	⚹♃	♉	14	**3:11 am** 12:11 am
16	**11:08 am** 8:08 am	□♃	♊	16	**3:43 pm** 12:43 pm
18	10:02 pm	△♃	♋	19	**4:42 am** 1:42 am
19	**1:02 am**	△♃	♋	19	**4:42 am** 1:42 am
21	**9:44 am** 6:44 am	☍♀	♌	21	**4:54 pm** 1:54 pm
23	10:39 pm	☍♃	♍	24	**3:24 am** 12:24 am
24	**1:39 am**	☍♃	♍	24	**3:24 am** 12:24 am
26	**3:39 am** 12:39 am	△♇	♎	26	**11:24 am** 8:24 am
28	**4:11 pm** 1:11 pm	△♃	♏	28	**4:16 pm** 1:16 pm
30	**12:10 pm** 9:10 am	⚹☿	♐	30	**6:08 pm** 3:08 pm

☽ Phases & Eclipses phase	day	ET / hr:mn / PT
New Moon	3	11:43 pm
New Moon	4	**2:43 am**
●	3/4	12° ♐ 22'
2nd Quarter	10	**8:36 pm** 5:36 pm
Full Moon	18	**11:36 pm** 8:36 pm
4th Quarter	26	**9:24 pm** 6:24 pm

Planet Ingress		day	ET / hr:mn / PT
♂	♐	13	**4:53 am** 1:53 am
☿	♑	13	**12:52 pm** 9:52 am
⚳	♉	21	**5:38 am** 2:38 am
☉	♑	21	**10:59 am** 7:59 am
♃	♓	28	**11:09 pm** 8:09 pm

Planetary Motion		day	ET / hr:mn / PT
♆	D	1	**8:22 am** 5:22 am
♀	℞	19	**5:36 am** 2:36 am
⚷	D	19	**11:33 am** 8:33 am

1 WEDNESDAY

☿⚻♅	**9:15 pm**	6:15 pm
☽□♄	**9:43 pm**	6:43 pm
☽⚺☉	**11:35 pm**	8:35 pm
☽☍♅		11:01 pm
☽⚺☿		11:36 pm

2 THURSDAY

☽☍♅	**2:01 am**	
☽⚺☿	**2:36 am**	
☽△♆	**3:58 pm**	12:58 pm
☽⚹♀	**5:52 pm**	2:52 pm
☽☌♂	**7:45 pm**	4:45 pm
☽⚹♇	**11:26 pm**	8:26 pm
☽□♃		9:22 pm

3 FRIDAY

☽□♃	**12:22 am**	
☉⚻♅	**10:14 am**	7:14 am
☽⚹♄	**9:46 pm**	6:46 pm
☽⚻♅		10:35 pm
☽☌☉		11:43 pm

4 SATURDAY

☽⚻♅	**1:35 am**	
☽☌☉	**2:43 am**	
☽☌☿	**7:43 am**	4:43 am
☽□♆	**3:22 pm**	12:22 pm
☽⚺♀	**6:55 pm**	3:55 pm
☽⚺♂	**9:22 pm**	6:22 pm
☽⚺♇	**10:50 pm**	7:50 pm
☽⚹♃		9:08 pm

Eastern time in bold type
Pacific time in medium type

5 SUNDAY

☽⚹♃	**12:08 am**	
☽⚺♄	**9:25 pm**	6:25 pm
☽△♅		9:56 pm

6 MONDAY

☽△♅	**12:56 am**	
☽⚺☉	**5:39 am**	2:39 am
♂⚹♇	**6:41 am**	3:41 am
☽⚺☿	**12:53 pm**	9:53 am
☽⚹♆	**3:09 pm**	12:09 pm
☽☌♀	**8:21 pm**	5:21 pm
☽☌♇	**10:56 pm**	7:56 pm
☽⚹♂	**11:42 pm**	8:42 pm
☽⚺♃		9:40 pm

7 TUESDAY

☽⚺♃	**12:40 am**	
☿□♆	**10:16 am**	7:16 am
☽☌♄	**10:43 pm**	7:43 pm
♂□♃		10:21 pm
☽□♅		11:01 pm

8 WEDNESDAY

♂□♃	**1:21 am**	
☽□♅	**2:01 am**	
☽⚹☉	**10:57 am**	7:57 am
☽⚺♆	**5:11 pm**	2:11 pm
☽⚹☿	**9:07 pm**	6:07 pm
☽⚺♀		9:15 pm
☽⚺♇		10:34 pm

9 THURSDAY

☽⚺♀	**12:15 am**	
☽⚺♇	**1:34 am**	
☽☌♃	**3:53 am**	12:53 am
☽□♂	**5:00 am**	2:00 am

10 FRIDAY

☽⚺♄	**3:18 am**	12:18 am
☽⚹♅	**6:22 am**	3:22 am
☿⚺♀	**7:50 am**	4:50 am
☿⚺♇	**12:56 pm**	9:56 am
☽□☉	**8:36 pm**	5:36 pm
☽☌♆	**10:50 pm**	7:50 pm

11 SATURDAY

☽⚹♀	**7:52 am**	4:52 am
☽⚹♇	**7:56 am**	4:56 am
☽□☿	**10:33 am**	7:33 am
☽⚺♃	**10:59 am**	7:59 am
♀☌♇	**11:29 am**	8:29 am
☿⚹♃	**2:24 pm**	11:24 am
☽△♂	**2:40 pm**	11:40 am
☉□♆		10:21 pm

12 SUNDAY

☉□♆	**1:21 am**	
☽⚹♄	**11:50 am**	8:50 am
☽⚺♅	**2:34 pm**	11:34 am

13 MONDAY

☽⚺♆	**8:16 am**	5:16 am
☽△☉	**11:03 am**	8:03 am
☽□♇	**6:01 pm**	3:01 pm
☽□♀	**7:02 pm**	4:02 pm
☿⚺♂	**7:16 pm**	4:16 pm
☽⚹♃	**9:52 pm**	6:52 pm

14 TUESDAY

☽⚻♂	**4:33 am**	1:33 am
☽△☿	**5:20 am**	2:20 am
☽□♄	**11:36 pm**	8:36 pm
☽☌♅		10:51 pm

15 WEDNESDAY

☽☌♅	**1:51 am**	
☽⚹♆	**8:21 pm**	5:21 pm

16 THURSDAY

☽⚻☉	**4:50 am**	1:50 am
☽△♇	**6:29 am**	3:29 am
☽△♀	**8:14 am**	5:14 am
☽□♃	**11:08 am**	8:08 am
☽☍♂	**8:56 pm**	5:56 pm
☉⚺♇		9:21 pm

17 FRIDAY

☉⚺♇	**12:21 am**	
☽⚻☿	**3:14 am**	12:14 am
☽△♄	**12:57 pm**	9:57 am
☽⚺♅	**2:36 pm**	11:36 am
☉⚺♀	**11:28 pm**	8:28 pm

18 SATURDAY

☽□♆	**9:24 am**	6:24 am
☽⚻♇	**7:38 pm**	4:38 pm
☽⚻♀	**9:35 pm**	6:35 pm
☽☍☉	**11:36 pm**	8:36 pm
☽△♃		10:02 pm

19 SUNDAY

☽△♃	**1:02 am**	
☽⚻♂	**1:43 pm**	10:43 am
☉⚹♃	**7:32 pm**	4:32 pm
☽☍☿		10:25 pm
☽⚻♄		11:17 pm

20 MONDAY

☽☍☿	**1:25 am**	
☽⚻♄	**2:17 am**	
☽⚹♅	**3:17 am**	12:17 am
☿⚺♄	**8:22 am**	5:22 am
☿△♅	**3:18 pm**	12:18 pm
☽△♆	**10:00 pm**	7:00 pm

21 TUESDAY

☽☍♇	**8:10 am**	5:10 am
☽☍♀	**9:44 am**	6:44 am
☽⚻♃	**2:12 pm**	11:12 am
☽⚻☉	**5:26 pm**	2:26 pm

22 WEDNESDAY

☽△♂	**5:24 am**	2:24 am
☽☍♄	**2:28 pm**	11:28 am
☽□♅	**2:50 pm**	11:50 am
☽⚻☿	**9:54 pm**	6:54 pm

23 THURSDAY

☽⚻♆	**9:12 am**	6:12 am
☽⚻♇	**7:07 pm**	4:07 pm
☽⚻♀	**7:50 pm**	4:50 pm
☽☍♃		10:39 pm
♄□♅		11:17 pm

24 FRIDAY

☽☍♃	**1:39 am**	
♄□♅	**2:17 am**	
☽△☉	**9:05 am**	6:05 am
☽□♂	**6:52 pm**	3:52 pm
☽△♅		9:24 pm
☽⚻♄		9:37 pm

25 SATURDAY

☽△♅	**12:24 am**	
☽⚻♄	**12:37 am**	
♀☌♇	**7:02 am**	4:02 am
☽△☿	**3:08 pm**	12:08 pm
☽☍♆	**6:07 pm**	3:07 pm

26 SUNDAY

☽△♀	**3:12 am**	12:12 am
☽△♇	**3:39 am**	12:39 am
☽⚻♃	**10:32 am**	7:32 am
☿⚹♆	**4:29 pm**	1:29 pm
☽□☉	**9:24 pm**	6:24 pm

27 MONDAY

☽⚹♂	**5:07 am**	2:07 am
☽⚻♅	**7:13 am**	4:13 am
☽△♄	**7:55 am**	4:55 am
☽⚻♆		9:04 pm

28 TUESDAY

☽⚻♆	**12:04 am**	
☽□☿	**3:57 am**	12:57 am
☽□♀	**7:19 am**	4:19 am
☽□♇	**9:06 am**	6:06 am
☽△♃	**4:11 pm**	1:11 pm
♂⚻♅	**8:04 pm**	5:04 pm

29 WEDNESDAY

☿☌♀	**5:27 am**	2:27 am
☽⚹☉	**5:43 am**	2:43 am
☽☍♅	**10:51 am**	7:51 am
☽⚺♂	**11:38 am**	8:38 am
☽□♄	**11:58 am**	8:58 am
♂⚹♄	**7:22 pm**	4:22 pm
☽△♆		11:51 pm

30 THURSDAY

☽△♆	**2:51 am**	
☿☌♇	**4:54 am**	1:54 am
☽⚹♀	**8:19 am**	5:19 am
☽⚹♇	**11:27 am**	8:27 am
☽⚹☿	**12:10 pm**	9:10 am
☽□♃	**6:42 pm**	3:42 pm

31 FRIDAY

☽⚺☉	**10:31 am**	7:31 am
☽⚻♅	**11:47 am**	8:47 am
☽⚹♄	**1:15 pm**	10:15 am
☽☌♂	**3:01 pm**	12:01 pm

DECEMBER 2021

DATE	SID. TIME	SUN	MOON	NODE	MERCURY	VENUS	MARS	JUPITER	SATURN	URANUS	NEPTUNE	PLUTO	CERES	PALLAS	JUNO	VESTA	CHIRON
1 W	4 40 17	8♐59 53	22♎49	1♊43	10♐00	20♑29	21♏23	25♒23	8♒58	11♉46R	20♓24D	25♑02	4♑12R	10♓31	5♐42	7♐47	8♈36R
2 Th	4 44 13	10 00 43	7♏23	1 44	11 35	21 04	22 04	25 31	9 03	11 44	20 24	25 04	3 58	10 39	6 04	8 20	8 35
3 F	4 48 10	11 01 35	22 18	1 44R	13 09	21 37	22 46	25 39	9 08	11 42	20 24	25 05	3 44	10 47	6 26	8 52	8 34
4 Sa	4 52 7	12 02 27	7♐28	1 44	14 43	22 09	23 27	25 48	9 13	11 39	20 24	25 07	3 31	10 55	6 47	9 25	8 33
5 Su	4 56 3	13 03 21	22 43	1 44	16 17	22 40	24 09	25 56	9 17	11 37	20 24	25 08	3 17	11 04	7 09	9 57	8 32
6 M	5 0 0	14 04 16	7♑52	1 43	17 51	23 08	24 50	26 05	9 23	11 35	20 25	25 10	3 03	11 13	7 32	10 29	8 31
7 T	5 3 56	15 05 12	22 24	1 41	19 25	23 36	25 32	26 13	9 28	11 34	20 25	25 11	2 50	11 22	7 54	11 02	8 31
8 W	5 7 53	16 06 09	7♒21	1 39	20 59	24 01	26 14	26 22	9 33	11 32	20 25	25 13	2 36	11 31	8 16	11 34	8 30
9 Th	5 11 49	17 07 06	21 48	1 37	22 33	24 25	26 55	26 32	9 38	11 30	20 25	25 15	2 23	11 41	8 38	12 07	8 30
10 F	5 15 46	18 08 04	5♓08	1 36	24 07	24 47	27 37	26 41	9 43	11 30	20 25	25 16	2 10	11 50	9 00	12 39	8 29
11 Sa	5 19 43	19 09 03	18 21	1 36D	25 41	25 07	28 19	26 50	9 49	11 28	20 26	25 18	1 58	12 01	9 23	13 12	8 28
12 Su	5 23 39	20 10 02	1♈19	1 36	27 16	25 25	29 01	26 59	9 54	11 24	20 26	25 20	1 45	12 11	9 45	13 44	8 28
13 M	5 27 36	21 11 01	13 40	1 37	28 50	25 40	29 43	27 09	10 00	11 23	20 26	25 21	1 33	12 22	10 08	14 17	8 27
14 T	5 31 32	22 12 01	25 53	1 39	0♑24	25 54	0♐25	27 19	10 05	11 21	20 27	25 23	1 21	12 33	10 30	14 49	8 27
15 W	5 35 29	23 13 02	7♉54	1 41	1 58	26 06	1 07	27 28	10 11	11 19	20 27	25 25	1 09	12 44	10 53	15 22	8 27
16 Th	5 39 25	24 14 03	19 48	1 42	3 33	26 15	1 49	27 38	10 16	11 17	20 28	25 27	0 57	12 55	11 15	15 54	8 27
17 F	5 43 22	25 15 05	1♊37	1 42R	5 07	26 22	2 31	27 48	10 22	11 16	20 28	25 28	0 46	13 07	11 38	16 26	8 27
18 Sa	5 47 18	26 16 08	13 25	1 42	6 42	26 27	3 13	27 59	10 28	11 14	20 29	25 30	0 35	13 19	12 01	16 59	8 26
19 Su	5 51 15	27 17 11	25 13	1 40	8 16	26 29R	3 55	28 09	10 34	11 13	20 29	25 32	0 25	13 31	12 23	17 31	8 26D
20 M	5 55 12	28 18 14	7♋05	1 37	9 50	26 29	4 37	28 19	10 40	11 11	20 30	25 34	0 14	13 43	12 46	18 04	8 26
21 T	5 59 8	29 19 19	19 01	1 32	11 25	26 26	5 19	28 30	10 46	11 10	20 30	25 35	0 04	13 56	13 09	18 36	8 26
22 W	6 3 5	0♑20 24	1♌04	1 27	12 59	26 21	6 01	28 41	10 52	11 09	20 31	25 37	29♐55	14 08	13 32	19 08	8 26
23 Th	6 7 1	1 21 29	13 15	1 21	14 33	26 14	6 44	28 51	10 58	11 07	20 31	25 39	29 45	14 21	13 55	19 41	8 26
24 F	6 10 58	2 22 35	25 37	1 16	16 06	26 04	7 26	29 02	11 04	11 06	20 32	25 41	29 36	14 34	14 18	20 13	8 27
25 Sa	6 14 54	3 23 42	8♍12	1 13	17 40	25 51	8 08	29 13	11 10	11 05	20 33	25 43	29 28	14 48	14 41	20 46	8 27
26 Su	6 18 51	4 24 49	21 03	1 10	19 13	25 36	8 51	29 24	11 16	11 03	20 35	25 45	29 19	15 02	15 04	21 18	8 27
27 M	6 22 47	5 25 57	4♎12	1 09D	20 45	25 18	9 33	29 35	11 22	11 02	20 36	25 47	29 12	15 15	15 27	21 50	8 28
28 T	6 26 44	6 27 05	17 43	1 10	22 16	24 59	10 16	29 46	11 29	11 01	20 37	25 48	29 04	15 29	15 50	22 22	8 28
29 W	6 30 41	7 28 14	1♏36	1 11	23 47	24 37	10 58	29 58	11 35	11 00	20 38	25 50	28 57	15 44	16 13	22 55	8 29
30 Th	6 34 37	8 29 24	15 53	1 12	25 17	24 12	11 41	0♓09	11 41	10 59	20 38	25 52	28 50	15 58	16 36	23 27	8 29
31 F	6 38 34	9 30 34	0♐32	1 13R	26 45	23 46	12 23	0 20	11 48	10 58	20 39	25 54	28 44	16 13	17 00	23 59	8 30

EPHEMERIS CALCULATED FOR 12 MIDNIGHT GREENWICH MEAN TIME. ALL OTHER DATA AND FACING ASPECTARIAN PAGE IN **EASTERN TIME (BOLD)** AND PACIFIC TIME (REGULAR).

JANUARY 2022

☽ Last Aspect day	ET	hr:mn / PT	asp	☽ Ingress sign day	ET	hr:mn / PT
1	**3:16 am**	12:16 am	□♆	♑ 1	**6:02 pm**	3:02 pm
3	**11:21 am**	8:21 am	☌♇	♒ 3	**5:44 pm**	2:44 pm
4	**7:45 pm**	4:45 pm	⚹♂	♓ 5	**7:17 pm**	4:17 pm
7	**5:23 pm**	2:23 pm	⚹♇	♈ 7		9:26 pm
7	**5:23 pm**	2:23 pm	⚹♇	♈ 8	**12:26 am**	
9		11:23 pm	□♇	♉ 10	**9:47 am**	6:47 am
10	**2:23 am**		□♇	♉ 10	**9:47 am**	6:47 am
12	**2:39 pm**	11:39 am	△♇	♊ 12	**10:08 pm**	7:08 pm
14	**9:22 pm**	6:22 pm	☍♂	♋ 15	**11:11 am**	8:11 am
17	**6:48 pm**	3:48 pm	☍☉	♌ 17	**11:03 pm**	8:03 pm
20	**3:15 am**	12:15 am	△♂	♍ 20	**9:02 am**	6:02 am
22	**2:46 pm**	11:46 am	□♂	♎ 22	**5:03 pm**	2:03 pm
24	**5:10 pm**	2:10 pm	□♇	♏ 24	**10:57 pm**	7:57 pm
26		9:28 pm	⚹☿	♐ 26		11:34 pm
27	**12:28 am**		⚹☿	♐ 27	**2:34 am**	
28	**2:00 pm**	11:00 am	□♆	♑ 29	**4:09 am**	1:09 am
30	**11:44 pm**	8:44 pm	☌♇	♒ 31	**4:43 am**	1:43 am

☽ Phases & Eclipses phase	day	ET	hr:mn / PT
New Moon	2	**1:33 pm**	10:33 am
2nd Quarter	9	**1:11 pm**	10:11 am
Full Moon	17	**6:48 pm**	3:48 pm
4th Quarter	25	**8:41 am**	5:41 am
New Moon	31		9:46 pm
New Moon	2/1	**12:46 am**	

Planet Ingress	day	ET	hr:mn / PT
☿ ♒	1		11:10 pm
☿ ♒	2	**2:10 am**	
⚶ ♑	10		9:19 pm
⚶ ♑	11	**12:19 am**	
☉ ♒	19	**9:39 pm**	6:39 pm
♂ ♑	24	**7:53 am**	4:53 am
☿ ♑	25	**10:05 pm**	7:05 pm

Planetary Motion		day	ET	hr:mn / PT
☿	℞	14	**6:41 am**	3:41 am
⚳	D	14	**4:20 pm**	1:20 pm
♅	D	18	**10:27 am**	7:27 am
♀	D	29	**3:46 am**	12:46 am

1 SATURDAY
☽□♆ **3:16 am** 12:16 am
☉△♅ **4:50 am** 1:50 am
☽⚺♀ **7:02 am** 4:02 am
☽⚺♇ **11:38 am** 8:38 am
☽⚺☿ **5:13 pm** 2:13 pm
☽⚹♃ **7:13 pm** 4:13 pm

2 SUNDAY
☉⚺♄ **7:12 am** 4:12 am
☽△♅ **11:20 am** 8:20 am
☽⚺♄ **1:10 pm** 10:10 am
☽☌☉ **1:33 pm** 10:33 am
☽⚺♂ **4:56 pm** 1:56 pm
☿⚺♃ **6:44 pm** 3:44 pm
☽⚹♆ 11:52 pm

3 MONDAY
☽⚹♆ **2:52 am**
☽☌♀ **4:59 am** 1:59 am
☽☌♇ **11:21 am** 8:21 am
☽⚺♃ **7:34 pm** 4:34 pm
☽☌☿ **9:37 pm** 6:37 pm

4 TUESDAY
☽□♅ **11:25 am** 8:25 am
☽☌♄ **1:44 pm** 10:44 am
☽⚺☉ **5:23 pm** 2:23 pm
☽⚹♂ **7:45 pm** 4:45 pm

5 WEDNESDAY
☽⚺♆ **3:41 am** 12:41 am
☽⚺♀ **3:59 am** 12:59 am
♀⚹♆ **11:03 am** 8:03 am
☽⚺♇ **12:39 pm** 9:39 am
☽☌♃ **9:57 pm** 6:57 pm

6 THURSDAY
☽⚺☿ **4:07 am** 1:07 am
☽⚹♅ **2:04 pm** 11:04 am
☽⚺♄ **5:01 pm** 2:01 pm
☽⚹☉ 9:41 pm
☽□♂ 10:55 pm

7 FRIDAY
☽⚹☉ **12:41 am**
☽□♂ **1:55 am**
☽⚹♀ **5:41 am** 2:41 am
☽☌♆ **7:40 am** 4:40 am
☽⚹♇ **5:23 pm** 2:23 pm

8 SATURDAY
☽⚺♃ **4:11 am** 1:11 am
☽⚹☿ **2:37 pm** 11:37 am
♀⚺♂ **5:48 pm** 2:48 pm
☉☌♀ **7:48 pm** 4:48 pm
☽⚺♅ **8:44 pm** 5:44 pm
☽⚹♄ 9:27 pm

9 SUNDAY
☽⚹♄ **12:27 am**
☉⚺♂ **4:32 am** 1:32 am
☽□♀ **11:01 am** 8:01 am

☽△♂ **12:58 pm** 9:58 am
☽□☉ **1:11 pm** 10:11 am
☽⚺♆ **3:52 pm** 12:52 pm
☽□♇ 11:23 pm

10 MONDAY
☽□♇ **2:23 am**
☽⚹♃ **2:48 pm** 11:48 am
☉⚹♆ **10:28 pm** 7:28 pm

11 TUESDAY
☽□☿ **4:38 am** 1:38 am
☽☌♅ **7:21 am** 4:21 am
☽□♄ **11:53 am** 8:53 am
♂□♆ **4:43 pm** 1:43 pm
☽△♀ **7:34 pm** 4:34 pm

12 WEDNESDAY
☽⚹♆ **3:38 am** 12:38 am
☽⚻♂ **4:19 am** 1:19 am
☽△☉ **6:20 am** 3:20 am
☽△♇ **2:39 pm** 11:39 am

13 THURSDAY
☽□♃ **4:24 am** 1:24 am
☽△☿ **7:10 pm** 4:10 pm
☽⚺♅ **8:12 pm** 5:12 pm
☽△♄ 10:26 pm

14 FRIDAY
☽△♄ **1:26 am**
☽⚻♀ **5:46 am** 2:46 am
☽□♆ **4:50 pm** 1:50 pm
☽☍♂ **9:22 pm** 6:22 pm
☽⚻☉ 10:10 pm

15 SATURDAY
☽⚻☉ **1:10 am**
☽⚻♇ **3:54 am** 12:54 am
☽△♃ **6:31 pm** 3:31 pm

16 SUNDAY
☽⚻☿ **7:12 am** 4:12 am
☽⚹♅ **8:58 am** 5:58 am
☉☌♇ **9:51 am** 6:51 am
☽⚻♄ **2:42 pm** 11:42 am
☽☍♀ **3:50 pm** 12:50 pm

17 MONDAY
☽△♆ **5:19 am** 2:19 am
☽⚻♂ **1:24 pm** 10:24 am
♀⚺♄ **2:44 pm** 11:44 am
☽☍♇ **4:08 pm** 1:08 pm
☽☍☉ **6:48 pm** 3:48 pm

18 TUESDAY
☽⚻♃ **7:15 am** 4:15 am
☽☍☿ **3:39 pm** 12:39 pm
☽□♅ **8:11 pm** 5:11 pm
☽⚻♀ 9:47 pm
☽☍♄ 11:19 pm

19 WEDNESDAY
☽⚻♀ **12:47 am**
☽☍♄ **2:19 am**
♂⚺♇ **1:30 pm** 10:30 am
☽⚻♆ **4:00 pm** 1:00 pm
☽⚻♇ 11:30 pm

20 THURSDAY
☽⚻♇ **2:30 am**
☽△♂ **3:15 am** 12:15 am
☽⚻☉ **10:02 am** 7:02 am
☽☍♃ **5:58 pm** 2:58 pm
☽⚻☿ **8:55 pm** 5:55 pm

21 FRIDAY
☽△♅ **5:28 am** 2:28 am
☽△♀ **8:19 am** 5:19 am
☽⚻♄ **11:54 am** 8:54 am
☿⚺♃ **11:00 pm** 8:00 pm
☽☍♆ 9:43 pm

22 SATURDAY
☽☍♆ **12:43 am**
☽△♇ **10:53 am** 7:53 am
☽□♂ **2:46 pm** 11:46 am
☽△☉ **10:43 pm** 7:43 pm
☽△☿ **11:47 pm** 8:47 pm
☽⚻♃ 11:37 pm

23 SUNDAY
☽⚻♃ **2:37 am**
☉☌☿ **5:28 am** 2:28 am
☽⚻♅ **12:45 pm** 9:45 am
☽□♀ **2:22 pm** 11:22 am
☽△♄ **7:26 pm** 4:26 pm

24 MONDAY
☽⚻♆ **7:23 am** 4:23 am
☽□♇ **5:10 pm** 2:10 pm
☽⚹♂ **11:48 pm** 8:48 pm
☽□☿ 9:51 pm

25 TUESDAY
☽□☿ **12:51 am**
☿⚺♂ **7:46 am** 4:46 am
☽□☉ **8:41 am** 5:41 am
☽△♃ **9:01 am** 6:01 am
☉⚺♃ **2:32 pm** 11:32 am
☽☍♅ **5:52 pm** 2:52 pm
☽⚹♀ **6:41 pm** 3:41 pm
☽□♄ 9:42 pm

26 WEDNESDAY
☽□♄ **12:42 am**
☽△♆ **11:47 am** 8:47 am
☽⚹♇ **9:10 pm** 6:10 pm
☽⚹☿ 9:28 pm

27 THURSDAY
☽⚹☿ **12:28 am**
☽⚺♂ **6:09 am** 3:09 am
☽□♃ **1:02 pm** 10:02 am
☽⚹☉ **3:47 pm** 12:47 pm
☽⚻♅ **8:43 pm** 5:43 pm
☽⚺♀ **9:08 pm** 6:08 pm

28 FRIDAY
☽⚹♄ **3:39 am** 12:39 am
☽□♆ **2:00 pm** 11:00 am
☽⚺♇ **11:02 pm** 8:02 pm
☽⚺☿ **11:03 pm** 8:03 pm
☿☌♇ **11:16 pm** 8:16 pm

29 SATURDAY
☽☌♂ **10:10 am** 7:10 am
☽⚹♃ **3:03 pm** 12:03 pm

☽⚺☉ **8:34 pm** 5:34 pm
☽△♅ **9:47 pm** 6:47 pm
☽☌♀ **10:08 pm** 7:08 pm

30 SUNDAY
☽⚺♄ **4:56 am** 1:56 am
☉□♅ **2:32 pm** 11:32 am
☽⚹♆ **2:48 pm** 11:48 am
☉⚺♀ **8:29 pm** 5:29 pm
☽☌☿ **9:26 pm** 6:26 pm
☽☌♇ **11:44 pm** 8:44 pm

31 MONDAY
☽⚺♂ **1:14 pm** 10:14 am
☽⚺♃ **4:22 pm** 1:22 pm
☽□♅ **10:25 pm** 7:25 pm
☽⚺♀ **10:58 pm** 7:58 pm
☽☌☉ 9:46 pm

Eastern time in bold type
Pacific time in medium type

JANUARY 2022

DATE	SID.TIME	SUN	MOON	NODE	MERCURY	VENUS	MARS	JUPITER	SATURN	URANUS	NEPTUNE	PLUTO	CERES	PALLAS	JUNO	VESTA	CHIRON
1 Sa	6 42 30	10♑31 44	15♐29	1♊12R	28♑11	23♑18R	13♐06	0♓33	11♒54	10♉57R	20♓40	25♑58	28♊38R	16♓28	17♑23	24♐32	8♈30
2 Su	6 46 27	11 32 55	0♑37	1 10	29 35	22 48	13 49	0 45	12 01	10 56	20 41	26 00	28 32	16 43	17 46	25 04	8 31
3 M	6 50 23	12 34 06	15 46	1 05	0♒57	22 16	14 31	0 56	12 07	10 55	20 42	26 02	28 27	16 58	18 10	25 36	8 32
4 T	6 54 20	13 35 17	0♒47	0 59	2 16	21 43	15 14	1 08	12 14	10 55	20 43	26 04	28 22	17 13	18 33	26 08	8 33
5 W	6 58 17	14 36 28	15 31	0 51	3 32	21 09	15 57	1 20	12 20	10 54	20 45	26 06	28 18	17 29	18 56	26 40	8 34
6 Th	7 2 13	15 37 38	29 50	0 44	4 43	20 34	16 40	1 33	12 27	10 53	20 46	26 08	28 14	17 45	19 20	27 13	8 34
7 F	7 6 10	16 38 48	13♓41	0 38	5 50	19 58	17 23	1 45	12 34	10 53	20 47	26 10	28 11	18 01	19 43	27 45	8 35
8 Sa	7 10 6	17 39 58	27 03	0 34	6 52	19 21	18 05	1 57	12 41	10 52	20 48	26 12	28 08	18 17	20 07	28 17	8 36
9 Su	7 14 3	18 41 07	9♈57	0 32D	7 47	18 44	18 48	2 09	12 47	10 52	20 49	26 14	28 05	18 33	20 30	28 49	8 38
10 M	7 17 59	19 42 16	22 27	0 32	8 35	18 08	19 31	2 22	12 54	10 51	20 51	26 16	28 03	18 49	20 54	29 21	8 39
11 T	7 21 56	20 43 24	4♉39	0 32	9 15	17 31	20 14	2 34	13 01	10 51	20 52	26 18	28 01	19 06	21 18	29 53	8 40
12 W	7 25 52	21 44 32	16 38	0 34R	9 46	16 55	20 57	2 47	13 08	10 50	20 53	26 20	28 00	19 23	21 41	0♑25	8 41
13 Th	7 29 49	22 45 40	28 28	0 34	10 08	16 20	21 40	3 00	13 15	10 50	20 55	26 22	27 59	19 40	22 05	0 57	8 42
14 F	7 33 45	23 46 46	10♊14	0 34	10 19R	15 46	22 24	3 12	13 22	10 49	20 56	26 24	27 58D	19 57	22 28	1 29	8 44
15 Sa	7 37 42	24 47 53	22 03	0 31	10 19	15 13	23 07	3 25	13 28	10 49	20 58	26 26	27 58	20 14	22 52	2 01	8 45
16 Su	7 41 39	25 48 58	3♋52	0 26	10 07	14 41	23 50	3 38	13 35	10 49	20 59	26 28	27 58	20 32	23 16	2 33	8 47
17 M	7 45 35	26 50 03	15 50	0 18	9 43	14 11	24 33	3 51	13 42	10 49	21 01	26 29	27 59	20 49	23 40	3 04	8 48
18 T	7 49 32	27 51 08	27 57	0 09	9 08	13 43	25 16	4 04	13 49	10 49D	21 02	26 31	28 00	21 07	24 03	3 36	8 50
19 W	7 53 28	28 52 12	10♌12	29♉57	8 22	13 17	26 00	4 17	13 56	10 49	21 04	26 33	28 01	21 25	24 27	4 08	8 51
20 Th	7 57 25	29 53 15	22 39	29 46	7 26	12 53	26 43	4 30	14 04	10 49	21 05	26 35	28 03	21 43	24 51	4 40	8 53
21 F	8 1 21	0♒54 18	5♍16	29 34	6 22	12 31	27 26	4 44	14 11	10 49	21 06	26 37	28 05	22 01	25 15	5 12	8 54
22 Sa	8 5 18	1 55 21	18 04	29 25	5 11	12 12	28 10	4 57	14 18	10 49	21 08	26 39	28 08	22 19	25 38	5 43	8 56
23 Su	8 9 15	2 56 22	1♎04	29 18	3 56	11 55	28 53	5 10	14 25	10 50	21 10	26 41	28 11	22 38	26 02	6 15	8 58
24 M	8 13 11	3 57 24	14 17	29 14	2 40	11 40	29 37	5 24	14 32	10 50	21 11	26 43	28 14	22 56	26 26	6 47	9 00
25 T	8 17 8	4 58 25	27 45	29 12D	1 23	11 28	0♑21	5 37	14 39	10 50	21 13	26 45	28 18	23 15	26 50	7 18	9 02
26 W	8 21 4	5 59 25	11♏30	29 12	0 09	11 19	1 04	5 51	14 46	10 51	21 15	26 47	28 22	23 34	27 14	7 50	9 04
27 Th	8 25 1	7 00 25	25 31	29 12R	29♑00	11 12	1 47	6 04	14 53	10 51	21 17	26 49	28 27	23 53	27 38	8 21	9 06
28 F	8 28 57	8 01 25	9♐49	29 12	27 57	11 07	2 31	6 18	15 00	10 51	21 19	26 51	28 32	24 12	28 01	8 53	9 08
29 Sa	8 32 54	9 02 24	24 23	29 09	27 01	11 05D	3 15	6 31	15 08	10 52	21 20	26 53	28 37	24 31	28 25	9 24	9 10
30 Su	8 36 50	10 03 23	9♑09	29 05	26 13	11 05	3 58	6 45	15 15	10 52	21 22	26 55	28 43	24 50	28 49	9 55	9 12
31 M	8 40 47	11 04 20	24 00	28 57	25 34	11 08	4 42	6 59	15 22	10 53	21 24	26 55	28 49	25 10	29 13	10 27	9 14

EPHEMERIS CALCULATED FOR 12 MIDNIGHT GREENWICH MEAN TIME. ALL OTHER DATA AND FACING ASPECTARIAN PAGE IN **EASTERN TIME (BOLD)** AND PACIFIC TIME (REGULAR).

FEBRUARY 2022

☽ Last Aspect day	ET / hr:mn / PT		asp	☽ Ingress sign	day	ET / hr:mn / PT	
1	**6:01 am**	3:01 am	☌ ♄	♓	2	**6:00 am**	3:00 am
4	**4:41 am**	1:41 am	⚹ ♇	♈	4	**9:57 am**	6:57 am
6	**12:21 pm**	9:21 am	□ ♇	♉	6	**5:52 pm**	2:52 pm
8	**11:48 pm**	8:48 pm	△ ♇	♊	9	**5:27 am**	2:27 am
11	**3:23 am**	12:23 am	△ ☉	♋	11	**6:27 pm**	3:27 pm
14	**5:27 am**	2:27 am	☍ ☿	♌	14	**6:17 am**	3:17 am
16	**11:56 am**	8:56 am	☍ ☉	♍	16	**3:42 pm**	12:42 pm
18	**6:20 pm**	3:20 pm	△ ♇	♎	18	**10:51 pm**	7:51 pm
20		9:02 pm	□ ♇	♏	21	**4:19 am**	1:19 am
21	**12:02 am**		□ ♇	♏	21	**4:19 am**	1:19 am
23	**4:24 am**	1:24 am	⚹ ♇	♐	23	**8:29 am**	5:29 am
24	**10:24 pm**	7:24 pm	□ ♆	♑	25	**11:27 am**	8:27 am
27	**9:49 am**	6:49 am	☌ ♇	♒	27	**1:36 pm**	10:36 am
28	**9:01 pm**	6:01 pm	☌ ♄	♓	3/1	**3:53 pm**	12:53 pm

☽ Phases & Eclipses phase	day	ET / hr:mn / PT	
New Moon	1/31		9:46 pm
New Moon	1	**12:46 am**	
2nd Quarter	8	**8:50 am**	5:50 am
Full Moon	16	**11:56 am**	8:56 am
4th Quarter	23	**5:32 pm**	2:32 pm

Planet Ingress		day	ET / hr:mn / PT	
⚵	♒	1	**6:04 pm**	3:04 pm
⚳	♊	8	**9:13 pm**	6:13 pm
♀	♈	13		9:53 pm
♀	♈	14	**12:53 am**	
☿	♒	14	**4:54 pm**	1:54 pm
☉	♓	18	**11:43 am**	8:43 am

Planetary Motion		day	ET / hr:mn / PT	
☿	D	3	**11:13 pm**	8:13 pm

1 TUESDAY
☽ ☌ ☉ **12:46 am**
☽ ☌ ♄ **6:01 am** 3:01 am
☽ ⊻ ♆ **3:46 pm** 12:46 pm
☽ ⊻ ☿ **9:05 pm** 6:05 pm
☽ ⊻ ♇ 9:57 pm

2 WEDNESDAY
☽ ⊻ ♇ **12:57 am**
☽ ⚹ ♂ **5:33 pm** 2:33 pm
☽ ☌ ♃ **6:57 pm** 3:57 pm
☽ ⚹ ♅ 9:30 pm
☽ ⚹ ♀ 10:35 pm

3 THURSDAY
☽ ⚹ ♅ **12:30 am**
☽ ⚹ ♀ **1:35 am**
☽ ⊻ ☉ **6:52 am** 3:52 am
☽ ⊻ ♄ **8:54 am** 5:54 am
☽ ☌ ♆ **6:54 pm** 3:54 pm
☽ ⚹ ☿ **11:55 pm** 8:55 pm

4 FRIDAY
☽ ⚹ ♇ **4:41 am** 1:41 am
♂ ⚹ ♃ **8:38 am** 5:38 am
☉ ☌ ♄ **2:05 pm** 11:05 am
☽ ⊻ ♃ 9:48 pm
☽ □ ♂ 10:27 pm

5 SATURDAY
☽ ⊻ ♃ **12:48 am**
☽ □ ♂ **1:27 am**
☽ ⊻ ♅ **5:53 am** 2:53 am
☽ □ ♀ **7:56 am** 4:56 am
☽ ⚹ ♄ **3:22 pm** 12:22 pm
☽ ⚹ ☉ **5:17 pm** 2:17 pm
☽ ⊻ ♆ 10:47 pm

6 SUNDAY
☽ ⊻ ♆ **1:47 am**
☽ □ ☿ **7:42 am** 4:42 am
☽ □ ♇ **12:21 pm** 9:21 am

7 MONDAY
☽ ⚹ ♃ **10:58 am** 7:58 am
☽ △ ♂ **2:12 pm** 11:12 am
☽ ☌ ♅ **3:22 pm** 12:22 pm
☽ △ ♀ **7:00 pm** 4:00 pm
☽ □ ♄ 11:01 pm

8 TUESDAY
☽ □ ♄ **2:01 am**
☽ □ ☉ **8:50 am** 5:50 am
♂ △ ♅ **9:57 am** 6:57 am
☽ ⚹ ♆ **12:40 pm** 9:40 am
☽ △ ☿ **8:48 pm** 5:48 pm
☽ △ ♇ **11:48 pm** 8:48 pm

9 WEDNESDAY
☽ □ ♃ 9:28 pm

10 THURSDAY
☽ □ ♃ **12:28 am**
☽ ⊻ ♅ **3:53 am** 12:53 am
☽ ⚻ ♂ **6:36 am** 3:36 am
☉ ⊻ ♆ **7:29 am** 4:29 am
☽ ⚻ ♀ **9:35 am** 6:35 am
☽ △ ♄ **3:20 pm** 12:20 pm
☽ □ ♆ 10:43 pm

11 FRIDAY
☽ □ ♆ **1:43 am**
☽ △ ☉ **3:23 am** 12:23 am
☿ ☌ ♇ **9:04 am** 6:04 am
☽ ⚻ ♇ **12:56 pm** 9:56 am
☽ ⚻ ☿ **1:11 pm** 10:11 am

12 SATURDAY
☽ △ ♃ **2:35 pm** 11:35 am
☽ ⚹ ♅ **4:49 pm** 1:49 pm
☽ ☍ ♂ **11:21 pm** 8:21 pm
☽ ☍ ♀ 9:45 pm

13 SUNDAY
☽ ☍ ♀ **12:45 am**
☽ ⚻ ♄ **4:33 am** 1:33 am
☽ △ ♆ **2:15 pm** 11:15 am
☽ ⚻ ☉ **9:09 pm** 6:09 pm
☽ ☍ ♇ 10:07 pm

14 MONDAY
☽ ☍ ♇ **1:07 am**
☽ ☍ ☿ **5:27 am** 2:27 am
☽ ⚻ ♃ 11:49 pm

15 TUESDAY
☽ ⚻ ♃ **2:49 am**
☽ □ ♅ **3:56 am** 12:56 am
☽ ⚻ ♂ **1:45 pm** 10:45 am
☽ ⚻ ♀ **2:02 pm** 11:02 am
☽ ☍ ♄ **3:38 pm** 12:38 pm
☉ ⊻ ♇ **10:17 pm** 7:17 pm
☽ ⚻ ♆ 9:31 pm

16 WEDNESDAY
☽ ⚻ ♆ **12:31 am**
♀ ☌ ♂ **9:29 am** 6:29 am
☽ ⚻ ♇ **10:53 am** 7:53 am
☽ ☍ ☉ **11:56 am** 8:56 am
☽ ⚻ ☿ **7:31 pm** 4:31 pm

17 THURSDAY
♂ ⊻ ♄ **3:34 am** 12:34 am
♀ ⊻ ♄ **9:09 am** 6:09 am
☽ ☍ ♃ **12:26 pm** 9:26 am
☽ △ ♅ **12:33 pm** 9:33 am
♃ ⚹ ♅ **7:13 pm** 4:13 pm
☽ ⚻ ♄ 9:11 pm
☽ △ ♀ 9:47 pm
☽ △ ♂ 10:13 pm

18 FRIDAY
☽ ⚻ ♄ **12:11 am**
☽ △ ♀ **12:47 am**
☽ △ ♂ **1:13 am**
☽ ☍ ♆ **8:22 am** 5:22 am
☽ △ ♇ **6:20 pm** 3:20 pm
☽ ⚻ ☉ **11:46 pm** 8:46 pm

19 SATURDAY
☽ △ ☿ **7:18 am** 4:18 am
☽ ⚻ ♅ **7:06 pm** 4:06 pm
☽ ⚻ ♃ **7:53 pm** 4:53 pm

20 SUNDAY
☽ △ ♄ **6:46 am** 3:46 am
☽ □ ♀ **9:33 am** 6:33 am
☽ □ ♂ **10:25 am** 7:25 am
☽ ⚻ ♆ **2:22 pm** 11:22 am
☽ □ ♇ 9:02 pm

21 MONDAY
☽ □ ♇ **12:02 am**
☽ △ ☉ **9:28 am** 6:28 am
☽ □ ☿ **5:28 pm** 2:28 pm
☽ ☍ ♅ 9:10 pm
☽ △ ♃ 10:45 pm

22 TUESDAY
☽ ☍ ♅ **12:10 am**
☽ △ ♃ **1:45 am**
☽ □ ♄ **11:53 am** 8:53 am
☽ ⚹ ♀ **4:55 pm** 1:55 pm
☽ ⚹ ♂ **5:58 pm** 2:58 pm
☽ △ ♆ **7:00 pm** 4:00 pm

23 WEDNESDAY
☽ ⚹ ♇ **4:24 am** 1:24 am
♂ ⚹ ♆ **2:12 pm** 11:12 am
☽ □ ☉ **5:32 pm** 2:32 pm
☽ ⚹ ☿ 11:17 pm

24 THURSDAY
☽ ⚹ ☿ **2:17 am**
☽ ⚻ ♅ **3:59 am** 12:59 am
☽ □ ♃ **6:19 am** 3:19 am
♀ ⚹ ♆ **11:04 am** 8:04 am
☽ ⚹ ♄ **3:45 pm** 12:45 pm
☿ □ ♅ **9:22 pm** 6:22 pm
☽ □ ♆ **10:24 pm** 7:24 pm
☽ ⊻ ♀ **11:00 pm** 8:00 pm
☽ ⊻ ♂ 9:06 pm

25 FRIDAY
☽ ⊻ ♂ **12:06 am**
☽ ⊻ ♇ **7:33 am** 4:33 am
☽ ⚹ ☉ 9:10 pm

26 SATURDAY
☽ ⚹ ☉ **12:10 am**
☽ △ ♅ **6:40 am** 3:40 am
☿ ⊻ ♃ **7:16 am** 4:16 am
☽ ⚹ ♃ **9:43 am** 6:43 am
☽ ⊻ ☿ **9:55 am** 6:55 am
☽ ⊻ ♄ **6:32 pm** 3:32 pm
☽ ⚹ ♆ 9:49 pm

27 SUNDAY
☽ ⚹ ♆ **12:49 am**
☽ ☌ ♀ **4:06 am** 1:06 am
☽ ☌ ♂ **5:06 am** 2:06 am
☽ ☌ ♇ **9:49 am** 6:49 am

28 MONDAY
☽ ⊻ ☉ **5:59 am** 2:59 am
☽ □ ♅ **8:50 am** 5:50 am
☽ ⊻ ♃ **12:37 pm** 9:37 am
☽ ☌ ☿ **5:11 pm** 2:11 pm
☽ ☌ ♄ **9:01 pm** 6:01 pm

Eastern time in bold type
Pacific time in medium type

FEBRUARY 2022

DATE	SID.TIME	SUN	MOON	NODE	MERCURY	VENUS	MARS	JUPITER	SATURN	URANUS	NEPTUNE	PLUTO	CERES	PALLAS	JUNO	VESTA	CHIRON
1 T	8 44 44	12≈05 17	8≈48	28ŏ47R.	25ŏ08R.	11ŏ13	5ŏ26	7ℋ13	15≈29	10ŏ54	21ℋ26	26ŏ57	28ŏ55	25ℋ29	29ŏ37	10ŏ58	9℉16
2 W	8 48 40	13 06 12	23 25	28 35	24 41	11 20	6 10	7 27	15 36	10 55	21 28	26 59	29 02	25 49	0≈01	11 29	9 18
3 Th	8 52 37	14 07 07	7ℋ42	28 23	24 28	11 30	6 54	7 40	15 43	10 55	21 30	27 01	29 09	26 09	0 25	12 01	9 21
4 F	8 56 33	15 08 00	21 42	28 12	24 23D	11 42	7 37	7 54	15 51	10 56	21 32	27 03	29 17	26 29	0 49	12 32	9 23
5 Sa	9 0 30	16 08 52	5℉01	28 04	24 25	11 56	8 21	8 08	15 58	10 57	21 33	27 05	29 25	26 49	1 13	13 03	9 25
6 Su	9 4 26	17 09 42	18 00	27 58	24 35	12 12	9 05	8 22	16 05	10 58	21 35	27 07	29 33	27 09	1 37	13 34	9 28
7 M	9 8 23	18 10 31	0ŏ35	27 55	24 51	12 30	9 49	8 36	16 12	10 59	21 37	27 08	29 41	27 30	2 01	14 05	9 30
8 T	9 12 19	19 11 19	12 50	27 54D	25 13	12 50	10 33	8 50	16 19	11 00	21 39	27 10	29 50	27 50	2 24	14 36	9 33
9 W	9 16 16	20 12 05	24 50	27 54R.	25 41	13 12	11 17	9 05	16 27	11 01	21 41	27 12	29 59	28 11	2 48	15 07	9 35
10 Th	9 20 13	21 12 50	6Ⅱ41	27 54	26 15	13 35	12 01	9 19	16 34	11 02	21 43	27 14	0Ⅱ09	28 31	3 12	15 38	9 38
11 F	9 24 9	22 13 33	18 28	27 52	26 53	14 01	12 45	9 33	16 41	11 03	21 45	27 16	0 18	28 52	3 36	16 09	9 40
12 Sa	9 28 6	23 14 14	0♋16	27 49	27 35	14 28	13 30	9 47	16 48	11 05	21 47	27 18	0 28	29 13	4 00	16 39	9 43
13 Su	9 32 2	24 14 54	12 11	27 42	28 21	14 57	14 14	10 01	16 55	11 06	21 49	27 19	0 39	29 34	4 24	17 10	9 45
14 M	9 35 59	25 15 33	24 15	27 33	29 11	15 27	14 58	10 16	17 02	11 07	21 52	27 21	0 49	29 55	4 48	17 41	9 48
15 T	9 39 55	26 16 10	6♌32	27 21	0≈05	15 59	15 42	10 30	17 10	11 09	21 54	27 23	1 00	0℉16	5 12	18 11	9 51
16 W	9 43 52	27 16 45	19 02	27 08	1 01	16 32	16 26	10 44	17 17	11 10	21 56	27 25	1 12	0 37	5 36	18 42	9 54
17 Th	9 47 48	28 17 19	1♍46	26 54	2 01	17 07	17 11	10 59	17 24	11 11	21 58	27 27	1 23	0 59	6 00	19 13	9 56
18 F	9 51 45	29 17 51	14 43	26 40	3 03	17 43	17 55	11 13	17 31	11 13	22 00	27 28	1 35	1 20	6 24	19 43	9 59
19 Sa	9 55 42	0ℋ18 22	27 52	26 29	4 07	18 20	18 39	11 27	17 38	11 15	22 02	27 30	1 47	1 42	6 47	20 13	10 02
20 Su	9 59 38	1 18 51	11≏13	26 20	5 14	18 59	19 24	11 42	17 45	11 16	22 04	27 32	2 00	2 03	7 11	20 44	10 05
21 M	10 3 35	2 19 19	24 43	26 14	6 23	19 39	20 08	11 56	17 52	11 18	22 06	27 33	2 12	2 25	7 35	21 14	10 08
22 T	10 7 31	3 19 46	8♏22	26 11	7 34	20 20	20 52	12 10	17 59	11 19	22 09	27 35	2 25	2 47	7 59	21 44	10 11
23 W	10 11 28	4 20 11	22 11	26 10	8 47	21 02	21 37	12 25	18 06	11 21	22 11	27 37	2 38	3 09	8 23	22 14	10 14
24 Th	10 15 24	5 20 35	6♐08	26 10	10 01	21 45	22 21	12 39	18 13	11 23	22 13	27 38	2 52	3 31	8 47	22 44	10 17
25 F	10 19 21	6 20 58	20 15	26 10	11 18	22 29	23 06	12 54	18 20	11 25	22 15	27 40	3 05	3 53	9 10	23 14	10 20
26 Sa	10 23 17	7 21 20	4♑30	26 08	12 35	23 14	23 51	13 08	18 27	11 27	22 17	27 42	3 19	4 15	9 34	23 44	10 23
27 Su	10 27 14	8 21 40	18 51	26 03	13 55	24 00	24 35	13 23	18 34	11 29	22 20	27 43	3 33	4 37	9 58	24 14	10 26
28 M	10 31 11	9 21 58	3≈15	25 55	15 15	24 47	25 20	13 37	18 41	11 31	22 22	27 45	3 48	5 00	10 22	24 44	10 29

EPHEMERIS CALCULATED FOR 12 MIDNIGHT GREENWICH MEAN TIME. ALL OTHER DATA AND FACING ASPECTARIAN PAGE IN **EASTERN TIME (BOLD)** AND PACIFIC TIME (REGULAR).

MARCH 2022

☽ Last Aspect day	ET / hr:mn / PT	asp	☽ Ingress sign	day	ET / hr:mn / PT
2/28	**9:01 pm** 6:01 pm	☌ ♄	♓	1	**3:53 pm** 12:53 pm
3	**4:45 pm** 1:45 pm	⚹ ♂	♈	3	**7:52 pm** 4:52 pm
5	**11:02 pm** 8:02 pm	□ ♇	♉	6	**3:00 am** 12:00 am
8	**9:35 am** 6:35 am	△ ♇	♊	8	**1:40 pm** 10:40 am
10	**11:43 am** 8:43 am	□ ♆	♋	10	11:24 pm
10	**11:43 am** 8:43 am	□ ♆	♋	11	**2:24 am**
13	**11:44 am** 8:44 am	☍ ♇	♌	13	**3:32 pm** 12:32 pm
15	**6:56 am** 3:56 am	☍ ♄	♍	15	9:59 pm
15	**6:56 am** 3:56 am	☍ ♄	♍	16	**12:59 am**
18	**4:11 am** 1:11 am	△ ♇	♎	18	**7:26 am** 4:26 am
20	**8:40 am** 5:40 am	□ ♇	♏	20	**11:45 am** 8:45 am
22	**12:01 pm** 9:01 am	⚹ ♇	♐	22	**2:59 pm** 11:59 am
24	**8:59 am** 5:59 am	□ ☿	♑	24	**5:54 pm** 2:54 pm
26	**7:51 pm** 4:51 pm	⚹ ☿	♒	26	**8:55 pm** 5:55 pm
28	**10:11 am** 7:11 am	☌ ♄	♓	28	9:32 pm
28	**10:11 am** 7:11 am	☌ ♄	♓	29	**12:32 am**
30	11:37 pm	⚹ ♇	♈	31	**5:30 am** 2:30 am
31	**2:37 am**	⚹ ♇	♈	31	**5:30 am** 2:30 am

☽ Phases & Eclipses phase	day	ET / hr:mn / PT
New Moon	2	**12:35 pm** 9:35 am
2nd Quarter	10	**5:45 am** 2:45 am
Full Moon	18	**3:18 am** 12:18 am
4th Quarter	24	10:37 pm
4th Quarter	25	**1:37 am**
New Moon	31	11:24 pm
New Moon	4/1	**2:24 am**

Planet Ingress		day	ET / hr:mn / PT
♂	♒	5	10:23 pm
♂	♒	6	**1:23 am**
♀	♒	5	10:30 pm
♀	♒	6	**1:30 am**
☿	♓	9	**8:32 pm** 5:32 pm
⚶	♒	10	**1:22 pm** 10:22 am
☉	♈	20	**11:33 am** 8:33 am
☿	♈	27	**3:44 am** 12:44 am

Planetary Motion	day	ET / hr:mn / PT

1 TUESDAY
☽ ⚺ ♆ **3:05 am** 12:05 am
☽ ⚺ ♀ **9:14 am** 6:14 am
☽ ⚺ ♂ **10:02 am** 7:02 am
☽ ⚺ ♇ **12:09 pm** 9:09 am
☉ ⚹ ♅ 9:05 pm

2 WEDNESDAY
☉ ⚹ ♅ **12:05 am**
☿ ☌ ♄ **11:33 am** 8:33 am
☽ ⚹ ♅ **11:43 am** 8:43 am
☽ ☌ ☉ **12:35 pm** 9:35 am
☽ ☌ ♃ **4:24 pm** 1:24 pm
☽ ⚺ ♄ 9:37 pm
☽ ⚺ ☿ 11:00 pm

3 THURSDAY
☽ ⚺ ♄ **12:37 am**
☽ ⚺ ☿ **2:00 am**
♂ ☌ ♇ **3:43 am** 12:43 am
☽ ☌ ♆ **6:37 am** 3:37 am
♀ ☌ ♇ **12:56 pm** 9:56 am
☽ ⚹ ♇ **4:03 pm** 1:03 pm
☽ ⚹ ♀ **4:15 pm** 1:15 pm
☽ ⚹ ♂ **4:45 pm** 1:45 pm

4 FRIDAY
☽ ⚺ ♅ **4:55 pm** 1:55 pm
☽ ⚺ ☉ **10:05 pm** 7:05 pm
☽ ⚺ ♃ **10:45 pm** 7:45 pm
☿ ⚺ ♆ **10:50 pm** 7:50 pm

5 SATURDAY
☽ ⚹ ♄ **6:56 am** 3:56 am
☉ ☌ ♃ **9:06 am** 6:06 am
☽ ⚺ ♆ **1:01 pm** 10:01 am
☽ ⚹ ☿ **2:49 pm** 11:49 am
☽ □ ♇ **11:02 pm** 8:02 pm
♀ ☌ ♂ 11:12 pm

6 SUNDAY
♀ ☌ ♂ **2:12 am**
☽ □ ♂ **3:06 am** 12:06 am
☽ □ ♀ **3:07 am** 12:07 am
☽ ☌ ♅ 10:38 pm

7 MONDAY
☽ ☌ ♅ **1:38 am**
☽ ⚹ ♃ **8:49 am** 5:49 am
☽ ⚹ ☉ **12:03 pm** 9:03 am
☽ □ ♄ **4:56 pm** 1:56 pm
☽ ⚹ ♆ **11:03 pm** 8:03 pm

8 TUESDAY
☽ □ ☿ **9:04 am** 6:04 am
☽ △ ♇ **9:35 am** 6:35 am
☿ ⚺ ♇ **1:05 pm** 10:05 am
☽ △ ♂ **5:40 pm** 2:40 pm
☽ △ ♀ **6:27 pm** 3:27 pm

9 WEDNESDAY
☽ ⚺ ♅ **1:35 pm** 10:35 am
☽ □ ♃ **10:07 pm** 7:07 pm

10 THURSDAY
☽ □ ☉ **5:45 am** 2:45 am
☽ △ ♄ **5:48 am** 2:48 am
☉ ⚺ ♄ **6:17 am** 3:17 am
☽ □ ♆ **11:43 am** 8:43 am
☽ ⚻ ♇ **10:23 pm** 7:23 pm

11 FRIDAY
☽ △ ☿ **7:00 am** 4:00 am
☽ ⚻ ♂ **10:34 am** 7:34 am
☽ ⚻ ♀ **12:19 pm** 9:19 am
☽ ⚹ ♅ 11:37 pm

12 SATURDAY
☽ ⚹ ♅ **2:37 am**
☽ △ ♃ **12:07 pm** 9:07 am
☽ ⚻ ♄ **6:59 pm** 3:59 pm
☽ △ ☉ **11:52 pm** 8:52 pm
☽ △ ♆ 9:25 pm

13 SUNDAY
☽ △ ♆ **12:25 am**
☿ ⚺ ♂ **5:44 am** 1:44 am
☉ ☌ ♆ **7:43 am** 4:43 am
☽ ☍ ♇ **11:44 am** 8:44 am

14 MONDAY
☽ ☍ ♂ **3:17 am** 12:17 am
☽ ⚻ ☿ **5:05 am** 2:05 am
☽ ☍ ♀ **6:00 am** 3:00 am
☽ □ ♅ **3:02 pm** 12:02 pm
☿ ⚺ ♀ **7:51 pm** 4:51 pm
☽ ⚻ ♃ 10:02 pm

15 TUESDAY
☽ ⚻ ♃ **1:02 am**
☽ ☍ ♄ **6:56 am** 3:56 am
☽ ⚻ ♆ **11:46 am** 8:46 am
☽ ⚻ ☉ **4:01 pm** 1:01 pm
☽ ⚻ ♇ **9:29 pm** 6:29 pm

16 WEDNESDAY
☽ ⚻ ♂ **3:35 pm** 12:35 pm
☽ ⚻ ♀ **7:09 pm** 4:09 pm
☽ ☍ ☿ **10:08 pm** 7:08 pm
☽ △ ♅ **11:25 pm** 8:25 pm

17 THURSDAY
☿ ⚹ ♅ **8:13 am** 5:13 am
☽ ☍ ♃ **9:44 am** 6:44 am
☽ ⚻ ♄ **2:44 pm** 11:44 am
☽ ☍ ♆ **7:02 pm** 4:02 pm

18 FRIDAY
☽ ☍ ☉ **3:18 am** 12:18 am
☽ △ ♇ **4:11 am** 1:11 am
☉ ⚹ ♇ **3:37 pm** 12:37 pm
☽ △ ♂ 9:29 pm

19 SATURDAY
☽ △ ♂ **12:29 am**
☽ △ ♀ **4:52 am** 1:52 am
☽ ⚻ ♅ **5:02 am** 2:02 am
♀ □ ♅ **7:16 am** 4:16 am
☽ ⚻ ☿ **11:20 am** 8:20 am
☽ ⚻ ♃ **3:43 pm** 12:43 pm

☽ △ ♄ **7:59 pm** 4:59 pm
☽ ⚻ ♆ **11:53 pm** 8:53 pm

20 SUNDAY
☽ □ ♇ **8:40 am** 5:40 am
☽ ⚻ ☉ **11:45 am** 8:45 am
☿ ☌ ♃ 11:06 pm

21 MONDAY
☿ ☌ ♃ **2:06 am**
☽ □ ♂ **7:17 am** 4:17 am
☽ ☍ ♅ **8:58 am** 5:58 am
☽ □ ♀ **12:34 pm** 9:34 am
☽ △ ♃ **8:09 pm** 5:09 pm
☽ △ ☿ **10:26 pm** 7:26 pm
☽ □ ♄ **11:49 pm** 8:49 pm

22 TUESDAY
☽ △ ♆ **3:26 am** 12:26 am
☿ ⚺ ♄ **9:48 am** 6:48 am
☽ ⚹ ♇ **12:01 pm** 9:01 am
♂ □ ♅ **4:44 pm** 1:44 pm
☽ △ ☉ **6:52 pm** 3:52 pm

23 WEDNESDAY
☽ ⚻ ♅ **12:10 pm** 9:10 am
☽ ⚹ ♂ **1:12 pm** 10:12 am
☿ ☌ ♆ **1:44 pm** 10:44 am
☽ ⚹ ♀ **7:29 pm** 4:29 pm
☽ □ ♃ **11:59 pm** 8:59 pm

24 THURSDAY
☽ ⚹ ♄ **3:09 am** 12:09 am
☽ □ ♆ **6:30 am** 3:30 am
☽ □ ☿ **8:59 am** 5:59 am

☽ ⚺ ♇ **3:00 pm** 12:00 pm
☽ □ ☉ 10:37 pm

25 FRIDAY
☽ □ ☉ **1:37 am**
☽ △ ♅ **3:16 pm** 12:16 pm
☽ ⚺ ♂ **6:59 pm** 3:59 pm
☽ ⚺ ♀ 11:22 pm

26 SATURDAY
☽ ⚺ ♀ **2:22 am**
☽ ⚹ ♃ **3:48 am** 12:48 am
☽ ⚺ ♄ **6:27 am** 3:27 am
☿ ⚹ ♇ **6:35 am** 3:35 am
☽ ⚹ ♆ **9:37 am** 6:37 am
☽ ☌ ♇ **6:04 pm** 3:04 pm
☽ ⚹ ☿ **7:51 pm** 4:51 pm

27 SUNDAY
♀ ⚺ ♃ **3:34 am** 12:34 am
☽ ⚹ ☉ **8:35 am** 5:35 am
☽ □ ♅ **6:38 pm** 3:38 pm
☽ ☌ ♂ 10:08 pm

28 MONDAY
☽ ☌ ♂ **1:08 am**
☽ ⚺ ♃ **8:02 am** 5:02 am
☽ ☌ ♀ **9:48 am** 6:48 am
☽ ☌ ♄ **10:11 am** 7:11 am
☽ ⚺ ♆ **1:10 pm** 10:10 am
♀ ☌ ♄ **3:27 pm** 12:27 pm
☽ ⚺ ♇ **9:40 pm** 6:40 pm

29 TUESDAY
☽ ⚺ ☿ **7:52 am** 4:52 am
☽ ⚺ ☉ **4:27 pm** 1:27 pm
☽ ⚹ ♅ **10:54 pm** 7:54 pm

30 WEDNESDAY
♀ ⚺ ♆ **8:15 am** 5:15 am
☽ ⚺ ♂ **8:27 am** 5:27 am
☽ ☌ ♃ **1:24 pm** 10:24 am
☽ ⚺ ♄ **3:04 pm** 12:04 pm
☽ ☌ ♆ **5:55 pm** 2:55 pm
☽ ⚺ ♀ **6:42 pm** 3:42 pm
☽ ⚹ ♇ 11:37 pm

31 THURSDAY
☽ ⚹ ♇ **2:37 am**
☽ ☌ ☿ **10:35 pm** 7:35 pm
☽ ☌ ☉ 11:24 pm

Eastern time in bold type
Pacific time in medium type

MARCH 2022

DATE	SID. TIME	SUN	MOON	NODE	MERCURY	VENUS	MARS	JUPITER	SATURN	URANUS	NEPTUNE	PLUTO	CERES	PALLAS	JUNO	VESTA	CHIRON
1 T	10 35 7	10♓42 15	17♒36	25♉45R	16♒55	25♑35	26♑04	13♓52	18♒48	11♉35	22♓24	27♑46	4♊02	5♈22	10♒46	25♈14	10♈32
2 W	10 39 4	11 42 31	1♓50	25 33	18 01	26 24	26 49	14 06	18 55	11 37	22 26	27 48	4 17	5 45	11 09	25 43	10 35
3 Th	10 43 0	12 42 44	15 50	25 21	19 26	27 13	27 34	14 21	19 02	11 39	22 29	27 50	4 32	6 07	11 33	26 13	10 39
4 F	10 46 57	13 42 56	29 30	25 10	20 52	28 03	28 19	14 35	19 08	11 41	22 31	27 51	4 48	6 30	11 57	26 42	10 42
5 Sa	10 50 53	14 43 06	12♈50	25 01	22 19	28 54	29 03	14 50	19 15	11 43	22 33	27 53	5 03	6 53	12 20	27 12	10 45
6 Su	10 54 50	15 43 13	25 46	24 55	23 48	29 46	29 48	15 04	19 22	11 46	22 35	27 54	5 19	7 15	12 44	27 41	10 48
7 M	10 58 46	16 43 19	8♉21	24 55D	25 18	0♒38	0♒33	15 19	19 29	11 48	22 38	27 55	5 35	7 38	13 07	28 11	10 51
8 T	11 2 43	17 43 23	20 38	24 50	26 49	1 31	1 18	15 33	19 35	11 50	22 40	27 57	5 51	8 01	13 31	28 40	10 55
9 W	11 6 39	18 43 25	2♊40	24 52	28 21	2 25	2 03	15 48	19 42	11 53	22 42	27 58	6 08	8 24	13 55	29 09	10 58
10 Th	11 10 36	19 43 24	14 32	24 51R	29 54	3 19	2 47	16 02	19 49	11 55	22 44	28 00	6 24	8 48	14 18	29 38	11 01
11 F	11 14 33	20 43 22	26 21	24 49	1♓28	4 13	3 32	16 17	19 55	11 58	22 47	28 02	6 41	9 11	14 42	0♉07	11 05
12 Sa	11 18 29	21 43 17	8♋12	24 45	3 04	5 09	4 17	16 31	20 02	12 00	22 49	28 04	6 58	9 34	15 05	0 36	11 08
13 Su	11 22 26	22 43 10	20 09	24 45	4 41	6 04	5 02	16 46	20 08	12 03	22 51	28 05	7 15	9 57	15 29	1 04	11 11
14 M	11 26 22	23 43 01	2♌17	24 39	6 19	7 01	5 47	17 00	20 14	12 05	22 54	28 06	7 33	10 21	15 52	1 33	11 15
15 T	11 30 19	24 42 50	14 40	24 30	7 58	7 58	6 32	17 15	20 21	12 08	22 56	28 07	7 50	10 44	16 15	2 02	11 18
16 W	11 34 15	25 42 36	27 20	24 21	9 38	8 55	7 17	17 29	20 27	12 10	22 58	28 09	8 08	11 08	16 39	2 30	11 21
17 Th	11 38 12	26 42 21	10♍19	24 14	11 20	9 53	8 02	17 44	20 34	12 13	23 00	28 10	8 26	11 32	17 02	2 59	11 25
18 F	11 42 8	27 42 03	23 35	24 00	13 02	10 51	8 47	17 58	20 40	12 16	23 03	28 11	8 44	11 55	17 25	3 27	11 28
19 Sa	11 46 5	28 41 43	7♎07	23 51	14 46	11 49	9 32	18 13	20 46	12 18	23 05	28 12	9 02	12 19	17 48	3 55	11 32
20 Su	11 50 2	29 41 22	20 53	23 45	16 31	12 48	10 17	18 27	20 52	12 21	23 07	28 12	9 21	12 43	18 12	4 23	11 35
21 M	11 53 58	0♈40 58	4♏48	23 41	18 18	13 48	11 02	18 41	20 58	12 24	23 09	28 13	9 39	13 07	18 35	4 51	11 39
22 T	11 57 55	1 40 33	18 51	23 39D	20 05	14 48	11 47	18 56	21 04	12 27	23 12	28 14	9 58	13 31	18 58	5 19	11 42
23 W	12 1 51	2 40 06	2♐57	23 39	21 54	15 48	12 33	19 10	21 10	12 30	23 14	28 15	10 17	13 55	19 21	5 47	11 46
24 Th	12 5 48	3 39 37	17 06	23 39	23 45	16 48	13 18	19 24	21 16	12 33	23 16	28 17	10 36	14 19	19 44	6 15	11 49
25 F	12 9 44	4 39 07	1♑14	23 41R	25 36	17 49	14 03	19 39	21 22	12 35	23 18	28 18	10 56	14 43	20 07	6 43	11 53
26 Sa	12 13 41	5 38 34	15 22	23 41	27 29	18 51	14 48	19 53	21 28	12 38	23 21	28 19	11 15	15 07	20 30	7 10	11 56
27 Su	12 17 37	6 38 01	29 28	23 38	29 23	19 52	15 33	20 07	21 34	12 41	23 23	28 20	11 35	15 32	20 53	7 38	12 00
28 M	12 21 34	7 37 25	13♒29	23 34	1♈18	20 54	16 19	20 21	21 40	12 44	23 25	28 20	11 54	15 56	21 16	8 05	12 03
29 T	12 25 31	8 36 47	27 24	23 21	3 15	21 56	17 04	20 36	21 46	12 47	23 27	28 21	12 14	16 20	21 39	8 32	12 07
30 W	12 29 27	9 36 08	11♓09	23 23	5 13	22 59	17 49	20 50	21 51	12 50	23 30	28 22	12 34	16 45	22 01	8 59	12 10
31 Th	12 33 24	10 35 27	24 42	23 13	7 12	24 02	18 34	21 04	21 57	12 52	23 32	28 23	12 54	17 09	22 24	9 26	12 14

EPHEMERIS CALCULATED FOR 12 MIDNIGHT GREENWICH MEAN TIME. ALL OTHER DATA AND FACING ASPECTARIAN PAGE IN **EASTERN TIME (BOLD)** AND PACIFIC TIME (REGULAR).

APRIL 2022

☽ Last Aspect day	ET / hr:mn / PT	asp	☽ Ingress sign day	ET / hr:mn / PT
2	**9:51 am** 6:51 am	□ ♇	♉ 2	**12:50 pm** 9:50 am
4	**9:53 pm** 6:53 pm	□ ♀	♊ 4	**11:04 pm** 8:04 pm
6	**11:15 pm** 8:15 pm	△ ♂	♋ 7	**11:30 am** 8:30 am
9	**9:01 pm** 6:01 pm	☍ ♇	♌ 9	9:00 pm
9	**9:01 pm** 6:01 pm	☍ ♇	♌ 10	**12:00 am**
12	**6:16 am** 3:16 am	☍ ♂	♍ 12	**10:07 am** 7:07 am
14	**2:11 pm** 11:11 am	△ ♇	♎ 14	**4:46 pm** 1:46 pm
16	**5:57 pm** 2:57 pm	□ ♇	♏ 16	**8:23 pm** 5:23 pm
18	**7:55 pm** 4:55 pm	⚹ ♇	♐ 18	**10:16 pm** 7:16 pm
20	**4:56 pm** 1:56 pm	□ ♃	♑ 20	**11:52 pm** 8:52 pm
22	**11:53 pm** 8:53 pm	☌ ♇	♒ 22	11:17 pm
22	**11:53 pm** 8:53 pm	☌ ♇	♒ 23	**2:17 am**
24	**8:33 pm** 5:33 pm	□ ☿	♓ 25	**6:15 am** 3:15 am
27	**9:36 am** 6:36 am	⚹ ♇	♈ 27	**12:10 pm** 9:10 am
29	**5:38 pm** 2:38 pm	□ ♇	♉ 29	**8:19 pm** 5:19 pm

☽ Phases & Eclipses phase	day	ET / hr:mn / PT
New Moon	3/31	11:24 pm
New Moon	1	**2:24 am**
2nd Quarter	8	11:48 pm
2nd Quarter	9	**2:48 am**
Full Moon	16	**2:55 pm** 11:55 am
4th Quarter	23	**7:56 am** 4:56 am
New Moon	30	**4:28 pm** 1:28 pm
●	30	10° ♉ 28'

Planet Ingress	day	ET / hr:mn / PT
♀ ♓	5	**11:18 am** 8:18 am
☿ ♉	10	**10:09 pm** 7:09 pm
♂ ♓	14	**11:06 pm** 8:06 pm
☉ ♉	19	**10:24 pm** 7:24 pm
⚵ ♓	20	**11:51 am** 8:51 am
☿ ♊	29	**6:23 pm** 3:23 pm
♀ ♉	30	**4:50 am** 1:50 am

Planetary Motion	day	ET / hr:mn / PT
♇ ℞	29	**2:38 pm** 11:38 am

1 FRIDAY
☽ ☌ ☉ **2:24 am**
☽ ⚺ ♅ **4:59 am** 1:59 am
☽ ⚹ ♂ **6:07 pm** 3:07 pm
☽ ⚺ ♃ **8:57 pm** 5:57 pm
☽ ⚹ ♄ **10:04 pm** 7:04 pm
☽ ⚺ ♆ 9:49 pm

2 SATURDAY
☽ ⚺ ♆ **12:49 am**
☽ ⚹ ♀ **6:24 am** 3:24 am
☽ □ ♇ **9:51 am** 6:51 am
☉ ⚺ ♅ **2:10 pm** 11:10 am
☿ ⚺ ♅ **4:49 pm** 1:49 pm
☉ ☌ ☿ **7:11 pm** 4:11 pm

3 SUNDAY
☽ ☌ ♅ **1:47 pm** 10:47 am
☽ ⚺ ☉ **3:43 pm** 12:43 pm
☽ ⚺ ☿ **5:50 pm** 2:50 pm
♀ ⚺ ♇ 9:16 pm

4 MONDAY
♀ ⚺ ♇ **12:16 am**
☽ □ ♂ **7:09 am** 4:09 am
☽ ⚹ ♃ **7:29 am** 4:29 am
☽ □ ♄ **7:58 am** 4:58 am
☽ ⚹ ♆ **10:36 am** 7:36 am
♂ ⚺ ♃ **2:47 pm** 11:47 am
☽ △ ♇ **8:00 pm** 5:00 pm
♂ ☌ ♄ **9:51 pm** 6:51 pm
☽ □ ♀ **9:53 pm** 6:53 pm

Eastern time in bold type
Pacific time in medium type

5 TUESDAY
♃ ⚺ ♄ **11:24 pm** 8:24 pm
☽ ⚺ ♅ 10:25 pm

6 WEDNESDAY
☽ ⚺ ♅ **1:25 am**
☽ ⚹ ☉ **8:32 am** 5:32 am
♂ ⚺ ♆ **5:34 pm** 2:34 pm
☽ ⚹ ☿ **5:57 pm** 2:57 pm
☽ △ ♄ **8:26 pm** 5:26 pm
☽ □ ♃ **8:42 pm** 5:42 pm
☽ □ ♆ **10:54 pm** 7:54 pm
☽ △ ♂ **11:15 pm** 8:15 pm

7 THURSDAY
☽ ⚻ ♇ **8:25 am** 5:25 am
☿ ⚹ ♄ **8:37 am** 5:37 am
☿ ⚺ ♃ **11:14 am** 8:14 am
☽ △ ♀ **4:20 pm** 1:20 pm
☿ ⚺ ♆ **10:33 pm** 7:33 pm

8 FRIDAY
☿ ⚹ ♂ **2:19 pm** 11:19 am
☽ ⚹ ♅ **2:28 pm** 11:28 am
☽ □ ☉ 11:48 pm

9 SATURDAY
☽ □ ☉ **2:48 am**
☽ ⚻ ♄ **9:35 am** 6:35 am
☽ △ ♃ **10:36 am** 7:36 am
☽ △ ♆ **11:46 am** 8:46 am
☽ ⚻ ♂ **4:01 pm** 1:01 pm
☽ □ ☿ **7:25 pm** 4:25 pm
☽ ☍ ♇ **9:01 pm** 6:01 pm

10 SUNDAY
☿ □ ♇ **4:45 am** 1:45 am
☽ ⚻ ♀ **10:37 am** 7:37 am
☽ □ ♅ 11:25 pm

11 MONDAY
☽ □ ♅ **2:25 am**
☽ △ ☉ **7:01 pm** 4:01 pm
☽ ☍ ♄ **8:50 pm** 5:50 pm
☽ ⚻ ♃ **10:30 pm** 7:30 pm
☽ ⚻ ♆ **10:42 pm** 7:42 pm

12 TUESDAY
☽ ☍ ♂ **6:16 am** 3:16 am
☽ ⚻ ♇ **7:21 am** 4:21 am
♃ ☌ ♆ **10:42 am** 7:42 am
☽ △ ☿ **4:55 pm** 1:55 pm
☉ ⚹ ♄ **8:14 pm** 5:14 pm
♂ ⚺ ♇ 9:30 pm
☽ ☍ ♀ 10:27 pm

13 WEDNESDAY
♂ ⚺ ♇ **12:30 am**
☽ ☍ ♀ **1:27 am**
☽ △ ♅ **11:15 am** 8:15 am
☉ ⚺ ♆ **7:48 pm** 4:48 pm

14 THURSDAY
☉ ⚺ ♃ **4:14 am** 1:14 am
☽ ⚻ ♄ **4:37 am** 1:37 am
☽ ☍ ♆ **6:11 am** 3:11 am
☽ ☍ ♃ **6:49 am** 3:49 am
☽ ⚻ ☉ **6:58 am** 3:58 am
☽ △ ♇ **2:11 pm** 11:11 am
☽ ⚻ ♂ **4:23 pm** 1:23 pm

15 FRIDAY
☽ ⚻ ☿ **8:12 am** 5:12 am
☽ ⚻ ♀ **11:48 am** 8:48 am
☽ ⚻ ♅ **4:37 pm** 1:37 pm

16 SATURDAY
☽ △ ♄ **9:06 am** 6:06 am
☽ ⚻ ♆ **10:26 am** 7:26 am
☽ ⚻ ♃ **11:45 am** 8:45 am
☽ ☍ ☉ **2:55 pm** 11:55 am
☽ □ ♇ **5:57 pm** 2:57 pm
☽ △ ♂ **10:55 pm** 7:55 pm

17 SUNDAY
☽ ☍ ☿ **6:43 pm** 3:43 pm
☽ △ ♀ **6:51 pm** 3:51 pm
☽ ☍ ♅ **7:28 pm** 4:28 pm
☿ ⚹ ♀ **9:09 pm** 6:09 pm
☿ ☌ ♅ 9:51 pm

18 MONDAY
☿ ☌ ♅ **12:51 am**
♀ ⚹ ♅ **3:15 am** 12:15 am
☉ □ ♇ **11:14 am** 8:14 am
☽ □ ♄ **11:31 am** 8:31 am
☽ △ ♆ **12:40 pm** 9:40 am
☽ △ ♃ **2:37 pm** 11:37 am
☽ ⚹ ♇ **7:55 pm** 4:55 pm
☽ ⚻ ☉ **8:32 pm** 5:32 pm

19 TUESDAY
☽ □ ♂ **3:30 am** 12:30 am
☽ ⚻ ♅ **9:15pm** 6:15pm
☽ □ ♀ 9:33 pm

20 WEDNESDAY
☽ □ ♀ **12:33 am**
☽ ⚻ ☿ **3:02 am** 12:02 am
☽ ⚹ ♄ **1:18 pm** 10:18 am
☽ □ ♆ **2:20 pm** 11:20 am
☽ □ ♃ **4:56 pm** 1:56 pm
☽ ⚺ ♇ **9:31 pm** 6:31 pm
☽ △ ☉ 10:43 pm

21 THURSDAY
☽ △ ☉ **1:43 am**
☽ ⚹ ♂ **7:53 am** 4:53 am
☽ △ ♅ **11:18 pm** 8:18 pm

22 FRIDAY
☽ ⚹ ♀ **6:43 am** 3:43 am
☽ △ ☿ **11:13 am** 8:13 am
☽ ⚺ ♄ **3:43 pm** 12:43 pm
☽ ⚹ ♆ **4:38 pm** 1:38 pm
☽ ⚹ ♃ **7:58 pm** 4:58 pm
☽ ☌ ♇ **11:53 pm** 8:53 pm

23 SATURDAY
☽ □ ☉ **7:56 am** 4:56 am
☽ ⚺ ♂ **1:24 pm** 10:24 am
☽ □ ♅ 11:35 pm

24 SUNDAY
☽ □ ♅ **2:35 am**
☿ □ ♄ **9:50 am** 6:50 am
☽ ⚺ ♀ **2:33 pm** 11:33 am
☿ ⚹ ♆ **6:37 pm** 3:37 pm
☽ ☌ ♄ **7:33 pm** 4:33 pm
☽ ⚺ ♆ **8:22 pm** 5:22 pm
☽ □ ☿ **8:33 pm** 5:33 pm
☽ ⚺ ♃ 9:32 pm

25 MONDAY
☽ ⚺ ♃ **12:32 am**
☽ ⚺ ♇ **3:46 am** 12:46 am
☽ ⚹ ☉ **4:09 pm** 1:09 pm
☽ ☌ ♂ **8:51 pm** 5:51 pm

26 TUESDAY
☽ ⚹ ♅ **7:39 am** 4:39 am
☽ ☌ ♀ 9:50 pm
☿ ⚹ ♃ 10:11 pm
☽ ⚺ ♄ 10:18 pm
☽ ☌ ♆ 11:02 pm

27 WEDNESDAY
☽ ☌ ♀ **12:50 am**
☿ ⚹ ♃ **1:11 am**
☽ ⚺ ♄ **1:18 am**
☽ ☌ ♆ **2:02 am**
♀ ⚺ ♄ **6:43 am** 3:43 am
☽ ☌ ♃ **7:07 am** 4:07 am
☽ ⚹ ☿ **7:35 am** 4:35 am
☽ ⚹ ♇ **9:36 am** 6:36 am
♀ ☌ ♆ **3:12 pm** 12:12 pm
☽ ⚺ ☉ 11:52 pm

28 THURSDAY
☽ ⚺ ☉ **2:52 am**
☽ ⚺ ♂ **6:45 am** 3:45 am
☿ △ ♇ **8:05 am** 5:05 am
☽ ⚺ ♅ **2:52 pm** 11:52 am

29 FRIDAY
☽ ⚹ ♄ **9:16 am** 6:16 am
☽ ⚺ ♆ **9:53 am** 6:53 am
☽ ⚺ ♀ **1:59 pm** 10:59 am
☽ ⚺ ♃ **4:01 pm** 1:01 pm
☽ □ ♇ **5:38 pm** 2:38 pm
☽ ⚺ ☿ **8:28 pm** 5:28 pm

30 SATURDAY
☽ ☌ ☉ **4:28 pm** 1:28 pm
♀ ☌ ♃ **5:14 pm** 2:14 pm
☽ ⚹ ♂ **7:23 pm** 4:23 pm
☽ ☌ ♅ 9:24 pm

APRIL 2022

DATE	SID. TIME	SUN	MOON	NODE	MERCURY	VENUS	MARS	JUPITER	SATURN	URANUS	NEPTUNE	PLUTO	CERES	PALLAS	JUNO	VESTA	CHIRON
1 F	12 37 20	11♈14 43	8♉00	23♉06R	9♈12	25♓05	19≈20	21♓18	22≈02	12♉53	23♓34	28♑24	13♑15	17♈34	22≈47	9≈53	12♈17
2 Sa	12 41 17	12 13 58	21 02	23 01	11 13	26 08	20 05	21 32	22 08	12 56	23 36	28 25	13 35	17 59	23 09	10 20	12 21
3 Su	12 45 13	13 13 10	3♊06	22 57	13 15	27 11	20 50	21 46	22 13	13 00	23 38	28 26	13 56	18 23	23 32	10 46	12 24
4 M	12 49 10	14 12 21	16 14	22 55D	15 22	28 15	21 35	22 00	22 19	13 03	23 41	28 26	14 16	18 48	23 54	11 13	12 28
5 T	12 53 6	15 11 29	28 27	22 55	17 22	29 19	22 21	22 14	22 24	13 06	23 43	28 27	14 37	19 13	24 17	11 39	12 31
6 W	12 57 3	16 10 35	10♋28	22 56	19 27	0♈23	23 06	22 28	22 29	13 09	23 45	28 28	14 58	19 38	24 39	12 06	12 35
7 Th	13 1 0	17 09 39	22 21	22 58	21 31	1 28	23 51	22 42	22 34	13 12	23 47	28 28	15 19	20 03	25 02	12 32	12 38
8 F	13 4 56	18 08 41	4♌11	23 00	23 36	2 32	24 37	22 56	22 39	13 15	23 49	28 29	15 40	20 28	25 24	12 58	12 42
9 Sa	13 8 53	19 07 40	16 02	23 01R	25 41	3 37	25 22	23 09	22 44	13 19	23 51	28 30	16 02	20 53	25 46	13 24	12 45
10 Su	13 12 49	20 06 37	28 00	23 00	27 45	4 42	26 07	23 23	22 49	13 22	23 53	28 30	16 23	21 18	26 08	13 49	12 49
11 M	13 16 46	21 05 32	10♍08	22 59	29 49	5 48	26 53	23 37	22 54	13 25	23 55	28 31	16 44	21 43	26 30	14 15	12 52
12 T	13 20 42	22 04 25	22 33	22 52	1♉52	6 53	27 38	23 50	22 59	13 28	23 57	28 31	17 06	22 08	26 52	14 40	12 56
13 W	13 24 39	23 03 15	5♎17	22 52	3 53	7 59	28 23	24 04	23 04	13 32	24 00	28 32	17 28	22 34	27 14	15 06	12 59
14 Th	13 28 35	24 02 03	18 22	22 47	5 53	9 04	29 09	24 18	23 08	13 35	24 02	28 32	17 50	22 59	27 36	15 31	13 03
15 F	13 32 32	25 00 49	1♏50	22 43	7 50	10 10	29 54	24 31	23 13	13 38	24 04	28 33	18 12	23 24	27 58	15 56	13 06
16 Sa	13 36 29	25 59 32	15 39	22 39	9 45	11 16	0♓40	24 45	23 18	13 42	24 06	28 33	18 34	23 50	28 20	16 21	13 10
17 Su	13 40 25	26 58 14	29 47	22 36	11 38	12 23	1 25	24 58	23 22	13 45	24 08	28 34	18 56	24 15	28 41	16 46	13 13
18 M	13 44 22	27 56 54	14♐08	22 35D	13 27	13 29	2 10	25 11	23 26	13 48	24 10	28 34	19 18	24 41	29 03	17 10	13 17
19 T	13 48 18	28 55 32	28 37	22 36	15 13	14 36	2 56	25 25	23 31	13 52	24 12	28 34	19 41	25 06	29 24	17 35	13 20
20 W	13 52 15	29 54 08	13♑10	22 37	16 56	15 43	3 41	25 38	23 35	13 55	24 13	28 35	20 03	25 32	29 46	17 59	13 23
21 Th	13 56 11	0♉52 42	27 40	22 38	18 35	16 50	4 26	25 51	23 39	13 58	24 15	28 35	20 26	25 57	0♓07	18 23	13 27
22 F	14 0 8	1 51 15	12≈04	22 38	20 09	17 57	5 12	26 04	23 43	14 02	24 17	28 35	20 48	26 23	0 29	18 47	13 30
23 Sa	14 4 4	2 49 47	26 18	22 39R	21 40	19 04	5 57	26 17	23 47	14 05	24 19	28 35	21 11	26 49	0 50	19 11	13 34
24 Su	14 8 1	3 48 16	10♓21	22 39	23 06	20 11	6 42	26 30	23 51	14 09	24 21	28 35	21 34	27 15	1 11	19 35	13 37
25 M	14 11 58	4 46 44	24 10	22 38	24 27	21 19	7 28	26 43	23 55	14 12	24 23	28 36	21 57	27 40	1 32	20 00	13 40
26 T	14 15 54	5 45 11	7♈46	22 36	25 44	22 26	8 13	26 56	23 59	14 16	24 25	28 36	22 20	28 06	1 53	20 22	13 44
27 W	14 19 51	6 43 36	21 08	22 34	26 57	23 34	8 59	27 09	24 02	14 19	24 27	28 36	22 43	28 32	2 14	20 45	13 47
28 Th	14 23 47	7 41 59	4♉16	22 32	28 04	24 42	9 44	27 22	24 06	14 22	24 28	28 36	23 06	28 58	2 34	21 08	13 50
29 F	14 27 44	8 40 20	17 10	22 30	29 06	25 50	10 29	27 34	24 10	14 26	24 30	28 36R	23 29	29 24	2 55	21 31	13 54
30 Sa	14 31 40	9 38 40	29 50	22 29	0♉04	26 58	11 16	27 47	24 13	14 29	24 32	28 36	23 53	29 50	3 16	21 53	13 57

EPHEMERIS CALCULATED FOR 12 MIDNIGHT GREENWICH MEAN TIME. ALL OTHER DATA AND FACING ASPECTARIAN PAGE IN **EASTERN TIME (BOLD)** AND PACIFIC TIME (REGULAR).

MAY 2022

Eastern time in bold type
Pacific time in medium type

D Last Aspect

day	ET / hr:mn / PT	asp
2	**6:13 am** 3:13 am	✱ □
4	**4:37 pm** 1:37 pm	⚹ □
6	**6:26 am** 3:26 am	△
8	**8:39 am** 5:39 am	□
9	9:00 pm	△
12	**12:00 am**	
14	**4:07 am** 1:07 am	
16	**5:28 am** 2:28 am	
17	11:59 pm 8:59 pm	
20	**8:00 am** 5:00 am	△

D Ingress

sign	day	ET / hr:mn / PT
Ⅱ	2	**6:47 am** 3:47 am
♋	4	**7:05 pm** 4:05 pm
♌	7	**7:50 am** 4:50 am
♍	9	**6:53 pm** 3:53 pm
≏	12	**2:34 am**
♏	14	**6:34 am** 3:34 am
♐	16	**7:50 am** 4:50 am
♑	18	**8:02 am** 5:02 am
♒	20	**8:53 am** 5:53 am

D Last Aspect

day	ET / hr:mn / PT	asp
22	**3:19 am** 12:19 am	
24	**4:33 pm** 1:33 pm	
26	11:20 am 8:20 am	
26	11:20 am 8:20 am	
29	10:11 am 7:11 am	
31	**4:10 pm** 1:10 pm	
31	**4:10 pm** 1:10 pm	

D Ingress

sign	day	ET / hr:mn / PT
✕	22	**11:49 am** 8:49 am
♈	24	**5:39 pm** 2:39 pm
♉	26	
♉	27	
Ⅱ	29	9:03 am
♋	31	
♌	6/1	**1:49 am**

Planet Ingress

	day	ET / hr:mn / PT
♀ ♈	2	**12:10 am** 9:10 am
♀ ♉	10	**7:22 am** 4:22 pm
♂ ♓	10	**3:11 am** 12:11 am
⊙ Ⅱ	20	**9:23 am** 6:23 am
☿ ♍	22	**9:15 am** 6:15 am
♀ Ⅱ	24	**5:46 am** 2:46 am
☿ ♋	24	**7:17 am** 4:17 pm
♀ ♋	28	**10:46 am** 7:46 am

D Phases & Eclipses

phase	day	ET / hr:mn / PT
2nd Quarter	8	**8:21 pm** 5:21 pm
Full Moon	15	9:14 pm
Full Moon	16	**12:14 am**
Full Moon	16	**12:14 am**
		15/16 25° ♏, 18'
4th Quarter	22	**2:43 pm** 11:43 am
New Moon	30	**7:30 am** 4:30 am

Planetary Motion

	day	ET / hr:mn / PT
♇ R	10	**7:47 am** 4:47 am

---

1 SUNDAY
- **12:24 am**
- **6:37 am** 3:37 am
- **7:33 pm** 4:33 pm
- **8:04 pm** 5:04 pm

2 MONDAY
- **3:19 am** 12:19 am
- **4:00 am** 1:00 am
- **6:13 am** 3:13 am
- **11:05 am** 8:05 am

3 TUESDAY
- **8:54 am** 5:54 am
- **10:41 am** 7:41 am
- **12:10 pm** 9:10 am
- **6:33 pm** 3:33 pm

4 WEDNESDAY
- **7:51 am** 4:51 am
- **8:16 am** 5:16 am
- **11:47 am** 8:47 am
- **4:14 pm** 1:14 pm
- **4:37 pm** 1:37 pm

5 THURSDAY
- **12:57 am**
- **2:33 am**
- **3:22 am** 12:22 am

- 10:13 pm
- 11:01 pm

6 FRIDAY
- **1:13 am**
- **2:01 am**
- **3:03 am** 12:03 am
- **3:34 am** 12:34 am
- **8:55 pm** 5:55 pm
- **9:13 pm** 6:13 pm

7 SATURDAY
- **4:59 am** 1:59 am
- **5:48 am** 2:48 am
- **6:26 am** 3:26 am
- **4:59 pm** 1:59 pm
- **8:02 pm** 5:02 pm

8 SUNDAY
- **1:41 am**
- **7:38 pm** 4:38 pm
- **8:21 pm** 5:21 pm

9 MONDAY
- **8:39 am** 5:39 am
- **8:50 am** 5:50 am
- **4:09 pm** 1:09 pm
- **6:30 pm** 3:30 pm

10 TUESDAY
- **4:10 am** 1:10 am
- **12:19 pm** 12:22 pm
- **11:27 pm** 8:27 pm

11 WEDNESDAY
- **8:17 am** 5:17 am
- **10:02 am** 7:02 am
- **5:10 pm** 2:10 pm
- **5:17 pm** 2:17 pm
- 9:00 pm

12 THURSDAY
- **12:00 am**
- **3:02 am** 12:02 am
- **10:54 am** 7:54 am
- **11:49 am** 8:49 am

13 FRIDAY
- **5:27 am** 2:27 am
- **4:28 am** 1:28 am
- **7:00 pm** 4:00 pm
- **9:54 pm** 6:54 pm
- **9:57 pm** 6:57 pm

14 SATURDAY
- **4:07 am** 1:07 am
- **7:42 am** 4:42 am
- **1:31 pm** 10:31 am

15 SUNDAY
- **6:55 am** 3:55 am
- **8:04 am** 5:04 am
- **2:49 pm** 11:49 am
- **3:15 pm** 12:15 pm
- **9:02 pm** 6:02 pm
- **10:14 pm** 7:14 pm

- 11:38 pm 8:38 pm
- 11:40 pm 8:40 pm

16 MONDAY
- **12:14 am**
- **5:28 am** 2:28 am
- **9:34 am** 6:34 am
- **1:19 pm** 10:19 am

17 TUESDAY
- **8:46 am** 5:46 am
- **11:31 am** 8:31 am
- **11:39 am** 8:39 am
- **11:51 am** 8:51 am
- **11:59 am** 8:59 am
- 11:33 pm
- 11:43 pm

18 WEDNESDAY
- **2:33 am**
- **2:43 am**
- **3:48 am** 12:48 am
- **5:39 am** 2:39 am
- **10:21 am** 7:21 am
- **12:00 pm** 9:00 am

19 THURSDAY
- **8:11 am** 5:11 am
- **11:06 am** 8:06 am
- **4:02 pm** 1:02 pm
- **9:33 pm** 6:33 pm

20 FRIDAY
- **12:41 pm**
- **12:43 pm**
- **3:07 pm** 12:07 pm
- **6:24 am** 3:24 am
- **8:00 am** 5:00 am
- **11:11 am** 8:11 am
- **11:54 am** 8:54 am

21 SATURDAY
- **11:16 am** 8:16 am
- **3:18 pm** 12:18 pm
- **10:40 pm** 7:40 pm

22 SUNDAY
- **3:17 am** 12:17 am
- **3:19 am** 12:19 am
- **8:39 am** 5:39 am
- **9:11 am** 6:11 am
- **12:12 pm** 9:12 am
- **3:40 pm** 12:40 pm
- **6:15 pm** 3:15 pm

23 MONDAY
- **2:33 am**
- **7:05 pm** 4:05 pm
- **3:54 pm** 12:54 pm
- **2:56 am** 11:56 pm
- **11:27 am** 8:27 am

24 TUESDAY
- **6:30 am** 3:30 am
- **7:06 am** 4:06 am
- **8:41 am** 5:41 am
- **8:45 am** 5:45 am

25 WEDNESDAY
- **8:54 am** 5:54 am
- **2:49 pm** 11:49 am
- **3:50 am** 12:50 am
- **5:33 pm** 2:33 pm
- **10:27 pm** 7:27 pm
- 10:03

26 THURSDAY
- **1:03 am**
- **5:49 am** 2:49 am
- **11:33 am** 8:33 am

27 FRIDAY
- **5:03 pm** 2:03 pm
- **5:06 pm** 2:06 pm
- **5:07 pm** 2:07 pm
- **10:16 pm** 7:16 pm
- **11:00 pm** 8:00 pm
- **11:29 pm** 8:29 pm

28 SATURDAY
- **2:29 am**
- **8:12 am** 5:12 am
- **2:56 pm** 11:56 am

29 SUNDAY
- **3:49 am** 12:49 am
- **3:51 am** 12:51 am
- **6:31 am** 3:31 am
- **7:15 am** 4:15 am

- **2:54 am**
- **6:50 am**

30 MONDAY
- **7:30 am** 4:30 am
- **10:00 pm** 7:00 pm

31 TUESDAY
- **10:11 am** 7:11 am
- **4:15 pm** 1:15 pm
- **8:12 pm** 5:12 pm
- **8:55 pm** 5:55 pm

- **2:34 am** 11:34 pm
- **4:10 pm** 1:10 pm
- **4:18 pm** 1:10 pm
- **6:03 pm** 3:03 pm
- **6:19 pm** 3:19 pm
- **10:30 pm** 7:30 pm

MAY 2022

DATE	SID.TIME	SUN	MOON	NODE	MERCURY	VENUS	MARS	JUPITER	SATURN	URANUS	NEPTUNE	PLUTO	CERES	PALLAS	JUNO	VESTA	CHIRON
1 Su	14 35 37	10Ⅱ36 58	12♌18	22♉28 58	0Ⅱ56	28♈06	12♓00	27♓59	24≈16	14♉33	24♓34	28♑36R	28Ⅱ16	0♊17	3♈36	22≈16	14♈00
2 M	14 39 33	11 35 14	24 33	22 28	1 43	29 14	12 45	28 12	24 20	14 36	24 35	28 36	28 40	0 43	3 57	22 38	14 03
3 T	14 43 30	12 33 29	6♍38	22 28	2 25	0♉30	13 30	28 24	24 23	14 40	24 37	28 36	25 04	1 09	4 17	23 00	14 05
4 W	14 47 27	13 31 42	18 36	22 29	3 02	1 31	14 16	28 36	24 26	14 43	24 39	28 36	25 27	1 35	4 37	23 22	14 10
5 Th	14 51 23	14 29 52	0♎27	22 30	3 33	2 39	15 01	28 49	24 29	14 47	24 40	28 36	25 51	2 01	4 57	23 43	14 13
6 F	14 55 20	15 28 01	12 16	22 30	3 59	3 48	15 46	29 01	24 32	14 50	24 42	28 36	26 15	2 28	5 17	24 05	14 16
7 Sa	14 59 16	16 26 09	24 08	22 31	4 20	4 57	16 31	29 13	24 35	14 54	24 43	28 35	26 39	2 54	5 37	24 26	14 19
8 Su	15 3 13	17 24 14	6♏05	22 31	4 36	6 05	17 17	29 25	24 37	14 57	24 45	28 35	27 03	3 21	5 57	24 47	14 22
9 M	15 7 9	18 22 17	18 12	22 32R	4 46	7 14	18 02	29 37	24 40	15 01	24 47	28 35	27 27	3 47	6 16	25 08	14 25
10 T	15 11 6	19 20 18	0♐29	22 32	4 51R	8 23	18 47	29 49	24 42	15 04	24 48	28 34	27 51	4 14	6 36	25 29	14 28
11 W	15 15 2	20 18 17	13 17	22 31	4 51	9 32	19 32	0♈00	24 45	15 08	24 50	28 34	28 15	4 40	6 55	25 49	14 31
12 Th	15 18 59	21 16 15	26 21	22 31	4 46	10 41	20 17	0 12	24 47	15 11	24 51	28 34	28 40	5 07	7 14	26 09	14 34
13 F	15 22 56	22 14 11	9♑50	22 31D	4 36	11 51	21 02	0 24	24 49	15 14	24 52	28 33	29 04	5 33	7 33	26 29	14 37
14 Sa	15 26 52	23 12 04	23 45	22 31	4 22	13 00	21 47	0 35	24 52	15 18	24 54	28 33	29 28	6 00	7 52	26 49	14 40
15 Su	15 30 49	24 09 57	8♒03	22 31R	4 04	14 09	22 32	0 46	24 54	15 21	24 55	28 33	29 53	6 27	8 11	27 08	14 43
16 M	15 34 45	25 07 47	22 41	22 31	3 42	15 19	23 17	0 58	24 56	15 25	24 57	28 32	0♋17	6 53	8 30	27 28	14 46
17 T	15 38 42	26 05 37	7♓33	22 31	3 16	16 28	24 02	1 09	24 58	15 28	24 58	28 32	0 42	7 20	8 49	27 47	14 49
18 W	15 42 38	27 03 25	22 30	22 31	2 48	17 38	24 47	1 20	24 59	15 31	24 59	28 31	1 06	7 47	9 07	28 06	14 51
19 Th	15 46 35	28 01 12	7♈24	22 30	2 17	18 47	25 32	1 31	25 01	15 35	25 00	28 31	1 31	8 14	9 25	28 24	14 54
20 F	15 50 31	28 58 57	22 11	22 30	1 45	19 57	26 17	1 42	25 03	15 38	25 02	28 30	1 56	8 41	9 44	28 42	14 57
21 Sa	15 54 28	29 56 41	6♉41	22 29	1 11	21 07	27 02	1 53	25 04	15 42	25 03	28 30	2 21	9 08	10 02	29 00	15 00
22 Su	15 58 25	0Ⅱ54 25	20 51	22 29D	0 36	22 16	27 47	2 03	25 06	15 45	25 04	28 29	2 45	9 35	10 20	29 18	15 02
23 M	16 2 21	1 52 07	4♊40	22 29	0 02	23 26	28 32	2 14	25 07	15 48	25 05	28 28	3 10	10 02	10 37	29 38	15 05
24 T	16 6 18	2 49 48	18 08	22 29	29♉28	24 36	29 17	2 24	25 08	15 52	25 06	28 28	3 35	10 29	10 55	29 53	15 08
25 W	16 10 14	3 47 28	1♋19	22 30	28 55	25 46	0♈01	2 35	25 09	15 55	25 08	28 27	4 00	10 56	11 13	0♓10	15 10
26 Th	16 14 11	4 45 07	14 07	22 31	28 24	26 56	0 46	2 45	25 10	15 58	25 09	28 26	4 25	11 23	11 30	0 27	15 13
27 F	16 18 7	5 42 45	26 42	22 32	27 55	28 07	1 31	2 55	25 11	16 02	25 10	28 26	4 51	11 50	11 47	0 43	15 15
28 Sa	16 22 4	6 40 22	9♍04	22 33	27 28	29 17	2 15	3 05	25 12	16 05	25 11	28 25	5 16	12 18	12 04	0 59	15 18
29 Su	16 26 0	7 37 58	21 16	22 33R	27 05	0♊27	3 00	3 15	25 13	16 08	25 12	28 24	5 41	12 45	12 21	1 15	15 20
30 M	16 29 57	8 35 33	3♎19	22 33	26 45	1 37	3 45	3 25	25 13	16 12	25 13	28 23	6 06	13 12	12 37	1 31	15 22
31 T	16 33 54	9 33 07	15 16	22 32	26 29	2 48	4 29	3 35	25 14	16 15	25 13	28 23	6 32	13 39	12 54	1 46	15 25

EPHEMERIS CALCULATED FOR 12 MIDNIGHT GREENWICH MEAN TIME. ALL OTHER DATA AND FACING ASPECTARIAN PAGE IN **EASTERN TIME (BOLD)** AND PACIFIC TIME (REGULAR).

JUNE 2022

☽ Last Aspect day	ET / hr:mn / PT		asp	☽ Ingress sign	day	ET / hr:mn / PT	
3	**11:15 am**	8:15 am	☍ ♇	♌	3	**2:38 pm**	11:38 am
5	**7:12 pm**	4:12 pm	□ ☿	♍	5		11:22 pm
5	**7:12 pm**	4:12 pm	□ ☿	♍	6	**2:22 am**	
8	**8:09 am**	5:09 am	△ ♇	♎	8	**11:23 am**	8:23 am
10	**1:36 pm**	10:36 am	□ ♇	♏	10	**4:41 pm**	1:41 pm
12	**5:40 pm**	2:40 pm	☍ ☿	♐	12	**6:31 pm**	3:31 pm
14	**10:58 am**	7:58 am	□ ♆	♑	14	**6:14 pm**	3:14 pm
16	**2:41 pm**	11:41 am	☌ ♇	♒	16	**5:44 pm**	2:44 pm
18	**2:50 pm**	11:50 am	△ ☉	♓	18	**7:01 pm**	4:01 pm
20	**11:11 pm**	8:11 pm	□ ☉	♈	20	**11:37 pm**	8:37 pm
23	**4:02 am**	1:02 am	□ ♇	♉	23	**7:58 am**	4:58 am
25	**3:02 pm**	12:02 pm	△ ♇	♊	25	**7:13 pm**	4:13 pm
27	**10:38 pm**	7:38 pm	□ ♆	♋	28	**7:53 am**	4:53 am
30	**4:14 pm**	1:14 pm	☍ ♇	♌	30	**8:40 pm**	5:40 pm

☽ Phases & Eclipses phase	day	ET / hr:mn / PT	
2nd Quarter	7	**10:48 am**	7:48 am
Full Moon	14	**7:52 am**	4:52 am
4th Quarter	20	**11:11 pm**	8:11 pm
New Moon	28	**10:52 pm**	7:52 pm

Planet Ingress		day	ET / hr:mn / PT	
☿	♊	13	**11:27 am**	8:27 am
☉	♋	21	**5:14 am**	2:14 am
♀	♊	22	**8:34 pm**	5:34 pm

Planetary Motion		day	ET / hr:mn / PT	
☿	D	3	**4:00 am**	1:00 am
♄	℞	4	**5:47 pm**	2:47 pm
♆	℞	28	**3:55 am**	12:55 am

1 WEDNESDAY
☽ □ ♃ **9:35 am** 6:35 am
☽ ✶ ♀ **11:24 am** 8:24 am
☽ □ ♂ **1:31 pm** 10:31 am
☽ ⊻ ☉ 10:33 pm

2 THURSDAY
☽ ⊻ ☉ **1:33 am**
☽ ✶ ♅ **11:05 am** 8:05 am

3 FRIDAY
☽ ⊼ ♄ **5:02 am** 2:02 am
☽ △ ♆ **5:05 am** 2:05 am
☽ ✶ ☿ **6:44 am** 3:44 am
☽ ☍ ♇ **11:15 am** 8:15 am
♀ ⊻ ♂ **5:18 pm** 2:18 pm
☽ △ ♃ **11:09 pm** 8:09 pm

4 SATURDAY
☽ △ ♂ **6:15 am** 3:15 am
☽ □ ♀ **6:47 am** 3:47 am
☽ ✶ ☉ **7:23 pm** 4:23 pm
☽ □ ♅ **11:47 pm** 8:47 pm

5 SUNDAY
☽ ☍ ♄ **5:03 pm** 2:03 pm
☽ ⊼ ♆ **5:10 pm** 2:10 pm
☽ □ ☿ **7:12 pm** 4:12 pm
☽ ⊼ ♇ **11:01 pm** 8:01 pm

6 MONDAY
☽ ⊼ ♃ **11:19 am** 8:19 am
☽ ⊼ ♂ **9:09 pm** 6:09 pm
☽ △ ♀ 9:05 pm

7 TUESDAY
☽ △ ♀ **12:05 am**
☉ ⊻ ♅ **5:36 am** 2:36 am
☽ △ ♅ **10:26 am** 7:26 am
☽ □ ☉ **10:48 am** 7:48 am
☽ ⊼ ♄ 11:34 pm
☽ ☍ ♆ 11:44 pm

8 WEDNESDAY
☽ ⊼ ♄ **2:34 am**
☽ ☍ ♆ **2:44 am**
☽ △ ☿ **5:56 am** 2:56 am
☽ △ ♇ **8:09 am** 5:09 am
☽ ☍ ♃ **8:26 pm** 5:26 pm

9 THURSDAY
☽ ☍ ♂ **8:16 am** 5:16 am
☽ ⊼ ♀ **1:08 pm** 10:08 am
☽ ⊼ ♅ **5:39 pm** 2:39 pm
☽ △ ☉ **9:57 pm** 6:57 pm

10 FRIDAY
☽ △ ♄ **8:27 am** 5:27 am
☽ ⊼ ♆ **8:41 am** 5:41 am
☽ ⊼ ☿ **1:27 pm** 10:27 am
☽ □ ♇ **1:36 pm** 10:36 am
☿ △ ♇ **5:21 pm** 2:21 pm
☽ ⊼ ♃ 10:38 pm

11 SATURDAY
☽ ⊼ ♃ **1:38 am**
☽ ⊼ ♂ **2:55 pm** 11:55 am
♀ ☌ ♅ **6:58 pm** 3:58 pm
☽ ☍ ♅ **9:05 pm** 6:05 pm
☽ ☍ ♀ **9:16 pm** 6:16 pm

12 SUNDAY
☽ ⊼ ☉ **4:29 am** 1:29 am
☽ □ ♄ **10:45 am** 7:45 am
☽ △ ♆ **11:01 am** 8:01 am
☽ ✶ ♇ **3:34 pm** 12:34 pm
☽ ☍ ☿ **5:40 pm** 2:40 pm

13 MONDAY
☽ △ ♃ **3:26 am** 12:26 am
☽ △ ♂ **6:05 pm** 3:05 pm
☽ ⊼ ♅ **9:40 pm** 6:40 pm
☽ ⊼ ♀ 10:47 pm

14 TUESDAY
☽ ⊼ ♀ **1:47 am**
☽ ☍ ☉ **7:52 am** 4:52 am
☽ ✶ ♄ **10:38 am** 7:38 am
☽ □ ♆ **10:58 am** 7:58 am
☽ ⊻ ♇ **3:18 pm** 12:18 pm
☽ ⊼ ☿ **7:55 pm** 4:55 pm

15 WEDNESDAY
☽ □ ♃ **3:21 am** 12:21 am
☽ □ ♂ **7:50 pm** 4:50 pm
☽ △ ♅ **9:10 pm** 6:10 pm

16 THURSDAY
☉ △ ♄ **3:13 am** 12:13 am
☽ △ ♀ **5:09 am** 2:09 am
☉ □ ♆ **9:41 am** 6:41 am
☽ ⊻ ♄ **9:58 am** 6:58 am
☽ ✶ ♆ **10:23 am** 7:23 am
☽ ⊼ ☉ **10:26 am** 7:26 am
☽ ☌ ♇ **2:41 pm** 11:41 am
☽ △ ☿ **10:30 pm** 7:30 pm
♂ ⊻ ♅ 10:37 pm

17 FRIDAY
♂ ⊻ ♅ **1:37 am**
☽ ✶ ♃ **3:28 am** 12:28 am
☽ □ ♅ **9:37 pm** 6:37 pm
☽ ✶ ♂ **10:35 pm** 7:35 pm

18 SATURDAY
☽ □ ♀ **10:10 am** 7:10 am
☽ ☌ ♄ **10:47 am** 7:47 am
☽ ⊻ ♆ **11:19 am** 8:19 am
☽ △ ☉ **2:50 pm** 11:50 am
☽ ⊻ ♇ **3:45 pm** 12:45 pm
♀ □ ♄ **5:32 pm** 2:32 pm
♀ ✶ ♆ 9:06 pm

19 SUNDAY
♀ ✶ ♆ **12:06 am**
☽ □ ☿ **4:01 am** 1:01 am
☉ ⊼ ♇ **4:10 am** 1:10 am
☽ ⊻ ♃ **5:45 am** 2:45 am
☽ ✶ ♅ 9:50 pm

20 MONDAY
☽ ✶ ♅ **12:50 am**
☿ ✶ ♃ **3:44 am** 12:44 am
☽ ⊻ ♂ **4:35 am** 1:35 am
☽ ⊻ ♄ **2:41 pm** 11:41 am
☽ ☌ ♆ **3:21 pm** 12:21 pm
☽ ✶ ♀ **7:11 pm** 4:11 pm
☽ ✶ ♇ **8:01 pm** 5:01 pm
☽ □ ☉ **11:11 pm** 8:11 pm

21 TUESDAY
♀ △ ♇ **4:23 am** 1:23 am
☽ ☌ ♃ **11:37 am** 8:37 am
☽ ✶ ☿ **2:34 pm** 11:34 am

22 WEDNESDAY
☽ ⊻ ♅ **7:50 am** 4:50 am
☽ ☌ ♂ **2:58 pm** 11:58 am
☽ ✶ ♄ **10:19 pm** 7:19 pm
☽ ⊻ ♆ **11:10 pm** 8:10 pm

23 THURSDAY
☽ □ ♇ **4:02 am** 1:02 am
☽ ⊻ ♀ **9:10 am** 6:10 am
☽ ✶ ☉ **12:12 pm** 9:12 am
☽ ⊻ ♃ **9:13 pm** 6:13 pm

24 FRIDAY
☽ ⊻ ☿ **6:48 am** 3:48 am
☽ ☌ ♅ **6:15 pm** 3:15 pm

25 SATURDAY
☽ ⊻ ♂ **5:14 am** 2:14 am
☽ □ ♄ **9:02 am** 6:02 am
☽ ✶ ♆ **10:05 am** 7:05 am
☽ △ ♇ **3:02 pm** 12:02 pm

26 SUNDAY
☽ ☌ ♀ **3:03 am** 12:03 am
☽ ⊻ ☉ **4:47 am** 1:47 am
☽ ✶ ♃ **9:27 am** 6:27 am

27 MONDAY
☽ ☌ ☿ **3:22 am** 12:22 am
☽ ⊻ ♅ **6:44 am** 3:44 am
♂ ✶ ♄ **6:29 pm** 3:29 pm
☽ △ ♄ **9:23 pm** 6:23 pm
☽ ✶ ♂ **9:35 pm** 6:35 pm
☽ □ ♆ **10:38 pm** 7:38 pm

28 TUESDAY
☽ ⊼ ♇ **3:33 am** 12:33 am
☿ ⊻ ♅ **5:02 am** 2:02 am
♂ ⊻ ♆ **3:08 pm** 12:08 pm
☉ □ ♃ **8:59 pm** 5:59 pm
☽ ⊻ ♀ **10:37 pm** 7:37 pm
☽ □ ♃ **10:44 pm** 7:44 pm
☽ ☌ ☉ **10:52 pm** 7:52 pm
♀ ✶ ♃ **11:52 pm** 8:52 pm

29 WEDNESDAY
☉ ⊻ ♀ **10:09 am** 7:09 am
☽ ✶ ♅ **7:48 pm** 4:48 pm
☽ ⊻ ☿ 11:00 pm

30 THURSDAY
☽ ⊻ ☿ **2:00 am**
☽ ⊼ ♄ **10:01 am** 7:01 am
☽ △ ♆ **11:28 am** 8:28 am
☽ □ ♂ **2:17 pm** 11:17 am
☽ ☍ ♇ **4:14 pm** 1:14 pm

Eastern time in bold type
Pacific time in medium type

JUNE 2022

DATE	SID.TIME	SUN	MOON	NODE	MERCURY	VENUS	MARS	JUPITER	SATURN	URANUS	NEPTUNE	PLUTO	CERES	PALLAS	JUNO	VESTA	CHIRON
1 W	16 37 50	10♊30 40	27♋08	22♉30R	26♉17R	3♉58	5♈14	3♈44	25♒14	16♉18	25♓14	28♑32R	6♋57	14♉07	13♈10	2♓01	15♈27
2 Th	16 41 47	11 28 12	8♌58	22 27	26 09	5 09	5 58	3 54	25 15	16 21	25 15	28 31	7 22	14 34	13 26	2 16	15 30
3 F	16 45 43	12 25 43	20 47	22 24	26 05D	6 19	6 42	4 03	25 15	16 25	25 16	28 30	7 48	15 02	13 42	2 30	15 32
4 Sa	16 49 40	13 23 12	2♍40	22 20	26 06	7 30	7 27	4 12	25 15R	16 28	25 17	28 29	8 13	15 29	13 58	2 44	15 34
5 Su	16 53 36	14 20 40	14 38	22 18	26 11	8 40	8 11	4 21	25 15	16 31	25 18	28 18	8 39	15 57	14 13	2 58	15 36
6 M	16 57 33	15 18 07	26 45	22 18	26 21	9 51	8 55	4 30	25 15	16 34	25 19	28 17	9 04	16 24	14 29	3 11	15 38
7 T	17 1 29	16 15 33	9♎06	22 14D	26 35	11 01	9 39	4 39	25 15	16 37	25 19	28 16	9 30	16 52	14 44	3 24	15 40
8 W	17 5 26	17 12 58	21 44	22 14	26 54	12 12	10 23	4 48	25 14	16 40	25 20	28 15	9 56	17 19	14 59	3 37	15 42
9 Th	17 9 23	18 10 21	4♏43	22 15	27 17	13 23	11 07	4 57	25 14	16 43	25 20	28 14	10 21	17 47	15 14	3 49	15 44
10 F	17 13 19	19 07 43	18 06	22 16	27 44	14 34	11 51	5 05	25 13	16 47	25 21	28 13	10 47	18 15	15 28	4 01	15 46
11 Sa	17 17 16	20 05 04	1♐56	22 18	28 16	15 45	12 35	5 13	25 13	16 50	25 22	28 12	11 13	18 42	15 42	4 12	15 48
12 Su	17 21 12	21 02 25	16 13	22 19R	28 52	16 56	13 19	5 21	25 13	16 53	25 23	28 11	11 39	19 10	15 56	4 24	15 50
13 M	17 25 9	21 59 44	0♑55	22 19	29 32	18 06	14 03	5 29	25 12	16 56	25 23	28 10	12 05	19 38	16 10	4 35	15 52
14 T	17 29 5	22 57 03	15 55	22 17	0♊16	19 17	14 47	5 37	25 11	16 59	25 24	28 09	12 30	20 06	16 24	4 45	15 54
15 W	17 33 2	23 54 21	1♒07	22 14	1 04	20 28	15 31	5 45	25 10	17 01	25 24	28 08	12 56	20 33	16 37	4 55	15 55
16 Th	17 36 59	24 51 38	16 20	22 10	1 56	21 40	16 14	5 53	25 09	17 04	25 25	28 07	13 22	21 01	16 51	5 05	15 57
17 F	17 40 55	25 48 55	1♓25	22 05	2 52	22 51	16 58	6 00	25 08	17 07	25 25	28 06	13 48	21 29	17 04	5 14	15 59
18 Sa	17 44 52	26 46 12	16 12	22 01	3 52	24 02	17 41	6 08	25 07	17 10	25 25	28 05	14 14	21 57	17 16	5 24	16 00
19 Su	17 48 48	27 43 28	0♈35	21 57	4 55	25 13	18 25	6 15	25 06	17 13	25 25	28 03	14 40	22 25	17 29	5 32	16 02
20 M	17 52 45	28 40 43	14 31	21 55	6 02	26 24	19 08	6 22	25 04	17 16	25 25	28 02	15 06	22 53	17 41	5 40	16 04
21 T	17 56 41	29 37 59	28 00	21 54D	7 12	27 36	19 51	6 29	25 03	17 19	25 26	28 01	15 33	23 21	17 53	5 48	16 05
22 W	18 0 38	0♋35 14	11♉04	21 54	8 26	28 47	20 35	6 35	25 01	17 21	25 26	28 00	15 59	23 49	18 05	5 56	16 06
23 Th	18 4 34	1 32 29	23 47	21 56	9 44	29 58	21 18	6 42	24 59	17 24	25 26	27 58	16 25	24 17	18 16	6 03	16 08
24 F	18 8 31	2 29 44	6♊11	21 57	11 05	1♊10	22 01	6 48	24 58	17 27	25 26	27 56	16 51	24 45	18 27	6 09	16 09
25 Sa	18 12 28	3 26 59	18 22	21 58R	12 29	2 21	22 44	6 55	24 56	17 29	25 27R	27 55	17 17	25 13	18 38	6 15	16 10
26 Su	18 16 24	4 24 14	0♋23	21 58	13 56	3 33	23 27	7 01	24 54	17 32	25 26	27 53	17 44	25 42	18 49	6 21	16 12
27 M	18 20 21	5 21 29	12 18	21 56	15 27	4 44	24 10	7 07	24 52	17 35	25 27	27 52	18 10	26 10	18 59	6 26	16 13
28 T	18 24 17	6 18 43	24 09	21 52	17 02	5 56	24 53	7 12	24 50	17 37	25 27	27 51	18 36	26 38	19 09	6 31	16 14
29 W	18 28 14	7 15 58	5♌58	21 45	18 39	7 07	25 35	7 18	24 47	17 40	25 27	27 50	19 03	27 06	19 19	6 35	16 15
30 Th	18 32 10	8 13 12	17 48	21 38	20 20	8 19	26 18	7 24	24 45	17 42	25 27	27 49	19 29	27 34	19 28	6 39	16 16

EPHEMERIS CALCULATED FOR 12 MIDNIGHT GREENWICH MEAN TIME. ALL OTHER DATA AND FACING ASPECTARIAN PAGE IN **EASTERN TIME (BOLD)** AND PACIFIC TIME (REGULAR).

JULY 2022

☽ Last Aspect day	ET / hr:mn / PT	asp	☽ Ingress sign day	ET / hr:mn / PT
3	**5:59 am** 2:59 am	△♂	♍ 3	**8:31 am** 5:31 am
5	**2:04 pm** 11:04 am	△♇	♎ 5	**6:25 pm** 3:25 pm
7	**9:04 pm** 6:04 pm	□♇	♏ 7	10:15 pm
7	**9:04 pm** 6:04 pm	□♇	♏ 8	**1:15 am**
9	9:34 pm	⚹♇	♐ 10	**4:34 am** 1:34 am
10	**12:34 am**	⚹♇	♐ 10	**4:34 am** 1:34 am
11	**9:42 pm** 6:42 pm	□♆	♑ 12	**5:01 am** 2:01 am
13	9:17 pm	☌♇	♒ 14	**4:13 am** 1:13 am
14	**12:17 am**	☌♇	♒ 14	**4:13 am** 1:13 am
15	9:36 pm	△♀	♓ 16	**4:18 am** 1:18 am
16	**12:36 am**	△♀	♓ 16	**4:18 am** 1:18 am

☽ Last Aspect day	ET / hr:mn / PT	asp	☽ Ingress sign day	ET / hr:mn / PT
17	11:43 pm	⚹♇	♈ 18	**7:17 am** 4:17 am
18	**2:43 am**	⚹♇	♈ 18	**7:17 am** 4:17 am
20	**10:19 am** 7:19 am	□☉	♉ 20	**2:23 pm** 11:23 am
22	**7:45 pm** 4:45 pm	△♇	♊ 22	10:11 pm
22	**7:45 pm** 4:45 pm	△♇	♊ 23	**1:11 am**
25	**4:14 am** 1:14 am	□♆	♋ 25	**1:54 pm** 10:54 am
27	**8:54 pm** 5:54 pm	☍♇	♌ 27	11:36 pm
27	**8:54 pm** 5:54 pm	☍♇	♌ 28	**2:36 am**
29	9:29 pm	☍♄	♍ 30	**2:11 pm** 11:11 am
30	**12:29 am**	☍♄	♍ 30	**2:11 pm** 11:11 am

☽ Phases & Eclipses phase	day	ET / hr:mn / PT
2nd Quarter	6	**10:14 pm** 7:14 pm
Full Moon	13	**2:38 pm** 11:38 am
4th Quarter	20	**10:19 am** 7:19 am
New Moon	28	**1:55 pm** 10:55 am

Planet Ingress		day	ET / hr:mn / PT
♀	♊	4	**11:16 pm** 8:16 pm
♂	♉	4	11:04 pm
♂	♉	5	**2:04 am**
☿	♋	4	11:25 pm
☿	♋	5	**2:25 am**
♀	♋	17	**9:32 pm** 6:32 pm
☿	♌	19	**8:35 am** 5:35 am
☉	♌	22	**4:07 pm** 1:07 pm
⚳	♌	23	**1:29 pm** 10:29 am

Planetary Motion		day	ET / hr:mn / PT
⚶	℞	7	**5:30 pm** 2:30 pm
⚷	℞	19	**11:21 am** 8:21 am
⚵	℞	24	11:48 pm
⚵	℞	25	**2:48 am**
♃	℞	28	**4:37 pm** 1:37 pm

1 FRIDAY
- ☽△♃ **11:49 am** 8:49 am
- ☽⚺☉ **4:46 pm** 1:46 pm
- ☽⚹♀ **5:59 pm** 2:59 pm
- ♂□♇ **10:14 pm** 7:14 pm

2 SATURDAY
- ☿△♄ **6:39 am** 3:39 am
- ☽□♅ **8:22 am** 5:22 am
- ☿□♆ **4:53 pm** 1:53 pm
- ☽☍♄ **9:55 pm** 6:55 pm
- ☽⚻♆ **11:31 pm** 8:31 pm
- ☽⚹☿ 9:43 pm

3 SUNDAY
- ☽⚹☿ **12:43 am**
- ☽⚻♇ **4:05 am** 1:05 am
- ☽△♂ **5:59 am** 2:59 am
- ☿⚻♇ **10:13 pm** 7:13 pm
- ☽⚻♃ **11:41 pm** 8:41 pm

4 MONDAY
- ☽⚹☉ **9:03 am** 6:03 am
- ☽□♀ **11:38 am** 8:38 am
- ☽△♅ **7:23 pm** 4:23 pm
- ☿⚹♂ 11:37 pm

5 TUESDAY
- ☿⚹♂ **2:37 am**
- ☽⚻♄ **8:02 am** 5:02 am
- ☽☍♆ **9:46 am** 6:46 am
- ☽△♇ **2:04 pm** 11:04 am
- ☽⚻♂ **7:22 pm** 4:22 pm
- ☽□☿ **9:20 pm** 6:20 pm

6 WEDNESDAY
- ☽☍♃ **9:13 am** 6:13 am
- ☽□☉ **10:14 pm** 7:14 pm
- ☽△♀ 10:54 pm

7 THURSDAY
- ☽△♀ **1:54 am**
- ☽⚻♅ **3:43 am** 12:43 am
- ☽△♄ **3:18 pm** 12:18 pm
- ☽⚻♆ **5:06 pm** 2:06 pm
- ☽□♇ **9:04 pm** 6:04 pm
- ♀⚺♅ **10:27 pm** 7:27 pm

8 FRIDAY
- ☽☍♂ **5:06 am** 2:06 am
- ☽△☿ **1:31 pm** 10:31 am
- ☽⚻♃ **3:23 pm** 12:23 pm
- ☿□♃ 11:14 pm

9 SATURDAY
- ☿□♃ **2:14 am**
- ☽△☉ **7:10 am** 4:10 am
- ☽☍♅ **8:34 am** 5:34 am
- ☽⚻♀ **11:38 am** 8:38 am
- ☽□♄ **7:04 pm** 4:04 pm
- ☽△♆ **8:56 pm** 5:56 pm
- ☽⚹♇ 9:34 pm

10 SUNDAY
- ☽⚹♇ **12:34 am**
- ☉⚹♅ **4:39 am** 1:39 am
- ☽⚻♂ **10:44 am** 7:44 am
- ☽△♃ **6:02 pm** 3:02 pm
- ☽⚻☿ 9:29 pm

11 MONDAY
- ☽⚻☿ **12:29 am**
- ☽⚻♅ **10:07 am** 7:07 am
- ☽⚻☉ **12:03 pm** 9:03 am
- ☽☍♀ **5:12 pm** 2:12 pm
- ☽⚹♄ **7:48 pm** 4:48 pm
- ☽□♆ **9:42 pm** 6:42 pm
- ☽⚺♇ 10:07 pm

12 TUESDAY
- ☽⚺♇ **1:07 am**
- ☽△♂ **1:12 pm** 10:12 am
- ☽□♃ **6:07 pm** 3:07 pm
- ♀△♄ 9:28 pm

13 WEDNESDAY
- ♀△♄ **12:28 am**
- ☽☍☿ **7:59 am** 4:59 am
- ☽△♅ **9:41 am** 6:41 am
- ☽☍☉ **2:38 pm** 11:38 am
- ☽⚺♄ **6:55 pm** 3:55 pm
- ☿⚹♅ **8:17 pm** 5:17 pm
- ☽⚻♀ **8:34 pm** 5:34 pm
- ☽⚹♆ **8:57 pm** 5:57 pm
- ☽☌♇ 9:17 pm
- ♀□♆ 10:24 pm

14 THURSDAY
- ☽☌♇ **12:17 am**
- ♀□♆ **1:24 am**
- ☽□♂ **2:39 pm** 11:39 am
- ☽⚹♃ **5:30 pm** 2:30 pm

15 FRIDAY
- ☽□♅ **9:16 am** 6:16 am
- ☽⚻☿ **3:25 pm** 12:25 pm
- ☽⚻☉ **5:30 pm** 2:30 pm
- ☽☌♄ **6:27 pm** 3:27 pm
- ♀⚻♇ **6:51 pm** 3:51 pm
- ☽⚺♆ **8:43 pm** 5:43 pm
- ☽⚺♇ 9:08 pm
- ☽△♀ 9:36 pm

16 SATURDAY
- ☽⚺♇ **12:08 am**
- ☽△♀ **12:36 am**
- ☉⚻♄ **7:34 am** 4:34 am
- ☿⚻♄ **11:55 am** 8:55 am
- ☉☌☿ **3:38 pm** 12:38 pm
- ☽⚹♂ **5:37 pm** 2:37 pm
- ☽⚺♃ **6:21 pm** 3:21 pm

17 SUNDAY
- ☿△♆ **3:52 am** 12:52 am
- ♂⚺♃ **9:58 am** 6:58 am
- ☽⚹♅ **11:01 am** 8:01 am
- ☉△♆ **6:55 pm** 3:55 pm
- ☽⚺♄ **8:31 pm** 5:31 pm
- ☽☌♆ **11:07 pm** 8:07 pm
- ☽△☉ **11:26 pm** 8:26 pm
- ☽△☿ 11:40 pm
- ☽⚹♇ 11:43 pm

18 MONDAY
- ☽△☿ **2:40 am**
- ☽⚹♇ **2:43 am**
- ☿☍♇ **3:01 am** 12:01 am
- ☽□♀ **8:15 am** 5:15 am
- ☽☌♃ **10:35 pm** 7:35 pm
- ☽⚺♂ 9:27 pm

19 TUESDAY
- ☽⚺♂ **12:27 am**
- ☽⚺♅ **4:35 pm** 1:35 pm
- ☉☍♇ **9:39 pm** 6:39 pm
- ☽⚹♄ 11:28 pm

20 WEDNESDAY
- ☽⚹♄ **2:28 am**
- ☽⚺♆ **5:30 am** 2:30 am
- ☽□♇ **9:20 am** 6:20 am
- ☽□☉ **10:19 am** 7:19 am
- ☽□☿ **8:19 pm** 5:19 pm
- ☽⚹♀ **9:17 pm** 6:17 pm

21 THURSDAY
- ☽⚺♃ **6:58 am** 3:58 am
- ☿⚺♀ **9:02 am** 6:02 am
- ☽☌♂ **12:06 pm** 9:06 am
- ☽☌♅ 11:14 pm

22 FRIDAY
- ☽☌♅ **2:14 am**
- ☽□♄ **12:18 pm** 9:18 am
- ☽⚹♆ **3:45 pm** 12:45 pm
- ☽△♇ **7:45 pm** 4:45 pm
- ☽⚹☉ 10:58 pm

23 SATURDAY
- ☽⚹☉ **1:58 am**
- ☿△♃ **1:52 pm** 10:52 am
- ☽⚺♀ **3:06 pm** 12:06 pm
- ☽⚹♃ **6:38 pm** 3:38 pm
- ☽⚹☿ **7:36 pm** 4:36 pm

24 SUNDAY
- ☽⚺♂ **3:26 am** 12:26 am
- ☽⚺♅ **2:36 pm** 11:36 am
- ☽△♄ 9:27 pm
- ♀□♃ 11:13 pm

25 MONDAY
- ☽△♄ **12:27 am**
- ♀□♃ **2:13 am**
- ☽□♆ **4:14 am** 1:14 am
- ☽⚻♇ **8:15 am** 5:15 am
- ☽⚺☉ **8:02 pm** 5:02 pm

26 TUESDAY
- ☽□♃ **7:35 am** 4:35 am
- ☽☌♀ **10:54 am** 7:54 am
- ☿□♂ **3:13 pm** 12:13 pm
- ☽⚹♂ **7:57 pm** 4:57 pm
- ☽⚺☿ **8:33 pm** 5:33 pm

27 WEDNESDAY
- ☽⚹♅ **3:36 am** 12:36 am
- ☽⚻♄ **12:56 pm** 9:56 am
- ☽△♆ **4:58 pm** 1:58 pm
- ☽☍♇ **8:54 pm** 5:54 pm

28 THURSDAY
- ☽☌☉ **1:55 pm** 10:55 am
- ☿□♅ **5:16 pm** 2:16 pm
- ☽△♃ **8:03 pm** 5:03 pm

29 FRIDAY
- ☽⚺♀ **6:04 am** 3:04 am
- ☽□♂ **11:38 am** 8:38 am
- ☽□♅ **3:48 pm** 12:48 pm
- ☽☌☿ **7:49 pm** 4:49 pm
- ☽☍♄ 9:29 pm

30 SATURDAY
- ☽☍♄ **12:29 am**
- ☽⚻♆ **4:42 am** 1:42 am
- ☽⚻♇ **8:30 am** 5:30 am
- ☿☍♄ 11:05 pm

31 SUNDAY
- ☿☍♄ **2:05 am**
- ☽⚺☉ **6:12 am** 3:12 am
- ☽⚻♃ **7:11 am** 4:11 am
- ☉△♃ **6:36 pm** 3:36 pm
- ☽⚹♀ **11:19 pm** 8:19 pm
- ☽△♂ 10:35 pm
- ☽△♅ 11:30 pm

Eastern time in bold type
Pacific time in medium type

JULY 2022

DATE	SID.TIME	SUN	MOON	NODE	MERCURY	VENUS	MARS	JUPITER	SATURN	URANUS	NEPTUNE	PLUTO	CERES	PALLAS	JUNO	VESTA	CHIRON
1 F	18 36 7	9♋10 26	29♋40	21♉29℞	22♊04	9♊31	27♈00	7♈29	24♒43℞	17♉45	25♓26℞	27♑48℞	19♋55	28♋03	19♈37	6♈43	16♈17
2 Sa	18 40 3	10 07 39	11♌37	21 12	23 51	10 43	27 43	7 34	24 40	17 47	25 26	27 47	20 22	28 31	19 46	6 46	16 18
3 Su	18 44 0	11 04 53	23 40	21 05	25 41	11 54	28 25	7 39	24 38	17 49	25 26	27 45	20 48	28 59	19 54	6 48	16 19
4 M	18 47 57	12 02 06	5♍51	21 00	27 33	13 06	29 07	7 44	24 35	17 52	25 26	27 44	21 15	29 28	20 03	6 50	16 20
5 T	18 51 53	12 59 19	18 14	20 57	29 29	14 18	29 49	7 48	24 32	17 54	25 26	27 43	21 41	29 56	20 10	6 52	16 20
6 W	18 55 50	13 56 31	0♎51	20 56 D	1♋27	15 30	0♉31	7 53	24 30	17 56	25 26	27 41	22 08	0♌25	20 18	6 53	16 21
7 Th	18 59 46	14 53 44	13 46	20 56	3 27	16 42	1 13	7 57	24 27	17 59	25 25	27 41	22 34	0 53	20 25	6 54℞	16 22
8 F	19 3 43	15 50 56	27 03	20 57℞	5 29	17 54	1 55	8 01	24 24	18 01	25 25	27 40	23 01	1 21	20 32	6 54	16 22
9 Sa	19 7 39	16 48 07	10♏44	20 57	7 33	19 06	2 37	8 05	24 21	18 03	25 25	27 37	23 27	1 50	20 38	6 54	16 23
10 Su	19 11 36	17 45 19	24 51	20 56	9 39	20 18	3 18	8 08	24 18	18 05	25 24	27 36	23 54	2 18	20 44	6 53	16 24
11 M	19 15 32	18 42 31	9♐24	20 53	11 46	21 30	4 00	8 12	24 15	18 07	25 24	27 34	24 20	2 47	20 50	6 52	16 24
12 T	19 19 29	19 39 43	24 19	20 47	13 54	22 42	4 41	8 15	24 11	18 09	25 24	27 33	24 47	3 15	20 56	6 50	16 24
13 W	19 23 26	20 36 54	9♑30	20 39	16 03	23 54	5 23	8 18	24 08	18 11	25 23	27 31	25 14	3 44	21 01	6 48	16 25
14 Th	19 27 22	21 34 06	24 47	20 30	18 12	25 06	6 04	8 21	24 05	18 13	25 23	27 30	25 40	4 12	21 06	6 45	16 25
15 F	19 31 19	22 31 19	9≈58	20 21	20 21	26 18	6 45	8 24	24 01	18 15	25 22	27 29	26 07	4 41	21 10	6 42	16 25
16 Sa	19 35 15	23 28 31	24 55	20 13	22 30	27 31	7 26	8 27	23 58	18 17	25 22	27 27	26 33	5 10	21 14	6 38	16 26
17 Su	19 39 12	24 25 44	9♓28	20 07	24 39	28 43	8 08	8 29	23 54	18 19	25 21	27 26	27 00	5 38	21 17	6 34	16 26
18 M	19 43 8	25 22 58	23 33	20 04	26 47	29 55	8 48	8 31	23 51	18 21	25 20	27 24	27 27	6 07	21 20	6 30	16 26
19 T	19 47 5	26 20 12	7♈08	20 02 D	28 54	1♋08	9 28	8 33	23 47	18 23	25 20	27 23	27 54	6 36	21 23	6 25	16 26
20 W	19 51 1	27 17 27	20 15	20 02	1♌00	2 20	10 09	8 35	23 43	18 24	25 19	27 21	28 20	7 04	21 26	6 20	16 26℞
21 Th	19 54 58	28 14 43	2♉56	20 02℞	3 05	3 33	10 49	8 37	23 39	18 26	25 18	27 20	28 47	7 33	21 28	6 13	16 26
22 F	19 58 55	29 11 59	15 18	20 02	5 08	4 45	11 29	8 38	23 36	18 28	25 18	27 19	29 14	8 02	21 29	6 07	16 26
23 Sa	20 2 51	0♌09 16	27 25	20 01	7 10	5 58	12 09	8 40	23 32	18 29	25 17	27 17	29 40	8 30	21 30	6 00	16 26
24 Su	20 6 48	1 06 35	9♊21	19 57	9 11	7 10	12 49	8 41	23 28	18 31	25 16	27 16	0♌07	8 59	21 31	5 52	16 26
25 M	20 10 44	2 03 53	21 12	19 50	11 10	8 23	13 29	8 42	23 24	18 32	25 15	27 14	0 34	9 28	21 31℞	5 44	16 25
26 T	20 14 41	3 01 13	3♋00	19 41	13 08	9 36	14 09	8 42	23 20	18 34	25 14	27 13	1 01	9 56	21 31	5 36	16 25
27 W	20 18 37	3 58 34	14 50	19 33	15 04	10 48	14 49	8 43	23 16	18 35	25 14	27 11	1 28	10 25	21 31	5 28	16 25
28 Th	20 22 34	4 55 55	26 43	19 25	16 58	12 01	15 28	8 43℞	23 11	18 36	25 13	27 10	1 54	10 54	21 30	5 18	16 24
29 F	20 26 30	5 53 17	8♌41	19 16	18 50	13 14	16 07	8 43	23 07	18 38	25 12	27 09	2 21	11 23	21 29	5 09	16 24
30 Sa	20 30 27	6 50 40	20 46	19 03	20 41	14 27	16 46	8 43	23 03	18 39	25 11	27 07	2 48	11 51	21 27	4 59	16 23
31 Su	20 34 24	7 48 03	2♍58	18 50	22 30	15 40	17 25	8 43	22 59	18 40	25 10	27 06	3 15	12 20	21 24	4 49	16 23

EPHEMERIS CALCULATED FOR 12 MIDNIGHT GREENWICH MEAN TIME. ALL OTHER DATA AND FACING ASPECTARIAN PAGE IN **EASTERN TIME (BOLD)** AND PACIFIC TIME (REGULAR).

AUGUST 2022

☽ Last Aspect day	ET / hr:mn / PT		asp	☽ Ingress sign	day	ET / hr:mn / PT	
1	**6:29 pm**	3:29 pm	△♇	♎	1		9:06 pm
1	**6:29 pm**	3:29 pm	△♇	♎	2	**12:06 am**	
3		11:20 pm	□♇	♏	4	**7:47 am**	4:47 am
4	**2:20 am**		□♇	♏	4	**7:47 am**	4:47 am
6	**7:24 am**	4:24 am	✶♇	♐	6	**12:39 pm**	9:39 am
8	**6:30 am**	3:30 am	□♆	♑	8	**2:39 pm**	11:39 am
10	**12:39 pm**	9:39 am	☍♀	♒	10	**2:45 pm**	11:45 am
12	**7:07 am**	4:07 am	□♂	♓	12	**2:44 pm**	11:44 am
14	**11:11 am**	8:11 am	✶♇	♈	14	**4:43 pm**	1:43 pm
16	**4:18 pm**	1:18 pm	□♇	♉	16	**10:22 pm**	7:22 pm
19	**7:06 am**	4:06 am	☌♂	♊	19	**8:06 am**	5:06 am
21	**6:06 pm**	3:06 pm	✶☉	♋	21	**8:29 pm**	5:29 pm
24	**5:40 am**	2:40 am	✶☿	♌	24	**9:09 am**	6:09 am
25		11:55 pm	☍♄	♍	26	**8:25 pm**	5:25 pm
26	**2:55 am**		☍♄	♍	26	**8:25 pm**	5:25 pm
28	**11:08 pm**	8:08 pm	△♇	♎	29	**5:45 am**	2:45 am
31	**6:43 am**	3:43 am	□♇	♏	31	**1:11 pm**	10:11 am

☽ Phases & Eclipses phase	day	ET / hr:mn / PT	
2nd Quarter	5	**7:07 am**	4:07 am
Full Moon	11	**9:36 pm**	6:36 pm
4th Quarter	18		9:36 pm
4th Quarter	19	**12:36 am**	
New Moon	27	**4:17 am**	1:17 am

Planet Ingress		day	ET / hr:mn / PT	
☿	♍	3		11:58 pm
☿	♍	4	**2:58 am**	
♀	♌	11	**2:30 pm**	11:30 am
♂	♊	20	**3:56 am**	12:56 am
⚶	♒	21	**6:33 am**	3:33 am
☉	♍	22	**11:16 pm**	8:16 pm
☿	♎	25	**9:03 pm**	6:03 pm

Planetary Motion		day	ET / hr:mn / PT	
♅	R	24	**9:54 am**	6:54 am

1 MONDAY

☽△♂	**1:35 am**	
☽△♅	**2:30 am**	
☿⚻♆	**7:23 am**	4:23 am
☽⚻♄	**10:30 am**	7:30 am
☽☍♆	**2:50 pm**	11:50 am
☽⚺☿	**4:03 pm**	1:03 pm
☽△♇	**6:29 pm**	3:29 pm
♂☌♅	**7:53 pm**	4:53 pm

2 TUESDAY

♀✶♅	**8:25 am**	5:25 am
☿⚻♇	**9:24 am**	6:24 am
☽☍♃	**4:27 pm**	1:27 pm
☽✶☉	**8:12 pm**	5:12 pm
♀✶♂	**10:00 pm**	7:00 pm

3 WEDNESDAY

☽⚻♅	**11:11 am**	8:11 am
☽⚻♂	**1:10 pm**	10:10 am
☽□♀	**1:54 pm**	10:54 am
☽△♄	**6:28 pm**	3:28 pm
☽⚻♆	**10:51 pm**	7:51 pm
☽□♇		11:20 pm

4 THURSDAY

☽□♇	**2:20 am**	
☽✶☿	**8:29 am**	5:29 am
☽⚻♃	**11:18 pm**	8:18 pm

5 FRIDAY

☽□☉	**7:07 am**	4:07 am
♀⚻♄	**12:23 pm**	9:23 am
☽☍♅	**5:13 pm**	2:13 pm
☽☍♂	**9:38 pm**	6:38 pm
☽□♄	**11:46 pm**	8:46 pm
☽△♀		9:56 pm

6 SATURDAY

☽△♀	**12:56 am**	
☽△♆	**4:08 am**	1:08 am
☽✶♇	**7:24 am**	4:24 am
☽□☿	**8:18 pm**	5:18 pm

7 SUNDAY

☽△♃	**3:12 am**	12:12 am
♀△♆	**12:43 pm**	9:43 am
☽△☉	**2:21 pm**	11:21 am
♂□♄	**3:57 pm**	12:57 pm
☽⚻♅	**8:17 pm**	5:17 pm
☽✶♄		11:11 pm
☽⚻♂		11:42 pm

8 MONDAY

☽✶♄	**2:11 am**	
☽⚻♂	**2:42 am**	
☽□♆	**6:30 am**	3:30 am
☽⚻♀	**8:08 am**	5:08 am
☽⚺♇	**9:35 am**	6:35 am
♀☍♇		10:18 pm

9 TUESDAY

♀☍♇	**1:18 am**	
☽△☿	**3:51 am**	12:51 am
☽□♃	**4:24 am**	1:24 am
☿⚻♃	**9:06 am**	6:06 am
☽⚻☉	**6:33 pm**	3:33 pm
☽△♅	**8:58 pm**	5:58 pm
☽⚺♄		11:23 pm

10 WEDNESDAY

☽⚺♄	**2:23 am**	
☽△♂	**5:12 am**	2:12 am
☽✶♆	**6:45 am**	3:45 am
☽☌♇	**9:45 am**	6:45 am
☽☍♀	**12:39 pm**	9:39 am

11 THURSDAY

☽✶♃	**4:08 am**	1:08 am
☉□♅	**8:53 am**	5:53 am
☽⚻☿	**9:05 am**	6:05 am
♂✶♆	**5:44 pm**	2:44 pm
☽□♅	**8:47 pm**	5:47 pm
☽☍☉	**9:36 pm**	6:36 pm
☽☌♄		10:58 pm

12 FRIDAY

☽☌♄	**1:58 am**	
☽⚺♆	**6:33 am**	3:33 am
☽□♂	**7:07 am**	4:07 am
☽⚺♇	**9:35 am**	6:35 am
☽⚻♀	**4:55 pm**	1:55 pm

13 SATURDAY

☽⚺♃	**4:19 am**	1:19 am
☽☍☿	**3:02 pm**	12:02 pm
☽✶♅	**9:49 pm**	6:49 pm
☽⚻☉		11:10 pm
☽⚺♄		11:58 pm

14 SUNDAY

☽⚻☉	**2:10 am**	
☽⚺♄	**2:58 am**	
☽☌♆	**7:58 am**	4:58 am
☽✶♂	**10:53 am**	7:53 am
☽✶♇	**11:11 am**	8:11 am
☉☍♄	**1:11 pm**	10:11 am
♂△♇	**5:28 pm**	2:28 pm
☽△♀	**11:53 pm**	8:53 pm

15 MONDAY

☽☌♃	**6:59 am**	3:59 am
☽⚻☿		9:41 pm
☽⚺♅		11:01 pm

16 TUESDAY

☽⚻☿	**12:41 am**	
☽⚺♅	**2:01 am**	
☽✶♄	**7:14 am**	4:14 am
☽△☉	**10:48 am**	7:48 am
☽⚺♆	**12:50 pm**	9:50 am
☿△♅	**1:46 pm**	10:46 am
☽□♇	**4:18 pm**	1:18 pm
☽⚺♂	**6:39 pm**	3:39 pm

17 WEDNESDAY

☽□♀	**11:54 am**	8:54 am
☽⚺♃	**1:32 pm**	10:32 am
☉⚻♆	**1:57 pm**	10:57 am

18 THURSDAY

♀△♃	**4:03 am**	1:03 am
☽☌♅	**10:20 am**	7:20 am
☿⚻♄	**3:06 pm**	12:06 pm
☽□♄	**3:34 pm**	12:34 pm
☽△☿	**3:37 pm**	12:37 pm
☽✶♆	**9:49 pm**	6:49 pm
☽□☉		9:36 pm
☽△♇		10:32 pm

19 FRIDAY

☽□☉	**12:36 am**	
☽△♇	**1:32 am**	
☽☌♂	**7:06 am**	4:06 am
☉⚻♇	**12:10 pm**	9:10 am
☽✶♃	**11:52 pm**	8:52 pm

20 SATURDAY

☽✶♀	**5:09 am**	2:09 am
☽⚺♅	**10:01 pm**	7:01 pm

21 SUNDAY

☽△♄	**3:04 am**	12:04 am
☿☍♆	**3:40 am**	12:40 am
☽□♆	**9:47 am**	6:47 am
☽□☿	**10:29 am**	7:29 am
☽⚻♇	**1:38 pm**	10:38 am
☽✶☉	**6:06 pm**	3:06 pm
☽⚺♂	**10:35 pm**	7:35 pm

22 MONDAY

☽□♃	**12:10 pm**	9:10 am
☿△♇	**5:59 pm**	2:59 pm
☽⚺♀		9:55 pm

23 TUESDAY

☽⚺♀	**12:55 am**	
☽✶♅	**10:51 am**	7:51 am
☽⚻♄	**3:30 pm**	12:30 pm
☽△♆	**10:26 pm**	7:26 pm
☽☍♇		11:17 pm

24 WEDNESDAY

☽☍♇	**2:17 am**	
☽✶☿	**5:40 am**	2:40 am
☽⚺☉	**12:07 pm**	9:07 am
☽✶♂	**2:16 pm**	11:16 am
☽△♃		9:10 pm

25 THURSDAY

☽△♃	**12:10 am**	
☽☌♀	**7:50 pm**	4:50 pm
☽□♅	**10:45 pm**	7:45 pm
☽☍♄		11:55 pm

26 FRIDAY

☽☍♄	**2:55 am**	
☽⚻♆	**9:53 am**	6:53 am
☽⚻♇	**1:39 pm**	10:39 am
☽⚺☿	**10:28 pm**	7:28 pm
♀□♅		9:34 pm
☉□♂		10:27 pm

27 SATURDAY

♀□♅	**12:34 am**	
☉□♂	**1:27 am**	
☽□♂	**4:11 am**	1:11 am
☽☌☉	**4:17 am**	1:17 am
☽⚻♃	**10:33 am**	7:33 am

28 SUNDAY

☽△♅	**8:47 am**	5:47 am
☽⚺♀	**12:17 pm**	9:17 am
☽⚻♄	**12:30 pm**	9:30 am
♀☍♄	**2:27 pm**	11:27 am
☽☍♆	**7:27 pm**	4:27 pm
☽△♇	**11:08 pm**	8:08 pm

29 MONDAY

☽☌☿	**12:10 pm**	9:10 am
☽△♂	**3:50 pm**	12:50 pm
☽⚺☉	**6:00 pm**	3:00 pm
☽☍♃	**7:00 pm**	4:00 pm

30 TUESDAY

☉⚻♃	**6:09 am**	3:09 am
☽⚻♅	**4:54 pm**	1:54 pm
☽△♄	**8:13 pm**	5:13 pm
☽✶♀		11:07 pm

31 WEDNESDAY

☽✶♀	**2:07 am**	
☽⚻♆	**3:08 am**	12:08 am
☽□♇	**6:43 am**	3:43 am
♀⚻♆	**12:37 pm**	9:37 am
☽⚺☿	**10:54 pm**	7:54 pm
☽⚻♂		10:16 pm
☽⚻♃		10:35 pm

Eastern time in bold type
Pacific time in medium type

AUGUST 2022

DATE	SID.TIME	SUN	MOON	NODE	MERCURY	VENUS	MARS	JUPITER	SATURN	URANUS	NEPTUNE	PLUTO	CERES	PALLAS	JUNO	VESTA	CHIRON
1 M	20 38 20	8♌45 27	15♍20	18♉40R	24♌18	16♋52	18♉04	8♈42R	22≈55R	18♉41	25♓08	27♑04R	3♑42	12♉49	21♈22R	4♈38R	16♈22R
2 T	20 42 17	9 42 52	27 51	18 31	26 04	18 05	18 42	8 41	22 51	18 43	25 07	27 03	4 09	13 18	21 19	4 27	16 21
3 W	20 46 13	10 40 18	10♎34	18 26	27 48	19 18	19 21	8 40	22 46	18 44	25 06	27 00	4 35	13 46	21 15	4 15	16 21
4 Th	20 50 10	11 37 44	23 32	18 23	29 31	20 31	20 00	8 39	22 42	18 45	25 05	26 59	5 02	14 15	21 11	4 04	16 20
5 F	20 54 6	12 35 10	6♏47	18 22	1♍11	21 44	20 38	8 38	22 37	18 46	25 04	26 58	5 29	14 44	21 07	3 51	16 19
6 Sa	20 58 3	13 32 38	20 22	18 22	2 51	22 58	21 16	8 36	22 33	18 47	25 02	26 57	5 56	15 13	21 02	3 39	16 18
7 Su	21 1 59	14 30 06	4♐19	18 22	4 28	24 11	21 54	8 35	22 29	18 48	25 01	26 56	6 23	15 41	20 57	3 26	16 17
8 M	21 5 56	15 27 35	18 38	18 22	6 04	25 24	22 31	8 33	22 24	18 48	25 00	26 55	6 50	16 10	20 51	3 13	16 16
9 T	21 9 53	16 25 05	3♑18	18 15	7 39	26 37	23 09	8 31	22 20	18 49	24 59	26 53	7 17	16 39	20 45	3 00	16 15
10 W	21 13 49	17 22 35	18 14	18 08	9 12	27 50	23 46	8 29	22 15	18 50	24 58	26 52	7 43	17 08	20 38	2 46	16 14
11 Th	21 17 46	18 20 07	3≈18	17 59	10 43	29 03	24 23	8 26	22 11	18 51	24 56	26 51	8 10	17 36	20 31	2 33	16 13
12 F	21 21 42	19 17 39	18 22	17 48	12 12	0♌17	25 00	8 23	22 06	18 51	24 55	26 50	8 37	18 05	20 24	2 19	16 13
13 Sa	21 25 39	20 15 13	3♓14	17 37	13 40	1 30	25 37	8 21	22 02	18 52	24 54	26 48	9 04	18 34	20 16	2 05	16 11
14 Su	21 29 35	21 12 47	17 47	17 27	15 06	2 44	26 13	8 17	21 57	18 52	24 52	26 47	9 31	19 02	20 08	1 50	16 10
15 M	21 33 32	22 10 23	1♈54	17 19	16 31	3 57	26 50	8 14	21 53	18 53	24 51	26 46	9 58	19 31	19 59	1 36	16 08
16 T	21 37 28	23 08 01	15 33	17 14	17 54	5 10	27 26	8 11	21 48	18 53	24 50	26 45	10 24	20 00	19 50	1 21	16 07
17 W	21 41 25	24 05 40	28 43	17 11	19 15	6 24	28 03	8 07	21 44	18 54	24 48	26 43	10 51	20 28	19 41	1 06	16 06
18 Th	21 45 22	25 03 20	11♉28	17 10D	20 34	7 37	28 39	8 03	21 39	18 54	24 47	26 42	11 18	20 57	19 31	0 52	16 04
19 F	21 49 18	26 01 02	23 52	17 10	21 51	8 51	29 13	7 59	21 35	18 54	24 46	26 41	11 45	21 25	19 21	0 37	16 03
20 Sa	21 53 15	26 58 46	5Ⅱ59	17 10R	23 07	10 05	29 48	7 55	21 30	18 55	24 44	26 40	12 12	21 54	19 11	0 22	16 01
21 Su	21 57 11	27 56 32	17 55	17 08	24 21	11 18	0Ⅱ23	7 51	21 26	18 55	24 43	26 38	12 38	22 23	19 00	0 07	16 00
22 M	22 1 8	28 54 19	29 46	16 58	25 32	12 32	0 58	7 46	21 21	18 55	24 41	26 37	13 05	22 51	18 49	29♓52	15 58
23 T	22 5 4	29 52 07	11♋35	16 50	26 42	13 46	1 33	7 42	21 17	18 55	24 40	26 36	13 32	23 20	18 37	29 37	15 56
24 W	22 9 1	0♍49 58	23 27	16 38	27 49	15 00	2 07	7 37	21 13	18 55R	24 38	26 35	13 59	23 48	18 25	29 22	15 55
25 Th	22 12 57	1 47 50	5♌25	16 26	28 55	16 13	2 42	7 32	21 08	18 55	24 37	26 34	14 26	24 17	18 13	29 07	15 53
26 F	22 16 54	2 45 43	17 32	16 13	29 57	17 27	3 16	7 27	21 04	18 55	24 35	26 33	14 52	24 45	18 00	28 52	15 51
27 Sa	22 20 51	3 43 38	29 47	16 01	0♎58	18 41	3 49	7 21	20 59	18 55	24 34	26 32	15 19	25 13	17 48	28 37	15 49
28 Su	22 24 47	4 41 35	12♍13	15 53	1 55	19 55	4 23	7 16	20 55	18 55	24 32	26 31	15 46	25 42	17 35	28 22	15 47
29 M	22 28 44	5 39 33	24 50	15 46	2 50	21 09	4 56	7 10	20 51	18 55	24 31	26 29	16 13	26 10	17 21	28 08	15 46
30 T	22 32 40	6 37 32	7♎37	15 42	3 42	22 23	5 29	7 05	20 47	18 55	24 30	26 28	16 39	26 38	17 08	27 53	15 44
31 W	22 36 37	7 35 33	20 35	15 37	4 31	23 37	6 01	6 59	20 42	18 54	24 29	26 27	17 06	27 06	16 54	27 39	15 42

EPHEMERIS CALCULATED FOR 12 MIDNIGHT GREENWICH MEAN TIME. ALL OTHER DATA AND FACING ASPECTARIAN PAGE IN EASTERN TIME (BOLD) AND PACIFIC TIME (REGULAR).

SEPTEMBER 2022

☽ Last Aspect day	ET / hr:mn / PT	asp	☽ Ingress sign	day	ET / hr:mn / PT
2	**1:22 pm** 10:22 am	□ ♀	♐	2	**6:39 pm** 3:39 pm
4	**9:51 pm** 6:51 pm	△ ♀	♑	4	**10:03 pm** 7:03 pm
6	**5:43 pm** 2:43 pm	☌ ♇	♒	6	**11:41 pm** 8:41 pm
8	**8:34 am** 5:34 am	☌ ♄	♓	8	9:42 pm
8	**8:34 am** 5:34 am	☌ ♄	♓	9	**12:42 am**
10	**8:29 pm** 5:29 pm	✶ ♇	♈	10	11:47 pm
10	**8:29 pm** 5:29 pm	✶ ♇	♈	11	**2:47 am**
12	9:53 pm	□ ♇	♉	13	**7:39 am** 4:39 am
13	**12:53 am**	□ ♇	♉	13	**7:39 am** 4:39 am
15	**8:59 am** 5:59 am	△ ♇	♊	15	**4:16 pm** 1:16 pm
17	**5:52 pm** 2:52 pm	□ ☉	♋	18	**3:59 am** 12:59 am
20	**11:57 am** 8:57 am	✶ ☉	♌	20	**4:38 pm** 1:38 pm
22	**7:07 am** 4:07 am	☍ ♄	♍	23	**3:53 am** 12:53 am
25	**8:49 am** 5:49 am	☌ ☿	♎	25	**12:43 pm** 9:43 am
27	**12:21 pm** 9:21 am	□ ♇	♏	27	**7:15 pm** 4:15 pm
29	**5:20 pm** 2:20 pm	✶ ♇	♐	29	9:03 pm
29	**5:20 pm** 2:20 pm	✶ ♇	♐	30	**12:03 am**

☽ Phases & Eclipses phase	day	ET / hr:mn / PT
2nd Quarter	3	**2:08 pm** 11:08 am
Full Moon	10	**5:59 am** 2:59 am
4th Quarter	17	**5:52 pm** 2:52 pm
New Moon	25	**5:55 pm** 2:55 pm

Planet Ingress		day	ET / hr:mn / PT
♀	♍	4	9:05 pm
♀	♍	5	**12:05 am**
♀	♋	5	10:04 pm
♀	♋	6	**1:04 am**
☉	♎	22	**9:04 pm** 6:04 pm
☿	♍	23	**8:04 am** 5:04 am
♀	♎	29	**3:49 am** 12:49 am
⚳	♍	29	**4:59 am** 1:59 am

Planetary Motion		day	ET / hr:mn / PT
☿	℞	9	**11:38 pm** 8:38 pm

1 THURSDAY
☽ ⚻ ♂ **1:16 am**
☽ ⚻ ♃ **1:35 am**
☽ ✶ ☉ **5:20 am** 2:20 am
♂ ✶ ♃ **7:52 am** 4:52 am
☽ ☍ ♅ **11:06 pm** 8:06 pm
☽ □ ♄ 11:02 pm
♀ ⚻ ♇ 11:33 pm

2 FRIDAY
☽ □ ♄ **2:02 am**
♀ ⚻ ♇ **2:33 am**
☽ △ ♆ **8:52 am** 5:52 am
☽ ✶ ♇ **12:23 pm** 9:23 am
☽ □ ♀ **1:22 pm** 10:22 am
☿ ☍ ♃ **9:49 pm** 6:49 pm

3 SATURDAY
☽ △ ♃ **6:10 am** 3:10 am
☽ ✶ ☿ **6:37 am** 3:37 am
☽ ☍ ♂ **8:23 am** 5:23 am
☽ □ ☉ **2:08 pm** 11:08 am

4 SUNDAY
☽ ⚻ ♅ **3:13 am** 12:13 am
☽ ✶ ♄ **5:50 am** 2:50 am
☽ □ ♆ **12:32 pm** 9:32 am
☽ ⚺ ♇ **3:57 pm** 12:57 pm
☽ △ ♀ **9:51 pm** 6:51 pm

5 MONDAY
☽ □ ♃ **8:44 am** 5:44 am
☽ □ ☿ **11:21 am** 8:21 am
☽ ⚻ ♂ **1:09 pm** 10:09 am
☽ △ ☉ **8:25 pm** 5:25 pm

6 TUESDAY
☽ △ ♅ **5:23 am** 2:23 am
☽ ⚺ ♄ **7:43 am** 4:43 am
☽ ✶ ♆ **2:21 pm** 11:21 am
☽ ☌ ♇ **5:43 pm** 2:43 pm

7 WEDNESDAY
☽ ⚻ ♀ **4:04 am** 1:04 am
☽ ✶ ♃ **9:45 am** 6:45 am
☽ △ ☿ **1:48 pm** 10:48 am
☽ △ ♂ **4:13 pm** 1:13 pm
☽ ⚻ ☉ 10:04 pm

8 THURSDAY
☽ ⚻ ☉ **1:04 am**
☽ □ ♅ **6:26 am** 3:26 am
☽ ☌ ♄ **8:34 am** 5:34 am
☽ ⚺ ♆ **3:17 pm** 12:17 pm
☽ ⚺ ♇ **6:41 pm** 3:41 pm

9 FRIDAY
☽ ☍ ♀ **9:39 am** 6:39 am
☽ ⚺ ♃ **10:26 am** 7:26 am
☽ ⚻ ☿ **3:24 pm** 12:24 pm
♀ ⚻ ♃ **6:06 pm** 3:06 pm
☽ □ ♂ **7:08 pm** 4:08 pm

10 SATURDAY
☽ ☍ ☉ **5:59 am** 2:59 am
☽ ✶ ♅ **7:51 am** 4:51 am
☽ ⚺ ♄ **9:52 am** 6:52 am
☽ ☌ ♆ **4:56 pm** 1:56 pm
☽ ✶ ♇ **8:29 pm** 5:29 pm

11 SUNDAY
☉ △ ♅ **9:09 am** 6:09 am
☽ ☌ ♃ **12:31 pm** 9:31 am
☽ ⚻ ♀ **5:05 pm** 2:05 pm
☽ ☍ ☿ **5:52 pm** 2:52 pm
☽ ✶ ♂ **11:56 pm** 8:56 pm
☿ ⚺ ♀ 9:49 pm

12 MONDAY
☿ ⚺ ♀ **12:49 am**
☽ ⚺ ♅ **11:27 am** 8:27 am
☉ ⚻ ♄ **12:09 pm** 9:09 am
☽ ✶ ♄ **1:25 pm** 10:25 am
☽ ⚻ ☉ **1:31 pm** 10:31 am
☽ ⚺ ♆ **9:02 pm** 6:02 pm
☽ □ ♇ 9:53 pm

13 TUESDAY
☽ □ ♇ **12:53 am**
☽ ⚺ ♃ **5:33 pm** 2:33 pm
☽ ⚻ ☿ **10:32 pm** 7:32 pm

14 WEDNESDAY
☽ △ ♀ **4:41 am** 1:41 am
☽ ⚺ ♂ **8:23 am** 5:23 am
☽ ☌ ♅ **6:34 pm** 3:34 pm
☽ □ ♄ **8:30 pm** 5:30 pm
☽ △ ☉ 10:31 pm

15 THURSDAY
☽ △ ☉ **1:31 am**
☽ ✶ ♆ **4:47 am** 1:47 am
☽ △ ♇ **8:59 am** 5:59 am
☽ ✶ ♃ 11:14 pm

16 FRIDAY
☽ ✶ ♃ **2:14 am**
☽ △ ☿ **5:36 am** 2:36 am
♀ □ ♂ **2:49 pm** 11:49 am
☉ ☍ ♆ **6:21 pm** 3:21 pm
☽ ☌ ♂ **8:52 pm** 5:52 pm
☽ □ ♀ **9:18 pm** 6:18 pm

17 SATURDAY
☽ ⚺ ♅ **5:13 am** 2:13 am
☽ △ ♄ **7:04 am** 4:04 am
☽ □ ♆ **3:54 pm** 12:54 pm
☽ □ ☉ **5:52 pm** 2:52 pm
☽ ⚻ ♇ **8:21 pm** 5:21 pm

18 SUNDAY
☽ □ ♃ **1:38 pm** 10:38 am
☽ □ ☿ **1:56 pm** 10:56 am
☿ ☍ ♃ **6:34 pm** 3:34 pm
☉ △ ♇ **11:58 pm** 8:58 pm

19 MONDAY
☽ ⚺ ♂ **11:41 am** 8:41 am
☽ ✶ ♀ **4:53 pm** 1:53 pm
☽ ✶ ♅ **5:43 pm** 2:43 pm
☽ ⚻ ♄ **7:25 pm** 4:25 pm
♀ △ ♅ 9:44 pm

20 TUESDAY
♀ △ ♅ **12:44 am**
☽ △ ♆ **4:25 am** 1:25 am
☽ ☍ ♇ **8:58 am** 5:58 am
☽ ✶ ☉ **11:57 am** 8:57 am
♀ ⚻ ♄ **4:12 pm** 1:12 pm
☽ ✶ ☿ **9:52 pm** 6:52 pm
☽ △ ♃ 10:32 pm

21 WEDNESDAY
☽ △ ♃ **1:32 am**
☽ ✶ ♂ 11:00 pm

22 THURSDAY
☽ ✶ ♂ **2:00 am**
☽ □ ♅ **5:36 am** 2:36 am
☽ ☍ ♄ **7:07 am** 4:07 am
☽ ⚺ ♀ **11:42 am** 8:42 am
☽ ⚻ ♆ **3:57 pm** 12:57 pm
☽ ⚻ ♇ **8:28 pm** 5:28 pm
☉ ☌ ☿ 11:50 pm

23 FRIDAY
☉ ☌ ☿ **2:50 am**
☽ ⚺ ☿ **4:13 am** 1:13 am
☽ ⚺ ☉ **4:28 am** 1:28 am
☽ ⚻ ♃ **11:50 am** 8:50 am

24 SATURDAY
♀ ☍ ♆ **4:51 am** 1:51 am
☽ □ ♂ **1:51 pm** 10:51 am
☽ △ ♅ **3:17 pm** 12:17 pm
☽ ⚻ ♄ **4:38 pm** 1:38 pm
☽ ☍ ♆ 10:10 pm

25 SUNDAY
☽ ☍ ♆ **1:10 am**
☽ ☌ ♀ **3:24 am** 12:24 am
☽ △ ♇ **5:35 am** 2:35 am
☽ ☌ ☿ **8:49 am** 5:49 am
☽ ☌ ☉ **5:55 pm** 2:55 pm
☽ ☍ ♃ **7:45 pm** 4:45 pm
♀ △ ♇ 10:46 pm

26 MONDAY
♀ △ ♇ **1:46 am**
♂ ⚺ ♅ **10:14 am** 7:14 am
☿ ☌ ♀ **1:59 pm** 10:59 am
☉ ☍ ♃ **3:33 pm** 12:33 pm
☽ ⚻ ♅ **10:31 pm** 7:31 pm
☽ △ ♂ **10:54 pm** 7:54 pm
☽ △ ♄ **11:44 pm** 8:44 pm

27 TUESDAY
☽ ⚻ ♆ **8:01 am** 5:01 am
☿ △ ♇ **8:56 am** 5:56 am
☽ ⚺ ☿ **12:10 pm** 9:10 am
☽ □ ♇ **12:21 pm** 9:21 am
☽ ⚺ ♀ **3:54 pm** 12:54 pm
☽ ⚻ ♃ 10:29 pm
♂ △ ♄ 10:49 pm

28 WEDNESDAY
☽ ⚻ ♃ **1:29 am**
♂ △ ♄ **1:49 am**
☽ ⚺ ☉ **4:31 am** 1:31 am

29 THURSDAY
☽ ☍ ♅ **3:49 am** 12:49 am
☽ □ ♄ **4:57 am** 1:57 am
☽ ⚻ ♂ **5:46 am** 2:46 am
☽ △ ♆ **1:03 pm** 10:03 am
☽ ✶ ☿ **2:58 pm** 11:58 am
☽ ✶ ♇ **5:20 pm** 2:20 pm
☽ ✶ ♀ 11:04 pm

30 FRIDAY
☽ ✶ ♀ **2:04 am**
☽ △ ♃ **5:38 am** 2:38 am
☽ ✶ ☉ **1:05 pm** 10:05 am

Eastern time in bold type
Pacific time in medium type

SEPTEMBER 2022

DATE	SID.TIME	SUN	MOON	NODE	MERCURY	VENUS	MARS	JUPITER	SATURN	URANUS	NEPTUNE	PLUTO	CERES	PALLAS	JUNO	VESTA	CHIRON
1 Th	22 40 33	8♍33 35	3♍46	15♉35 D	5♎17	24Ω01	6♊34	6♈53 Rx	20♒38 Rx	18♉54 Rx	24♓28 Rx	26♑26 Rx	17Ω33	27♉34	16♓40 Rx	27♒25 Rx	15♈40 Rx
2 F	22 44 30	9 31 39	17 09	15 34	5 59	26 05	7 06	6 46	20 34	18 53	24 26	26 25	17 59	28 02	16 26	27 11	15 38
3 Sa	22 48 26	10 29 44	0✗46	15 35 Rx	6 37	27 19	7 37	6 40	20 30	18 53	24 24	26 25	18 26	28 30	16 12	26 58	15 36
4 Su	22 52 23	11 27 51	14 39	15 35	7 11	28 33	8 09	6 33	20 26	18 53	24 23	26 24	18 53	28 58	15 57	26 44	15 33
5 M	22 56 20	12 25 59	28 47	15 34	7 41	29 47	8 40	6 27	20 22	18 52	24 21	26 23	19 19	29 26	15 43	26 31	15 31
6 T	23 0 16	13 24 08	13♑10	15 31	8 06	1♍02	9 11	6 20	20 18	18 51	24 20	26 22	19 46	29 54	15 28	26 18	15 29
7 W	23 4 13	14 22 19	27 45	15 25	8 27	2 16	9 42	6 13	20 14	18 51	24 18	26 21	20 12	0♊22	15 13	26 06	15 27
8 Th	23 8 9	15 20 32	12≈26	15 17	8 42	3 30	10 12	6 06	20 10	18 50	24 16	26 20	20 39	0 50	14 59	25 54	15 25
9 F	23 12 6	16 18 45	27 08	15 09	8 51	4 44	10 42	5 59	20 06	18 49	24 15	26 20	21 06	1 17	14 44	25 42	15 22
10 Sa	23 16 2	17 17 01	11♓42	14 59	8 55 Rx	5 59	11 11	5 52	20 03	18 49	24 13	26 19	21 32	1 45	14 29	25 30	15 20
11 Su	23 19 59	18 15 18	26 01	14 51	8 53	7 13	11 41	5 45	19 59	18 48	24 11	26 18	21 59	2 12	14 14	25 19	15 18
12 M	23 23 55	19 13 37	9♈59	14 45	8 45	8 27	12 10	5 38	19 55	18 47	24 10	26 17	22 25	2 40	13 59	25 08	15 15
13 T	23 27 52	20 11 58	23 34	14 40	8 30	9 42	12 38	5 30	19 52	18 46	24 08	26 16	22 51	3 07	13 44	24 58	15 13
14 W	23 31 49	21 10 21	6♉43	14 38 D	8 08	10 56	13 07	5 23	19 48	18 45	24 07	26 16	23 18	3 34	13 30	24 48	15 11
15 Th	23 35 45	22 08 46	19 29	14 38	7 39	12 11	13 35	5 15	19 45	18 44	24 05	26 15	23 44	4 01	13 15	24 38	15 08
16 F	23 39 42	23 07 13	1♊55	14 39	7 04	13 25	14 02	5 07	19 41	18 43	24 04	26 14	24 11	4 28	13 00	24 29	15 06
17 Sa	23 43 38	24 05 42	14 04	14 40 Rx	6 22	14 40	14 29	5 00	19 38	18 42	24 02	26 14	24 37	4 55	12 46	24 20	15 03
18 Su	23 47 35	25 04 14	26 03	14 41	5 34	15 54	14 56	4 52	19 35	18 41	24 00	26 13	25 03	5 22	12 32	24 12	15 01
19 M	23 51 31	26 02 48	7♋55	14 40	4 41	17 09	15 22	4 44	19 32	18 39	23 58	26 13	25 29	5 49	12 17	24 04	14 58
20 T	23 55 28	27 01 24	19 46	14 37	3 43	18 23	15 48	4 36	19 29	18 38	23 57	26 12	25 56	6 16	12 03	23 56	14 56
21 W	23 59 24	28 00 02	1Ω43	14 32	2 42	19 38	16 14	4 28	19 26	18 37	23 55	26 12	26 22	6 42	11 50	23 49	14 53
22 Th	0 3 21	28 58 42	13 43	14 26	1 38	20 52	16 39	4 20	19 23	18 36	23 53	26 11	26 48	7 09	11 36	23 43	14 51
23 F	0 7 18	29 57 24	25 56	14 18	0 33	22 07	17 04	4 12	19 20	18 34	23 52	26 11	27 14	7 35	11 23	23 36	14 48
24 Sa	0 11 14	0≏56 09	8♍22	14 10	29♍17	23 22	17 28	4 04	19 17	18 33	23 50	26 10	27 40	8 01	11 10	23 31	14 45
25 Su	0 15 11	1 54 55	21 02	14 02	28 26	24 37	17 52	3 56	19 14	18 31	23 48	26 10	28 06	8 27	10 57	23 25	14 43
26 M	0 19 7	2 53 43	3≏57	13 56	27 28	25 51	18 15	3 48	19 12	18 30	23 47	26 09	28 32	8 53	10 44	23 21	14 40
27 T	0 23 4	3 52 34	17 05	13 51	26 35	27 06	18 38	3 40	19 09	18 28	23 45	26 09	28 58	9 19	10 32	23 16	14 37
28 W	0 27 0	4 51 26	0♏25	13 49 D	25 48	28 21	19 01	3 32	19 07	18 27	23 43	26 09	29 24	9 44	10 20	23 12	14 35
29 Th	0 30 57	5 50 20	13 58	13 48	25 10	29 36	19 23	3 24	19 04	18 25	23 42	26 08	29 50	10 10	10 08	23 09	14 32
30 F	0 34 53	6 49 17	27 40	13 48	24 41	0≏50	19 44	3 16	19 02	18 24	23 40	26 08	0♍16	10 35	9 57	23 06	14 29

EPHEMERIS CALCULATED FOR 12 MIDNIGHT GREENWICH MEAN TIME. ALL OTHER DATA AND FACING ASPECTARIAN PAGE IN **EASTERN TIME (BOLD)** AND PACIFIC TIME (REGULAR).

OCTOBER 2022

☽ Last Aspect day	ET / hr:mn / PT		asp	☽ Ingress sign	day	ET / hr:mn / PT	
1	**5:46 pm**	2:46 pm	□ ☿	♑	2	**3:38 am**	12:38 am
3	**11:49 pm**	8:49 pm	☌ ♇	♒	4	**6:20 am**	3:20 am
5	**6:46 pm**	3:46 pm	△ ♂	♓	6	**8:47 am**	5:47 am
8	**7:10 am**	4:10 am	☍ ☿	♈	8	**11:57 am**	8:57 am
10	**10:02 am**	7:02 am	□ ♇	♉	10	**5:04 pm**	2:04 pm
12	**5:42 pm**	2:42 pm	△ ♇	♊	12		10:08 pm
12	**5:42 pm**	2:42 pm	△ ♇	♊	13	**1:08 am**	
14		9:11 pm	☌ ♂	♋	15	**12:11 pm**	9:11 am
15	**12:11 am**		☌ ♂	♋	15	**12:11 pm**	9:11 am
17	**4:56 pm**	1:56 pm	☍ ♇	♌	17		9:45 pm
17	**4:56 pm**	1:56 pm	☍ ♇	♌	18	**12:45 am**	
20	**6:35 am**	3:35 am	✶ ☉	♍	20	**12:25 pm**	9:25 am
22	**2:17 pm**	11:17 am	△ ♇	♎	22	**9:24 pm**	6:24 pm
24	**8:36 pm**	5:36 pm	□ ♇	♏	25	**3:18 am**	12:18 am
26		9:27 pm	✶ ♇	♐	27	**6:55 am**	3:55 am
27	**12:27 am**		✶ ♇	♐	27	**6:55 am**	3:55 am
29	**9:10 am**	6:10 am	□ ♃	♑	29	**9:21 am**	6:21 am
31	**11:14 am**	8:14 am	✶ ♃	♒	31	**11:43 am**	8:43 am

☽ Phases & Eclipses phase	day	ET / hr:mn / PT	
2nd Quarter	2	**8:14 pm**	5:14 pm
Full Moon	9	**4:55 pm**	1:55 pm
4th Quarter	17	**1:15 pm**	10:15 am
New Moon	25	**6:49 am**	3:49 am
●	25	2° ♏ 00'	
2nd Quarter	31		11:37 pm
2nd Quarter	11/1	**2:37 am**	

Planet Ingress		day	ET / hr:mn / PT	
☿	♎	10	**7:51 pm**	4:51 pm
♀	♏	23	**3:52 am**	12:52 am
☉	♏	23	**6:36 am**	3:36 am
♃	♓	27		10:10 pm
♃	♓	28	**1:10 am**	
☿	♏	29	**3:22 pm**	12:22 pm

Planetary Motion		day	ET / hr:mn / PT	
☿	D	2	**5:07 am**	2:07 am
⚴	D	5	**2:10 pm**	11:10 am
♇	D	8	**5:56 pm**	2:56 pm
♄	D	22		9:07 pm
♄	D	23	**12:07 am**	
⚵	D	23	**9:05 am**	6:05 am
♂	℞	30	**9:26 am**	6:26 am

1 SATURDAY
- ☽ ⚻ ♅ **7:43 am** 4:43 am
- ☽ ✶ ♄ **8:48 am** 5:48 am
- ☽ ☍ ♂ **11:03 am** 8:03 am
- ♀ ☍ ♃ **2:12 pm** 11:12 am
- ☽ □ ♆ **4:45 pm** 1:45 pm
- ☽ □ ☿ **5:46 pm** 2:46 pm
- ☽ ⚺ ♇ **9:02 pm** 6:02 pm

2 SUNDAY
- ☽ □ ♃ **8:37 am** 5:37 am
- ☽ □ ♀ **10:35 am** 7:35 am
- ☽ □ ☉ **8:14 pm** 5:14 pm

3 MONDAY
- ☽ △ ♅ **10:37 am** 7:37 am
- ☽ ⚺ ♄ **11:39 am** 8:39 am
- ☽ ⚻ ♂ **3:12 pm** 12:12 pm
- ☽ ✶ ♆ **7:31 pm** 4:31 pm
- ☽ △ ☿ **8:59 pm** 5:59 pm
- ☽ ☌ ♇ **11:49 pm** 8:49 pm

4 TUESDAY
- ☽ ✶ ♃ **10:48 am** 7:48 am
- ☽ △ ♀ **6:04 pm** 3:04 pm
- ☽ △ ☉ 11:31 pm

5 WEDNESDAY
- ☽ △ ☉ **2:31 am**
- ☽ □ ♅ **12:58 pm** 9:58 am
- ☽ ☌ ♄ **2:00 pm** 11:00 am
- ☽ △ ♂ **6:46 pm** 3:46 pm
- ☽ ⚺ ♆ **9:51 pm** 6:51 pm
- ☽ ⚻ ☿ 10:06 pm
- ☽ ⚺ ♇ 11:14 pm

6 THURSDAY
- ☽ ⚻ ☿ **1:06 am**
- ☽ ⚺ ♇ **2:14 am**
- ☽ ⚺ ♃ **12:49 pm** 9:49 am
- ☿ △ ♇ **11:56 pm** 8:56 pm
- ☽ ⚻ ♀ 10:28 pm

7 FRIDAY
- ☽ ⚻ ♀ **1:28 am**
- ☽ ⚻ ☉ **8:54 am** 5:54 am
- ☽ ✶ ♅ **3:35 pm** 12:35 pm
- ☽ ⚺ ♄ **4:39 pm** 1:39 pm
- ☽ □ ♂ **10:40 pm** 7:40 pm
- ☽ ☌ ♆ 9:40 pm

8 SATURDAY
- ☽ ☌ ♆ **12:40 am**
- ☽ ✶ ♇ **5:14 am** 2:14 am
- ☽ ☍ ☿ **7:10 am** 4:10 am
- ☽ ☌ ♃ **3:37 pm** 12:37 pm

9 SUNDAY
- ☽ ☍ ♀ **10:20 am** 7:20 am
- ☽ ☍ ☉ **4:55 pm** 1:55 pm
- ☽ ⚺ ♅ **7:39 pm** 4:39 pm
- ☽ ✶ ♄ **8:48 pm** 5:48 pm

10 MONDAY
- ☽ ✶ ♂ **4:14 am** 1:14 am
- ☽ ⚺ ♆ **5:09 am** 2:09 am
- ☽ □ ♇ **10:02 am** 7:02 am
- ☽ ⚻ ☿ **4:47 pm** 1:47 pm
- ☽ ⚺ ♃ **8:25 pm** 5:25 pm

11 TUESDAY
- ☉ ⚻ ♅ **5:13 am** 2:13 am
- ☉ △ ♄ **9:07 pm** 6:07 pm
- ☽ ⚻ ♀ **10:29 pm** 7:29 pm
- ♂ □ ♆ 10:46 pm
- ☽ ☌ ♅ 11:20 pm

12 WEDNESDAY
- ♂ □ ♆ **1:46 am**
- ☽ ☌ ♅ **2:20 am**
- ☿ ☍ ♃ **3:24 am** 12:24 am
- ☽ □ ♄ **3:37 am** 12:37 am
- ☽ ⚻ ☉ **4:10 am** 1:10 am
- ☽ ✶ ♆ **12:25 pm** 9:25 am
- ☽ ⚺ ♂ **12:38 pm** 9:38 am
- ☽ △ ♇ **5:42 pm** 2:42 pm

13 THURSDAY
- ☽ ✶ ♃ **4:08 am** 1:08 am
- ☽ △ ☿ **7:29 am** 4:29 am
- ♀ ⚻ ♅ **12:57 pm** 9:57 am
- ♀ △ ♄ 11:21 pm

14 FRIDAY
- ♀ △ ♄ **2:21 am**
- ☽ ⚺ ♅ **12:07 pm** 9:07 am
- ☽ △ ♄ **1:33 pm** 10:33 am
- ☽ △ ♀ **2:51 pm** 11:51 am
- ☽ △ ☉ **7:23 pm** 4:23 pm
- ☽ □ ♆ **10:46 pm** 7:46 pm
- ☽ ☌ ♂ 9:11 pm

15 SATURDAY
- ☽ ☌ ♂ **12:11 am**
- ☽ ⚻ ♇ **4:26 am** 1:26 am
- ☽ □ ♃ **2:44 pm** 11:44 am

16 SUNDAY
- ☽ □ ☿ **3:19 am** 12:19 am
- ☉ ⚻ ♆ **11:39 am** 8:39 am
- ☽ ✶ ♅ 9:09 pm
- ☽ ⚻ ♄ 10:44 pm

17 MONDAY
- ☽ ✶ ♅ **12:09 am**
- ☽ ⚻ ♄ **1:44 am**
- ☽ □ ♀ **10:14 am** 7:14 am
- ☽ △ ♆ **11:04 am** 8:04 am
- ☽ □ ☉ **1:15 pm** 10:15 am
- ☽ ⚺ ♂ **1:35 pm** 10:35 am
- ☽ ☍ ♇ **4:56 pm** 1:56 pm
- ♀ ⚻ ♆ **6:00 pm** 3:00 pm
- ☉ △ ♂ **6:05 pm** 3:05 pm
- ☽ △ ♃ 11:44 pm

18 TUESDAY
- ☽ △ ♃ **2:44 am**
- ♀ △ ♂ **10:20 pm** 7:20 pm
- ☽ ✶ ☿ 10:16 pm

19 WEDNESDAY
- ☽ ✶ ☿ **1:16 am**
- ☉ □ ♇ **9:33 am** 6:33 am
- ☽ □ ♅ **12:17 pm** 9:17 am
- ☽ ☍ ♄ **1:59 pm** 10:59 am
- ☽ ⚻ ♆ **11:02 pm** 8:02 pm
- ♀ □ ♇ 11:03 pm
- ☽ ✶ ♂ 11:23 pm

20 THURSDAY
- ♀ □ ♇ **2:03 am**
- ☽ ✶ ♂ **2:23 am**
- ☽ ⚻ ♇ **4:53 am** 1:53 am
- ☽ ✶ ♀ **5:13 am** 2:13 am
- ☽ ✶ ☉ **6:35 am** 3:35 am
- ☽ ⚻ ♃ **1:50 pm** 10:50 am

21 FRIDAY
- ☽ ⚺ ☿ **8:54 pm** 5:54 pm
- ☽ △ ♅ **10:19 pm** 7:19 pm
- ☽ ⚻ ♄ 9:06 pm

22 SATURDAY
- ☽ ⚻ ♄ **12:06 am**
- ☿ ⚻ ♅ **7:24 am** 4:24 am
- ☽ ☍ ♆ **8:37 am** 5:37 am
- ☽ □ ♂ **12:27 pm** 9:27 am
- ☽ △ ♇ **2:17 pm** 11:17 am
- ☉ ☌ ♀ **5:17 pm** 2:17 pm
- ☽ ⚺ ☉ **8:38 pm** 5:38 pm
- ☽ ⚺ ♀ **8:43 pm** 5:43 pm
- ☿ △ ♄ **9:00 pm** 6:00 pm
- ☽ ☍ ♃ **10:17 pm** 7:17 pm

23 SUNDAY
- ♀ ⚻ ♃ **11:58 am** 8:58 am
- ☉ ⚻ ♃ **4:21 pm** 1:21 pm

24 MONDAY
- ☽ ⚻ ♅ **5:18 am** 2:18 am
- ☽ △ ♄ **7:08 am** 4:08 am
- ☽ ☌ ☿ **12:01 pm** 9:01 am
- ☽ ⚻ ♆ **3:07 pm** 12:07 pm
- ☽ △ ♂ **7:12 pm** 4:12 pm
- ☽ □ ♇ **8:36 pm** 5:36 pm

25 TUESDAY
- ☽ ⚻ ♃ **3:46 am** 12:46 am
- ☽ ☌ ☉ **6:49 am** 3:49 am
- ☽ ☌ ♀ **8:04 am** 5:04 am
- ☿ ⚻ ♆ **12:30 pm** 9:30 am

26 WEDNESDAY
- ☽ ☍ ♅ **9:34 am** 6:34 am
- ☽ □ ♄ **11:30 am** 8:30 am
- ☽ △ ♆ **7:04 pm** 4:04 pm
- ☽ ⚺ ☿ **11:17 pm** 8:17 pm
- ☽ ⚻ ♂ **11:19 pm** 8:19 pm
- ☿ △ ♂ **11:37 pm** 8:37 pm
- ☽ ✶ ♇ 9:27 pm

27 THURSDAY
- ☽ ✶ ♇ **12:27 am**
- ☽ △ ♃ **7:01 am** 4:01 am
- ☿ □ ♇ **9:09 am** 6:09 am
- ☽ ⚺ ☉ **2:11 pm** 11:11 am
- ☽ ⚺ ♀ **4:30 pm** 1:30 pm

28 FRIDAY
- ☽ ⚻ ♅ **12:13 pm** 9:13 am
- ☽ ✶ ♄ **2:17 pm** 11:17 am
- ☽ □ ♆ **9:37 pm** 6:37 pm
- ☽ ☍ ♂ 10:59 pm

29 SATURDAY
- ☽ ☍ ♂ **1:59 am**
- ☽ ⚺ ♇ **3:01 am** 12:01 am
- ☽ ✶ ☿ **8:34 am** 5:34 am
- ☽ □ ♃ **9:10 am** 6:10 am
- ☿ ⚻ ♃ **1:32 pm** 10:32 am
- ☽ ✶ ☉ **8:20 pm** 5:20 pm
- ☽ ✶ ♀ **11:41 pm** 8:41 pm

30 SUNDAY
- ☽ △ ♅ **2:21 pm** 11:21 am
- ☽ ⚺ ♄ **4:36 pm** 1:36 pm
- ☽ ✶ ♆ **11:51 pm** 8:51 pm

31 MONDAY
- ☽ ⚻ ♂ **4:19 am** 1:19 am
- ☽ ☌ ♇ **5:23 am** 2:23 am
- ☽ ✶ ♃ **11:14 am** 8:14 am
- ☽ □ ☿ **5:37 pm** 2:37 pm
- ☽ □ ☉ 11:37 pm

Eastern time in bold type
Pacific time in medium type

OCTOBER 2022

DATE	SID.TIME	SUN	MOON	NODE	MERCURY	VENUS	MARS	JUPITER	SATURN	URANUS	NEPTUNE	PLUTO	CERES	PALLAS	JUNO	VESTA	CHIRON
1 Sa	0 38 50	7≏48 15	11✗'32	13♉50	24♍22R	2≏05	20Ⅱ05	3♈08R	19≈00R	18♉22R	23♓39R	26♑08R	0♉42	11♋00	9♋46R	23≈03R	14♈27R
2 Su	0 42 47	8 47 14	25 32	13 51	24 13D	3 20	20 25	3 00	18 58	18 20	23 37	26 08	1 08	11 25	9 36	23 02	14 24
3 M	0 46 43	9 46 16	9♑39	13 52R	24 14	4 35	20 45	2 52	18 56	18 18	23 35	26 07	1 34	11 50	9 26	23 00	14 21
4 T	0 50 40	10 45 19	23 51	13 51	24 26	5 50	21 04	2 44	18 54	18 17	23 34	26 07	1 59	12 15	9 16	22 59	14 19
5 W	0 54 36	11 44 24	8≈08	13 49	24 47	7 05	21 23	2 36	18 52	18 15	23 32	26 07	2 25	12 39	9 07	22 58D	14 16
6 Th	0 58 33	12 43 31	22 25	13 45	25 19	8 20	21 41	2 29	18 50	18 13	23 31	26 07	2 50	13 03	8 58	22 58	14 14
7 F	1 2 29	13 42 39	6♓38	13 41	26 00	9 35	21 59	2 21	18 48	18 11	23 29	26 07	3 16	13 27	8 50	22 59	14 11
8 Sa	1 6 26	14 41 49	20 44	13 37	26 49	10 50	22 16	2 13	18 47	18 09	23 28	26 07D	3 41	13 51	8 42	22 59	14 08
9 Su	1 10 22	15 41 01	4♈38	13 33	27 46	12 04	22 32	2 06	18 45	18 07	23 26	26 07	4 07	14 15	8 35	23 01	14 05
10 M	1 14 19	16 40 15	18 17	13 33	28 50	13 19	22 48	1 58	18 44	18 05	23 25	26 07	4 32	14 38	8 28	23 02	14 02
11 T	1 18 15	17 39 31	1♉37	13 28D	0≏00	14 34	23 03	1 51	18 43	18 03	23 23	26 07	4 57	15 02	8 21	23 04	14 00
12 W	1 22 12	18 38 49	14 38	13 27	1 17	15 49	23 18	1 43	18 42	18 01	23 22	26 07	5 23	15 25	8 15	23 06	13 57
13 Th	1 26 9	19 38 10	27 19	13 27	2 37	17 04	23 32	1 36	18 41	17 59	23 20	26 07	5 48	15 47	8 10	23 10	13 54
14 F	1 30 5	20 37 32	9Ⅱ44	13 29	4 03	18 19	23 45	1 29	18 40	17 57	23 19	26 07	6 13	16 10	8 05	23 14	13 52
15 Sa	1 34 2	21 36 57	21 54	13 31	5 31	19 35	23 58	1 22	18 39	17 55	23 18	26 08	6 38	16 32	8 00	23 17	13 50
16 Su	1 37 58	22 36 24	3♋54	13 32	7 03	20 50	24 10	1 15	18 38	17 53	23 16	26 08	7 03	16 54	7 56	23 22	13 46
17 M	1 41 55	23 35 54	15 47	13 33R	8 37	22 05	24 21	1 08	18 37	17 50	23 15	26 08	7 28	17 16	7 52	23 27	13 44
18 T	1 45 51	24 35 26	27 39	13 33	10 13	23 20	24 31	1 01	18 37	17 48	23 13	26 08	7 53	17 38	7 49	23 32	13 41
19 W	1 49 48	25 35 00	9♌35	13 33	11 51	24 35	24 41	0 55	18 36	17 46	23 12	26 08	8 18	17 59	7 47	23 37	13 38
20 Th	1 53 45	26 34 36	21 38	13 31	13 30	25 50	24 50	0 48	18 36	17 44	23 11	26 09	8 43	18 20	7 45	23 43	13 36
21 F	1 57 41	27 34 14	3♍54	13 30	15 09	27 05	24 59	0 42	18 36	17 41	23 09	26 09	9 07	18 41	7 43	23 50	13 33
22 Sa	2 1 38	28 33 55	16 25	13 27	16 50	28 20	25 06	0 35	18 35	17 39	23 08	26 09	9 32	19 01	7 42	23 57	13 30
23 Su	2 5 34	29 33 38	29 15	13 25	18 31	29 35	25 13	0 29	18 35D	17 37	23 07	26 10	9 56	19 21	7 42D	24 04	13 28
24 M	2 9 31	0♏33 23	12≏23	13 22D	20 12	0♏51	25 19	0 23	18 35	17 34	23 06	26 10	10 21	19 41	7 42	24 11	13 25
25 T	2 13 27	1 33 10	25 51	13 22	21 54	2 06	25 24	0 18	18 35	17 32	23 04	26 11	10 45	20 00	7 42	24 19	13 23
26 W	2 17 24	2 32 59	9♏35	13 22D	23 35	3 21	25 28	0 12	18 36	17 30	23 03	26 11	11 10	20 19	7 43	24 28	13 20
27 Th	2 21 20	3 32 50	23 35	13 23	25 17	4 36	25 31	0 06	18 36	17 27	23 02	26 12	11 34	20 38	7 45	24 36	13 18
28 F	2 25 17	4 32 43	7✗45	13 22	26 58	5 51	25 34	0 01	18 37	17 25	23 01	26 12	11 58	20 56	7 47	24 46	13 15
29 Sa	2 29 13	5 32 37	22 02	13 23	28 39	7 06	25 36	29♓56	18 37	17 23	23 00	26 13	12 22	21 14	7 49	24 55	13 13
30 Su	2 33 10	6 32 34	6♑21	13 24	0♏19	8 22	25 37R	29 51	18 38	17 20	22 59	26 14	12 46	21 32	7 52	25 05	13 10
31 M	2 37 7	7 32 32	20 40	13 24	2 00	9 37	25 37	29 46	18 38	17 18	22 58	26 14	13 10	21 49	7 56	25 15	13 08

EPHEMERIS CALCULATED FOR 12 MIDNIGHT GREENWICH MEAN TIME. ALL OTHER DATA AND FACING ASPECTARIAN PAGE IN **EASTERN TIME (BOLD)** AND PACIFIC TIME (REGULAR).

NOVEMBER 2022

☽ Last Aspect / ☽ Ingress (first)

☽ Last Aspect day	ET / hr:mn / PT	asp	☽ Ingress sign day	ET / hr:mn / PT
2	7:08 am 4:08 am	△ ♂	♈ 2	2:46 pm 11:46 am
4	6:05 pm 3:05 pm	□ ♀	♉ 4	7:57 pm ... 9:15 pm
5	5:30 am 2:30 am	⚹ ♀	♊ 6	...
6	5:30 am 2:30 am		♋ 9	8:37 am 5:37 am
7	7:00 am 4:00 am		♌ 11	7:22 pm 4:22 pm
11	5:28 am 2:28 am		♍ 14	7:48 am 4:48 am
13	5:41 am 2:41 am		♎ 16	8:04 pm 5:04 pm
16	6:55 am 3:55 am		♏ 19	5:58 am 2:58 am
19	3:47 am 12:47 am		♐ 21	12:16 pm 9:16 am
21	6:14 am 3:14 am			

☽ Last Aspect / ☽ Ingress (second)

☽ Last Aspect day	ET / hr:mn / PT	asp	☽ Ingress sign day	ET / hr:mn / PT
23	1:16 pm 10:16 am		♑ 23	3:16 pm 12:16 pm
25	2:22 pm 11:22 am		♒ 25	4:18 pm 1:18 pm
27	3:11 pm 12:11 pm		♓ 27	5:07 pm 2:07 pm
28	10:53 pm		♈ 29	7:15 pm 4:15 pm
28	1:53 am		♓ 29	7:15 pm 4:15 pm

☽ Phases & Eclipses

phase	day	ET / hr:mn / PT
2nd Quarter 10/31		11:37 pm
2nd Quarter	1	2:37 am
Full Moon	8	6:02 am 3:02 am
	8	16° ♉ 01'
4th Quarter	16	8:27 am 5:27 am
New Moon	23	5:57 pm 2:57 pm
2nd Quarter	30	9:37 am 6:37 am

Planet Ingress

		ET / hr:mn / PT
♀ ♐	15	10:09 pm
♀ ♐	16	1:09 am
☿ ♐	17	3:42 am 12:42 am
☿ ♐	20	4:25 pm 1:25 pm
⊙ ♐	22	3:20 am 12:20 am

Planetary Motion

		ET / hr:mn / PT
♀ D	23	6:02 pm 3:02 pm
♀ D	30	3:33 pm 12:33 pm

Eastern time in bold type
Pacific time in medium type

NOVEMBER 2022

DATE	SID.TIME	SUN	MOON	NODE	MERCURY	VENUS	MARS	JUPITER	SATURN	URANUS	NEPTUNE	PLUTO	CERES	PALLAS	JUNO	VESTA	CHIRON
1 T	2 41 3	8 ♏ 32 32	4 ≈ 54	13 ♉ 24 ℞	3 ♏ 40	10 ♏ 52	25 ♊ 36 ℞	29 ♓ 42 ℞	18 ≈ 39	17 ♉ 15 ℞	22 ♓ 57 ℞	26 ♑ 15	13 ♍ 34	22 ♋ 06	8 ♊ 00	25 ≈ 26	13 ♈ 05 ℞
2 W	2 45 0	9 32 33	19 02	13 24	5 19	12 07	25 34	29 37	18 40	17 13	22 56	26 15	13 57	22 22	8 04	25 37	13 03
3 Th	2 48 56	10 32 36	3 ♓ 02	13 24	6 58	13 23	25 28	29 33	18 41	17 10	22 55	26 16	14 21	22 38	8 09	25 48	13 01
4 F	2 52 53	11 32 40	16 52	13 24 D	8 37	14 38	25 23	29 29	18 43	17 08	22 54	26 17	14 44	22 54	8 15	25 59	12 58
5 Sa	2 56 49	12 32 45	0 ♈ 30	13 24	10 15	15 53	25 19	29 25	18 44	17 06	22 53	26 18	15 08	23 09	8 21	26 11	12 56
6 Su	3 0 46	13 32 53	13 56	13 24	11 53	17 08	25 13	29 21	18 45	17 03	22 52	26 19	15 31	23 24	8 27	26 24	12 54
7 M	3 4 42	14 33 02	27 09	13 24	13 31	18 23	25 06	29 18	18 47	17 00	22 51	26 19	15 54	23 38	8 34	26 36	12 52
8 T	3 8 39	15 33 13	10 ♉ 07	13 24 ℞	15 08	19 39	24 58	29 14	18 48	16 58	22 50	26 20	16 17	23 52	8 41	26 49	12 49
9 W	3 12 36	16 33 25	22 52	13 24	16 44	20 54	24 49	29 11	18 50	16 55	22 49	26 21	16 40	24 05	8 49	27 02	12 47
10 Th	3 16 32	17 33 39	5 ♊ 23	13 24	18 21	22 09	24 40	29 08	18 52	16 53	22 48	26 22	17 03	24 18	8 58	27 16	12 45
11 F	3 20 29	18 33 56	17 42	13 23	19 57	23 24	24 29	29 05	18 54	16 51	22 48	26 23	17 26	24 30	9 06	27 29	12 43
12 Sa	3 24 25	19 34 14	29 49	13 22	21 32	24 40	24 18	29 03	18 56	16 48	22 47	26 24	17 48	24 42	9 16	27 43	12 41
13 Su	3 28 22	20 34 34	11 ♋ 47	13 21	23 08	25 55	24 06	29 00	18 58	16 46	22 46	26 25	18 11	24 53	9 25	27 58	12 39
14 M	3 32 18	21 34 56	23 41	13 20	24 43	27 10	23 53	28 58	19 00	16 43	22 45	26 26	18 33	25 04	9 35	28 12	12 37
15 T	3 36 15	22 35 19	5 ♌ 32	13 19	26 17	28 25	23 39	28 56	19 02	16 41	22 45	26 27	18 56	25 14	9 46	28 27	12 35
16 W	3 40 12	23 35 45	17 26	13 19 D	27 52	29 41	23 25	28 55	19 04	16 38	22 44	26 28	19 18	25 24	9 57	28 42	12 33
17 Th	3 44 8	24 36 12	29 28	13 19	29 28	0 ♐ 56	23 09	28 53	19 07	16 36	22 44	26 29	19 40	25 33	10 08	28 58	12 31
18 F	3 48 5	25 36 41	11 ♍ 41	13 19	1 ♐ 00	2 11	22 53	28 52	19 09	16 33	22 43	26 30	20 02	25 41	10 20	29 13	12 29
19 Sa	3 52 1	26 37 12	24 11	13 19	2 34	3 27	22 36	28 50	19 12	16 31	22 43	26 31	20 24	25 49	10 32	29 29	12 28
20 Su	3 55 58	27 37 45	7 ♎ 01	13 23	4 07	4 42	22 19	28 50	19 15	16 28	22 42	26 33	20 45	25 56	10 45	29 45	12 26
21 M	3 59 54	28 38 20	20 14	13 23	5 40	5 57	22 01	28 49	19 18	16 26	22 42	26 34	21 07	26 03	10 58	0 ♓ 02	12 26
22 T	4 3 51	29 38 56	3 ♏ 52	13 24 ℞	7 13	7 12	21 42	28 48	19 21	16 24	22 41	26 35	21 28	26 09	11 11	0 18	12 23
23 W	4 7 47	0 ♐ 39 34	17 53	13 23	8 46	8 28	21 22	28 48 D	19 24	16 21	22 41	26 36	21 49	26 14	11 25	0 35	12 21
24 Th	4 11 44	1 40 13	2 ♐ 16	13 23	10 19	9 43	21 02	28 48	19 27	16 19	22 40	26 37	22 10	26 19	11 39	0 52	12 19
25 F	4 15 40	2 40 54	16 53	13 21	11 51	10 58	20 42	28 48	19 30	16 16	22 40	26 39	22 31	26 23	11 54	1 10	12 18
26 Sa	4 19 37	3 41 36	1 ♑ 40	13 24	13 24	12 14	20 21	28 48	19 33	16 14	22 40	26 40	22 52	26 26	12 09	1 27	12 16
27 Su	4 23 34	4 42 20	16 27	13 16	14 56	13 29	19 59	28 49	19 37	16 12	22 40	26 41	23 13	26 29	12 24	1 45	12 15
28 M	4 27 30	5 43 04	1 ≈ 09	13 11	16 28	14 44	19 37	28 50	19 40	16 09	22 39	26 43	23 33	26 31	12 40	2 03	12 14
29 T	4 31 27	6 43 50	15 38	13 11	18 00	16 00	19 15	28 51	19 44	16 07	22 39	26 44	23 53	26 32	12 56	2 22	12 12
30 W	4 35 23	7 44 36	29 51	13 09 D	19 32	17 15	19 15	28 52	19 47	16 05	22 39	26 46	24 14	26 33 ℞	13 12	2 40	12 11

DECEMBER 2022

☽ Last Aspect day	ET / hr:mn / PT	asp	☽ Ingress sign	day	ET / hr:mn / PT
1	9:44 pm 6:44 pm	☌ ♃	♈	1	11:41 pm 8:41 pm
3	9:46 pm	□ ♇	♉	4	6:38 am 3:38 am
4	12:46 am	□ ♇	♉	4	6:38 am 3:38 am
6	2:02 pm 11:02 am	⚹ ♃	♊	6	3:49 pm 12:49 pm
8	10:13 pm	□ ♃	♋	8	11:49 pm
9	1:13 am	□ ♃	♋	9	2:49 am
11	1:49 pm 10:49 am	△ ♃	♌	11	3:09 pm 12:09 pm
13	10:52 am 7:52 am	△ ☉	♍	14	3:45 am 12:45 am
16	2:13 pm 11:13 am	☍ ♃	♎	16	2:49 pm 11:49 am
18	5:35 pm 2:35 pm	□ ♇	♏	18	10:31 pm 7:31 pm
20	9:45 pm 6:45 pm	⚹ ♇	♐	20	11:12 pm

☽ Last Aspect day	ET / hr:mn / PT	asp	☽ Ingress sign	day	ET / hr:mn / PT
20	9:45 pm 6:45 pm	⚹ ♇	♐	21	2:12 am
22	3:16 pm 12:16 pm	□ ♆	♑	22	11:49 pm
22	3:16 pm 12:16 pm	□ ♆	♑	23	2:49 am
24	10:11 pm 7:11 pm	☌ ♇	♒	24	11:14 pm
24	10:11 pm 7:11 pm	☌ ♇	♒	25	2:14 am
26	1:19 pm 10:19 am	☌ ♄	♓	26	11:34 pm
26	1:19 pm 10:19 am	☌ ♄	♓	27	2:34 am
28	10:21 pm	⚹ ♇	♈	29	5:36 am 2:36 am
29	1:21 am	⚹ ♇	♈	29	5:36 am 2:36 am
31	7:44 am 4:44 am	□ ♇	♉	31	12:08 pm 9:08 am

☽ Phases & Eclipses phase	day	ET / hr:mn / PT
Full Moon	7	11:08 pm 8:08 pm
4th Quarter	16	3:56 am 12:56 am
New Moon	23	5:17 am 2:17 am
2nd Quarter	29	8:21 pm 5:21 pm

Planet Ingress	day	ET / hr:mn / PT
☿ ♑	6	5:08 pm 2:08 pm
♀ ♑	9	10:54 pm 7:54 pm
⚳ ♎	18	6:34 pm 3:34 pm
♃ ♈	20	9:32 am 6:32 am
☉ ♑	21	4:48 pm 1:48 pm

Planetary Motion		day	ET / hr:mn / PT
♆	D	3	7:15 pm 4:15 pm
⚷	D	23	4:31 am 1:31 am
☿	℞	29	4:32 am 1:32 am

1 THURSDAY
- ♀ ☍ ♂ **12:28 am**
- ☽ □ ♂ **3:42 am** 12:42 am
- ☽ □ ♀ **4:08 am** 1:08 am
- ☽ ⚺ ♄ **5:43 am** 2:43 am
- ☽ □ ☿ **9:23 am** 6:23 am
- ☽ ☌ ♆ **10:36 am** 7:36 am
- ☽ ⚹ ♇ **5:59 pm** 2:59 pm
- ☿ □ ♆ **8:08 pm** 5:08 pm
- ☽ ☌ ♃ **9:44 pm** 6:44 pm
- ♀ ⚹ ♄ **10:09 pm** 7:09 pm

2 FRIDAY
- ☽ △ ☉ **7:10 pm** 4:10 pm

3 SATURDAY
- ☽ ⚺ ♅ **4:36 am** 1:36 am
- ☽ ⚹ ♂ **8:11 am** 5:11 am
- ☽ ⚹ ♄ **12:06 pm** 9:06 am
- ☽ △ ♀ **3:57 pm** 12:57 pm
- ☽ ⚺ ♆ **4:56 pm** 1:56 pm
- ☽ △ ☿ **10:53 pm** 7:53 pm
- ☽ □ ♇ 9:46 pm
- ♀ □ ♆ 11:12 pm

4 SUNDAY
- ☽ □ ♇ **12:46 am**
- ♀ □ ♆ **2:12 am**
- ☽ ⚺ ♃ **4:44 am** 1:44 am
- ☿ ⚺ ♇ **3:11 pm** 12:11 pm

5 MONDAY
- ☽ ⚻ ☉ **7:50 am** 4:50 am
- ☽ ☌ ♅ **12:38 pm** 9:38 am
- ☽ ⚺ ♂ **2:50 pm** 11:50 am
- ☽ □ ♄ **8:54 pm** 5:54 pm
- ☽ ⚹ ♆ 10:37 pm
- ☿ □ ♃ 11:05 pm

6 TUESDAY
- ☽ ⚹ ♆ **1:37 am**
- ☿ □ ♃ **2:05 am**
- ☽ ⚻ ♀ **6:55 am** 3:55 am
- ☽ △ ♇ **9:51 am** 6:51 am
- ☽ ⚹ ♃ **2:02 pm** 11:02 am
- ☽ ⚻ ☿ **3:38 pm** 12:38 pm

7 WEDNESDAY
- ♀ ⚺ ♇ **12:33 pm** 9:33 am
- ☉ ⚻ ♅ **5:35 pm** 2:35 pm
- ☽ ⚺ ♅ **10:40 pm** 7:40 pm
- ☽ ☍ ☉ **11:08 pm** 8:08 pm
- ☽ ☌ ♂ **11:19 pm** 8:19 pm
- ☉ ☍ ♂ 9:42 pm

8 THURSDAY
- ☉ ☍ ♂ **12:42 am**
- ☽ △ ♄ **7:41 am** 4:41 am
- ☽ □ ♆ **12:13 pm** 9:13 am
- ☽ ⚻ ♇ **8:49 pm** 5:49 pm
- ♂ ⚺ ♅ **10:05 pm** 7:05 pm
- ☽ ☍ ♀ 9:29 pm
- ☽ □ ♃ 10:13 pm

9 FRIDAY
- ☽ ☍ ♀ **12:29 am**
- ☽ □ ♃ **1:13 am**
- ♀ □ ♃ **7:55 am** 4:55 am
- ☽ ☍ ☿ **10:55 am** 7:55 am

10 SATURDAY
- ☽ ⚺ ♂ **9:16 am** 6:16 am
- ☽ ⚹ ♅ **10:17 am** 7:17 am
- ☽ ⚻ ☉ **4:30 pm** 1:30 pm
- ☽ ⚻ ♄ **8:03 pm** 5:03 pm
- ☽ △ ♆ 9:18 pm

11 SUNDAY
- ☽ △ ♆ **12:18 am**
- ☽ ☍ ♇ **9:11 am** 6:11 am
- ☽ △ ♃ **1:49 pm** 10:49 am
- ☽ ⚻ ♀ **7:54 pm** 4:54 pm

12 MONDAY
- ☽ ⚻ ☿ **7:47 am** 4:47 am
- ☉ ⚹ ♄ **1:12 pm** 10:12 am
- ☽ ⚹ ♂ **8:04 pm** 5:04 pm
- ☽ □ ♅ **10:47 pm** 7:47 pm

13 TUESDAY
- ☽ ☍ ♄ **9:09 am** 6:09 am
- ☽ △ ☉ **10:52 am** 7:52 am
- ☽ ⚻ ♆ **1:01 pm** 10:01 am
- ☽ ⚻ ♇ **9:59 pm** 6:59 pm
- ☽ ⚻ ♃ 11:46 pm

14 WEDNESDAY
- ☽ ⚻ ♃ **2:46 am**
- ☉ □ ♆ **12:10 pm** 9:10 am
- ☽ △ ♀ **3:32 pm** 12:32 pm

15 THURSDAY
- ☽ △ ☿ **4:02 am** 1:02 am
- ☽ □ ♂ **6:29 am** 3:29 am
- ☽ △ ♅ **10:41 am** 7:41 am
- ☽ ⚻ ♄ **9:18 pm** 6:18 pm
- ☿ ⚻ ♂ **10:12 pm** 7:12 pm
- ☽ ☍ ♆ 9:41 pm

16 FRIDAY
- ☽ ☍ ♆ **12:41 am**
- ☽ □ ☉ **3:56 am** 12:56 am
- ☽ △ ♇ **9:25 am** 6:25 am
- ☽ ☍ ♃ **2:13 pm** 11:13 am

17 SATURDAY
- ☽ □ ♀ **8:28 am** 5:28 am
- ☽ △ ♂ **2:44 pm** 11:44 am
- ☿ △ ♅ **4:37 pm** 1:37 pm
- ☽ ⚻ ♅ **8:03 pm** 5:03 pm
- ☽ □ ☿ **8:26 pm** 5:26 pm

18 SUNDAY
- ☽ △ ♄ **6:31 am** 3:31 am
- ☽ ⚻ ♆ **9:20 am** 6:20 am
- ☽ ⚹ ☉ **5:03 pm** 2:03 pm
- ☽ □ ♇ **5:35 pm** 2:35 pm
- ☽ ⚻ ♃ **10:17 pm** 7:17 pm
- ☉ ⚺ ♇ 9:26 pm

19 MONDAY
- ☉ ⚺ ♇ **12:26 am**
- ♀ ⚻ ♂ **12:37 pm** 9:37 am
- ☽ ⚻ ♂ **7:30 pm** 4:30 pm
- ☽ ⚹ ♀ **8:22 pm** 5:22 pm
- ☽ ☍ ♅ 10:33 pm

20 TUESDAY
- ☽ ☍ ♅ **1:33 am**
- ☽ ⚹ ☿ **6:58 am** 3:58 am
- ☽ □ ♄ **11:41 am** 8:41 am
- ☽ △ ♆ **2:01 pm** 11:01 am
- ☽ ⚹ ♇ **9:45 pm** 6:45 pm
- ☽ ⚺ ☉ 10:06 pm
- ☽ △ ♃ 11:19 pm

21 WEDNESDAY
- ☽ ⚺ ☉ **1:06 am**
- ☽ △ ♃ **2:19 am**
- ☉ □ ♃ **7:50 pm** 4:50 pm
- ☽ ☍ ♂ **8:48 pm** 5:48 pm

22 THURSDAY
- ☽ ⚺ ♀ **3:15 am** 12:15 am
- ☽ ⚻ ♅ **3:23 am** 12:23 am
- ♀ △ ♅ **4:48 am** 1:48 am
- ☽ ⚺ ☿ **12:15 pm** 9:15 am
- ☽ ⚹ ♄ **1:19 pm** 10:19 am
- ☽ □ ♆ **3:16 pm** 12:16 pm
- ☽ ⚺ ♇ **10:40 pm** 7:40 pm

23 FRIDAY
- ☽ □ ♃ **3:13 am** 12:13 am
- ☽ ☌ ☉ **5:17 am** 2:17 am
- ☿ ⚺ ♄ **8:08 am** 5:08 am
- ☽ ⚻ ♂ **7:51 pm** 4:51 pm

24 SATURDAY
- ☽ △ ♅ **3:02 am** 12:02 am
- ☽ ☌ ♀ **7:16 am** 4:16 am
- ☽ ⚺ ♄ **1:09 pm** 10:09 am
- ☽ ☌ ☿ **2:32 pm** 11:32 am
- ☽ ⚹ ♆ **2:48 pm** 11:48 am
- ☿ ⚹ ♆ **8:17 pm** 5:17 pm
- ☽ ☌ ♇ **10:11 pm** 7:11 pm
- ☽ ⚹ ♃ 11:56 pm

25 SUNDAY
- ☽ ⚹ ♃ **2:56 am**
- ☽ ⚺ ☉ **8:07 am** 5:07 am
- ☽ △ ♂ **6:34 pm** 3:34 pm
- ☽ □ ♅ 11:35 pm

26 MONDAY
- ☽ □ ♅ **2:35 am**
- ☽ ⚺ ♀ **11:24 am** 8:24 am
- ☽ ☌ ♄ **1:19 pm** 10:19 am
- ☽ ⚺ ♆ **2:46 pm** 11:46 am
- ☽ ⚺ ☿ **4:24 pm** 1:24 pm
- ☽ ⚺ ♇ **10:28 pm** 7:28 pm

27 TUESDAY
- ☽ ⚺ ♃ **3:39 am** 12:39 am
- ♀ ⚺ ♄ **11:53 am** 8:53 am
- ☽ ⚹ ☉ **12:23 pm** 9:23 am
- ☽ □ ♂ **6:54 pm** 3:54 pm

28 WEDNESDAY
- ♀ ⚹ ♆ **3:32 am** 12:32 am
- ☽ ⚹ ♅ **4:02 am** 1:02 am
- ☽ ⚺ ♄ **3:51 pm** 12:51 pm
- ☽ ☌ ♆ **5:05 pm** 2:05 pm
- ☽ ⚹ ♀ **6:25 pm** 3:25 pm
- ☽ ⚹ ☿ **7:43 pm** 4:43 pm
- ☽ ⚹ ♇ 10:21 pm

29 THURSDAY
- ☽ ⚹ ♇ **1:21 am**
- ☽ ☌ ♃ **7:11 am** 4:11 am
- ☿ ☌ ♀ **8:58 am** 5:58 am
- ☽ □ ☉ **8:21 pm** 5:21 pm
- ☽ ⚹ ♂ **10:17 pm** 7:17 pm

30 FRIDAY
- ☽ ⚺ ♅ **8:45 am** 5:45 am
- ☉ ⚻ ♂ **6:21 pm** 3:21 pm
- ☽ ⚹ ♄ **9:52 pm** 6:52 pm
- ☽ ⚺ ♆ **10:51 pm** 7:51 pm
- ☽ □ ☿ 10:00 pm

31 SATURDAY
- ☽ □ ☿ **1:00 am**
- ☽ □ ♀ **5:59 am** 2:59 am
- ☽ □ ♇ **7:44 am** 4:44 am
- ☽ ⚺ ♃ **2:20 pm** 11:20 am
- ♀ ☌ ♇ 9:25 pm

Eastern time in bold type
Pacific time in medium type

DECEMBER 2022

DATE	SID.TIME	SUN	MOON	NODE	MERCURY	VENUS	MARS	JUPITER	SATURN	URANUS	NEPTUNE	PLUTO	CERES	PALLAS	JUNO	VESTA	CHIRON
1 Th	4 39 20	8♐45 24	13♓46	13♉09	21♐03	18♐30	18♊53R	28♓53	19≈51	16♉03R	22♓39R	26♑47	24♍34	26♋33R	13♈29	2♓59	12♈10R
2 F	4 43 16	9 46 12	27 23	13 10	22 34	19 46	18 30	28 55	19 55	16 00	22 39	26 50	24 53	26 32	13 46	3 18	12 09
3 Sa	4 47 13	10 47 01	10♈42	13 12	24 06	21 01	18 07	28 56	19 59	15 58	22 39	26 50	25 13	26 30	14 03	3 37	12 08
4 Su	4 51 10	11 47 51	23 45	13 13	25 36	22 16	17 44	28 58	20 03	15 56	22 39D	26 53	25 32	26 28	14 21	3 56	12 06
5 M	4 55 6	12 48 41	6♉35	13 15R	27 07	23 31	17 21	29 01	20 07	15 54	22 39	26 54	25 52	26 25	14 39	4 16	12 05
6 T	4 59 3	13 49 33	19 12	13 15	28 37	24 47	16 58	29 03	20 11	15 52	22 39	26 56	26 11	26 22	14 57	4 35	12 04
7 W	5 2 59	14 50 26	1♊39	13 13	0♑07	26 02	16 34	29 06	20 15	15 50	22 39	26 57	26 30	26 17	15 16	4 55	12 04
8 Th	5 6 56	15 51 20	13 56	13 10	1 36	27 17	16 11	29 09	20 20	15 48	22 39	26 59	26 48	26 12	15 35	5 15	12 03
9 F	5 10 52	16 52 15	26 04	13 05	3 05	28 32	15 48	29 11	20 24	15 46	22 39	27 01	27 07	26 06	15 55	5 35	12 02
10 Sa	5 14 49	17 53 10	8♋06	12 59	4 33	29 48	15 25	29 14	20 29	15 44	22 39	27 02	27 25	25 59	16 14	5 56	12 01
11 Su	5 18 45	18 54 07	20 02	12 52	6 01	1♑03	15 03	29 18	20 33	15 42	22 40	27 04	27 43	25 52	16 34	6 16	12 00
12 M	5 22 42	19 55 05	1♌54	12 45	7 27	2 18	14 40	29 21	20 38	15 40	22 40	27 05	28 01	25 44	16 54	6 37	12 00
13 T	5 26 39	20 56 04	13 45	12 38	8 53	3 34	14 18	29 25	20 42	15 38	22 40	27 07	28 19	25 35	17 15	6 58	11 59
14 W	5 30 35	21 57 03	25 39	12 33	10 17	4 49	13 57	29 29	20 47	15 36	22 40	27 09	28 36	25 26	17 36	7 19	11 59
15 Th	5 34 32	22 58 04	7♍38	12 30	11 40	6 04	13 35	29 33	20 52	15 34	22 41	27 11	28 54	25 15	17 57	7 40	11 58
16 F	5 38 28	23 59 06	19 47	12 29D	13 01	7 19	13 14	29 38	20 57	15 32	22 41	27 12	29 11	25 04	18 18	8 01	11 58
17 Sa	5 42 25	25 00 09	2≏11	12 29	14 20	8 35	12 54	29 42	21 02	15 30	22 42	27 14	29 27	24 53	18 40	8 23	11 57
18 Su	5 46 21	26 01 12	14 55	12 30	15 36	9 50	12 34	29 47	21 07	15 29	22 42	27 16	29 44	24 41	19 02	8 44	11 57
19 M	5 50 18	27 02 17	28 03	12 31	16 50	11 05	12 14	29 52	21 12	15 27	22 43	27 17	0≏00	24 28	19 24	9 06	11 57
20 T	5 54 14	28 03 22	11♏38	12 32R	18 01	12 20	11 55	29 57	21 18	15 25	22 43	27 19	0 16	24 14	19 46	9 28	11 56
21 W	5 58 11	29 04 29	25 41	12 31	19 08	13 36	11 37	0♈02	21 23	15 24	22 44	27 21	0 32	24 00	20 09	9 50	11 56
22 Th	6 2 8	0♑06 36	10♐25	12 28	20 10	14 51	11 20	0 08	21 28	15 22	22 44	27 23	0 48	23 45	20 32	10 12	11 56
23 F	6 6 4	1 06 44	25 05	12 23	21 08	16 06	11 03	0 13	21 34	15 21	22 45	27 25	1 03	23 30	20 55	10 35	11 56
24 Sa	6 10 1	2 07 52	10♑13	12 16	21 59	17 21	10 46	0 19	21 39	15 19	22 46	27 26	1 18	23 14	21 18	10 57	11 56
25 Su	6 13 57	3 09 01	25 26	12 08	22 44	18 37	10 31	0 25	21 45	15 18	22 46	27 28	1 33	22 57	21 42	11 20	11 56
26 M	6 17 54	4 10 09	10≈32	12 00	23 22	19 52	10 16	0 31	21 50	15 16	22 47	27 30	1 48	22 40	22 06	11 42	11 56D
27 T	6 21 50	5 11 18	25 24	11 53	23 51	21 07	10 02	0 37	21 56	15 15	22 48	27 32	2 02	22 23	22 30	12 05	11 56
28 W	6 25 47	6 12 27	9♓52	11 48	24 11	22 23	9 49	0 44	22 02	15 14	22 49	27 34	2 16	22 05	22 54	12 28	11 56
29 Th	6 29 44	7 13 36	23 56	11 45	24 21R	23 37	9 36	0 51	22 07	15 12	22 50	27 36	2 30	21 46	23 19	12 51	11 57
30 F	6 33 40	8 14 45	7♈33	11 44D	24 19	24 53	9 25	0 57	22 13	15 11	22 50	27 36	2 43	21 28	23 44	13 14	11 57
31 Sa	6 37 37	9 15 54	20 46	11 44	24 07	26 08	9 14	1 04	22 19	15 10	22 51	27 38	2 56	21 09	24 09	13 38	11 58

EPHEMERIS CALCULATED FOR 12 MIDNIGHT GREENWICH MEAN TIME. ALL OTHER DATA AND FACING ASPECTARIAN PAGE IN **EASTERN TIME (BOLD)** AND PACIFIC TIME (REGULAR).

JANUARY 2023

☽ Last Aspect day	ET / hr:mn	PT	asp	☽ Ingress sign	day	ET / hr:mn	PT
2	**5:16 pm**	2:16 pm	△♇	♊	2	**9:44 pm**	6:44 pm
4	**7:08 pm**	4:08 pm	□♆	♋	5	**9:15 am**	6:15 am
7	**5:23 pm**	2:23 pm	☍♇	♌	7	**9:40 pm**	6:40 pm
9	**8:52 pm**	5:52 pm	☍♄	♍	10	**10:15 am**	7:15 am
12	**6:06 pm**	3:06 pm	△♇	♎	12	**9:56 pm**	6:56 pm
15	**3:40 am**	12:40 am	□♇	♏	15	**7:08 am**	4:08 am
17	**9:27 am**	6:27 am	⚹♇	♐	17	**12:33 pm**	9:33 am
19	**5:09 am**	2:09 am	⚹♄	♑	19	**2:11 pm**	11:11 am
21	**10:52 am**	7:52 am	☌♇	♒	21	**1:29 pm**	10:29 am
23	**5:19 am**	2:19 am	☌♀	♓	23	**12:36 pm**	9:36 am
25	**11:12 am**	8:12 am	⚹♇	♈	25	**1:48 pm**	10:48 am
27	**4:01 pm**	1:01 pm	□♇	♉	27	**6:42 pm**	3:42 pm
29		9:52 pm	△♇	♊	30	**3:35 am**	12:35 am
30	**12:52 am**		△♇	♊	30	**3:35 am**	12:35 am

☽ Phases & Eclipses phase	day	ET / hr:mn	PT
Full Moon	6	**6:08 pm**	3:08 pm
4th Quarter	14	**9:10 pm**	6:10 pm
New Moon	21	**3:53 pm**	12:53 pm
2nd Quarter	28	**10:19 am**	7:19 am

Planet Ingress		day	ET / hr:mn	PT
♀	♒	2	**9:09 pm**	6:09 pm
✱	♈	12		10:30 pm
✱	♈	13	**1:30 am**	
☉	♒	20	**3:30 am**	12:30 am
♀	♓	26	**9:33 pm**	6:33 pm

Planetary Motion		day	ET / hr:mn	PT
♂	D	12	**3:56 pm**	12:56 pm
☿	D	18	**8:12 am**	5:12 am
♅	D	22	**5:59 pm**	2:59 pm

1 SUNDAY
♀ ☌ ♇ **12:25 am**
☽ ⚺ ♂ **5:09 am** 2:09 am
☽ △ ☉ **8:42 am** 5:42 am
☽ ☌ ♅ **4:52 pm** 1:52 pm
☿ ⚹ ♆ 10:44 pm

2 MONDAY
☿ ⚹ ♆ **1:44 am**
☽ □ ♄ **7:15 am** 4:15 am
☽ △ ☿ **7:30 am** 4:30 am
☽ ⚹ ♆ **7:53 am** 4:53 am
☿ ⚺ ♄ **10:59 am** 7:59 am
☽ △ ♇ **5:16 pm** 2:16 pm
☽ △ ♀ **9:48 pm** 6:48 pm
☽ ⚹ ♃ 9:37 pm

3 TUESDAY
☽ ⚹ ♃ **12:37 am**
☽ ☌ ♂ **2:47 pm** 11:47 am
☽ ⚻ ☉ 9:30 pm

4 WEDNESDAY
☽ ⚻ ☉ **12:30 am**
☽ ⚺ ♅ **3:30 am** 12:30 am
♀ ⚹ ♃ **4:08 am** 1:08 am
☽ ⚻ ☿ **2:10 pm** 11:10 am
☽ △ ♄ **6:54 pm** 3:54 pm
☽ □ ♆ **7:08 pm** 4:08 pm

5 THURSDAY
☽ ⚻ ♇ **4:50 am** 1:50 am
☉ △ ♅ **11:43 am** 8:43 am

☽ □ ♃ **12:50 pm** 9:50 am
☽ ⚻ ♀ **4:16 pm** 1:16 pm
☽ ⚺ ♂ 11:08 pm
♄ ⚺ ♆ 11:56 pm

6 FRIDAY
☽ ⚺ ♂ **2:08 am**
♄ ⚺ ♆ **2:56 am**
☽ ⚹ ♅ **3:30 pm** 12:30 pm
☽ ☍ ☉ **6:08 pm** 3:08 pm
☽ ☍ ☿ **8:36 pm** 5:36 pm

7 SATURDAY
☽ △ ♆ **7:30 am** 4:30 am
☽ ⚻ ♄ **7:42 am** 4:42 am
☉ ☌ ☿ **7:57 am** 4:57 am
☽ ☍ ♇ **5:23 pm** 2:23 pm
☽ △ ♃ 11:00 pm

8 SUNDAY
☽ △ ♃ **2:00 am**
☽ ☍ ♀ **11:52 am** 8:52 am
☽ ⚹ ♂ **2:19 pm** 11:19 am
☿ △ ♅ **6:23 pm** 3:23 pm

9 MONDAY
☽ ⚻ ☿ **3:05 am** 12:05 am
☽ □ ♅ **4:02 am** 1:02 am
♀ △ ♂ **10:22 am** 7:22 am
☽ ⚻ ☉ **12:26 pm** 9:26 am
☽ ⚻ ♆ **8:13 pm** 5:13 pm
☽ ☍ ♄ **8:52 pm** 5:52 pm

10 TUESDAY
☽ ⚻ ♇ **6:09 am** 3:09 am
☽ ⚻ ♃ **3:17 pm** 12:17 pm
☽ □ ♂ 11:36 pm

11 WEDNESDAY
☽ □ ♂ **2:36 am**
☽ ⚻ ♀ **7:25 am** 4:25 am
☽ △ ☿ **9:58 am** 6:58 am
☽ △ ♅ **4:17 pm** 1:17 pm
☿ ⚺ ♀ **10:02 pm** 7:02 pm

12 THURSDAY
☽ △ ☉ **6:08 am** 3:08 am
☽ ☍ ♆ **8:21 am** 5:21 am
☽ ⚻ ♄ **9:25 am** 6:25 am
☽ △ ♇ **6:06 pm** 3:06 pm

13 FRIDAY
☽ ☍ ♃ **3:34 am** 12:34 am
☉ ⚹ ♆ **9:11 am** 6:11 am
☽ △ ♂ **1:46 pm** 10:46 am
☽ □ ☿ **4:55 pm** 1:55 pm
☽ △ ♀ 9:58 pm
☉ ⚺ ♄ 10:47 pm
☽ ⚻ ♅ 11:54 pm

14 SATURDAY
☽ △ ♀ **12:58 am**
☉ ⚺ ♄ **1:47 am**
☽ ⚻ ♅ **2:54 am**
☽ ⚻ ♆ **6:22 pm** 3:22 pm
☽ △ ♄ **7:47 pm** 4:47 pm

♀ □ ♅ **8:22 pm** 5:22 pm
☽ □ ☉ **9:10 pm** 6:10 pm

15 SUNDAY
☽ □ ♇ **3:40 am** 12:40 am
☽ ⚻ ♃ **1:07 pm** 10:07 am
☽ ⚻ ♂ **10:08 pm** 7:08 pm
☽ ⚹ ☿ **10:47 pm** 7:47 pm

16 MONDAY
☽ ☍ ♅ **10:17 am** 7:17 am
☽ □ ♀ **2:09 pm** 11:09 am
☽ △ ♆ 9:48 pm
☿ ⚻ ♂ 10:42 pm
☽ □ ♄ 11:27 pm

17 TUESDAY
☽ △ ♆ **12:48 am**
☿ ⚻ ♂ **1:42 am**
☽ □ ♄ **2:27 am**
☽ ⚹ ☉ **7:36 am** 4:36 am
☽ ⚹ ♇ **9:27 am** 6:27 am
☽ △ ♃ **6:41 pm** 3:41 pm
☽ ⚺ ☿ 11:21 pm
☽ ☍ ♂ 11:39 pm

18 WEDNESDAY
☽ ⚺ ☿ **2:21 am**
☽ ☍ ♂ **2:39 am**
☉ ☌ ♇ **9:44 am** 6:44 am
☽ ⚻ ♅ **1:42 pm** 10:42 am
☽ ⚹ ♀ **10:05 pm** 7:05 pm

19 THURSDAY
☽ □ ♆ **3:17 am** 12:17 am
☽ ⚹ ♄ **5:09 am** 2:09 am
☽ ⚺ ♇ **11:24 am** 8:24 am
☽ ⚺ ☉ **1:13 pm** 10:13 am
☽ □ ♃ **8:29 pm** 5:29 pm

20 FRIDAY
☽ ☌ ☿ **3:30 am** 12:30 am
☽ ⚻ ♂ **3:42 am** 12:42 am
☽ △ ♅ **1:55 pm** 10:55 am
☿ ⚻ ♂ **8:06 pm** 5:06 pm
☽ ⚺ ♀ 11:10 pm

21 SATURDAY
☽ ⚺ ♀ **2:10 am**
☽ ⚹ ♆ **3:01 am** 12:01 am
☽ ⚺ ♄ **5:04 am** 2:04 am
☽ ☌ ♇ **10:52 am** 7:52 am
♀ ⚺ ♆ **12:43 pm** 9:43 am
☽ ☌ ☉ **3:53 pm** 12:53 pm
☽ ⚹ ♃ **8:09 pm** 5:09 pm

22 SUNDAY
☽ △ ♂ **3:02 am** 12:02 am
☽ ⚺ ☿ **3:36 am** 12:36 am
☽ □ ♅ **12:49 pm** 9:49 am
♀ ☌ ♄ **5:13 pm** 2:13 pm
☽ ⚺ ♆ 11:03 pm

23 MONDAY
☽ ⚺ ♆ **2:03 am**
☽ ☌ ♄ **4:25 am** 1:25 am
☽ ☌ ♀ **5:19 am** 2:19 am

☽ ⚺ ♇ **10:02 am** 7:02 am
☽ ⚺ ☉ **6:30 pm** 3:30 pm
☽ ⚺ ♃ **7:59 pm** 4:59 pm
☽ □ ♂ 11:56 pm

24 TUESDAY
☽ □ ♂ **2:56 am**
☽ ⚹ ☿ **4:59 am** 1:59 am
☽ ⚹ ♅ **12:43 pm** 9:43 am
☉ ⚹ ♃ **8:30 pm** 5:30 pm
☽ ☌ ♆ 11:42 pm

25 WEDNESDAY
☽ ☌ ♆ **2:42 am**
☽ ⚺ ♄ **5:30 am** 2:30 am
☽ ⚺ ♀ **10:45 am** 7:45 am
☽ ⚹ ♇ **11:12 am** 8:12 am
♀ ⚺ ♇ **3:59 pm** 12:59 pm
☽ ☌ ♃ **10:18 pm** 7:18 pm
☽ ⚹ ☉ **11:59 pm** 8:59 pm

26 THURSDAY
☽ ⚹ ♂ **5:40 am** 2:40 am
☽ □ ☿ **10:08 am** 7:08 am
☽ ⚺ ♅ **3:38 pm** 12:38 pm

27 FRIDAY
☽ ⚺ ♆ **6:50 am** 3:50 am
☽ ⚹ ♄ **10:13 am** 7:13 am
☽ □ ♇ **4:01 pm** 1:01 pm
☽ ⚹ ♀ **8:56 pm** 5:56 pm

28 SATURDAY
☽ ⚺ ♃ **4:39 am** 1:39 am
☽ □ ☉ **10:19 am** 7:19 am

☽ ⚺ ♂ **12:34 pm** 9:34 am
☽ △ ☿ **8:44 pm** 5:44 pm
☽ ☌ ♅ **10:37 pm** 7:37 pm

29 SUNDAY
☽ ⚹ ♆ **3:02 pm** 12:02 pm
☽ □ ♄ **7:03 pm** 4:03 pm
☉ △ ♂ **8:45 pm** 5:45 pm
☿ △ ♅ **9:16 pm** 6:16 pm
☽ △ ♇ 9:52 pm

30 MONDAY
☽ △ ♇ **12:52 am**
☽ □ ♀ **12:24 pm** 9:24 am
☽ ⚹ ♃ **3:01 pm** 12:01 pm
☽ ☌ ♂ **11:27 pm** 8:27 pm
☽ △ ☉ 10:24 pm

31 TUESDAY
☽ △ ☉ **1:24 am**
☽ ⚺ ♅ **9:06 am** 6:06 am
☽ ⚻ ☿ **12:27 pm** 9:27 am
♀ ⚺ ♃ **6:14 pm** 3:14 pm
☽ □ ♆ 11:21 pm

Eastern time in bold type
Pacific time in medium type

JANUARY 2023

DATE	SID. TIME	SUN	MOON	NODE	MERCURY	VENUS	MARS	JUPITER	SATURN	URANUS	NEPTUNE	PLUTO	CERES	PALLAS	JUNO	VESTA	CHIRON
1 Su	6 41 33	10♑17 02	3♋39	11♉45R	23♑42R	27♑23	9♊04R	1♈12	22♒25	15♉09R	22♓52	27♑39	3♎09	20♏49R	24♐34	14♓01	11♈58
2 M	6 45 30	11 18 11	16 14	11 45	23 06	28 38	8 55	1 19	22 31	15 08	22 53	27 41	3 22	20 30	25 00	14 25	11 59
3 T	6 49 26	12 19 19	28 36	11 44	22 18	29 53	8 46	1 26	22 37	15 07	22 54	27 43	3 34	20 10	25 25	14 49	12 00
4 W	6 53 23	13 20 27	10♌48	11 39	21 20	1♒08	8 39	1 34	22 43	15 06	22 55	27 45	3 46	19 50	25 51	15 12	12 00
5 Th	6 57 19	14 21 35	22 53	11 33	20 13	2 23	8 32	1 42	22 49	15 05	22 56	27 47	3 58	19 30	26 17	15 36	12 01
6 F	7 1 16	15 22 43	4♍52	11 23	18 59	3 39	8 26	1 50	22 56	15 04	22 57	27 49	4 09	19 10	26 43	16 00	12 01
7 Sa	7 5 13	16 23 51	16 47	11 13	17 40	4 54	8 21	1 58	23 02	15 03	22 59	27 51	4 20	18 50	27 10	16 24	12 02
8 Su	7 9 9	17 24 59	28 41	10 58	16 20	6 09	8 17	2 06	23 08	15 02	23 00	27 53	4 31	18 29	27 37	16 48	12 03
9 M	7 13 6	18 26 06	10♎33	10 44	15 00	7 24	8 14	2 14	23 15	15 02	23 01	27 55	4 41	18 09	28 03	17 12	12 04
10 T	7 17 2	19 27 14	22 26	10 32	13 42	8 39	8 11	2 23	23 21	15 01	23 02	27 57	4 51	17 49	28 30	17 37	12 05
11 W	7 20 59	20 28 21	4♏21	10 13	12 31	9 54	8 09	2 32	23 28	15 00	23 03	27 59	5 01	17 29	28 58	18 01	12 06
12 Th	7 24 55	21 29 29	16 21	10 08	11 26	11 09	8 08 D	2 40	23 34	15 00	23 05	28 01	5 10	17 09	29 25	18 26	12 07
13 F	7 28 52	22 30 36	28 30	10 08	10 30	12 24	8 08	2 49	23 41	14 59	23 06	28 03	5 19	16 49	29 53	18 50	12 08
14 Sa	7 32 48	23 31 43	10♐51	10 08	9 42	13 39	8 09	2 58	23 47	14 59	23 07	28 05	5 28	16 29	0♑20	19 15	12 09
15 Su	7 36 45	24 32 50	23 29	10 04 D	9 05	14 54	8 11	3 08	23 54	14 58	23 09	28 07	5 36	16 10	0 48	19 40	12 10
16 M	7 40 42	25 33 57	6♑28	10 06 R	8 37	16 09	8 14	3 17	24 00	14 58	23 10	28 09	5 44	15 51	1 16	20 05	12 11
17 T	7 44 38	26 35 04	19 53	10 02	8♑09	17 24	8 18	3 26	24 07	14 57	23 11	28 11	5 52	15 32	1 44	20 29	12 12
18 W	7 48 35	27 36 10	3♒47	9 58	8 08 D	18 39	8 22	3 36	24 14	14 57	23 13	28 12	5 59	15 13	2 13	20 54	12 14
19 Th	7 52 31	28 37 17	18 10	9 51	8 09	19 54	8 27	3 46	24 21	14 57	23 14	28 14	6 06	14 55	2 41	21 20	12 15
20 F	7 56 28	29 38 23	3♓00	9 41	8 17	21 08	8 32	3 56	24 27	14 57	23 16	28 16	6 12	14 38	3 10	21 45	12 16
21 Sa	8 0 24	0♒39 29	18 11	9 30	8 32	22 23	8 39	4 06	24 34	14 57	23 17	28 18	6 18	14 20	3 39	22 10	12 18
22 Su	8 4 21	1 40 34	3♈32	9 18	8 54	23 38	8 46	4 16	24 41	14 56 D	23 19	28 20	6 23	14 04	4 08	22 35	12 20
23 M	8 8 17	2 41 38	18 53	9 07	9 22	24 53	8 53	4 26	24 48	14 56	23 20	28 22	6 29	13 47	4 37	23 01	12 21
24 T	8 12 14	3 42 42	4♉00	8 59	9 56	26 08	9 02	4 36	24 55	14 56	23 22	28 24	6 33	13 32	5 06	23 26	12 23
25 W	8 16 11	4 43 44	18 46	8 53	10 35	27 23	9 10	4 47	25 02	14 57	23 23	28 26	6 38	13 16	5 36	23 52	12 25
26 Th	8 20 7	5 44 46	3♊03	8 51	11 19	28 37	9 20	4 57	25 09	14 57	23 25	28 28	6 42	13 02	6 05	24 17	12 27
27 F	8 24 4	6 45 46	16 51	8 50	12 07	29 52	9 30	5 08	25 16	14 57	23 27	28 30	6 45	12 48	6 35	24 43	12 28
28 Sa	8 28 0	7 46 46	0♋10	8 50	12 58	1♓07	9 41	5 19	25 23	14 57	23 29	28 32	6 48	12 34	7 05	25 08	12 30
29 Su	8 31 57	8 47 44	13 03	8 50	13 54	2 21	9 52	5 30	25 30	14 57	23 31	28 34	6 51	12 22	7 35	25 34	12 32
30 M	8 35 53	9 48 41	25 35	8 49	14 52	3 36	10 04	5 41	25 37	14 58	23 32	28 36	6 53	12 09	8 05	26 00	12 34
31 T	8 39 50	10 49 37	7♌51	8 47	15 53	4 51	10 16	5 52	25 44	14 58	23 34	28 38	6 55	11 58	8 36	26 26	12 36

EPHEMERIS CALCULATED FOR 12 MIDNIGHT GREENWICH MEAN TIME. ALL OTHER DATA AND FACING ASPECTARIAN PAGE IN **EASTERN TIME (BOLD)** AND PACIFIC TIME (REGULAR).

FEBRUARY 2023

☽ Last Aspect day	ET / hr:mn / PT		asp	☽ Ingress sign	day	ET / hr:mn / PT	
1	**6:58 am**	3:58 am	△♄	♋	1	**3:11 pm**	12:11 pm
3		10:19 pm	☍♇	♌	4	**3:48 am**	12:48 am
4	**1:19 am**		☍♇	♌	4	**3:48 am**	12:48 am
6	**9:15 am**	6:15 am	☍♄	♍	6	**4:14 pm**	1:14 pm
8		10:40 pm	△♇	♎	9	**3:47 am**	12:47 am
9	**1:40 am**		△♇	♎	9	**3:47 am**	12:47 am
11	**11:41 am**	8:41 am	□♇	♏	11	**1:34 pm**	10:34 am
13	**6:52 pm**	3:52 pm	⚹♇	♐	13	**8:31 pm**	5:31 pm
15	**8:06 pm**	5:06 pm	⚹♄	♑	15		9:00 pm
15	**8:06 pm**	5:06 pm	⚹♄	♑	16	**12:00 am**	
17	**11:18 pm**	8:18 pm	☌♇	♒	17		9:35 pm
17	**11:18 pm**	8:18 pm	☌♇	♒	18	**12:35 am**	
19	**9:00 pm**	6:00 pm	☌♄	♓	19	**11:56 pm**	8:56 pm
21	**11:06 pm**	8:06 pm	⚹♇	♈	21		9:14 pm
21	**11:06 pm**	8:06 pm	⚹♇	♈	22	**12:14 am**	
23		11:22 pm	□♇	♉	24	**3:29 am**	12:29 am
24	**2:22 am**		□♇	♉	24	**3:29 am**	12:29 am
26	**9:42 am**	6:42 am	△♇	♊	26	**10:48 am**	7:48 am
28	**8:07 pm**	5:07 pm	△♄	♋	28	**9:40 pm**	6:40 pm

☽ Phases & Eclipses phase	day	ET / hr:mn / PT	
Full Moon	5	**1:29 pm**	10:29 am
4th Quarter	13	**11:01 am**	8:01 am
New Moon	19		11:06 pm
New Moon	20	**2:06 am**	
2nd Quarter	27	**3:06 am**	12:06 am

Planet Ingress		day	ET / hr:mn / PT	
⚵	♈	7	**11:47 pm**	8:47 pm
☿	♒	11	**6:22 am**	3:22 am
☉	♓	18	**5:34 pm**	2:34 pm
♀	♈	19		11:56 pm
♀	♈	20	**2:56 am**	

Planetary Motion		day	ET / hr:mn / PT	
⚳	℞	3	**2:13 pm**	11:13 am
⚴	D	16	**9:26 am**	6:26 am

1 WEDNESDAY
☽□♆	**2:21 am**	
☽△♄	**6:58 am**	3:58 am
☽⊼♇	**12:33 pm**	9:33 am

2 THURSDAY
☽□♃	**3:55 am**	12:55 am
☽△♀	**7:15 am**	4:15 am
☽⊻♂	**12:42 pm**	9:42 am
☽⊼☉	**7:12 pm**	4:12 pm
☽⚹♅	**9:27 pm**	6:27 pm

3 FRIDAY
☽☍☿	**7:09 am**	3:09 am
☽△♆	**3:02 pm**	12:02 pm
☽⊼♄	**8:09 pm**	5:09 pm
☉□♅	**9:50 pm**	6:50 pm
☽☍♇		10:19 pm

4 SATURDAY
☽☍♇	**1:19 am**	
☽△♃	**5:34 pm**	2:34 pm
♀□♂	**10:29 pm**	7:29 pm
☽⚹♂		11:35 pm
☽⊼♀		11:58 pm

5 SUNDAY
☽⚹♂	**2:35 am**	
☽⊼♀	**2:58 am**	
☽□♅	**10:08 am**	7:08 am
☽☍☉	**1:29 pm**	10:29 am
☽⊼☿		11:37 pm

6 MONDAY
☽⊼☿	**2:37 am**	
☽⊼♆	**3:44 am**	12:44 am
☽☍♄	**9:15 am**	6:15 am
☿⚹♆	**1:26 pm**	10:26 am
☽⊼♇	**1:56 pm**	10:56 am

7 TUESDAY
☽⊼♃	**6:51 am**	3:51 am
☽□♂	**4:05 pm**	1:05 pm
☽☍♀	**10:01 pm**	7:01 pm
☽△♅	**10:16 pm**	7:16 pm
♀⚹♅		9:29 pm

8 WEDNESDAY
♀⚹♅	**12:29 am**	
☽⊼☉	**6:58 am**	3:58 am
☽☍♆	**3:40 pm**	12:40 pm
☽△☿	**9:30 pm**	6:30 pm
☽⊼♄	**9:32 pm**	6:32 pm
☿⊻♄	**9:49 pm**	6:49 pm
☽△♇		10:40 pm

9 THURSDAY
☽△♇	**1:40 am**	
☽☍♃	**7:02 pm**	4:02 pm

10 FRIDAY
☽△♂	**4:25 am**	1:25 am
☽⊼♅	**9:08 am**	6:08 am
☿☌♇	**12:16 pm**	9:16 am
☽⊼♀	**3:18 pm**	12:18 pm
☽△☉	**10:39 pm**	7:39 pm
☽⊼♆		11:04 pm

11 SATURDAY
☽⊼♆	**2:04 am**	
☽△♄	**8:07 am**	5:07 am
☽□♇	**11:41 am**	8:41 am
☽□☿	**2:27 pm**	11:27 am

12 SUNDAY
☽⊼♃	**5:07 am**	2:07 am
☽⊼♂	**2:28 pm**	11:28 am
☽☍♅	**5:43 pm**	2:43 pm
☉⊻♆	**6:37 pm**	3:37 pm

13 MONDAY
☽△♀	**5:16 am**	2:16 am
☽△♆	**9:49 am**	6:49 am
☽□☉	**11:01 am**	8:01 am
☽□♄	**3:53 pm**	12:53 pm
☽⚹♇	**6:52 pm**	3:52 pm

14 TUESDAY
☽⚹☿	**3:39 am**	12:39 am
☽△♃	**11:56 am**	8:56 am
☽☍♂	**9:06 pm**	6:06 pm
☽⊼♅	**10:59 pm**	7:59 pm

15 WEDNESDAY
♀☌♆	**7:25 am**	4:25 am
☽□♆	**2:06 pm**	11:06 am
☽□♀	**2:43 pm**	11:43 am
☽⚹☉	**7:03 pm**	4:03 pm
☽⚹♄	**8:06 pm**	5:06 pm
☽⊻♇	**10:33 pm**	7:33 pm

16 THURSDAY
☉☌♄	**11:48 am**	8:48 am
☽⊻☿	**12:17 pm**	9:17 am
☽□♃	**3:11 pm**	12:11 pm
☽⊼♂		9:12 pm
☽△♅		9:55 pm

17 FRIDAY
☽⊼♂	**12:12 am**	
☽△♅	**12:55 am**	
☽⚹♆	**3:16 pm**	12:16 pm
☽⚹♀	**8:06 pm**	5:06 pm
☿⚹♃	**9:13 pm**	6:13 pm
☽⊻♄	**9:15 pm**	6:15 pm
☉⊻♇	**10:23 pm**	7:23 pm
☽☌♇	**11:18 pm**	8:18 pm
☽⊻☉	**11:22 pm**	8:22 pm

18 SATURDAY
♂⊻♅	**9:51 am**	6:51 am
♀⊻♄	**11:32 am**	8:32 am
☽⚹♃	**3:51 pm**	12:51 pm
☽☌☿	**5:35 pm**	2:35 pm
☽□♅		9:42 pm
☽△♂		10:01 pm

19 SUNDAY
☽□♅	**12:42 am**	
☽△♂	**1:01 am**	
♀⚹♇	**12:05 pm**	9:05 am
☽⊻♆	**2:48 pm**	11:48 am
☽☌♄	**9:00 pm**	6:00 pm
☽⊻♇	**10:45 pm**	7:45 pm
☽⊻♀	**11:40 pm**	8:40 pm
☽☌☉		11:06 pm

20 MONDAY
☽☌☉	**2:06 am**	
☽⊻♃	**3:57 pm**	12:57 pm
☽⊻☿	**10:24 pm**	7:24 pm
☽⚹♅		9:20 pm
☽□♂		10:44 pm

21 TUESDAY
☽⚹♅	**12:20 am**	
☽□♂	**1:44 am**	
☽☌♆	**2:52 pm**	11:52 am
☿□♅	**5:22 pm**	2:22 pm
☽⊻♄	**9:35 pm**	6:35 pm
☽⚹♇	**11:06 pm**	8:06 pm

22 WEDNESDAY
☽☌♀	**4:26 am**	1:26 am
☽⊻☉	**6:07 am**	3:07 am
☿△♂	**3:14 pm**	12:14 pm
☽☌♃	**5:48 pm**	2:48 pm
☽⊻♅		11:01 pm

23 THURSDAY
☽⊻♅	**2:01 am**	
☽⚹♂	**4:44 am**	1:44 am
☽⚹☿	**6:03 am**	3:03 am
☽⊻♆	**5:34 pm**	2:34 pm
☽⚹♄		10:06 pm
☽□♇		11:22 pm

24 FRIDAY
☽⚹♄	**1:06 am**	
☽□♇	**2:22 am**	
☽⊻♀	**1:12 pm**	10:12 am
☽⚹☉	**2:02 pm**	11:02 am
☽⊻♃	**11:19 pm**	8:19 pm

25 SATURDAY
☽☌♅	**7:25 am**	4:25 am
☽⊻♂	**11:51 am**	8:51 am
☽□☿	**7:16 pm**	4:16 pm
☽⚹♆		9:15 pm

26 SUNDAY
☽⚹♆	**12:15 am**	
☽□♄	**8:45 am**	5:45 am
☽△♇	**9:42 am**	6:42 am
☉⊻♀	**11:11 am**	8:11 am

27 MONDAY
☽□☉	**3:06 am**	12:06 am
☽⚹♀	**3:24 am**	12:24 am
☽⚹♃	**9:08 am**	6:08 am
☿⊻♆	**11:03 am**	8:03 am
☽⊻♅	**4:51 pm**	1:51 pm
☽☌♂	**11:21 pm**	8:21 pm

28 TUESDAY
☽□♆	**10:46 am**	7:46 am
☽△☿	**2:27 pm**	11:27 am
☽△♄	**8:07 pm**	5:07 pm
☽⊼♇	**8:40 pm**	5:40 pm

Eastern time in bold type
Pacific time in medium type

FEBRUARY 2023

DATE	SID.TIME	SUN	MOON	NODE	MERCURY	VENUS	MARS	JUPITER	SATURN	URANUS	NEPTUNE	PLUTO	CERES	PALLAS	JUNO	VESTA	CHIRON
1 W	8 43 46	11≈50 31	19♊56	8♉42 R	16♑57	6♓45	10♊17	6♈17	25≈51	14♉59	23♓36	28♑40	6♋57	11♋47 R	9♋06	26♓52	12♈38
2 Th	8 47 43	12 51 25	1♋42	8 35	18 03	7 20	10 30	6 15	25 58	14 59	23 38	28 42	6 58	11 37	9 37	27 18	12 40
3 F	8 51 40	13 52 17	13 47	8 24	19 12	8 34	10 43	6 26	26 05	15 00	23 40	28 44	6 58	11 28	10 07	27 44	12 42
4 Sa	8 55 36	14 53 08	25 39	8 11	20 22	9 49	10 57	6 38	26 13	15 00	23 41	28 46	6 58	11 19	10 38	28 10	12 45
5 Su	8 59 33	15 53 58	7♌31	7 56	21 35	11 03	11 12	6 49	26 20	15 01	23 43	28 48	6 58	11 11	11 09	28 36	12 47
6 M	9 3 29	16 54 46	19 25	7 41	22 49	12 18	11 27	7 01	26 27	15 02	23 45	28 51	6 57	11 03	11 40	29 02	12 49
7 T	9 7 26	17 55 34	1♍23	7 27	24 04	13 32	11 43	7 13	26 34	15 02	23 47	28 51	6 56	10 56	12 11	29 28	12 51
8 W	9 11 22	18 56 20	13 25	7 15	25 21	14 46	11 59	7 25	26 41	15 03	23 49	28 53	6 54	10 50	12 42	29 55	12 54
9 Th	9 15 19	19 57 05	25 32	7 06	26 40	16 01	12 15	7 37	26 48	15 03	23 51	28 55	6 52	10 45	13 14	0♈21	12 56
10 F	9 19 15	20 57 49	7≏48	7 00	28 00	17 15	12 32	7 49	26 56	15 05	23 53	28 57	6 50	10 40	13 45	0 47	12 58
11 Sa	9 23 12	21 58 32	20 13	6 56	29 21	18 29	12 49	8 01	27 03	15 06	23 55	28 59	6 47	10 36	14 17	1 14	13 01
12 Su	9 27 9	22 59 14	2♏53	6 56 D	0≈43	19 43	13 07	8 13	27 10	15 07	23 57	29 01	6 44	10 33	14 48	1 40	13 03
13 M	9 31 5	23 59 54	15 50	6 55	2 07	20 58	13 25	8 25	27 17	15 08	23 59	29 02	6 40	10 30	15 20	2 07	13 06
14 T	9 35 2	25 00 34	29 09	6 54	3 32	22 12	13 44	8 38	27 25	15 09	24 01	29 04	6 36	10 27	15 52	2 33	13 08
15 W	9 38 58	26 01 13	12✗51	6 54	4 57	23 26	14 03	8 50	27 32	15 10	24 03	29 06	6 31	10 27	16 24	3 00	13 11
16 Th	9 42 55	27 01 51	27 00	6 51	6 24	24 40	14 22	9 03	27 39	15 12	24 05	29 08	6 26	10 26 D	16 56	3 26	13 14
17 F	9 46 51	28 02 27	11♐34	6 45	7 52	25 54	14 42	9 15	27 46	15 13	24 07	29 10	6 20	10 26	17 28	3 53	13 16
18 Sa	9 50 48	29 03 02	26 30	6 40	9 21	27 08	15 02	9 28	27 54	15 14	24 09	29 11	6 14	10 26	18 00	4 20	13 19
19 Su	9 54 45	0♓03 36	11≈39	6 27	10 51	28 22	15 23	9 41	28 01	15 16	24 11	29 13	6 08	10 28	18 33	4 46	13 22
20 M	9 58 41	1 04 09	26 53	6 16	12 22	29 36	15 44	9 54	28 08	15 17	24 14	29 15	6 01	10 29	19 05	5 13	13 24
21 T	10 2 38	2 04 39	11✗59	6 07	13 53	0♈49	16 05	10 07	28 16	15 18	24 16	29 17	5 54	10 32	19 38	5 40	13 27
22 W	10 6 34	3 05 09	26 49	5 59	15 26	2 03	16 27	10 20	28 23	15 20	24 18	29 18	5 46	10 35	20 10	6 07	13 30
23 Th	10 10 31	4 05 36	11♈14	5 54	17 00	3 17	16 49	10 33	28 30	15 21	24 20	29 20	5 38	10 39	20 43	6 34	13 33
24 F	10 14 27	5 06 01	25 11	5 55 D	18 35	4 31	17 11	10 46	28 37	15 23	24 22	29 22	5 30	10 43	21 16	7 01	13 36
25 Sa	10 18 24	6 06 25	8♉39	5 51	20 10	5 44	17 33	10 59	28 44	15 25	24 24	29 23	5 21	10 48	21 49	7 27	13 39
26 Su	10 22 20	7 06 47	21 39	5 52	21 47	6 58	17 56	11 12	28 52	15 26	24 27	29 25	5 12	10 53	22 22	7 54	13 42
27 M	10 26 17	8 07 07	4♊17	5 53 R	23 24	8 11	18 19	11 25	28 59	15 28	24 29	29 26	5 02	10 59	22 55	8 21	13 45
28 T	10 30 13	9 07 25	16 35	5 52	25 03	9 25	18 43	11 39	29 06	15 30	24 31	29 28	4 53	11 06	23 28	8 48	13 48

EPHEMERIS CALCULATED FOR 12 MIDNIGHT GREENWICH MEAN TIME. ALL OTHER DATA AND FACING ASPECTARIAN PAGE IN **EASTERN TIME (BOLD)** AND PACIFIC TIME (REGULAR).

MARCH 2023

☽ Last Aspect day	ET / hr:mn / PT		asp	☽ Ingress sign	day	ET / hr:mn / PT	
3	**9:22 am**	6:22 am	☍♇	♌	3	**10:16 am**	7:16 am
5	**10:18 pm**	7:18 pm	☍♄	♍	5	**10:38 pm**	7:38 pm
8	**9:07 am**	6:07 am	△♇	♎	8	**9:44 am**	6:44 am
10	**6:37 pm**	3:37 pm	□♇	♏	10	**7:06 pm**	4:06 pm
12		11:58 pm	⚹♇	♐	13	**3:21 am**	12:21 am
13	**2:58 am**		⚹♇	♐	13	**3:21 am**	12:21 am
15	**4:50 am**	1:50 am	△♀	♑	15	**8:06 am**	5:06 am
17	**10:14 am**	7:14 am	☌♇	♒	17	**10:25 am**	7:25 am
19	**6:33 am**	3:33 am	△♂	♓	19	**11:12 am**	8:12 am
21	**11:58 am**	8:58 am	⚹♇	♈	21	**12:01 pm**	9:01 am
23	**1:13 pm**	10:13 am	⚹♂	♉	23	**2:42 pm**	11:42 am
25	**12:19 pm**	9:19 am	⚹♆	♊	25	**8:42 pm**	5:42 pm
27	**9:39 pm**	6:39 pm	□♆	♋	28	**6:22 am**	3:22 am
30	**9:45 am**	6:45 am	△♆	♌	30	**6:31 pm**	3:31 pm

☽ Phases & Eclipses phase	day	ET / hr:mn / PT	
Full Moon	7	**7:40 am**	4:40 am
4th Quarter	14	**10:08 pm**	7:08 pm
New Moon	21	**1:23 pm**	10:23 am
2nd Quarter	28	**10:32 pm**	7:32 pm

Planet Ingress		day	ET / hr:mn / PT	
☿	♓	2	**5:52 pm**	2:52 pm
♄	♓	7	**8:35 am**	5:35 am
⚵	♉	11	**11:15 am**	8:15 am
♀	♉	16	**6:34 pm**	3:34 pm
☿	♈	18		9:24 pm
☿	♈	19	**12:24 am**	
☉	♈	20	**5:24 pm**	2:24 pm
⚳	♍	22	**11:38 pm**	8:38 pm
♇	♒	23	**8:13 am**	5:13 am
♂	♋	25	**7:45 am**	4:45 am

Planetary Motion

day	ET / hr:mn / PT

1 WEDNESDAY
☽△☉ **8:10 pm** 5:10 pm
☽□♀ **9:50 pm** 6:50 pm
☽□♃ **10:04 pm** 7:04 pm
♀☌♃ 9:36 pm

2 THURSDAY
♀☌♃ **12:36 am**
☽⚹♅ **5:03 am** 2:03 am
☿☌♄ **9:34 am** 6:34 am
☿⚺♇ **11:21 am** 8:21 am
☽⚺♂ **1:39 pm** 10:39 am
☽△♆ **11:23 pm** 8:23 pm
☉⚺♃ 9:40 pm

3 FRIDAY
☉⚺♃ **12:40 am**
☽⚻♄ **9:19 am** 6:19 am
☽☍♇ **9:22 am** 6:22 am
☽⚻☿ **1:01 pm** 10:01 am
♄⚺♇ **5:26 pm** 2:26 pm

4 SATURDAY
☽△♃ **11:56 am** 8:56 am
☽⚻☉ **2:27 pm** 11:27 am
☽△♀ **5:28 pm** 2:28 pm
☽□♅ **5:54 pm** 2:54 pm
♀⚺♅ **9:46 pm** 6:46 pm

5 SUNDAY
☽⚹♂ **4:26 am** 1:26 am
☽⚻♆ **12:06 pm** 9:06 am
☽⚻♇ **9:54 pm** 6:54 pm
☽☍♄ **10:18 pm** 7:18 pm

6 MONDAY
☉⚹♅ **8:42 am** 5:42 am
☽☍☿ **11:32 am** 8:32 am
☽⚻♃ 10:00 pm

7 TUESDAY
☽⚻♃ **1:00 am**
☽△♅ **5:51 am** 2:51 am
☽☍☉ **7:40 am** 4:40 am
☽⚻♀ **11:53 am** 8:53 am
☽□♂ **6:06 pm** 3:06 pm
☽☍♆ **11:39 pm** 8:39 pm

8 WEDNESDAY
☽△♇ **9:07 am** 6:07 am
☽⚻♄ **9:58 am** 6:58 am

9 THURSDAY
☽⚻☿ **8:10 am** 5:10 am
☽☍♃ **12:27 pm** 9:27 am
☽⚻♅ **4:15 pm** 1:15 pm
☽⚻☉ **10:52 pm** 7:52 pm

10 FRIDAY
☽☍♀ **4:07 am** 1:07 am
☽△♂ **6:00 am** 3:00 am
☽⚻♆ **9:30 am** 6:30 am
☿⚺♃ **5:04 pm** 2:04 pm
☽□♇ **6:37 pm** 3:37 pm
☽△♄ **7:51 pm** 4:51 pm

11 SATURDAY
♀⚹♂ **10:05 am** 7:05 am
☿⚹♅ **4:04 pm** 1:04 pm
☽⚻♃ **9:55 pm** 6:55 pm
☽☍♅ 9:43 pm
☽△☿ 11:07 pm

12 SUNDAY
☽☍♅ **12:43 am**
☽△☿ **3:07 am**
☽△☉ **12:32 pm** 9:32 am
♀⚺♆ **3:09 pm** 12:09 pm
☽⚻♂ **4:43 pm** 1:43 pm
☽△♆ **6:18 pm** 3:18 pm
☽⚻♀ **6:37 pm** 3:37 pm
☽⚹♇ 11:58 pm

13 MONDAY
☽⚹♇ **2:58 am**
☽□♄ **4:34 am** 1:34 am

14 TUESDAY
☽△♃ **5:57 am** 2:57 am
☽⚻♅ **7:49 am** 4:49 am
☽□☿ **5:38 pm** 2:38 pm
♂□♆ **7:39 pm** 4:39 pm
☽□☉ **10:08 pm** 7:08 pm
☽□♆ **11:38 pm** 8:38 pm
☽☍♂ **11:45 pm** 8:45 pm

15 WEDNESDAY
☽△♀ **4:50 am** 1:50 am
☽⚺♇ **7:49 am** 4:49 am
☽⚹♄ **9:41 am** 6:41 am
☉☌♆ **7:39 pm** 4:39 pm

16 THURSDAY
☽□♃ **10:17 am** 7:17 am
☽△♅ **11:22 am** 8:22 am
☿☌♆ **1:13 pm** 10:13 am
☉□♂ **2:10 pm** 11:10 am
♀□♇ **3:59 pm** 12:59 pm
☿□♂ 9:49 pm
☽⚹♆ 11:26 pm

17 FRIDAY
☿□♂ **12:49 am**
☽⚹♆ **2:26 am**
☽⚻♂ **4:04 am** 1:04 am
☽⚹☿ **4:28 am** 1:28 am
☽⚹☉ **4:37 am** 1:37 am
☉☌☿ **6:45 am** 3:45 am
☽☌♇ **10:14 am** 7:14 am
☽□♀ **11:50 am** 8:50 am
☽⚺♄ **12:20 pm** 9:20 am
♀⚹♄ **6:25 pm** 3:25 pm

18 SATURDAY
☽⚹♃ **12:27 pm** 9:27 am
☽□♅ **12:50 pm** 9:50 am
☿⚹♇ **11:24 pm** 8:24 pm

19 SUNDAY
☽⚺♆ **3:30 am** 12:30 am
☽△♂ **6:33 am** 3:33 am
☽⚺☉ **9:02 am** 6:02 am
☽⚺♇ **11:05 am** 8:05 am
☽⚺☿ **12:52 pm** 9:52 am
☽☌♄ **1:28 pm** 10:28 am
☽⚹♀ **4:54 pm** 1:54 pm
☿⚺♄ **5:30 pm** 2:30 pm
♃⚺♅ **6:06 pm** 3:06 pm

20 MONDAY
☽⚹♅ **1:34 pm** 10:34 am
☽⚺♃ **1:49 pm** 10:49 am
☉⚹♇ **4:12 pm** 1:12 pm

21 TUESDAY
☽☌♆ **4:20 am** 1:20 am
☽□♂ **8:55 am** 5:55 am
☽⚹♇ **11:58 am** 8:58 am
☽☌☉ **1:23 pm** 10:23 am
☽⚺♄ **2:43 pm** 11:43 am
☽☌☿ **9:34 pm** 6:34 pm
☽⚺♀ **10:17 pm** 7:17 pm

22 WEDNESDAY
☿⚺♀ **9:14 am** 6:14 am
☉⚺♄ **11:00 am** 8:00 am
☽⚺♅ **3:19 pm** 12:19 pm
☽☌♃ **4:17 pm** 1:17 pm

23 THURSDAY
☽⚺♆ **6:44 am** 3:44 am
☽⚹♂ **1:13 pm** 10:13 am
☽□♇ **2:42 pm** 11:42 am
☽⚹♄ **5:57 pm** 2:57 pm
☽⚺☉ **8:05 pm** 5:05 pm

24 FRIDAY
☽☌♀ **6:31 am** 3:31 am
☽⚺☿ **9:45 am** 6:45 am
☽☌♅ **7:52 pm** 4:52 pm
☽⚺♃ **9:40 pm** 6:40 pm

25 SATURDAY
♂⚻♇ **9:34 am** 6:34 am
☽⚹♆ **12:19 pm** 9:19 am
☽△♇ **8:46 pm** 5:46 pm
☽⚺♂ **9:12 pm** 6:12 pm
☽□♄ 9:38 pm

26 SUNDAY
☽□♄ **12:38 am**
☽⚹☉ **7:03 am** 4:03 am
☽⚺♀ **7:25 pm** 4:25 pm

27 MONDAY
☽⚹☿ **3:39 am** 12:39 am
☽⚺♅ **4:08 am** 1:08 am
☿⚺♅ **6:45 am** 3:45 am
☽⚹♃ **6:57 am** 3:57 am
☽□♆ **9:39 pm** 6:39 pm
☿☌♃ 11:50 pm

28 TUESDAY
☿☌♃ **2:50 am**
☽⚻♇ **6:32 am** 3:32 am
☽☌♂ **9:19 am** 6:19 am
☽△♄ **11:04 am** 8:04 am
☽□☉ **10:32 pm** 7:32 pm

29 WEDNESDAY
☽⚹♀ **12:50 pm** 9:50 am
☽⚹♅ **3:40 pm** 12:40 pm
☽□♃ **7:35 pm** 4:35 pm
☽□☿ 11:30 pm

30 THURSDAY
☽□☿ **2:30 am**
☽△♆ **9:45 am** 6:45 am
♂△♄ **3:03 pm** 12:03 pm
♀☌♅ **6:26 pm** 3:26 pm
☽☍♇ **6:46 pm** 3:46 pm
☽⚻♄ **11:51 pm** 8:51 pm
☽⚺♂ 9:10 pm

31 FRIDAY
☽⚺♂ **12:10 am**
☽△☉ **4:29 pm** 1:29 pm
☿⚺♆ 10:39 pm

Eastern time in bold type
Pacific time in medium type

MARCH 2023

DATE	SID. TIME	SUN	MOON	NODE	MERCURY	VENUS	MARS	JUPITER	SATURN	URANUS	NEPTUNE	PLUTO	CERES	PALLAS	JUNO	VESTA	CHIRON
1 W	10 34 10	10♓07 41	28♊40	5♉50R	26≈43	10♈38	19♊31	11♈52	29≈13	15♉32	24♓33	29♑31	4≈42R	11♋13	24♏01	9♈15	13♈51
2 Th	10 38 7	11 07 55	10♋36	5 46	28 23	11 52	19 37	12 06	29 20	15 34	24 35	29 33	4 32	11 20	24 34	9 42	13 54
3 F	10 42 3	12 08 06	22 28	5 39	0♓05	13 05	19 55	12 19	29 28	15 36	24 38	29 34	4 21	11 29	25 08	10 09	13 57
4 Sa	10 46 0	13 08 16	4♌19	5 31	1 48	14 18	20 19	12 33	29 35	15 38	24 40	29 36	4 10	11 37	25 41	10 36	14 00
5 Su	10 49 56	14 08 24	16 12	5 21	3 31	15 31	20 44	12 46	29 42	15 40	24 42	29 37	3 59	11 46	26 15	11 03	14 03
6 M	10 53 53	15 08 30	28 11	5 11	5 16	16 44	21 09	13 00	29 49	15 42	24 44	29 39	3 47	11 56	26 48	11 31	14 06
7 T	10 57 49	16 08 34	10♍15	5 01	7 02	17 58	21 35	13 14	29 56	15 44	24 47	29 40	3 35	12 06	27 22	11 58	14 10
8 W	11 1 46	17 08 36	22 27	4 53	8 49	19 10	22 00	13 27	0♓03	15 46	24 49	29 42	3 23	12 17	27 56	12 25	14 13
9 Th	11 5 42	18 08 36	4♎47	4 47	10 37	20 23	22 26	13 41	0 10	15 48	24 51	29 43	3 11	12 28	28 29	12 52	14 16
10 F	11 9 39	19 08 35	17 17	4 43	12 26	21 36	22 52	13 55	0 17	15 50	24 53	29 45	2 58	12 39	29 03	13 19	14 19
11 Sa	11 13 36	20 08 32	29 57	4 42D	14 17	22 49	23 18	14 09	0 24	15 52	24 56	29 46	2 45	12 51	29 37	13 46	14 23
12 Su	11 17 32	21 08 27	12♏50	4 42	16 08	24 02	23 45	14 23	0 31	15 55	24 58	29 47	2 32	13 03	0♐11	14 13	14 26
13 M	11 21 29	22 08 20	25 56	4 43	18 01	25 14	24 11	14 37	0 38	15 57	25 00	29 49	2 19	13 16	0 45	14 41	14 29
14 T	11 25 25	23 08 12	9♐19	4 44	19 54	26 27	24 38	14 51	0 45	15 59	25 02	29 50	2 06	13 29	1 19	15 08	14 32
15 W	11 29 22	24 08 02	22 59	4 45R	21 49	27 39	25 05	15 05	0 52	16 02	25 05	29 51	1 52	13 42	1 53	15 35	14 36
16 Th	11 33 18	25 07 50	6♑59	4 44	23 45	28 52	25 32	15 19	0 59	16 04	25 07	29 52	1 39	13 56	2 27	16 02	14 39
17 F	11 37 15	26 07 37	21 17	4 42	25 42	0♉04	26 00	15 33	1 06	16 06	25 09	29 54	1 25	14 10	3 02	16 29	14 43
18 Sa	11 41 11	27 07 22	5≈51	4 38	27 40	1 17	26 27	15 47	1 12	16 09	25 12	29 55	1 11	14 25	3 36	16 57	14 46
19 Su	11 45 8	28 07 06	20 36	4 33	29 38	2 29	26 55	16 01	1 19	16 12	25 14	29 56	0 58	14 40	4 10	17 24	14 49
20 M	11 49 5	29 06 47	5♓27	4 28	1♈38	3 41	27 23	16 15	1 26	16 14	25 16	29 57	0 44	14 55	4 45	17 51	14 53
21 T	11 53 1	0♈06 27	20 14	4 23	3 38	4 53	27 51	16 30	1 33	16 17	25 18	29 58	0 30	15 11	5 19	18 19	14 56
22 W	11 56 58	1 06 04	4♈49	4 18	5 38	6 05	28 20	16 44	1 39	16 20	25 21	29 59	0 16	15 27	5 53	18 46	15 00
23 Th	12 0 54	2 05 40	19 07	4 16	7 39	7 17	28 48	16 58	1 46	16 22	25 23	0≈01	0 02	15 43	6 28	19 13	15 03
24 F	12 4 51	3 05 13	3♉02	4 15D	9 40	8 29	29 17	17 12	1 52	16 25	25 25	0 02	29♑48	16 00	7 03	19 40	15 07
25 Sa	12 8 47	4 04 45	16 32	4 16	11 41	9 41	29 46	17 27	1 59	16 28	25 27	0 03	29 34	16 17	7 37	20 08	15 10
26 Su	12 12 44	5 04 14	29 38	4 17	13 41	10 52	0♋15	17 41	2 05	16 31	25 30	0 04	29 21	16 34	8 12	20 35	15 13
27 M	12 16 40	6 03 41	12♊20	4 19	15 41	12 04	0 44	17 55	2 12	16 33	25 32	0 05	29 07	16 52	8 46	21 02	15 17
28 T	12 20 37	7 03 06	24 44	4 20	17 40	13 15	1 13	18 10	2 18	16 36	25 34	0 06	28 54	17 09	9 21	21 30	15 21
29 W	12 24 34	8 02 28	6♋52	4 21R	19 38	14 27	1 43	18 24	2 25	16 39	25 36	0 07	28 40	17 27	9 56	21 57	15 24
30 Th	12 28 30	9 01 48	18 51	4 20	21 33	15 38	2 12	18 38	2 31	16 42	25 39	0 07	28 27	17 46	10 31	22 24	15 27
31 F	12 32 27	10 01 06	0♌44	4 19	23 27	16 49	2 42	18 53	2 37	16 45	25 41	0 07	28 14	18 04	11 06	22 52	15 31

EPHEMERIS CALCULATED FOR 12 MIDNIGHT GREENWICH MEAN TIME. ALL OTHER DATA AND FACING ASPECTARIAN PAGE IN **EASTERN TIME (BOLD)** AND PACIFIC TIME (REGULAR).

APRIL 2023

☽ Last Aspect				☽ Ingress			
day	ET / hr:mn / PT		asp	sign	day	ET / hr:mn / PT	
1		11:03 pm	△☿	♍	2	**6:57 am**	3:57 am
2	**2:03 am**		△☿	♍	2	**6:57 am**	3:57 am
4	**9:50 am**	6:50 am	☍♆	♎	4	**5:51 pm**	2:51 pm
6	**8:43 am**	5:43 am	☍♃	♏	6		11:29 pm
6	**8:43 am**	5:43 am	☍♃	♏	7	**2:29 am**	
9	**5:09 am**	2:09 am	☍♀	♐	9	**8:57 am**	5:57 am
11	**6:48 am**	3:48 am	□♆	♑	11	**1:33 pm**	10:33 am
13	**10:14 am**	7:14 am	⚹♆	♒	13	**4:42 pm**	1:42 pm
15	**11:16 am**	8:16 am	⚹☉	♓	15	**6:57 pm**	3:57 pm
17	**2:57 pm**	11:57 am	☌♆	♈	17	**9:09 pm**	6:09 pm
19		9:13 pm	☌☉	♉	19		9:30 pm
20	**12:13 am**		☌☉	♉	20	**12:30 am**	
21	**11:41 pm**	8:41 pm	⚹♆	♊	22	**6:11 am**	3:11 am
24	**8:15 am**	5:15 am	□♆	♋	24	**2:58 pm**	11:58 am
26	**7:41 pm**	4:41 pm	△♆	♌	26		11:30 pm
26	**7:41 pm**	4:41 pm	△♆	♌	27	**2:30 am**	
29	**6:53 am**	3:53 am	△♃	♍	29	**2:59 pm**	11:59 am

☽ Phases & Eclipses			
phase	day	ET / hr:mn / PT	
Full Moon	5		9:34 pm
Full Moon	6	**12:34 am**	
4th Quarter	13	**5:11 am**	2:11 am
New Moon	19		9:13 pm
New Moon	20	**12:13 am**	
●	20	29° ♈ 50'	
2nd Quarter	27	**5:20 pm**	2:20 pm

Planet Ingress				
		day	ET / hr:mn / PT	
☿	♉	3	**12:22 pm**	9:22 am
♀	♊	10		9:47 pm
♀	♊	11	**12:47 am**	
⚶	♉	15	**1:01 pm**	10:01 am
☉	♉	20	**4:14 am**	1:14 am

Planetary Motion				
		day	ET / hr:mn / PT	
☿	℞	21	**4:35 am**	1:35 am

1 SATURDAY
☿ ⚺ ♆ **1:39 am**
☽ □ ♅ **4:30 am** 1:30 am
☽ □ ♀ **8:06 am** 5:06 am
☽ △ ♃ **9:25 am** 6:25 am
☽ ⚻ ♆ **10:28 pm** 7:28 pm
♀ ⚺ ♃ 9:18 pm
☽ △ ☿ 11:03 pm

2 SUNDAY
♀ ⚺ ♃ **12:18 am**
☽ △ ☿ **2:03 am**
☽ ⚻ ♇ **7:16 am** 4:16 am
☽ ☍ ♄ **12:44 pm** 9:44 am
☽ ⚹ ♂ **3:08 pm** 12:08 pm

3 MONDAY
☽ ⚻ ☉ **9:49 am** 6:49 am
☿ □ ♇ **2:55 pm** 11:55 am
☽ △ ♅ **4:28 pm** 1:28 pm
☽ ⚻ ♃ **10:12 pm** 7:12 pm
☽ △ ♀ 11:04 pm

4 TUESDAY
☽ △ ♀ **2:04 am**
☽ ☍ ♆ **9:50 am** 6:50 am
☽ △ ♇ **6:13 pm** 3:13 pm
☽ ⚻ ☿ **10:16 pm** 7:16 pm
☽ ⚻ ♄ **11:54 pm** 8:54 pm

5 WEDNESDAY
☽ □ ♂ **4:12 am** 1:12 am
☿ ⚹ ♄ **12:21 pm** 9:21 am
☽ ☍ ☉ 9:34 pm
☽ ⚻ ♅ 11:21 pm

6 THURSDAY
☽ ☍ ☉ **12:34 am**
☽ ⚻ ♅ **2:21 am**
☽ ☍ ♃ **8:43 am** 5:43 am
☽ ⚻ ♀ **5:06 pm** 2:06 pm
☽ ⚻ ♆ **6:57 pm** 3:57 pm
☉ ⚺ ♅ 9:42 pm
☽ □ ♇ 11:54 pm

7 FRIDAY
☉ ⚺ ♅ **12:42 am**
☽ □ ♇ **2:54 am**
☽ △ ♄ **8:44 am** 5:44 am
☽ ☍ ☿ **1:53 pm** 10:53 am
♀ ⚹ ♆ **1:58 pm** 10:58 am
☽ △ ♂ **2:42 pm** 11:42 am
☿ ⚹ ♂ 11:29 pm

8 SATURDAY
☿ ⚹ ♂ **2:29 am**
☽ ☍ ♅ **9:56 am** 6:56 am
☽ ⚻ ☉ **12:27 pm** 9:27 am
☽ ⚻ ♃ **4:51 pm** 1:51 pm
☽ △ ♆ 10:50 pm

9 SUNDAY
☽ △ ♆ **1:50 am**
☽ ☍ ♀ **5:09 am** 2:09 am
☽ ⚹ ♇ **9:23 am** 6:23 am
☽ □ ♄ **3:21 pm** 12:21 pm
☽ ⚻ ♂ **10:51 pm** 7:51 pm
☽ ⚻ ☿ 10:23 pm

10 MONDAY
☽ ⚻ ☿ **1:23 am**
☽ ⚻ ♅ **3:29 pm** 12:29 pm
☽ △ ☉ **9:48 pm** 6:48 pm
☽ △ ♃ **10:55 pm** 7:55 pm

11 TUESDAY
♀ △ ♇ **6:14 am** 3:14 am
☽ □ ♆ **6:48 am** 3:48 am
☽ ⚺ ♇ **2:01 pm** 11:01 am
☽ ⚻ ♀ **2:43 pm** 11:43 am
☉ ☌ ♃ **6:07 pm** 3:07 pm
☽ ⚹ ♄ **8:08 pm** 5:08 pm

12 WEDNESDAY
☽ ☍ ♂ **5:03 am** 2:03 am
☽ △ ☿ **9:35 am** 6:35 am
☽ △ ♅ **7:24 pm** 4:24 pm

13 THURSDAY
☽ □ ♃ **3:20 am** 12:20 am
☽ □ ☉ **5:11 am** 2:11 am
☽ ⚹ ♆ **10:14 am** 7:14 am
☽ ☌ ♇ **5:11 pm** 2:11 pm
☽ △ ♀ **10:23 pm** 7:23 pm
☽ ⚺ ♄ **11:28 pm** 8:28 pm

14 FRIDAY
☽ ⚻ ♂ **9:47 am** 6:47 am
♀ □ ♄ **12:38 pm** 9:38 am
☽ □ ☿ **3:16 pm** 12:16 pm
☽ □ ♅ **10:08 pm** 7:08 pm

15 SATURDAY
☽ ⚹ ♃ **6:36 am** 3:36 am
☽ ⚹ ☉ **11:16 am** 8:16 am
☽ ⚺ ♆ **12:41 pm** 9:41 am
☽ ⚺ ♇ **7:27 pm** 4:27 pm
☽ ☌ ♄ 10:58 pm

16 SUNDAY
☽ ☌ ♄ **1:58 am**
☽ □ ♀ **4:58 am** 1:58 am
☉ ⚺ ♆ **8:43 am** 5:43 am
☽ △ ♂ **1:49 pm** 10:49 am
☽ ⚹ ☿ **7:24 pm** 4:24 pm
☽ ⚹ ♅ 9:25 pm

17 MONDAY
☽ ⚹ ♅ **12:25 am**
☽ ⚺ ♃ **9:35 am** 6:35 am
☽ ☌ ♆ **2:57 pm** 11:57 am
☽ ⚺ ☉ **5:06 pm** 2:06 pm
☽ ⚹ ♇ **9:42 pm** 6:42 pm

18 TUESDAY
☽ ⚺ ♄ **4:34 am** 1:34 am
☽ ⚹ ♀ **11:47 am** 8:47 am
☽ □ ♂ **6:16 pm** 3:16 pm
☽ ⚺ ☿ **11:15 pm** 8:15 pm

19 WEDNESDAY
☽ ⚺ ♅ **3:20 am** 12:20 am
☽ ☌ ♃ **1:27 pm** 10:27 am
☽ ⚺ ♆ **6:12 pm** 3:12 pm
☽ ☌ ☉ 9:13 pmc
☽ □ ♇ 10:04 pm

20 THURSDAY
☽ ☌ ☉ **12:13 am**
☽ □ ♇ **1:04 am**
☽ ⚹ ♄ **8:30 am** 5:30 am
☉ □ ♇ **12:27 pm** 9:27 am
☽ ⚺ ♀ **8:29 pm** 5:29 pm
☽ ⚹ ♂ 9:37 pm

21 FRIDAY
☽ ⚹ ♂ **12:37 am**
☽ ☌ ☿ **4:05 am** 1:05 am
☽ ☌ ♅ **8:09 am** 5:09 am
☽ ⚺ ♃ **7:32 pm** 4:32 pm
☽ ⚹ ♆ **11:41 pm** 8:41 pm

22 SATURDAY
☽ △ ♇ **6:49 am** 3:49 am
☽ ⚺ ☉ **10:14 am** 7:14 am
☽ □ ♄ **3:00 pm** 12:00 pm

23 SUNDAY
☽ ☌ ♀ **8:43 am** 5:43 am
☽ ⚺ ♂ **10:06 am** 7:06 am
☽ ⚺ ☿ **10:54 am** 7:54 am
☽ ⚺ ♅ **3:55 pm** 12:55 pm
☿ ⚹ ♂ **11:19 pm** 8:19 pm

24 MONDAY
☽ ⚹ ♃ **4:49 am** 1:49 am
☿ ⚺ ♀ **5:04 am** 2:04 am
☽ □ ♆ **8:15 am** 5:15 am
♀ ⚺ ♂ **12:50 pm** 9:50 am
☽ ⚻ ♇ **3:40 pm** 12:40 pm
☽ ⚹ ☉ 9:11 pm
☽ △ ♄ 9:40 pm

25 TUESDAY
☽ ⚹ ☉ **12:11 am**
☽ △ ♄ **12:40 am**
☉ ⚹ ♄ **6:48 am** 3:48 am
☽ ⚹ ☿ **7:47 pm** 4:47 pm
☽ ☌ ♂ **11:08 pm** 8:08 pm
☽ ⚺ ♀ 10:00 pm
☽ ⚹ ♅ 11:45 pm

26 WEDNESDAY
☽ ⚺ ♀ **1:00 am**
☽ ⚹ ♅ **2:45 am**
☽ □ ♃ **5:09 pm** 2:09 pm
☽ △ ♆ **7:41 pm** 4:41 pm
♀ ⚺ ♅ **8:35 pm** 5:35 pm

27 THURSDAY
☽ ☍ ♇ **3:13 am** 12:13 am
☽ ⚻ ♄ **12:54 pm** 9:54 am
☽ □ ☉ **5:20 pm** 2:20 pm

28 FRIDAY
☽ □ ☿ **5:44 am** 2:44 am
☽ ⚺ ♂ **2:22 pm** 11:22 am
☽ □ ♅ **3:26 pm** 12:26 pm
☽ ⚹ ♀ **7:42 pm** 4:42 pm

29 SATURDAY
☽ △ ♃ **6:53 am** 3:53 am
☽ ⚻ ♆ **8:20 am** 5:20 am
☽ ⚻ ♇ **3:43 pm** 12:43 pm
♂ ⚹ ♅ **4:05 pm** 1:05 pm
☽ ☍ ♄ 10:41 pm

30 SUNDAY
☽ ☍ ♄ **1:41 am**
☽ △ ☉ **10:59 am** 7:59 am
☽ △ ☿ **3:05 pm** 12:05 pm

Eastern time in bold type
Pacific time in medium type

April 2023

DATE	SID.TIME	SUN	MOON	NODE	MERCURY	VENUS	MARS	JUPITER	SATURN	URANUS	NEPTUNE	PLUTO	CERES	PALLAS	JUNO	VESTA	CHIRON
1 Sa	12 36 23	11♈00 21	12♌36	4♉16℞	25♈18	18♉01	3♊12	19♈07	2♓44	16♉48	25♓43	0♒08	28♍01℞	18♌23	11♊41	23♈19	15♈35
2 Su	12 40 20	11 59 34	24 31	4 13	27 06	19 12	3 42	19 22	2 50	16 51	25 45	0 09	27 48	18 42	12 15	23 46	15 38
3 M	12 44 16	12 58 45	6♍33	4 09	28 51	20 22	4 12	19 36	2 56	16 54	25 48	0 10	27 36	19 02	12 50	24 13	15 42
4 T	12 48 13	13 57 54	18 45	4 06	0♉32	21 33	4 42	19 51	3 02	16 57	25 50	0 11	27 24	19 21	13 25	24 41	15 45
5 W	12 52 9	14 57 00	1♎07	4 03	2 09	22 44	5 13	20 05	3 08	17 00	25 52	0 12	27 12	19 41	14 01	25 09	15 49
6 Th	12 56 6	15 56 05	13 42	4 03	3 41	23 55	5 43	20 20	3 14	17 03	25 54	0 12	27 00	20 01	14 35	25 35	15 52
7 F	13 0 2	16 55 07	26 30	4 00D	5 09	25 05	6 14	20 34	3 20	17 06	25 56	0 13	26 48	20 21	15 10	26 03	15 56
8 Sa	13 3 59	17 54 07	9♏32	4 00	6 32	26 16	6 45	20 48	3 26	17 09	25 58	0 14	26 37	20 42	15 45	26 30	15 59
9 Su	13 7 56	18 53 06	22 46	4 01	7 49	27 26	7 16	21 03	3 32	17 12	26 01	0 14	26 26	21 02	16 21	26 57	16 03
10 M	13 11 52	19 52 02	6✓14	4 02	9 01	28 36	7 47	21 17	3 37	17 15	26 03	0 15	26 16	21 23	16 56	27 24	16 06
11 T	13 15 49	20 50 57	19 53	4 03	10 08	29 46	8 18	21 31	3 43	17 19	26 05	0 16	26 05	21 44	17 31	27 52	16 10
12 W	13 19 45	21 49 51	3♑44	4 04℞	11 08	0♊56	8 49	21 46	3 49	17 22	26 07	0 16	25 55	22 06	18 06	28 19	16 13
13 Th	13 23 42	22 48 42	17 46	4 04	12 03	2 06	9 20	22 01	3 54	17 25	26 09	0 17	25 45	22 27	18 41	28 46	16 17
14 F	13 27 38	23 47 32	1≈57	4 03	12 51	3 16	9 52	22 15	4 00	17 28	26 11	0 17	25 36	22 49	19 16	29 13	16 20
15 Sa	13 31 35	24 46 20	16 16	4 01	13 34	4 25	10 23	22 30	4 05	17 32	26 13	0 18	25 27	23 10	19 52	29 41	16 24
16 Su	13 35 32	25 45 07	0♓38	4 03	14 10	5 35	10 55	22 44	4 11	17 35	26 15	0 18	25 18	23 32	20 27	0♉08	16 27
17 M	13 39 28	26 43 51	15 00	4 02	14 40	6 44	11 26	22 59	4 16	17 38	26 17	0 19	25 10	23 54	21 02	0 35	16 31
18 T	13 43 25	27 42 34	29 19	4 01	15 03	7 53	11 58	23 13	4 22	17 41	26 19	0 19	25 02	24 17	21 38	1 02	16 34
19 W	13 47 21	28 41 15	13♈29	4 01	15 21	9 02	12 30	23 28	4 27	17 45	26 21	0 20	24 55	24 39	22 13	1 30	16 38
20 Th	13 51 18	29 39 54	27 25	4 00D	15 32	10 11	13 02	23 42	4 32	17 48	26 23	0 20	24 48	25 02	22 48	1 57	16 41
21 F	13 55 14	0♉38 31	11♉05	4 00	15 37℞	11 20	13 34	23 57	4 37	17 51	26 25	0 20	24 41	25 24	23 24	2 24	16 45
22 Sa	13 59 11	1 37 07	24 26	4 01	15 36	12 29	14 06	24 11	4 42	17 55	26 27	0 21	24 34	25 47	23 59	2 51	16 48
23 Su	14 3 7	2 35 40	7♊27	4 01	15 30	13 37	14 39	24 25	4 47	17 58	26 29	0 21	24 29	26 10	24 34	3 18	16 52
24 M	14 7 4	3 34 12	20 10	4 01℞	15 18	14 46	15 11	24 40	4 52	18 02	26 31	0 21	24 23	26 33	25 10	3 45	16 55
25 T	14 11 0	4 32 41	2♋35	4 01	15 00	15 54	15 43	24 54	4 57	18 05	26 33	0 21	24 18	26 57	25 45	4 12	16 58
26 W	14 14 57	5 31 08	14 46	4 01	14 39	17 02	16 16	25 08	5 02	18 08	26 35	0 22	24 13	27 20	26 20	4 40	17 02
27 Th	14 18 54	6 29 33	26 46	4 01D	14 13	18 10	16 49	25 23	5 06	18 12	26 37	0 22	24 09	27 43	26 56	5 07	17 05
28 F	14 22 50	7 27 56	8♌41	4 01	13 43	19 18	17 22	25 37	5 11	18 15	26 38	0 22	24 05	28 07	27 31	5 34	17 09
29 Sa	14 26 47	8 26 17	20 34	4 01	13 10	20 26	17 54	25 51	5 15	18 19	26 40	0 22	24 02	28 31	28 07	6 01	17 12
30 Su	14 30 43	9 24 36	2♍30	4 01	12 35	21 33	18 27	26 06	5 20	18 22	26 42	0 22	23 58	28 55	28 42	6 28	17 15

EPHEMERIS CALCULATED FOR 12 MIDNIGHT GREENWICH MEAN TIME. ALL OTHER DATA AND FACING ASPECTARIAN PAGE IN **EASTERN TIME (BOLD)** AND PACIFIC TIME (REGULAR).

☽ Last Aspect day	ET / hr:mn / PT	asp	☽ Ingress sign	day	ET / hr:mn / PT
1	**7:53 pm** 4:53 pm	☍♆	♎	1	11:09 pm
1	**7:53 pm** 4:53 pm	☍♆	♎	2	**2:09 am**
4	**5:17 am** 2:17 am	☍♃	♏	4	**10:32 am** 7:32 am
6	**10:38 am** 7:38 am	△♆	♐	6	**4:04 pm** 1:04 pm
8	**4:28 pm** 1:28 pm	△♃	♑	8	**7:33 pm** 4:33 pm
10	**7:52 pm** 4:52 pm	□♃	♒	10	**10:05 pm** 7:05 pm
12	**11:15 pm** 8:15 pm	⚹♃	♓	12	9:39 pm
12	**11:15 pm** 8:15 pm	⚹♃	♓	13	**12:39 am**
14	**10:56 pm** 7:56 pm	☌♆	♈	15	**3:56 am** 12:56 am
17	**5:10 am** 2:10 am	□♂	♉	17	**8:28 am** 5:28 am
19	**1:51 pm** 10:51 am	⚹♂	♊	19	**2:48 pm** 11:48 am
21	**6:12 pm** 3:12 pm	□♆	♋	21	**11:28 pm** 8:28 pm
24	**5:12 am** 2:12 am	△♆	♌	24	**10:35 am** 7:35 am
25	11:38 pm	□♅	♍	26	**11:05 pm** 8:05 pm
26	**2:38 am**	□♅	♍	26	**11:05 pm** 8:05 pm
29	**5:46 am** 2:46 am	☍♆	♎	29	**10:51 am** 7:51 am
31	**10:53 am** 7:53 am	□♀	♏	31	**7:45 pm** 4:45 pm

☽ Phases & Eclipses phase	day	ET / hr:mn / PT
Full Moon	5	**1:34 pm** 10:34 am
☊	5	14° ♏ 58'
4th Quarter	12	**10:28 am** 7:28 am
New Moon	19	**11:53 am** 8:53 am
2nd Quarter	27	**11:22 am** 8:22 am

Planet Ingress		day	ET / hr:mn / PT
⚵	♊	1	9:50 pm
⚵	♊	2	**12:50 am**
♀	♌	2	**1:03 pm** 10:03 am
♀	♋	7	**10:25 am** 7:25 am
♃	♉	16	**1:20 pm** 10:20 am
♂	♌	20	**11:31 am** 8:31 am
☉	♊	21	**3:09 am** 12:09 am

Planetary Motion		day	ET / hr:mn / PT
♇	℞	1	**1:09 pm** 10:09 am
⚳	D	6	**3:24 pm** 12:24 pm
☿	D	14	**11:17 pm** 8:17 pm

1 MONDAY
☽△♅ **3:38 am** 12:38 am
☽⚹♂ **5:08 am** 2:08 am
☽□♀ **1:31 pm** 10:31 am
☉☌☿ **7:28 pm** 4:28 pm
☽⚻♃ **7:30 pm** 4:30 pm
☽☍♆ **7:53 pm** 4:53 pm
☽△♇ 11:51 pm

2 TUESDAY
☽△♇ **2:51 am**
☽⚻♄ **12:46 pm** 9:46 am
♃⚺♆ **6:03 pm** 3:03 pm
☽⚻☿ **10:26 pm** 7:26 pm
☽⚻☉ 11:09 pm

3 WEDNESDAY
☽⚻☉ **2:09 am**
☽⚻♅ **1:26 pm** 10:26 am
☽□♂ **5:10 pm** 2:10 pm

4 THURSDAY
☽△♀ **3:54 am** 12:54 am
☽⚻♆ **4:43 am** 1:43 am
☽☍♃ **5:17 am** 2:17 am
☽□♇ **11:12 am** 8:12 am
♀□♆ **1:40 pm** 10:40 am
☽△♄ **8:53 pm** 5:53 pm
♀⚹♃ 9:03 pm

5 FRIDAY
♀⚹♃ **12:03 am**
☽☍☿ **3:15 am** 12:15 am

☽☍☉ **1:34 pm** 10:34 am
☽☍♅ **8:13 pm** 5:13 pm
☽△♂ 10:51 pm

6 SATURDAY
☽△♂ **1:51 am**
☽△♆ **10:38 am** 7:38 am
☽⚻♃ **11:59 am** 8:59 am
☽⚻♀ **2:28 pm** 11:28 am
☽⚹♇ **4:41 pm** 1:41 pm
☽□♄ 11:12 pm

7 SUNDAY
☽□♄ **2:12 am**
☽⚻☿ **5:58 am** 2:58 am
♀⚻♇ **6:10 pm** 3:10 pm
☽⚻☉ **9:50 pm** 6:50 pm
☽⚻♅ 9:34 pm

8 MONDAY
☽⚻♅ **12:34 am**
☽⚻♂ **7:55 am** 4:55 am
☽□♆ **2:22 pm** 11:22 am
☽△♃ **4:28 pm** 1:28 pm
☽⚺♇ **8:09 pm** 5:09 pm
☽☍♀ **10:20 pm** 7:20 pm

9 TUESDAY
☽⚹♄ **5:39 am** 2:39 am
☽△☿ **7:28 am** 4:28 am
☉☌♅ **3:56 pm** 12:56 pm

10 WEDNESDAY
☽△♅ **3:32 am** 12:32 am
☽△☉ **4:20 am** 1:20 am
☽☍♂ **12:38 pm** 9:38 am
☽⚹♆ **5:03 pm** 2:03 pm
☽□♃ **7:52 pm** 4:52 pm
☽☌♇ **10:40 pm** 7:40 pm

11 THURSDAY
☽⚻♀ **5:01 am** 2:01 am
☽⚺♄ **8:20 am** 5:20 am
☽□☿ **8:45 am** 5:45 am

12 FRIDAY
☿⚹♄ **4:42 am** 1:42 am
☽□♅ **6:12 am** 3:12 am
☽□☉ **10:28 am** 7:28 am
☽⚻♂ **5:13 pm** 2:13 pm
☽⚺♆ **7:40 pm** 4:40 pm
☿⚹♀ **10:44 pm** 7:44 pm
☽⚹♃ **11:15 pm** 8:15 pm
☽⚺♇ 10:13 pm
♀△♄ 11:57 pm

13 SATURDAY
☽⚺♇ **1:13 am**
♀△♄ **2:57 am**
☽⚹☿ **10:44 am** 7:44 am
☽☌♄ **11:12 am** 8:12 am
☽△♀ **11:51 am** 8:51 am

14 SUNDAY
☽⚹♅ **9:22 am** 6:22 am
☽⚹☉ **5:17 pm** 2:17 pm

☽△♂ **10:30 pm** 7:30 pm
☽☌♆ **10:56 pm** 7:56 pm

15 MONDAY
☽⚺♃ **3:22 am** 12:22 am
☽⚹♇ **4:29 am** 1:29 am
♂△♆ **9:44 am** 6:44 am
☽⚺☿ **2:05 pm** 11:05 am
☽⚺♄ **2:54 pm** 11:54 am
☽□♀ **7:42 pm** 4:42 pm

16 TUESDAY
☽⚺♅ **1:37 pm** 10:37 am
☽⚺☉ 10:30 pm

17 WEDNESDAY
☽⚺☉ **1:30 am**
☽⚺♆ **3:25 am** 12:25 am
☽□♂ **5:10 am** 2:10 am
☽☌♃ **8:47 am** 5:47 am
☽□♇ **9:00 am** 6:00 am
☽☌☿ **7:27 pm** 4:27 pm
☽⚹♄ **7:57 pm** 4:57 pm
♃□♇ **9:11 pm** 6:11 pm

18 THURSDAY
☉⚹♆ **5:00 am** 2:00 am
☽⚹♀ **5:18 am** 2:18 am
☽☌♅ **7:28 pm** 4:28 pm
☿⚹♄ 11:40 pm

19 FRIDAY
☿⚹♄ **2:40 am**
☽⚹♆ **9:39 am** 6:39 am
☽☌☉ **11:53 am** 8:53 am

☽⚹♂ **1:51 pm** 10:51 am
☽△♇ **3:20 pm** 12:20 pm
☽⚺♃ **4:06 pm** 1:06 pm
☽□♄ 11:58 pm

20 SATURDAY
☽□♄ **2:58 am**
☽⚺☿ **3:33 am** 12:33 am
☽⚺♀ **5:28 pm** 2:28 pm
♂☍♇ **11:12 pm** 8:12 pm

21 SUNDAY
☽⚺♅ **3:32 am** 12:32 am
☉△♇ **9:58 am** 6:58 am
☽□♆ **6:12 pm** 3:12 pm
☽⚻♇ 9:00 pm
☽⚺☉ 10:11 pm
☽⚺♂ 10:12 pm
☽⚹♃ 10:54 pm
☉⚹♂ 10:57 pm

22 MONDAY
☽⚻♇ **12:00 am**
☽⚺☉ **1:11 am**
☽⚺♂ **1:12 am**
☽⚹♃ **1:54 am**
☉⚹♂ **1:57 am**
☽△♄ **12:24 pm** 9:24 am
☉⚺♃ **12:55 pm** 9:55 am
☽⚹☿ **3:07 pm** 12:07 pm
♂□♃ 10:13 pm

23 TUESDAY
♂□♃ **1:13 am**
☽☌♀ **8:45 am** 5:45 am
☽⚹♅ **2:07 pm** 11:07 am

24 WEDNESDAY
☽△♆ **5:12 am** 2:12 am
☽☍♇ **11:04 am** 8:04 am
☽□♃ **2:13 pm** 11:13 am
☽☌♂ **3:21 pm** 12:21 pm
☽⚹☉ **5:31 pm** 2:31 pm
☽⚻♄ 9:09 pm

25 THURSDAY
☽⚻♄ **12:09 am**
☽□☿ **6:11 am** 3:11 am
☽⚺♀ 11:33 pm
☽□♅ 11:38 pm

26 FRIDAY
☽⚺♀ **2:33 am**
☽□♅ **2:38 am**
♀⚹♅ **3:37 am** 12:37 am
☽⚻♆ **5:45 pm** 2:45 pm
☽⚻♇ **11:31 pm** 8:31 pm

27 SATURDAY
☽△♃ **3:53 am** 12:53 am
☽⚺♂ **6:57 am** 3:57 am
☽□☉ **11:22 am** 8:22 am
☽☍♄ **12:53 pm** 9:53 am
☽△☿ **11:07 pm** 8:07 pm

28 SUNDAY
☉□♄ **6:46 am** 3:46 am
☽△♅ **3:12 pm** 12:12 pm
☽⚹♀ **8:19 pm** 5:19 pm

29 MONDAY
☽☍♆ **5:46 am** 2:46 am
☽△♇ **11:13 am** 8:13 am
☽⚻♃ **4:33 pm** 1:33 pm
☽⚹♂ **9:21 pm** 6:21 pm
☽⚻♄ 9:18 pm

30 TUESDAY
☽⚻♄ **12:18 am**
☽△☉ **3:39 am** 12:39 am
☽⚻☿ **2:50 pm** 11:50 am
☽⚻♅ 10:29 pm

31 WEDNESDAY
☽⚻♅ **1:29 am**
☽□♀ **10:53 am** 7:53 am
☽⚻♆ **3:02 pm** 12:02 pm
☽□♇ **8:02 pm** 5:02 pm
☽☍♃ 11:04 pm

Eastern time in bold type
Pacific time in medium type

MAY 2023

DATE	SID.TIME	SUN	MOON	NODE	MERCURY	VENUS	MARS	JUPITER	SATURN	URANUS	NEPTUNE	PLUTO	CERES	PALLAS	JUNO	VESTA	CHIRON
1 M	14 34 40	10♉22 52	14♏34	4♉02R	11♉57R	22♊40	19♋00	26♈20	5♓24	18♉26	26♓44	0♒22R	23♍56R	29♋19	29♊17	6♋55	17♈19
2 T	14 38 36	11 21 07	26 49	4 02	11 19	23 48	19 33	26 34	5 29	18 29	26 46	0 22	23 54	29 43	29 53	7 22	17 22
3 W	14 42 33	12 19 19	9♐19	4 03	10 40	24 55	20 06	26 48	5 33	18 32	26 47	0 22	23 52	0♌07	0♋28	7 49	17 25
4 Th	14 46 29	13 17 30	22 06	4 04	10 02	26 01	20 39	27 02	5 37	18 36	26 49	0 22	23 51	0 31	1 03	8 16	17 28
5 F	14 50 26	14 15 39	5♑12	4 04	9 24	27 08	21 12	27 17	5 41	18 39	26 51	0 22	23 50	0 56	1 39	8 43	17 32
6 Sa	14 54 23	15 13 46	18 35	4 03	8 48	28 14	21 45	27 31	5 45	18 43	26 52	0 22	23 49D	1 20	2 15	9 09	17 35
7 Su	14 58 19	16 11 52	2♒16	4 03	8 14	29 20	22 19	27 45	5 49	18 46	26 54	0 21	23 49	1 45	2 50	9 36	17 38
8 M	15 02 16	17 09 56	16 10	4 01	7 43	0♋26	22 52	27 59	5 53	18 50	26 56	0 21	23 49	2 09	3 25	10 03	17 41
9 T	15 06 12	18 07 59	0♓16	3 59	7 15	1 32	23 26	28 13	5 57	18 53	26 57	0 21	23 50	2 34	4 01	10 30	17 44
10 W	15 10 09	19 06 00	14 29	3 58	6 50	2 38	23 59	28 27	6 00	18 57	26 59	0 21	23 51	2 59	4 36	10 57	17 48
11 Th	15 14 05	20 04 00	28 45	3 56	6 29	3 43	24 33	28 41	6 04	19 00	27 00	0 21	23 52	3 24	5 12	11 24	17 51
12 F	15 18 02	21 01 58	13♈02	3 55D	6 13	4 48	25 06	28 55	6 07	19 04	27 02	0 20	23 54	3 49	5 47	11 50	17 54
13 Sa	15 21 59	21 59 55	27 15	3 55	6 01	5 53	25 40	29 09	6 11	19 07	27 03	0 20	23 57	4 14	6 22	12 17	17 57
14 Su	15 25 55	22 57 51	11♉23	3 56	5 54	6 58	26 14	29 23	6 14	19 11	27 05	0 20	23 59	4 39	6 58	12 44	18 00
15 M	15 29 52	23 55 46	25 24	3 57	5 51D	8 02	26 48	29 36	6 17	19 14	27 06	0 19	24 02	5 04	7 33	13 10	18 03
16 T	15 33 48	24 53 39	9♊16	3 59	5 53	9 06	27 22	29 50	6 21	19 18	27 08	0 19	24 06	5 30	8 08	13 37	18 06
17 W	15 37 45	25 51 31	22 58	4♉00R	5 59	10 10	27 56	0♉04	6 24	19 21	27 09	0 19	24 10	5 55	8 44	14 04	18 09
18 Th	15 41 41	26 49 22	6♋28	4 00	6 10	11 14	28 30	0 17	6 27	19 25	27 11	0 18	24 14	6 21	9 19	14 30	18 12
19 F	15 45 38	27 47 12	19 45	3 59	6 25	12 17	29 04	0 31	6 30	19 28	27 12	0 18	24 19	6 46	9 54	14 57	18 15
20 Sa	15 49 34	28 45 00	2♌49	3 57	6 45	13 21	29 38	0 45	6 32	19 31	27 13	0 17	24 24	7 12	10 30	15 24	18 17
21 Su	15 53 31	29 42 47	15 38	3 54	7 09	14 24	0♌12	0 58	6 35	19 35	27 14	0 17	24 29	7 37	11 05	15 50	18 20
22 M	15 57 28	0♊40 33	28 12	3 50	7 38	15 26	0 46	1 12	6 38	19 38	27 16	0 16	24 35	8 03	11 40	16 17	18 23
23 T	16 01 24	1 38 17	10♍33	3 45	8 10	16 28	1 21	1 25	6 40	19 42	27 17	0 16	24 41	8 29	12 16	16 43	18 26
24 W	16 05 21	2 35 59	22 42	3 41	8 47	17 31	1 55	1 39	6 43	19 45	27 18	0 15	24 47	8 55	12 51	17 10	18 29
25 Th	16 09 17	3 33 40	4♎42	3 37	9 27	18 32	2 29	1 52	6 45	19 49	27 19	0 14	24 54	9 21	13 26	17 36	18 31
26 F	16 13 14	4 31 20	16 36	3 34	10 11	19 34	3 04	2 05	6 47	19 52	27 21	0 14	25 01	9 47	14 01	18 02	18 34
27 Sa	16 17 10	5 28 57	28 28	3 33D	10 59	20 35	3 38	2 18	6 49	19 55	27 22	0 13	25 09	10 13	14 37	18 29	18 37
28 Su	16 21 07	6 26 34	10♏24	3 32	11 50	21 35	4 13	2 32	6 52	19 59	27 23	0 12	25 16	10 39	15 12	18 55	18 39
29 M	16 25 03	7 24 09	22 27	3 33	12 45	22 36	4 48	2 45	6 53	20 02	27 24	0 12	25 25	11 05	15 47	19 21	18 42
30 T	16 29 00	8 21 42	4♐42	3 35	13 43	23 36	5 22	2 58	6 55	20 05	27 25	0 11	25 33	11 31	16 22	19 47	18 44
31 W	16 32 57	9 19 15	17 15	3 36	14 45	24 35	5 57	3 11	6 57	20 09	27 26	0 10	25 42	11 57	16 57	20 14	18 47

EPHEMERIS CALCULATED FOR 12 MIDNIGHT GREENWICH MEAN TIME. ALL OTHER DATA AND FACING ASPECTARIAN PAGE IN **EASTERN TIME (BOLD)** AND PACIFIC TIME (REGULAR).

☽ Last Aspect day	ET / hr:mn / PT	asp	☽ Ingress sign	day	ET / hr:mn / PT
2	**8:51 pm** 5:51 pm	△♀	♐	2	10:03 pm
2	**8:51 pm** 5:51 pm	△♀	♐	3	**1:03 am**
4	**11:24 pm** 8:24 pm	□♆	♑	5	**3:31 am** 12:31 am
6	9:40 pm	⚹♆	♒	7	**4:42 am** 1:42 am
7	**12:40 am**	⚹♆	♒	7	**4:42 am** 1:42 am
8	9:24 pm	□☿	♓	9	**6:14 am** 3:14 am
9	**12:24 am**	□☿	♓	9	**6:14 am** 3:14 am
11	**9:20 am** 6:20 am	⚹♇	♈	11	**9:20 am** 6:20 am
13	**2:27 pm** 11:27 am	□♇	♉	13	**2:31 pm** 11:31 am
15	**9:36 pm** 6:36 pm	△♇	♊	15	**9:46 pm** 6:46 pm

☽ Last Aspect day	ET / hr:mn / PT	asp	☽ Ingress sign	day	ET / hr:mn / PT
17	11:24 pm	□♆	♋	18	**6:58 am** 3:58 am
18	**2:24 am**	□♆	♋	18	**6:58 am** 3:58 am
20	**5:43 pm** 2:43 pm	☍♇	♌	20	**6:04 pm** 3:04 pm
22	**1:01 pm** 10:01 am	□♅	♍	23	**6:35 am** 3:35 am
25	**6:24 pm** 3:24 pm	△♇	♎	25	**6:57 pm** 3:57 pm
28	**4:19 am** 1:19 am	□♇	♏	28	**4:55 am** 1:55 am
30	**10:20 am** 7:20 am	⚹♇	♐	30	**10:59 am** 7:59 am

☽ Phases & Eclipses phase	day	ET / hr:mn / PT
Full Moon	3	**11:42 pm** 8:42 pm
4th Quarter	10	**3:31 pm** 12:31 pm
New Moon	17	9:37 pm
New Moon	18	**12:37 am**
2nd Quarter	26	**3:50 am** 12:50 am

Planet Ingress		day	ET / hr:mn / PT
♀	♌	5	**9:46 am** 6:46 am
♇	♑	11	**5:47 am** 2:47 am
☿	♊	11	**6:27 am** 3:27 am
⚳	♎	21	**7:30 am** 4:30 am
☉	♋	21	**10:58 am** 7:58 am
⚵	♋	22	**7:40 am** 4:40 am
⚶	♊	22	**3:17 pm** 12:17 pm
☿	♋	26	**8:24 pm** 5:24 pm

Planetary Motion		day	ET / hr:mn / PT
♄	℞	17	**1:27 pm** 10:27 am
♆	℞	30	**5:07 pm** 2:07 pm

1 THURSDAY
- ☽☍♃ **2:04 am**
- ☽□♂ **8:11 am** 5:11 am
- ☽△♄ **8:30 am** 5:30 am
- ♂⚻♄ **3:31 pm** 12:31 pm
- ☽⚻☉ **3:50 pm** 12:50 pm
- ☽☍☿ 11:53 pm

2 FRIDAY
- ☽☍☿ **2:53 am**
- ☽☍♅ **8:10 am** 5:10 am
- ♀△♆ **6:42 pm** 3:42 pm
- ☽△♆ **8:42 pm** 5:42 pm
- ☽△♀ **8:51 pm** 5:51 pm
- ☽⚹♇ 10:16 pm

3 SATURDAY
- ☽⚹♇ **1:16 am**
- ☽⚻♃ **7:48 am** 4:48 am
- ☽□♄ **1:07 pm** 10:07 am
- ☽△♂ **2:59 pm** 11:59 am
- ☽☍☉ **11:42 pm** 8:42 pm

4 SUNDAY
- ☽⚻☿ **11:12 am** 8:12 am
- ☽⚻♅ **11:35 am** 8:35 am
- ☿☌♅ **3:49 pm** 12:49 pm
- ☽□♆ **11:24 pm** 8:24 pm

5 MONDAY
- ☽⚻♀ **3:05 am** 12:05 am
- ☽⚺♇ **3:40 am** 12:40 am
- ☽△♃ **10:44 am** 7:44 am

- ♀☍♇ **12:05 pm** 9:05 am
- ☽⚹♄ **3:12 pm** 12:12 pm
- ☽⚻♂ **7:00 pm** 4:00 pm

6 TUESDAY
- ☽⚻☉ **4:51 am** 1:51 am
- ☽△♅ **1:10 pm** 10:10 am
- ☽△☿ **5:34 pm** 2:34 pm
- ☽⚹♆ 9:40 pm

7 WEDNESDAY
- ☽⚹♆ **12:40 am**
- ☽☌♇ **4:48 am** 1:48 am
- ☽☍♀ **7:39 am** 4:39 am
- ☽□♃ **12:35 pm** 9:35 am
- ☽⚺♄ **4:23 pm** 1:23 pm
- ☽☍♂ **10:11 pm** 7:11 pm

8 THURSDAY
- ☽△☉ **9:29 am** 6:29 am
- ☽□♅ **2:37 pm** 11:37 am
- ☽□☿ 9:24 pm
- ☽⚺♆ 11:10 pm

9 FRIDAY
- ☽□☿ **12:24 am**
- ☽⚺♆ **2:10 am**
- ☽⚺♇ **6:17 am** 3:17 am
- ☽⚻♀ **12:41 pm** 9:41 am
- ☽⚹♃ **3:02 pm** 12:02 pm
- ☿⚹♆ **5:14 pm** 2:14 pm
- ☽☌♄ **6:16 pm** 3:16 pm
- ☽⚻♂ 11:20 pm

10 SATURDAY
- ☽⚻♂ **2:20 am**
- ☽□☉ **3:31 pm** 12:31 pm
- ☽⚹♅ **5:21 pm** 2:21 pm

11 SUNDAY
- ☽☌♆ **5:09 am** 2:09 am
- ☿△♇ **6:26 am** 3:26 am
- ☽⚹♇ **9:20 am** 6:20 am
- ☽⚹☿ **9:43 am** 6:43 am
- ♀□♃ **11:40 am** 8:40 am
- ☽⚺♃ **7:16 pm** 4:16 pm
- ☉⚺♅ **7:37 pm** 4:37 pm
- ☽△♀ **7:40 pm** 4:40 pm
- ☽⚺♄ **9:53 pm** 6:53 pm

12 MONDAY
- ☽△♂ **8:35 am** 5:35 am
- ☽⚺♅ **10:04 pm** 7:04 pm
- ☽⚹☉ **11:59 pm** 8:59 pm

13 TUESDAY
- ♀⚻♄ **5:59 am** 2:59 am
- ☽⚺♆ **10:12 am** 7:12 am
- ☽□♇ **2:27 pm** 11:27 am
- ☽⚺☿ **10:35 pm** 7:35 pm
- ☽☌♃ 10:40 pm

14 WEDNESDAY
- ☽☌♃ **1:40 am**
- ☽⚹♄ **3:36 am** 12:36 am
- ☽□♀ **5:08 am** 2:08 am
- ☽□♂ **5:15 pm** 2:15 pm
- ☿⚺♃ 9:24 pm

15 THURSDAY
- ☿⚺♃ **12:24 am**
- ☽☌♅ **4:55 am** 1:55 am
- ☽⚺☉ **11:04 am** 8:04 am
- ☿□♄ **12:09 pm** 9:09 am
- ☽⚹♆ **5:19 pm** 2:19 pm
- ☽△♇ **9:36 pm** 6:36 pm

16 FRIDAY
- ☽⚺♃ **10:12 am** 7:12 am
- ☽□♄ **11:20 am** 8:20 am
- ☽☌☿ **3:12 pm** 12:12 pm
- ☽⚹♀ **4:57 pm** 1:57 pm

17 SATURDAY
- ☽⚹♂ **4:14 am** 1:14 am
- ☿⚹♀ **11:29 am** 8:29 am
- ☽⚺♅ **1:45 pm** 10:45 am
- ☽☌☉ 9:37 pm
- ☽□♆ 11:24 pm

18 SUNDAY
- ☽☌☉ **12:37 am**
- ☽□♆ **2:24 am**
- ☽⚻♇ **6:43 am** 3:43 am
- ☽⚹♃ **8:45 pm** 5:45 pm
- ☽△♄ **9:00 pm** 6:00 pm
- ☉□♆ **11:54 pm** 8:54 pm

19 MONDAY
- ☽⚺♀ **7:02 am** 4:02 am
- ☽⚺☿ **11:41 am** 8:41 am
- ♃⚹♄ **11:53 am** 8:53 am

- ☽⚺♂ **5:28 pm** 2:28 pm
- ☽⚹♅ 9:33 pm

20 TUESDAY
- ☽⚹♅ **12:33 am**
- ☽△♆ **1:24 pm** 10:24 am
- ☽⚺☉ **4:37 pm** 1:37 pm
- ☽☍♇ **5:43 pm** 2:43 pm

21 WEDNESDAY
- ☉⚻♇ **6:20 am** 3:20 am
- ☽⚻♄ **8:30 am** 5:30 am
- ☽□♃ **9:15 am** 6:15 am
- ☿⚹♂ **11:23 am** 8:23 am
- ☽☌♀ **11:08 pm** 8:08 pm

22 THURSDAY
- ☽☌♂ **8:41 am** 5:41 am
- ☽⚹☿ **11:51 am** 8:51 am
- ☽□♅ **1:01 pm** 10:01 am
- ☿⚺♅ **6:37 pm** 3:37 pm
- ☽⚻♆ 10:52 pm

23 FRIDAY
- ☽⚻♆ **1:52 am**
- ☽⚻♇ **6:08 am** 3:08 am
- ☽⚹☉ **10:24 am** 7:24 am
- ☽☍♄ **9:07 pm** 6:07 pm
- ☽△♃ **10:53 pm** 7:53 pm

24 SATURDAY
- ☽⚺♀ **3:59 pm** 12:59 pm
- ☽⚺♂ 9:33 pm
- ☽△♅ 10:53 pm

25 SUNDAY
- ☽⚺♂ **12:33 am**
- ☽△♅ **1:53 am**
- ☽□☿ **1:25 pm** 10:25 am
- ☽☍♆ **2:20 pm** 11:20 am
- ☽△♇ **6:24 pm** 3:24 pm
- ☿□♆ **6:36 pm** 3:36 pm

26 MONDAY
- ☽□☉ **3:50 am** 12:50 am
- ♂□♅ **5:23 am** 2:23 am
- ☽⚻♄ **9:04 am** 6:04 am
- ☽⚻♃ **11:44 am** 8:44 am
- ☿⚻♇ **5:07 pm** 2:07 pm

27 TUESDAY
- ☽⚹♀ **6:56 am** 3:56 am
- ☽⚻♅ **12:58 pm** 9:58 am
- ☽⚹♂ **2:26 pm** 11:26 am
- ☽⚻♆ 9:35 pm

28 WEDNESDAY
- ☽⚻♆ **12:35 am**
- ☽□♇ **4:19 am** 1:19 am
- ☽△☿ **11:32 am** 8:32 am
- ☽△☉ **5:49 pm** 2:49 pm
- ☽△♄ **6:07 pm** 3:07 pm
- ☽☍♃ **9:29 pm** 6:29 pm
- ☉△♄ **9:43 pm** 6:43 pm

29 THURSDAY
- ☽□♀ **5:32 pm** 2:32 pm
- ☽☍♅ **8:22 pm** 5:22 pm

- ☽□♂ 9:05 pm
- ☿△♄ 11:24 pm

30 FRIDAY
- ☽□♂ **12:05 am**
- ☿△♄ **2:24 am**
- ☽△♆ **6:58 am** 3:58 am
- ☽⚹♇ **10:20 am** 7:20 am
- ☽□♄ **11:08 pm** 8:08 pm
- ☉☌☿ 10:06 pm
- ☽⚻☉ 11:48 pm
- ☽⚻☿ 11:58 pm

Eastern time in bold type
Pacific time in medium type

JUNE 2023

DATE	SID. TIME	SUN	MOON	NODE	MERCURY	VENUS	MARS	JUPITER	SATURN	URANUS	NEPTUNE	PLUTO	CERES	PALLAS	JUNO	VESTA	CHIRON
1 Th	16 36 53	10Ⅱ16 45	0♏08	3♉37R	15♉49	25♊35	6♋32	3♉24	6♓59	20♉12	27♓27	0≈09R	25♌51	12♎23	17♊32	20♈40	18♈49
2 F	16 40 50	11 14 15	13 24	3 37	16 57	26 33	7 07	3 37	7 00	20 15	27 28	0 09	26 00	12 50	18 07	21 06	18 52
3 Sa	16 44 46	12 11 44	27 04	3 35	18 08	27 32	7 41	3 49	7 02	20 19	27 29	0 08	26 10	13 16	18 42	21 32	18 54
4 Su	16 48 43	13 09 11	11✗07	3 31	19 21	28 30	8 16	4 02	7 03	20 22	27 30	0 07	26 20	13 42	19 18	21 58	18 57
5 M	16 52 39	14 06 38	25 27	3 26	20 38	29 27	8 51	4 15	7 05	20 25	27 30	0 06	26 30	14 09	19 53	22 24	18 59
6 T	16 56 36	15 04 03	10♑01	3 20	21 58	0♋24	9 26	4 28	7 06	20 28	27 31	0 05	26 41	14 35	20 27	22 50	19 01
7 W	17 0 32	16 01 28	24 41	3 14	23 20	1 21	10 01	4 40	7 07	20 32	27 31	0 04	26 52	15 02	21 02	23 16	19 04
8 Th	17 4 29	16 58 52	9≈20	3 08	24 46	2 17	10 36	4 53	7 08	20 35	27 32	0 03	27 03	15 28	21 37	23 42	19 06
9 F	17 8 26	17 56 16	23 52	3 04	26 14	3 13	11 12	5 05	7 09	20 38	27 33	0 02	27 15	15 55	22 12	24 08	19 08
10 Sa	17 12 22	18 53 38	8✵12	3 02D	27 45	4 08	11 47	5 17	7 10	20 41	27 34	0 01	27 26	16 22	22 47	24 33	19 10
11 Su	17 16 19	19 51 01	22 17	3 01	29 18	5 02	12 22	5 30	7 11	20 44	27 35	0 00	27 39	16 48	23 22	24 59	19 12
12 M	17 20 15	20 48 22	6♈07	3 02	0Ⅱ55	5 56	12 57	5 42	7 11	20 47	27 35	29♑59	27 51	17 15	23 57	25 25	19 14
13 T	17 24 12	21 45 44	19 41	3 03	2 34	6 50	13 33	5 54	7 12	20 51	27 36	29 58	28 03	17 42	24 32	25 51	19 16
14 W	17 28 8	22 43 05	3♉02	3 04R	4 16	7 43	14 08	6 06	7 12	20 54	27 37	29 57	28 16	18 08	25 06	26 16	19 18
15 Th	17 32 5	23 40 25	16 09	3 03	6 01	8 35	14 43	6 18	7 12	20 57	27 37	29 56	28 29	18 35	25 41	26 42	19 20
16 F	17 36 1	24 37 45	29 04	3 00	7 48	9 26	15 19	6 30	7 12	21 00	27 38	29 55	28 43	19 02	26 15	27 07	19 20
17 Sa	17 39 58	25 35 05	11Ⅱ47	2 55	9 38	10 17	15 54	6 41	7 13R	21 03	27 38	29 54	28 56	19 29	26 50	27 33	19 24
18 Su	17 43 55	26 32 24	24 20	2 47	11 30	11 08	16 30	6 53	7 13	21 06	27 39	29 53	29 10	19 56	27 25	27 58	19 26
19 M	17 47 51	27 29 42	6♋42	2 38	13 25	11 57	17 05	7 04	7 13	21 09	27 39	29 52	29 24	20 22	27 59	28 24	19 27
20 T	17 51 48	28 27 00	18 54	2 28	15 22	12 46	17 41	7 16	7 12	21 12	27 39	29 51	29 38	20 49	28 34	28 49	19 29
21 W	17 55 44	29 24 17	0♌58	2 18	17 22	13 34	18 17	7 28	7 12	21 15	27 40	29 49	29 53	21 16	29 09	29 14	19 30
22 Th	17 59 41	0♋21 34	12 55	2 08	19 24	14 22	18 53	7 39	7 12	21 18	27 40	29 48	0♍08	21 43	29 43	29 40	19 31
23 F	18 3 37	1 18 50	24 47	2 01	21 27	15 08	19 28	7 50	7 11	21 20	27 40	29 47	0 23	22 10	0♋18	0♉05	19 32
24 Sa	18 7 34	2 16 05	6♍37	1 55	23 33	15 54	20 04	8 02	7 11	21 23	27 40	29 46	0 38	22 37	0 52	0 30	19 34
25 Su	18 11 30	3 13 20	18 31	1 52	25 40	16 39	20 40	8 13	7 10	21 26	27 41	29 45	0 53	23 04	1 26	0 55	19 35
26 M	18 15 27	4 10 34	0♎32	1 51D	27 48	17 22	21 16	8 24	7 09	21 29	27 41	29 43	1 09	23 31	2 01	1 20	19 37
27 T	18 19 24	5 07 47	12 45	1 51	29 58	18 05	21 52	8 34	7 08	21 32	27 41	29 42	1 25	23 58	2 35	1 45	19 38
28 W	18 23 20	6 05 00	25 15	1 51R	2♋08	18 47	22 28	8 45	7 07	21 34	27 41	29 41	1 41	24 26	3 09	2 10	19 40
29 Th	18 27 17	7 02 13	8♏08	1 51	4 19	19 28	23 04	8 56	7 06	21 37	27 41	29 40	1 57	24 53	3 44	2 35	19 41
30 F	18 31 13	7 59 25	21 27	1 50	6 30	20 08	23 40	9 06	7 05	21 39	27 41R	29 38	2 14	25 20	4 18	3 00	19 43

EPHEMERIS CALCULATED FOR 12 MIDNIGHT GREENWICH MEAN TIME. ALL OTHER DATA AND FACING ASPECTARIAN PAGE IN **EASTERN TIME (BOLD)** AND PACIFIC TIME (REGULAR).

JULY 2023

Phases & Eclipses

phase	day	ET / hr:mn / PT
Full Moon	3	7:39 am 4:39 am
4th Quarter	9	9:48 pm 6:48 pm
New Moon	17	2:32 pm 11:32 am
2nd Quarter	25	6:07 pm 3:07 pm

Planetary Motion

	day	ET / hr:mn / PT
♀ R	22	9:33 pm 6:33 pm
♅ R	23	8:42 am 5:42 am

Eastern time in bold type
Pacific time in medium type

JULY 2023

DATE	SID.TIME	SUN	MOON	NODE	MERCURY	VENUS	MARS	JUPITER	SATURN	URANUS	NEPTUNE	PLUTO	CERES	PALLAS	JUNO	VESTA	CHIRON
1 Sa	18 35 10	8♋56 36	5♐'14	1♉46R	8♋41	20♌47	24♋16	9♉17	7♓04R	21♉42	27♓41R	29♑37R	2♎30	25♍47	4♋52	3♊25	19♈45
2 Su	18 39 6	9 53 48	19 28	1 40	10 52	21 24	24 52	9 27	7 03	21 45	27 41	29 36	2 47	26 11	5 26	3 49	19 46
3 M	18 43 3	10 50 59	4♑06	1 31	13 02	22 00	25 28	9 38	7 01	21 47	27 41	29 34	3 04	26 41	6 00	4 14	19 47
4 T	18 47 0	11 48 10	19 01	1 22	15 11	22 36	26 04	9 48	7 00	21 50	27 41	29 33	3 21	27 09	6 34	4 39	19 48
5 W	18 50 56	12 45 21	4≈05	1 12	17 19	23 09	26 41	9 58	6 58	21 52	27 41	29 32	3 39	27 36	7 08	5 03	19 49
6 Th	18 54 53	13 42 32	19 07	1 03	19 26	23 42	27 17	10 08	6 56	21 55	27 41	29 30	3 56	28 03	7 42	5 28	19 50
7 F	18 58 49	14 39 43	3♓58	0 56	21 32	24 13	27 53	10 17	6 55	21 57	27 41	29 29	4 14	28 30	8 16	5 53	19 51
8 Sa	19 2 46	15 36 55	18 32	0 51	23 36	24 42	28 29	10 27	6 53	22 00	27 40	29 28	4 32	28 58	8 49	6 16	19 51
9 Su	19 6 42	16 34 06	2♈45	0 49	25 39	25 11	29 06	10 37	6 51	22 02	27 40	29 26	4 50	29 25	9 23	6 41	19 52
10 M	19 10 39	17 31 18	16 34	0 48R	27 40	25 37	29 42	10 46	6 49	22 04	27 40	29 25	5 08	29 52	9 57	7 05	19 53
11 T	19 14 35	18 28 31	0♉03	0 48R	29 39	26 02	0♍19	10 56	6 46	22 07	27 40	29 23	5 26	0♎19	10 31	7 29	19 54
12 W	19 18 32	19 25 44	13 11	0 48	1♌37	26 25	0 55	11 05	6 44	22 09	27 39	29 22	5 45	0 47	11 04	7 53	19 54
13 Th	19 22 29	20 22 58	26 04	0 46	3 33	26 47	1 32	11 14	6 42	22 11	27 39	29 21	6 04	1 14	11 38	8 17	19 55
14 F	19 26 25	21 20 12	8♊42	0 41	5 26	27 07	2 08	11 23	6 39	22 13	27 38	29 19	6 22	1 41	12 11	8 41	19 55
15 Sa	19 30 22	22 17 26	21 10	0 34	7 18	27 25	2 45	11 32	6 37	22 15	27 38	29 18	6 41	2 09	12 45	9 05	19 56
16 Su	19 34 18	23 14 41	3♋27	0 24	9 08	27 41	3 22	11 40	6 34	22 17	27 38	29 16	7 01	2 36	13 18	9 28	19 56
17 M	19 38 15	24 11 57	15 37	0 11	10 57	27 55	3 58	11 49	6 32	22 19	27 37	29 15	7 20	3 04	13 52	9 52	19 57
18 T	19 42 11	25 09 13	27 40	29♉58	12 43	28 07	4 35	11 58	6 29	22 21	27 37	29 14	7 39	3 31	14 25	10 16	19 57
19 W	19 46 8	26 06 29	9♌38	29 44	14 27	28 17	5 12	12 06	6 26	22 23	27 36	29 12	7 59	3 58	14 58	10 39	19 57
20 Th	19 50 4	27 03 45	21 31	29 31	16 10	28 26	5 49	12 14	6 23	22 25	27 35	29 11	8 19	4 26	15 32	11 03	19 58
21 F	19 54 1	28 01 02	3♍21	29 20	17 51	28 31	6 26	12 22	6 20	22 27	27 35	29 09	8 39	4 53	16 05	11 26	19 58
22 Sa	19 57 58	28 58 19	15 11	29 12	19 29	28 35	7 03	12 30	6 17	22 29	27 34	29 08	8 59	5 21	16 38	11 50	19 58
23 Su	20 1 54	29 55 36	27 04	29 07	21 06	28 36R	7 40	12 38	6 14	22 31	27 33	29 06	9 19	5 48	17 11	12 13	19 58R
24 M	20 5 51	0♌52 54	9♎04	29 04	22 42	28 35	8 17	12 45	6 11	22 33	27 32	29 05	9 39	6 16	17 44	12 36	19 58
25 T	20 9 47	1 50 12	21 15	29 03	24 15	28 32	8 54	12 53	6 08	22 34	27 31	29 04	9 59	6 43	18 17	12 59	19 58
26 W	20 13 44	2 47 31	3♏42	29 03	25 46	28 26	9 31	13 00	6 04	22 36	27 31	29 02	10 20	7 11	18 50	13 22	19 58
27 Th	20 17 40	3 44 49	16 32	29 02	27 16	28 18	10 08	13 07	6 01	22 37	27 30	29 01	10 40	7 38	19 23	13 45	19 57
28 F	20 21 37	4 42 09	29 47	29 00	28 43	28 07	10 45	13 14	5 57	22 39	27 30	29 00	11 01	8 06	19 55	14 08	19 57
29 Sa	20 25 33	5 39 28	13♐31	28 57	0♍09	27 54	11 22	13 21	5 54	22 41	27 29	28 58	11 22	8 33	20 28	14 30	19 57
30 Su	20 29 30	6 36 49	27 44	28 51	1 32	27 39	12 00	13 28	5 50	22 42	27 28	28 56	11 43	9 01	21 01	14 53	19 57
31 M	20 33 27	7 34 10	12♑26	28 42	2 54	27 21	12 37	13 35	5 46	22 44	27 27	28 55	12 04	9 28	21 33	15 15	19 56

EPHEMERIS CALCULATED FOR 12 MIDNIGHT GREENWICH MEAN TIME. ALL OTHER DATA AND FACING ASPECTARIAN PAGE IN **EASTERN TIME (BOLD)** AND PACIFIC TIME (REGULAR).

AUGUST 2023

☽ Last Aspect day	ET / hr:mn / PT		asp	☽ Ingress sign	day	ET / hr:mn / PT	
2	**5:15 pm**	2:15 pm	☍♀	♓	2	**11:05 pm**	8:05 pm
4	**9:21 pm**	6:21 pm	✶♇	♈	4	**11:19 pm**	8:19 pm
6		9:13 pm	□♇	♉	6		11:25 pm
7	**12:13 am**		□♇	♉	7	**2:25 am**	
9	**6:39 am**	3:39 am	△♇	♊	9	**9:05 am**	6:05 am
11	**1:27 pm**	10:27 am	□♆	♋	11	**6:52 pm**	3:52 pm
14	**3:46 am**	12:46 am	☍♇	♌	14	**6:36 am**	3:36 am
16	**5:38 am**	2:38 am	☌☉	♍	16	**7:14 pm**	4:14 pm
19	**4:51 am**	1:51 am	△♇	♎	19	**7:53 am**	4:53 am
21	**4:31 pm**	1:31 pm	✶☉	♏	21	**7:22 pm**	4:22 pm
23		10:10 pm	✶♇	♐	24	**4:07 am**	1:07 am
24	**1:10 am**		✶♇	♐	24	**4:07 am**	1:07 am
26	**7:56 am**	4:56 am	□♂	♑	27	**9:05 am**	6:05 am
28	**7:49 am**	4:49 am	☌♇	♒	28	**10:32 am**	7:32 am
29	**11:04 pm**	8:04 pm	□♅	♓	30	**9:56 am**	6:56 am

☽ Phases & Eclipses phase	day	ET / hr:mn / PT	
Full Moon	1	**2:32 pm**	11:32 am
4th Quarter	8	**6:28 am**	3:28 am
New Moon	16	**5:38 am**	2:38 am
2nd Quarter	24	**5:57 am**	2:57 am
Full Moon	30	**9:36 pm**	6:36 pm

Planet Ingress	day	ET / hr:mn / PT	
✱ ♌	15	**3:29 pm**	12:29 pm
☉ ♍	23	**5:01 am**	2:01 am
♂ ♎	27	**9:20 am**	6:20 am

Planetary Motion		day	ET / hr:mn / PT	
☿	℞	23	**3:59 pm**	12:59 pm
♅	℞	28	**10:39 pm**	7:39 pm

1 TUESDAY
☽ ⚻ ☿ **7:37 am** 4:37 am
☽ ⚺ ♄ **8:54 am** 5:54 am
☽ ☍ ☉ **2:32 pm** 11:32 am
♂ △ ♃ **4:45 pm** 1:45 pm
☽ □ ♃ **9:38 pm** 6:38 pm
☽ ⚻ ♂ **9:48 pm** 6:48 pm
☿ ☍ ♄ **10:18 pm** 7:18 pm

2 WEDNESDAY
☽ □ ♅ **11:44 am** 8:44 am
☽ ☍ ♀ **5:15 pm** 2:15 pm
☽ ⚺ ♆ **7:00 pm** 4:00 pm
☽ ⚺ ♇ **9:16 pm** 6:16 pm

3 THURSDAY
☽ ☌ ♄ **7:53 am** 4:53 am
☽ ☍ ☿ **11:03 am** 8:03 am
☽ ⚻ ☉ **4:59 pm** 1:59 pm
☽ ✶ ♃ **9:20 pm** 6:20 pm
☽ ☍ ♂ **11:15 pm** 8:15 pm

4 FRIDAY
☽ ✶ ♅ **11:35 am** 8:35 am
☽ ⚻ ♀ **3:49 pm** 12:49 pm
☽ ☌ ♆ **7:00 pm** 4:00 pm
☽ ✶ ♇ **9:21 pm** 6:21 pm

5 SATURDAY
☽ ⚺ ♄ **8:18 am** 5:18 am
☽ ⚻ ☿ **4:14 pm** 1:14 pm
☽ △ ☉ **9:40 pm** 6:40 pm
☽ ⚺ ♃ **11:03 pm** 8:03 pm

6 SUNDAY
☽ ⚻ ♂ **3:03 am** 12:03 am
☽ ⚺ ♅ **1:57 pm** 10:57 am
☽ △ ♀ **4:35 pm** 1:35 pm
☉ □ ♃ **8:03 pm** 5:03 pm
☽ ⚺ ♆ **9:43 pm** 6:43 pm
☽ □ ♇ 9:13 pm

7 MONDAY
☽ □ ♇ **12:13 am**
☽ ✶ ♄ **11:46 am** 8:46 am
☽ △ ☿ 10:10 pm

8 TUESDAY
☽ △ ☿ **1:10 am**
☽ ☌ ♃ **4:11 am** 1:11 am
☽ □ ☉ **6:28 am** 3:28 am
☽ △ ♂ **10:46 am** 7:46 am
☽ ☌ ♅ **7:50 pm** 4:50 pm
☽ □ ♀ **8:21 pm** 5:21 pm

9 WEDNESDAY
☽ ✶ ♆ **4:00 am** 1:00 am
☽ △ ♇ **6:39 am** 3:39 am
♀ □ ♅ **7:08 am** 4:08 am
☽ □ ♄ **6:45 pm** 3:45 pm
☿ △ ♃ **8:47 pm** 5:47 pm

10 THURSDAY
☽ ⚺ ♃ **12:51 pm** 9:51 am
☽ □ ☿ **2:02 pm** 11:02 am
☽ ✶ ☉ **7:37 pm** 4:37 pm

☽ □ ♂ **10:28 pm** 7:28 pm
☽ ✶ ♀ 11:52 pm

11 FRIDAY
☽ ✶ ♀ **2:52 am**
☽ ⚺ ♅ **5:03 am** 2:03 am
☽ □ ♆ **1:27 pm** 10:27 am
☽ ⚻ ♇ **4:13 pm** 1:13 pm

12 SATURDAY
☽ △ ♄ **4:37 am** 1:37 am
♀ ⚺ ♂ **8:15 pm** 5:15 pm
☽ ✶ ♃ 9:06 pm

13 SUNDAY
☽ ✶ ♃ **12:06 am**
☽ ✶ ☿ **5:26 am** 2:26 am
☉ ☌ ♀ **7:16 am** 4:16 am
☽ ⚺ ♀ **11:17 am** 8:17 am
☽ ⚺ ☉ **11:51 am** 8:51 am
☽ ✶ ♂ **12:56 pm** 9:56 am
☽ ✶ ♅ **4:30 pm** 1:30 pm
☽ △ ♆ 9:57 pm

14 MONDAY
☽ △ ♆ **12:57 am**
☽ ☍ ♇ **3:46 am** 12:46 am
☽ ⚻ ♄ **4:12 pm** 1:12 pm
☉ ⚺ ♂ 10:10 pm

15 TUESDAY
☉ ⚺ ♂ **1:10 am**
☽ □ ♃ **12:44 pm** 9:44 am
☿ ⚺ ♀ **1:04 pm** 10:04 am
☽ ☌ ♀ **8:44 pm** 5:44 pm

☽ ⚺ ☿ **9:34 pm** 6:34 pm
☉ □ ♅ **10:35 pm** 7:35 pm

16 WEDNESDAY
☽ ⚺ ♂ **4:48 am** 1:48 am
☽ □ ♅ **5:04 am** 2:04 am
☽ ☌ ☉ **5:38 am** 2:38 am
♂ △ ♅ **9:53 am** 6:53 am
☽ ⚻ ♆ **1:26 pm** 10:26 am
☽ ⚻ ♇ **4:17 pm** 1:17 pm

17 THURSDAY
☽ ☍ ♄ **4:32 am** 1:32 am
☽ △ ♃ 10:48 pm

18 FRIDAY
☽ △ ♃ **1:48 am**
☽ ⚺ ♀ **6:35 am** 3:35 am
☽ ☌ ☿ **1:09 pm** 10:09 am
☽ △ ♅ **5:51 pm** 2:51 pm
☽ ☌ ♂ **8:57 pm** 5:57 pm
☽ ⚺ ☉ **11:42 pm** 8:42 pm
☽ ☍ ♆ 11:01 pm

19 SATURDAY
☽ ☍ ♆ **2:01 am**
☽ △ ♇ **4:51 am** 1:51 am
☽ ⚻ ♄ **4:43 pm** 1:43 pm

20 SUNDAY
☉ ⚻ ♆ **3:40 am** 12:40 am
☽ ⚻ ♃ **2:19 pm** 11:19 am
☽ ✶ ♀ **4:07 pm** 1:07 pm
☽ ⚺ ☿ 11:50 pm

21 MONDAY
☽ ⚺ ☿ **2:50 am**
☽ ⚻ ♅ **5:47 am** 2:47 am
☽ ⚺ ♂ **12:02 pm** 9:02 am
☽ ⚻ ♆ **1:34 pm** 10:34 am
☉ ⚻ ♇ **2:07 pm** 11:07 am
☽ □ ♇ **4:19 pm** 1:19 pm
☽ ✶ ☉ **4:31 pm** 1:31 pm

22 TUESDAY
☽ △ ♄ **3:33 am** 12:33 am
♀ □ ♃ **8:16 am** 5:16 am
♂ ☍ ♆ **4:34 pm** 1:34 pm
☽ □ ♀ 9:10 pm
☽ ☍ ♃ 9:48 pm

23 WEDNESDAY
☽ □ ♀ **12:10 am**
☽ ☍ ♃ **12:48 am**
☽ ✶ ☿ **1:03 pm** 10:03 am
☽ ☍ ♅ **3:19 pm** 12:19 pm
☽ △ ♆ **10:33 pm** 7:33 pm
☽ ✶ ♂ 9:09 pm
☽ ✶ ♇ 10:10 pm

24 THURSDAY
☽ ✶ ♂ **12:09 am**
☽ ✶ ♇ **1:10 am**
☽ □ ☉ **5:57 am** 2:57 am
☽ □ ♄ **11:29 am** 8:29 am
♂ △ ♇ **8:23 pm** 5:23 pm

25 FRIDAY
☽ △ ♀ **5:27 am** 2:27 am
☽ ⚻ ♃ **7:49 am** 4:49 am

☽ □ ☿ **6:43 pm** 3:43 pm
☽ ⚻ ♅ **9:12 pm** 6:12 pm

26 SATURDAY
☽ □ ♆ **3:49 am** 12:49 am
☽ ⚺ ♇ **6:16 am** 3:16 am
☽ □ ♂ **7:56 am** 4:56 am
☽ △ ☉ **2:39 pm** 11:39 am
☽ ✶ ♄ **3:39 pm** 12:39 pm

27 SUNDAY
☉ ☍ ♄ **4:28 am** 1:28 am
☽ ⚻ ♀ **7:28 am** 4:28 am
☽ △ ♃ **10:58 am** 7:58 am
☽ △ ☿ **8:00 pm** 5:00 pm
☽ △ ♅ **11:22 pm** 8:22 pm

28 MONDAY
☽ ✶ ♆ **5:29 am** 2:29 am
☽ ☌ ♇ **7:49 am** 4:49 am
☽ △ ♂ **11:39 am** 8:39 am
☽ ⚺ ♄ **4:29 pm** 1:29 pm
☽ ⚻ ☉ **7:08 pm** 4:08 pm

29 TUESDAY
☽ ☍ ♀ **6:56 am** 3:56 am
☽ □ ♃ **11:11 am** 8:11 am
☽ ⚻ ☿ **6:18 pm** 3:18 pm
☽ □ ♅ **11:04 pm** 8:04 pm

30 WEDNESDAY
☽ ⚺ ♆ **4:56 am** 1:56 am
☽ ⚺ ♇ **7:14 am** 4:14 am
☽ ⚻ ♂ **1:07 pm** 10:07 am

☽ ☌ ♄ **3:33 pm** 12:33 pm
☽ ☍ ☉ **9:36 pm** 6:36 pm

31 THURSDAY
☽ ⚻ ♀ **5:33 am** 2:33 am
☽ ✶ ♃ **10:25 am** 7:25 am
☽ ☍ ☿ **3:29 pm** 12:29 pm
☽ ✶ ♅ **10:20 pm** 7:20 pm

Eastern time in bold type
Pacific time in medium type

AUGUST 2023

DATE	SID. TIME	SUN	MOON	NODE	MERCURY	VENUS	MARS	JUPITER	SATURN	URANUS	NEPTUNE	PLUTO	CERES	PALLAS	JUNO	VESTA	CHIRON
1 T	20 37 23	8♌31 31	27♐29	28♉32R	4♍14	27♌01R	13♍14	13♉41	5♓43R	22♉45	27♓26R	28♑54R	12♎25	9♋56	22♋06	15♊38	19♈56R
2 W	20 41 20	9 28 53	12♑45	28 21	5 31	26 39	13 51	13 47	5 39	22 46	27 25	28 52	12 47	10 23	22 38	16 00	19 55
3 Th	20 45 16	10 26 16	28 02	28 11	6 47	26 15	14 28	13 53	5 35	22 48	27 24	28 51	13 08	10 51	23 11	16 22	19 55
4 F	20 49 13	11 23 40	13♒16	28 04	8 00	25 49	15 06	13 59	5 31	22 49	27 23	28 49	13 30	11 18	23 43	16 45	19 54
5 Sa	20 53 9	12 21 05	27 59	27 59	9 11	25 20	15 44	14 05	5 27	22 50	27 22	28 48	13 51	11 46	24 15	17 07	19 54
6 Su	20 57 6	13 18 31	12♓23	27 56	10 20	24 50	16 21	14 11	5 23	22 51	27 20	28 47	14 13	12 13	24 47	17 29	19 53
7 M	21 1 2	14 15 59	26 21	27 55D	11 26	24 19	16 59	14 16	5 19	22 52	27 20	28 45	14 35	12 41	25 20	17 50	19 52
8 T	21 4 59	15 13 28	9♈52	27 55R	12 30	23 46	17 36	14 21	5 15	22 53	27 19	28 44	14 57	13 08	25 52	18 12	19 52
9 W	21 8 56	16 10 58	23 00	27 54	13 31	23 11	18 14	14 26	5 11	22 54	27 18	28 43	15 19	13 36	26 24	18 34	19 51
10 Th	21 12 52	17 08 29	5♉47	27 50	14 30	22 36	18 52	14 31	5 07	22 55	27 17	28 41	15 41	14 04	26 56	18 55	19 50
11 F	21 16 49	18 06 02	18 17	27 44	15 25	22 00	19 29	14 36	5 03	22 56	27 16	28 40	16 03	14 31	27 28	19 17	19 49
12 Sa	21 20 45	19 03 36	0♊35	27 35	16 18	21 23	20 07	14 41	4 58	22 57	27 14	28 39	16 25	14 59	27 59	19 38	19 48
13 Su	21 24 42	20 01 12	12 42	27 35	17 08	20 46	20 45	14 45	4 54	22 58	27 13	28 37	16 48	15 26	28 31	19 59	19 47
14 M	21 28 38	20 58 49	24 43	27 24	17 54	20 08	21 23	14 49	4 50	22 59	27 12	28 36	17 10	15 54	29 03	20 20	19 46
15 T	21 32 35	21 56 27	6♋39	27 12	18 37	19 31	22 01	14 53	4 45	23 00	27 10	28 35	17 33	16 21	29 34	20 41	19 45
16 W	21 36 31	22 54 06	18 32	27 00	19 16	18 54	22 39	14 57	4 41	23 00	27 09	28 33	17 55	16 49	0♌06	21 02	19 44
17 Th	21 40 28	23 51 47	0♌23	26 49	19 51	18 18	23 17	15 01	4 37	23 01	27 08	28 32	18 18	17 17	0 37	21 22	19 42
18 F	21 44 25	24 49 29	12 13	26 39	20 22	17 43	23 55	15 05	4 32	23 02	27 07	28 31	18 41	17 44	1 09	21 43	19 41
19 Sa	21 48 21	25 47 12	24 06	26 32	20 49	17 08	24 33	15 08	4 28	23 02	27 05	28 30	19 04	18 12	1 40	22 03	19 40
20 Su	21 52 18	26 44 56	6♍02	26 27	21 12	16 35	25 11	15 11	4 23	23 02	27 04	28 28	19 27	18 39	2 11	22 24	19 39
21 M	21 56 14	27 42 42	18 06	26 25D	21 29	16 05	25 49	15 14	4 19	23 03	27 04	28 27	19 50	19 07	2 43	22 44	19 37
22 T	22 0 11	28 40 28	0♎19	26 25	21 42	15 33	26 27	15 17	4 14	23 03	27 02	28 26	20 13	19 35	3 14	23 04	19 36
23 W	22 4 7	29 38 16	12 48	26 27R	21 49R	15 04	27 05	15 19	4 10	23 04	27 01	28 25	20 36	20 02	3 45	23 24	19 34
24 Th	22 8 4	0♍36 05	25 35	26 26	21 51	14 38	27 44	15 22	4 05	23 04	27 00	28 24	20 59	20 30	4 16	23 43	19 33
25 F	22 12 0	1 33 55	8♏46	26 26	21 47	14 13	28 22	15 24	4 01	23 04	26 58	28 23	21 23	20 57	4 46	24 03	19 31
26 Sa	22 15 57	2 31 47	22 23	26 25	21 38	13 50	29 00	15 26	3 56	23 04	26 57	28 21	21 46	21 25	5 17	24 23	19 30
27 Su	22 19 54	3 29 40	6♐28	26 21	21 22	13 30	29 39	15 28	3 52	23 04	26 55	28 20	22 09	21 52	5 48	24 42	19 28
28 M	22 23 50	4 27 34	21 00	26 15	21 00	13 12	0♎17	15 29	3 47	23 04	26 54	28 19	22 33	22 20	6 19	25 01	19 26
29 T	22 27 47	5 25 29	5♑56	26 08	20 33	12 56	0 56	15 31	3 43	23 05R	26 52	28 18	22 57	22 48	6 49	25 20	19 24
30 W	22 31 43	6 23 25	21 07	26 01	20 00	12 43	1 34	15 32	3 38	23 05	26 51	28 17	23 20	23 15	7 20	25 39	19 23
31 Th	22 35 40	7 21 23	6♒24	25 54	19 21	12 32	2 13	15 33	3 34	23 04	26 49	28 16	23 44	23 43	7 50	25 57	19 21

EPHEMERIS CALCULATED FOR 12 MIDNIGHT GREENWICH MEAN TIME. ALL OTHER DATA AND FACING ASPECTARIAN PAGE IN **EASTERN TIME (BOLD)** AND PACIFIC TIME (REGULAR).

SEPTEMBER 2023

☽ Last Aspect day	ET / hr:mn	PT	asp	☽ Ingress sign	day	ET / hr:mn	PT
1	**6:36 am**	3:36 am	⚹♇	♈	1	**9:25 am**	6:25 am
3	**7:57 am**	4:57 am	□♇	♉	3	**11:00 am**	8:00 am
5	**12:46 pm**	9:46 am	△♇	♊	5	**4:07 pm**	1:07 pm
7	**6:22 pm**	3:22 pm	□♆	♋	7		10:00 pm
7	**6:22 pm**	3:22 pm	□♆	♋	8	**1:00 am**	
10	**8:47 am**	5:47 am	☍♇	♌	10	**12:36 pm**	9:36 am
12	**11:06 am**	8:06 am	□♅	♍	12		10:18 pm
12	**11:06 am**	8:06 am	□♅	♍	13	**1:18 am**	
15	**9:49 am**	6:49 am	△♇	♎	15	**1:44 pm**	10:44 am
17	**9:06 pm**	6:06 pm	□♇	♏	17		9:58 pm
17	**9:06 pm**	6:06 pm	□♇	♏	18	**12:58 am**	
20	**6:21 am**	3:21 am	⚹♇	♐	20	**10:06 am**	7:06 am
22	**3:32 pm**	12:32 pm	□☉	♑	22	**4:20 pm**	1:20 pm
24	**4:05 pm**	1:05 pm	☌♇	♒	24	**7:29 pm**	4:29 pm
26	**8:38 am**	5:38 am	□♅	♓	26	**8:18 pm**	5:18 pm
28	**4:58 pm**	1:58 pm	⚹♇	♈	28	**8:17 pm**	5:17 pm
30	**5:50 pm**	2:50 pm	□♇	♉	30	**9:18 pm**	6:18 pm

☽ Phases & Eclipses phase	day	ET / hr:mn	PT
4th Quarter	6	**6:21 pm**	3:21 pm
New Moon	14	**9:40 pm**	6:40 pm
2nd Quarter	22	**3:32 pm**	12:32 pm
Full Moon	29	**5:58 am**	2:58 am

Planet Ingress		day	ET / hr:mn	PT
♀	♎	13	**12:38 pm**	9:38 am
⚵	♋	13	**7:28 pm**	4:28 pm
⚳	♏	15	**8:50 am**	5:50 am
☉	♎	22		11:50 pm
☉	♎	23	**2:50 am**	

Planetary Motion		day	ET / hr:mn	PT
♀	D	3	**9:20 pm**	6:20 pm
♃	℞	4	**10:10 am**	7:10 am
☿	D	15	**4:21 pm**	1:21 pm

1 FRIDAY
☽ ☌ ♆ **4:13 am** 1:13 am
☽ ⚹ ♇ **6:36 am** 3:36 am
☽ ☍ ♂ **2:50 pm** 11:50 am
☽ ⚺ ♄ **2:56 pm** 11:56 am
♂ ⚻ ♄ **5:01 pm** 2:01 pm
☽ ⚻ ☉ 9:46 pm

2 SATURDAY
☽ ⚻ ☉ **12:46 am**
☽ △ ♀ **5:19 am** 2:19 am
☽ ⚺ ♃ **10:47 am** 7:47 am
☽ ⚻ ☿ **1:25 pm** 10:25 am
☽ ⚺ ♅ **11:15 pm** 8:15 pm

3 SUNDAY
☽ ⚺ ♆ **5:24 am** 2:24 am
☽ □ ♇ **7:57 am** 4:57 am
☽ ⚹ ♄ **4:36 pm** 1:36 pm
☽ ⚻ ♂ **7:10 pm** 4:10 pm

4 MONDAY
☿ △ ♃ **6:29 am** 3:29 am
☽ △ ☉ **7:12 am** 4:12 am
☽ □ ♀ **8:08 am** 5:08 am
☽ △ ☿ **1:35 pm** 10:35 am
☽ ☌ ♃ **2:06 pm** 11:06 am
☉ ⚺ ♀ **8:42 pm** 5:42 pm

5 TUESDAY
☽ ☌ ♅ **3:28 am** 12:28 am
☽ ⚹ ♆ **9:59 am** 6:59 am
☽ △ ♇ **12:46 pm** 9:46 am
☽ □ ♄ **9:50 pm** 6:50 pm

6 WEDNESDAY
☽ △ ♂ **3:45 am** 12:45 am
☉ ☌ ☿ **7:09 am** 4:09 am
☽ ⚹ ♀ **3:06 pm** 12:06 pm
☽ □ ☿ **4:46 pm** 1:46 pm
☽ □ ☉ **6:21 pm** 3:21 pm
☽ ⚺ ♃ **9:12 pm** 6:12 pm

7 THURSDAY
☽ ⚺ ♅ **11:30 am** 8:30 am
☿ ⚺ ♀ **12:18 pm** 9:18 am
☽ □ ♆ **6:22 pm** 3:22 pm
☽ ⚻ ♇ **9:22 pm** 6:22 pm

8 FRIDAY
☽ △ ♄ **6:43 am** 3:43 am
☉ △ ♃ **7:13 am** 4:13 am
☽ □ ♂ **4:34 pm** 1:34 pm
☽ ⚹ ☿ **10:57 pm** 7:57 pm
☽ ⚺ ♀ 11:02 pm

9 SATURDAY
☽ ⚺ ♀ **2:02 am**
☽ ⚹ ♃ **7:38 am** 4:38 am
☽ ⚹ ☉ **9:49 am** 6:49 am
☽ ⚹ ♅ **10:34 pm** 7:34 pm

10 SUNDAY
☽ △ ♆ **5:36 am** 2:36 am
☽ ☍ ♇ **8:47 am** 5:47 am
☽ ⚻ ♄ **6:09 pm** 3:09 pm

11 MONDAY
☿ ⚺ ♂ **3:22 am** 12:22 am
☽ ⚺ ☿ **7:37 am** 4:37 am
☽ ⚹ ♂ **8:06 am** 5:06 am
☽ ☌ ♀ **3:32 pm** 12:32 pm
☽ □ ♃ **7:54 pm** 4:54 pm

12 TUESDAY
☽ ⚺ ☉ **3:37 am** 12:37 am
☽ □ ♅ **11:06 am** 8:06 am
☽ ⚻ ♆ **6:07 pm** 3:07 pm
☽ ⚻ ♇ **9:24 pm** 6:24 pm

13 WEDNESDAY
☽ ☍ ♄ **6:31 am** 3:31 am
☽ ☌ ☿ **6:04 pm** 3:04 pm
☽ ⚺ ♂ 9:22 pm

14 THURSDAY
☽ ⚺ ♂ **12:22 am**
☽ ⚺ ♀ **5:56 am** 2:56 am
☽ △ ♃ **8:27 am** 5:27 am
☽ ☌ ☉ **9:40 pm** 6:40 pm
☽ △ ♅ **11:38 pm** 8:38 pm

15 FRIDAY
☽ ☍ ♆ **6:30 am** 3:30 am
☽ △ ♇ **9:49 am** 6:49 am
☽ ⚻ ♄ **6:32 pm** 3:32 pm
☉ △ ♅ **9:24 pm** 6:24 pm

16 SATURDAY
☽ ⚺ ☿ **5:45 am** 2:45 am
☽ ☌ ♂ **3:53 pm** 12:53 pm
☽ ⚹ ♀ **7:57 pm** 4:57 pm
☽ ⚻ ♃ **8:12 pm** 5:12 pm
♀ □ ♃ 11:10 pm

17 SUNDAY
♀ □ ♃ **2:10 am**
☽ ⚻ ♅ **11:09 am** 8:09 am
☽ ⚺ ☉ **2:27 pm** 11:27 am
☽ ⚻ ♆ **5:47 pm** 2:47 pm
☽ □ ♇ **9:06 pm** 6:06 pm

18 MONDAY
☽ △ ♄ **5:19 am** 2:19 am
☽ ⚹ ☿ **5:52 pm** 2:52 pm

19 TUESDAY
☽ ⚺ ♂ **5:31 am** 2:31 am
☽ ☍ ♃ **6:16 am** 3:16 am
☉ ☍ ♆ **7:17 am** 4:17 am
☽ □ ♀ **8:29 am** 5:29 am
♂ ⚻ ♃ **6:48 pm** 3:48 pm
☽ ☍ ♅ **8:46 pm** 5:46 pm

20 WEDNESDAY
☽ △ ♆ **3:06 am** 12:06 am
☽ ⚹ ☉ **4:47 am** 1:47 am
☽ ⚹ ♇ **6:21 am** 3:21 am
☽ □ ♄ **1:58 pm** 10:58 am
☉ △ ♇ 10:21 pm

21 THURSDAY
☉ △ ♇ **1:21 am**
☽ □ ☿ **5:13 am** 2:13 am
☽ ⚻ ♃ **1:47 pm** 10:47 am
☽ ⚹ ♂ **4:12 pm** 1:12 pm
☽ △ ♀ **6:25 pm** 3:25 pm

22 FRIDAY
☽ ⚻ ♅ **3:40 am** 12:40 am
☽ □ ♆ **9:37 am** 6:37 am
☽ ⚺ ♇ **12:46 pm** 9:46 am
☽ □ ☉ **3:32 pm** 12:32 pm
☽ ⚹ ♄ **7:44 pm** 4:44 pm

23 SATURDAY
☽ △ ☿ **2:24 pm** 11:24 am
☽ △ ♃ **6:12 pm** 3:12 pm
☽ □ ♂ **11:17 pm** 8:17 pm
☽ □ ⚷ 9:07 pm
☽ ⚻ ♀ 10:04 pm

24 SUNDAY
☽ ⚻ ♀ **1:04 am**
☽ △ ♅ **7:27 am** 4:27 am
☽ ⚹ ♆ **1:03 pm** 10:03 am
☽ ☌ ♇ **4:05 pm** 1:05 pm
☽ △ ☉ **10:26 pm** 7:26 pm
☽ ⚺ ♄ **10:29 pm** 7:29 pm
☉ ⚻ ♄ **11:10 pm** 8:10 pm

25 MONDAY
☿ △ ♃ **8:10 am** 5:10 am
☽ □ ♃ **7:49 pm** 4:49 pm
☽ ⚻ ☿ **9:02 pm** 6:02 pm

26 TUESDAY
☽ △ ♂ **3:13 am** 12:13 am
☽ ☍ ♀ **4:47 am** 1:47 am
☽ □ ♅ **8:38 am** 5:38 am
☽ ⚺ ♆ **2:00 pm** 11:00 am
☽ ⚺ ♇ **5:00 pm** 2:00 pm
☽ ☌ ♄ **11:01 pm** 8:01 pm
☽ ⚻ ☉ 11:33 pm

27 WEDNESDAY
☽ ⚻ ☉ **2:33 am**
☽ ⚹ ♃ **7:46 pm** 4:46 pm
☽ ☍ ☿ 11:18 pm

28 THURSDAY
☽ ☍ ☿ **2:18 am**
☽ ⚻ ♂ **5:30 am** 2:30 am
☽ ⚻ ♀ **7:06 am** 4:06 am
☽ ⚹ ♅ **8:35 am** 5:35 am
☽ ☌ ♆ **1:54 pm** 10:54 am
☽ ⚹ ♇ **4:58 pm** 1:58 pm
☽ ⚺ ♄ **10:49 pm** 7:49 pm

29 FRIDAY
☽ ☍ ☉ **5:58 am** 2:58 am
♀ □ ♅ **1:53 pm** 10:53 am
☽ ⚺ ♃ **7:46 pm** 4:46 pm

30 SATURDAY
☿ ⚺ ♂ **4:35 am** 1:35 am
☽ ☍ ♂ **8:20 am** 5:20 am
☽ ⚻ ☿ **8:36 am** 5:36 am
☽ ⚺ ♅ **9:06 am** 6:06 am
☽ △ ♀ **10:08 am** 7:08 am
☿ △ ♅ **12:55 pm** 9:55 am
☽ ⚺ ♆ **2:35 pm** 11:35 am
☽ □ ♇ **5:50 pm** 2:50 pm
☽ ⚹ ♄ **11:45 pm** 8:45 pm
♂ ⚻ ♅ 9:38 pm

Eastern time in bold type
Pacific time in medium type

SEPTEMBER 2023

DATE	SID.TIME	SUN	MOON	NODE	MERCURY	VENUS	MARS	JUPITER	SATURN	URANUS	NEPTUNE	PLUTO	CERES	PALLAS	JUNO	VESTA	CHIRON
1 F	22 39 36	8♍19 23	21♓36	25♉48R	18♍37R	12♌23R	2♎51	15♉34	3♓29R	23♉04R	26♓46R	28♑15R	24♒08	24♍10	8♌20	26♊16	19♈19R
2 Sa	22 43 33	9 17 24	6♈33	25 45	17 48	12 17	3 30	15 34	3 25	23 04	26 45	28 14	24 32	24 38	8 50	26 34	19 17
3 Su	22 47 29	10 15 27	21 07	25 43D	16 55	12 14	4 09	15 35	3 20	23 04	26 43	28 13	24 56	25 05	9 21	26 52	19 15
4 M	22 51 26	11 13 32	5♉15	25 45	16 00	12 12D	4 47	15 35R	3 16	23 03	26 42	28 12	25 20	25 33	9 51	27 10	19 13
5 T	22 55 23	12 11 39	18 54	25 45	15 02	12 13	5 26	15 34	3 11	23 03	26 40	28 11	25 44	26 01	10 21	27 28	19 11
6 W	22 59 19	13 09 48	2♊07	25 46R	14 04	12 17	6 05	15 34	3 07	23 03	26 38	28 10	26 08	26 28	10 50	27 46	19 09
7 Th	23 3 16	14 07 59	14 56	25 46	13 06	12 22	6 44	15 33	3 02	23 02	26 37	28 09	26 32	26 56	11 20	28 03	19 07
8 F	23 7 12	15 06 12	27 26	25 46	12 10	12 30	7 23	15 32	2 58	23 02	26 35	28 08	26 56	27 23	11 50	28 21	19 05
9 Sa	23 11 9	16 04 27	9♋41	25 45	11 16	12 40	8 02	15 31	2 53	23 02	26 34	28 08	27 20	27 51	12 20	28 38	19 03
10 Su	23 15 5	17 02 44	21 44	25 39	10 27	12 52	8 41	15 29	2 49	23 01	26 32	28 06	27 45	28 18	12 49	28 55	19 01
11 M	23 19 2	18 01 03	3♌40	25 33	9 44	13 07	9 20	15 28	2 45	23 00	26 30	28 06	28 09	28 46	13 18	29 11	18 58
12 T	23 22 58	18 59 24	15 32	25 26	9 07	13 21	9 59	15 26	2 40	23 00	26 29	28 05	28 33	29 13	13 48	29 28	18 56
13 W	23 26 55	19 57 47	27 23	25 20	8 37	13 41	10 38	15 24	2 36	22 59	26 27	28 04	28 58	29 41	14 17	29 44	18 54
14 Th	23 30 52	20 56 12	9♍15	25 13	8 16	14 01	11 17	15 22	2 32	22 58	26 25	28 04	29 22	0♎08	14 46	0♋00	18 51
15 F	23 34 48	21 54 39	21 09	25 09R	8 04D	14 23	11 56	15 19	2 28	22 57	26 24	28 03	29 47	0 36	15 15	0 16	18 49
16 Sa	23 38 45	22 53 07	3♎08	25 05	8 00	14 47	12 36	15 17	2 24	22 57	26 22	28 02	0♓11	1 03	15 44	0 32	18 47
17 Su	23 42 41	23 51 38	15 13	25 03D	8 06	15 12	13 15	15 14	2 20	22 56	26 20	28 02	0 36	1 31	16 13	0 47	18 44
18 M	23 46 38	24 50 10	27 27	25 02	8 22	15 39	13 54	15 11	2 16	22 55	26 19	28 01	1 01	1 58	16 42	1 03	18 42
19 T	23 50 34	25 48 44	9♏51	25 03	8 47	16 08	14 34	15 08	2 12	22 54	26 17	28 00	1 26	2 26	17 10	1 18	18 39
20 W	23 54 31	26 47 20	22 28	25 05	9 21	16 38	15 13	15 05	2 08	22 53	26 16	28 00	1 50	2 53	17 39	1 33	18 37
21 Th	23 58 27	27 45 57	5♐27	25 06	10 04	17 09	15 53	15 01	2 04	22 52	26 14	27 59	2 15	3 21	18 07	1 47	18 34
22 F	0 2 24	28 44 36	18 51	25 07R	10 55	17 42	16 32	14 57	2 00	22 50	26 12	27 59	2 40	3 48	18 36	2 01	18 32
23 Sa	0 6 21	29 43 17	2♑05	25 08	11 54	18 16	17 12	14 53	1 56	22 49	26 10	27 58	3 05	4 16	19 04	2 16	18 29
24 Su	0 10 17	0♎42 00	16 01	25 07	13 00	18 52	17 52	14 49	1 53	22 47	26 09	27 58	3 30	4 43	19 32	2 29	18 27
25 M	0 14 14	1 40 44	0♒18	25 05	14 12	19 29	18 31	14 45	1 49	22 45	26 07	27 57	3 55	5 11	20 00	2 43	18 24
26 T	0 18 10	2 39 30	14 56	25 03	15 31	20 07	19 11	14 40	1 45	22 44	26 05	27 57	4 20	5 38	20 28	2 56	18 22
27 W	0 22 7	3 38 18	29 49	25 00	16 54	20 46	19 51	14 36	1 42	22 43	26 04	27 56	4 45	6 06	20 56	3 09	18 19
28 Th	0 26 3	4 37 07	14♓49	24 57	18 22	21 27	20 31	14 31	1 38	22 42	26 02	27 56	5 10	6 33	21 23	3 22	18 17
29 F	0 30 0	5 35 58	29 49	24 55	19 54	22 09	21 10	14 27	1 35	22 41	26 01	27 56	5 35	7 00	21 51	3 35	18 14
30 Sa	0 33 56	6 34 51	14♈40	24 54D	21 30	22 51	21 50	14 23	1 32	22 40	25 59	27 55	6 00	7 28	22 18	3 47	18 11

EPHEMERIS CALCULATED FOR 12 MIDNIGHT GREENWICH MEAN TIME. ALL OTHER DATA AND FACING ASPECTARIAN PAGE IN **EASTERN TIME (BOLD)** AND PACIFIC TIME (REGULAR).

OCTOBER 2023

☽ Last Aspect day	ET / hr:mn / PT	asp	☽ Ingress sign	day	ET / hr:mn / PT
2	**9:20 pm** 6:20 pm	△♇	♊	2	10:03 pm
2	**9:20 pm** 6:20 pm	△♇	♊	3	**1:03 am**
4	11:34 pm	✶♀	♋	5	**8:32 am** 5:32 am
5	**2:34 am**	✶♀	♋	5	**8:32 am** 5:32 am
7	**3:12 pm** 12:12 pm	☍♇	♌	7	**7:24 pm** 4:24 pm
10	**5:37 am** 2:37 am	✶♂	♍	10	**8:02 am** 5:02 am
12	**4:10 pm** 1:10 pm	△♇	♎	12	**8:22 pm** 5:22 pm
15	**3:01 am** 12:01 am	□♇	♏	15	**7:04 am** 4:04 am
17	**11:44 am** 8:44 am	✶♇	♐	17	**3:36 pm** 12:36 pm
19	**3:02 pm** 12:02 pm	✶☉	♑	19	**9:55 pm** 6:55 pm
21	11:00 pm	□☿	♒	21	11:06 pm
22	**2:00 am**	□☿	♒	22	**2:06 am**
23	**3:04 pm** 12:04 pm	□♅	♓	24	**4:33 am** 1:33 am
25	11:39 pm	✶♇	♈	26	**6:02 am** 3:02 am
26	**2:39 am**	✶♇	♈	26	**6:02 am** 3:02 am
28	**4:20 am** 1:20 am	□♇	♉	28	**7:44 am** 4:44 am
30	**7:36 am** 4:36 am	△♇	♊	30	**11:08 am** 8:08 am

☽ Phases & Eclipses phase	day	ET / hr:mn / PT
4th Quarter	6	**9:48 am** 6:48 am
New Moon	14	**1:55 pm** 10:55 am
	14	21° ♎ 08'
2nd Quarter	21	**11:29 pm** 8:29 pm
Full Moon	28	**4:24 pm** 1:24 pm
	28	5° ♉ 09'

Planet Ingress		day	ET / hr:mn / PT
☿	♎	4	**8:09 pm** 5:09 pm
♀	♍	8	**9:11 pm** 6:11 pm
♂	♏	11	9:04 pm
♂	♏	12	**12:04 am**
✳	♍	17	**9:27 am** 6:27 am
☿	♏	21	11:49 pm
☿	♏	22	**2:49 am**
☉	♏	23	**12:21 pm** 9:21 am

Planetary Motion		day	ET / hr:mn / PT
♇	D	10	**9:10 pm** 6:10 pm

1 SUNDAY
♂⚻♅ **12:38 am**
☿⚺♀ **7:38 am** 4:38 am
☽⚻☉ **11:05 am** 8:05 am
☽☌♃ **9:37 pm** 6:37 pm

2 MONDAY
☿☍♆ **11:34 am** 8:34 am
☽☌♅ **11:57 am** 8:57 am
☽⚻♂ **1:50 pm** 10:50 am
☽□♀ **4:07 pm** 1:07 pm
☽✶♆ **5:47 pm** 2:47 pm
☽△☿ **6:41 pm** 3:41 pm
☽△♇ **9:20 pm** 6:20 pm

3 TUESDAY
☽□♄ **3:29 am** 12:29 am
☿△♇ **3:20 pm** 12:20 pm
☽△☉ **8:03 pm** 5:03 pm
♀⚻♆ **8:21 pm** 5:21 pm
☽⚺♃ 11:44 pm

4 WEDNESDAY
☽⚺♃ **2:44 am**
☽⚺♅ **6:22 pm** 3:22 pm
☽△♂ **11:33 pm** 8:33 pm
☽□♆ 9:37 pm
☽✶♀ 11:34 pm

5 THURSDAY
☽□♆ **12:37 am**
☽✶♀ **2:34 am**
☽⚻♇ **4:31 am** 1:31 am

Eastern time in bold type
Pacific time in medium type

☽□☿ **10:33 am** 7:33 am
☽△♄ **10:55 am** 7:55 am
☿⚻♄ **1:03 pm** 10:03 am
♂⚻♆ **7:09 pm** 4:09 pm

6 FRIDAY
♀⚻♇ **8:50 am** 5:50 am
☽□☉ **9:48 am** 6:48 am
☽✶♃ **11:30 am** 8:30 am

7 SATURDAY
☽✶♅ **4:22 am** 1:22 am
☉⚻♃ **5:04 am** 2:04 am
☽△♆ **10:58 am** 7:58 am
☽□♂ **1:25 pm** 10:25 am
☽☍♇ **3:12 pm** 12:12 pm
☽⚺♀ **5:27 pm** 2:27 pm
☽⚻♄ **9:41 pm** 6:41 pm

8 SUNDAY
☽✶☿ **7:47 am** 4:47 am
♂□♇ **9:05 pm** 6:05 pm
☽□♃ **10:55 pm** 7:55 pm

9 MONDAY
☽✶☉ **3:07 am** 12:07 am
☽□♅ **4:36 pm** 1:36 pm
☽⚻♆ **11:21 pm** 8:21 pm
♀☍♄ 11:11 pm

10 TUESDAY
♀☍♄ **2:11 am**
☽⚻♇ **3:45 am** 12:45 am
☽✶♂ **5:37 am** 2:37 am

☽☍♄ **10:06 am** 7:06 am
☽☌♀ **10:46 am** 7:46 am

11 WEDNESDAY
☽⚺☿ **7:08 am** 4:08 am
☽△♃ **11:06 am** 8:06 am
☽⚺☉ **9:18 pm** 6:18 pm

12 THURSDAY
☽△♅ **5:01 am** 2:01 am
☿⚻♃ **8:32 am** 5:32 am
☽☍♆ **11:42 am** 8:42 am
☽△♇ **4:10 pm** 1:10 pm
☽⚺♂ **9:34 pm** 6:34 pm
☽⚻♄ **10:13 pm** 7:13 pm

13 FRIDAY
☽⚺♀ **3:49 am** 12:49 am
♂△♄ **8:29 am** 5:29 am
☽⚻♃ **10:16 pm** 7:16 pm

14 SATURDAY
☽☌☿ **4:58 am** 1:58 am
☽☌☉ **1:55 pm** 10:55 am
☽⚻♅ **4:03 pm** 1:03 p
☽⚻♆ **10:34 pm** 7:34 pm

15 SUNDAY
☽□♇ **3:01 am** 12:01 am
☽△♄ **8:41 am** 5:41 am
☽☌♂ **11:35 am** 8:35 am
☉⚻♅ **3:44 pm** 12:44 pm
☽✶♀ **6:51 pm** 3:51 pm

16 MONDAY
☽☍♃ **7:31 am** 4:31 am
☽⚺☿ **11:29 pm** 8:29 pm
☽☍♅ 10:01 pm

17 TUESDAY
☽☍♅ **1:01 am**
☽⚺☉ **3:54 am** 12:54 am
☽△♆ **7:20 am** 4:20 am
☿⚻♅ **10:48 am** 7:48 am
☽✶♇ **11:44 am** 8:44 am
☽□♄ **5:02 pm** 2:02 pm
☽⚺♂ **11:03 pm** 8:03 pm

18 WEDNESDAY
☽□♀ **7:15 am** 4:15 am
☽⚻♃ **2:35 pm** 11:35 am
☉⚻♆ **11:40 pm** 8:40 pm

19 THURSDAY
☽⚻♅ **7:45 am** 4:45 am
☿⚻♆ **10:12 am** 7:12 am
☽□♆ **1:53 pm** 10:53 am
☽✶☿ **2:25 pm** 11:25 am
☽✶☉ **3:02 pm** 12:02 pm
☽⚺♇ **6:12 pm** 3:12 pm
☽✶♄ **11:10 pm** 8:10 pm
☉☌☿ 10:38 pm

20 FRIDAY
☉☌☿ **1:38 am**
☽✶♂ **7:54 am** 4:54 am
☽△♀ **4:59 pm** 1:59 pm
☽△♃ **7:30 pm** 4:30 pm
☿□♇ **8:51 pm** 5:51 pm

21 SATURDAY
☉□♇ **10:09 am** 7:09 am
☽△♅ **12:21 pm** 9:21 am
☽✶♆ **6:17 pm** 3:17 pm
☽☌♇ **10:33 pm** 7:33 pm
☽□☉ **11:29 pm** 8:29 pm
♀△♃ 9:32 pm
☽□☿ 11:00 pm

22 SUNDAY
♀△♃ **12:32 am**
☽□☿ **2:00 am**
☽⚺♄ **3:13 am** 12:13 am
☿△♄ **12:12 pm** 9:12 am
☽□♂ **2:21 pm** 11:21 am
☽□♃ **10:27 pm** 7:27 pm
☽⚻♀ 9:17 pm

23 MONDAY
☽⚻♀ **12:17 am**
☽□♅ **3:04 pm** 12:04 pm
☽⚺♆ **8:53 pm** 5:53 pm
☽⚺♇ 10:07 pm

24 TUESDAY
☽⚺♇ **1:07 am**
☉△♄ **3:14 am** 12:14 am
☽☌♄ **5:34 am** 2:34 am
☽△☉ **5:45 am** 2:45 am
☽△☿ **10:57 am** 7:57 am
☽△♂ **6:58 pm** 3:58 pm
☽✶♃ **11:57 pm** 8:57 pm

25 WEDNESDAY
☽☍♀ **5:52 am** 2:52 am
☽✶♅ **4:35 pm** 1:35 pm
☽☌♆ **10:22 pm** 7:22 pm
☽✶♇ 11:39 pm

26 THURSDAY
☽✶♇ **2:39 am**
☽⚺♄ **6:59 am** 3:59 am
☽⚻☉ **10:50 am** 7:50 am
☽⚻☿ **6:36 pm** 3:36 pm
☽⚻♂ **10:49 pm** 7:49 pm
☽⚺♃ 9:54 pm

27 FRIDAY
☽⚺♃ **12:54 am**
☽⚻♀ **11:00 am** 8:00 am
☽⚺♅ **5:57 pm** 2:57 pm
☽⚺♆ **11:53 pm** 8:53 pm

28 SATURDAY
☽□♇ **4:20 am** 1:20 am
☽✶♄ **8:40 am** 5:40 am
♂☍♃ **12:03 pm** 9:03 am
☽☍☉ **4:24 pm** 1:24 pm
☿☍♃ **11:44 pm** 8:44 pm
☽☌♃ 11:37 pm

29 SUNDAY
☽☌♃ **2:37 am**
☽☍☿ **3:00 am** 12:00 am
☽☍♂ **3:30 am** 12:30 am
☿☌♂ **10:22 am** 7:22 am

☽△♀ **5:33 pm** 2:33 pm
☽☌♅ **8:36 pm** 5:36 pm
☽✶♆ 11:51 pm

30 MONDAY
☽✶♆ **2:51 am**
☽△♇ **7:36 am** 4:36 am
☽□♄ **12:04 pm** 9:04 am
☽⚻☉ 9:22 pm

31 TUESDAY
☽⚻☉ **12:22 am**
☽⚺♃ **6:28 am** 3:28 am
♀△♅ **8:51 am** 5:51 am
☽⚻♂ **10:48 am** 7:48 am
☽⚻☿ **2:31 pm** 11:31 am
☽⚺♅ 10:53 pm

OCTOBER 2023

DATE	SID.TIME	SUN	MOON	NODE	MERCURY	VENUS	MARS	JUPITER	SATURN	URANUS	NEPTUNE	PLUTO	CERES	PALLAS	JUNO	VESTA	CHIRON
1 Su	0 37 53	7≏33 47	29♈13	24♈54R	23♍09	23♌35	22≏30	14♉26R	1♓29R	22♉38R	25♓57R	27♑55R	6♏25	7≏55	22♌46	3♋59	18♈09R
2 M	0 41 50	8 32 44	13♉24	24 54	24 48	24 20	23 10	14 21	1 25	22 37	25 56	27 54	6 50	8 22	23 13	4 11	18 06
3 T	0 45 46	9 31 44	27 10	24 55	26 31	25 05	23 50	14 16	1 22	22 35	25 54	27 54	7 16	8 50	23 40	4 22	18 03
4 W	0 49 43	10 30 46	10♊29	24 57	28 15	25 52	24 30	14 10	1 19	22 34	25 53	27 54	7 41	9 17	24 07	4 34	18 01
5 Th	0 53 39	11 29 50	23 24	24 58	29 59	26 39	25 11	14 04	1 16	22 32	25 51	27 54	8 06	9 44	24 34	4 45	17 58
6 F	0 57 36	12 28 57	5♋58	24 58R	1≏45	27 28	25 51	13 59	1 14	22 30	25 49	27 54	8 32	10 12	25 01	4 55	17 55
7 Sa	1 1 32	13 28 06	18 14	24 58	3 31	28 17	26 31	13 53	1 11	22 28	25 48	27 54	8 57	10 39	25 27	5 05	17 52
8 Su	1 5 29	14 27 17	0♌18	24 58	5 17	29 07	27 11	13 47	1 08	22 27	25 46	27 54	9 22	11 06	25 54	5 15	17 50
9 M	1 9 25	15 26 31	12 13	24 57	7 04	29 57	27 52	13 40	1 05	22 25	25 45	27 54	9 48	11 33	26 20	5 25	17 47
10 T	1 13 22	16 25 46	24 04	24 56	8 50	0♍49	28 32	13 34	1 03	22 23	25 43	27 54	10 13	12 01	26 46	5 34	17 44
11 W	1 17 19	17 25 04	5♍55	24 55	10 36	1 41	29 13	13 28	1 01	22 21	25 42	27 54	10 38	12 28	27 12	5 43	17 41
12 Th	1 21 15	18 24 24	17 49	24 54	12 22	2 34	29 53	13 21	0 58	22 19	25 40	27 54 D	11 04	12 55	27 38	5 52	17 39
13 F	1 25 12	19 23 47	29 49	24 53	14 08	3 28	0♏34	13 14	0 56	22 17	25 39	27 54	11 29	13 22	28 04	6 00	17 36
14 Sa	1 29 8	20 23 11	11♎57	24 52	15 53	4 22	1 14	13 07	0 54	22 15	25 37	27 54	11 55	13 49	28 30	6 09	17 33
15 Su	1 33 5	21 22 38	24 16	24 52 D	17 37	5 17	1 55	13 00	0 52	22 13	25 36	27 54	12 20	14 17	28 55	6 16	17 31
16 M	1 37 1	22 22 06	6♏45	24 52	19 21	6 12	2 36	12 53	0 50	22 11	25 34	27 54	12 46	14 44	29 21	6 24	17 28
17 T	1 40 58	23 21 37	19 28	24 53	21 04	7 08	3 16	12 46	0 48	22 09	25 33	27 54	13 12	15 11	29 46	6 30	17 25
18 W	1 44 54	24 21 10	2♐23	24 53R	22 47	8 04	3 57	12 39	0 46	22 07	25 31	27 54	13 37	15 38	0♍11	6 37	17 22
19 Th	1 48 51	25 20 44	15 32	24 53	24 29	9 01	4 38	12 31	0 44	22 05	25 30	27 54	14 03	16 05	0 36	6 43	17 20
20 F	1 52 47	26 20 20	28 55	24 53	26 11	9 59	5 19	12 24	0 43	22 03	25 28	27 54	14 28	16 32	1 01	6 49	17 17
21 Sa	1 56 44	27 19 58	12♑33	24 52	27 51	10 57	6 00	12 16	0 41	22 01	25 27	27 55	14 54	16 59	1 25	6 55	17 14
22 Su	2 0 41	28 19 38	26 26	24 52 D	29 32	11 56	6 41	12 08	0 40	21 58	25 26	27 55	15 20	17 26	1 50	7 00	17 12
23 M	2 4 37	29 19 20	10♒33	24 53	1♏11	12 55	7 22	12 01	0 39	21 56	25 25	27 56	15 45	17 53	2 14	7 05	17 09
24 T	2 8 34	0♏19 03	24 52	24 53	2 50	13 54	8 03	11 53	0 37	21 54	25 23	27 56	16 11	18 20	2 39	7 09	17 06
25 W	2 12 30	1 18 47	9♓20	24 53	4 29	14 54	8 44	11 45	0 36	21 52	25 22	27 56	16 37	18 47	3 03	7 13	17 04
26 Th	2 16 27	2 18 34	23 54	24 54	6 06	15 55	9 25	11 37	0 35	21 49	25 21	27 57	17 02	19 14	3 26	7 16	17 01
27 F	2 20 23	3 18 22	8♈58	24 54	7 44	16 55	10 07	11 29	0 34	21 47	25 20	27 57	17 28	19 41	3 50	7 20	16 59
28 Sa	2 24 20	4 18 12	22 59	24 55R	9 20	17 57	10 48	11 21	0 34	21 45	25 18	27 58	17 54	20 07	4 14	7 22	16 56
29 Su	2 28 16	5 18 03	7♉17	24 54	10 57	18 58	11 29	11 13	0 33	21 42	25 17	27 58	18 19	20 34	4 37	7 25	16 53
30 M	2 32 13	6 17 57	21 19	24 54	12 32	20 00	12 11	11 05	0 32	21 40	25 16	27 59	18 45	21 01	5 00	7 27	16 51
31 T	2 36 10	7 17 53	5♊01	24 52	14 08	21 03	12 52	10 57	0 32	21 38	25 15	27 59	19 11	21 28	5 23	7 28	16 48

EPHEMERIS CALCULATED FOR 12 MIDNIGHT GREENWICH MEAN TIME. ALL OTHER DATA AND FACING ASPECTARIAN PAGE IN **EASTERN TIME (BOLD)** AND PACIFIC TIME (REGULAR).

NOVEMBER 2023

☽ Last Aspect day	ET / hr:mn / PT	asp	☽ Ingress sign	day	ET / hr:mn / PT
1	**8:36 am** 5:36 am	□ ♆	♋	1	**5:30 pm** 2:30 pm
3	**11:28 pm** 8:28 pm	☍ ♇	♌	4	**3:21 am** 12:21 am
5	11:25 pm	□ ☿	♍	6	**2:39 pm** 11:39 am
6	**2:25 am**	□ ☿	♍	6	**2:39 pm** 11:39 am
8	**11:55 pm** 8:55 pm	⚹ ☿	♎	9	**3:08 am** 12:08 am
11	**10:05 am** 7:05 am	□ ♇	♏	11	**1:39 pm** 10:39 am
13	**6:03 pm** 3:03 pm	⚹ ♇	♐	13	**9:23 pm** 6:23 pm
15	**5:57 pm** 2:57 pm	□ ♆	♑	15	11:41 pm
15	**5:57 pm** 2:57 pm	□ ♆	♑	16	**2:41 am**
18	**3:27 am** 12:27 am	☌ ♇	♒	18	**6:28 am** 3:28 am
20	**5:50 am** 2:50 am	□ ☉	♓	20	**9:29 am** 6:29 am
22	**10:10 am** 7:10 am	△ ♂	♈	22	**12:19 pm** 9:19 am
24	**12:40 pm** 9:40 am	□ ♀	♉	24	**3:29 pm** 12:29 pm
26	**4:52 pm** 1:52 pm	△ ♇	♊	26	**7:40 pm** 4:40 pm
28	**8:03 pm** 5:03 pm	☍ ☿	♋	28	10:54 pm
28	**8:03 pm** 5:03 pm	☍ ☿	♋	29	**1:54 am**

☽ Phases & Eclipses phase	day	ET / hr:mn / PT
4th Quarter	5	**3:37 am** 1:37 am
New Moon	13	**4:27 am** 1:27 am
2nd Quarter	20	**5:50 am** 2:50 am
Full Moon	27	**4:16 am** 1:16 am

Planet Ingress		day	ET / hr:mn / PT
♀	♎	8	**4:30 am** 1:30 am
☿	♐	9	10:25 pm
☿	♐	10	**1:25 am**
♀	♏	19	**4:03 am** 1:03 am
☉	♐	22	**9:03 am** 6:03 am
♂	♐	24	**5:15 am** 2:15 am
⚳	♐	24	9:14 pm
⚳	♐	25	**12:14 am**

Planetary Motion		day	ET / hr:mn / PT
⚶	℞	2	**9:50 pm** 6:50 pm
♄	D	4	**3:03 am** 12:03 am

1 WEDNESDAY
☽ ⚺ ♅ **1:53 am**
☽ □ ♀ **3:26 am** 12:26 am
☽ □ ♆ **8:36 am** 5:36 am
☽ ⚻ ♇ **1:47 pm** 10:47 am
☽ △ ♄ **6:29 pm** 3:29 pm

2 THURSDAY
☽ △ ☉ **12:23 pm** 9:23 am
☽ ⚹ ♃ **1:31 pm** 10:31 am
☽ △ ♂ **10:01 pm** 7:01 pm
☉ ☍ ♃ 10:02 pm

3 FRIDAY
☉ ☍ ♃ **1:02 am**
☽ △ ☿ **6:49 am** 3:49 am
☽ ⚹ ♅ **10:36 am** 7:36 am
☽ ⚹ ♀ **5:49 pm** 2:49 pm
☽ △ ♆ **5:50 pm** 2:50 pm
♀ ☍ ♆ **6:06 pm** 3:06 pm
☽ ☍ ♇ **11:28 pm** 8:28 pm

4 SATURDAY
☽ ⚻ ♄ **4:22 am** 1:22 am
☿ ☍ ♅ **12:07 pm** 9:07 am
☽ □ ♃ **11:46 pm** 8:46 pm

5 SUNDAY
☽ □ ☉ **3:37 am** 1:37 am
☽ □ ♂ **12:00 pm** 9:00 am
☽ □ ♅ **9:11 pm** 6:11 pm
☽ □ ☿ 11:25 pm

6 MONDAY
☽ □ ☿ **2:25 am**
☽ ⚻ ♆ **4:48 am** 1:48 am
♀ △ ♇ **9:38 am** 6:38 am
☽ ⚻ ♇ **10:44 am** 7:44 am
☽ ⚺ ♀ **10:50 am** 7:50 am
☽ ☍ ♄ **3:42 pm** 12:42 pm
☿ △ ♆ **8:37 pm** 5:37 pm

7 TUESDAY
☽ △ ♃ **10:43 am** 7:43 am
☽ ⚹ ☉ **9:54 pm** 6:54 pm

8 WEDNESDAY
☽ ⚹ ♂ **4:29 am** 1:29 am
☽ △ ♅ **9:40 am** 6:40 am
♀ ⚻ ♄ **4:13 pm** 1:13 pm
☽ ☍ ♆ **5:20 pm** 2:20 pm
☿ ⚹ ♇ **7:17 pm** 4:17 pm
☽ △ ♇ **11:20 pm** 8:20 pm
☽ ⚹ ☿ **11:55 pm** 8:55 pm

9 THURSDAY
☽ ⚻ ♄ **4:12 am** 1:12 am
☽ ☌ ♀ **5:23 am** 2:23 am
☽ ⚻ ♃ **10:05 pm** 7:05 pm

10 FRIDAY
☿ □ ♄ **10:07 am** 7:07 am
☽ ⚺ ☉ **2:51 pm** 11:51 am
☽ ⚺ ♂ **7:29 pm** 4:29 pm
☽ ⚻ ♅ **8:43 pm** 5:43 pm

11 SATURDAY
☽ ⚻ ♆ **4:13 am** 1:13 am
☽ □ ♇ **10:05 am** 7:05 am
☽ △ ♄ **2:43 pm** 11:43 am
♂ ☍ ♅ **4:11 pm** 1:11 pm
☽ ⚺ ☿ **6:34 pm** 3:34 pm
☽ ⚺ ♀ **9:22 pm** 6:22 pm

12 SUNDAY
☽ ☍ ♃ **7:09 am** 4:09 am

13 MONDAY
☽ ☌ ☉ **4:27 am** 1:27 am
☽ ☍ ♅ **5:05 am** 2:05 am
☽ ☌ ♂ **7:18 am** 4:18 am
☽ △ ♆ **12:20 pm** 9:20 am
☉ ☍ ♅ **12:21 pm** 9:21 am
☽ ⚹ ♇ **6:03 pm** 3:03 pm
☽ □ ♄ **10:28 pm** 7:28 pm

14 TUESDAY
☽ ☌ ☿ **9:04 am** 6:04 am
☽ ⚹ ♀ **9:44 am** 6:44 am
☽ ⚻ ♃ **1:32 pm** 10:32 am

15 WEDNESDAY
☿ ⚹ ♀ **7:48 am** 4:48 am
☽ ⚻ ♅ **10:52 am** 7:52 am
☽ ⚺ ☉ **2:44 pm** 11:44 am
☽ ⚺ ♂ **4:05 pm** 1:05 pm
☽ □ ♆ **5:57 pm** 2:57 pm
☿ ⚻ ♃ **10:35 pm** 7:35 pm
☽ ⚺ ♇ **11:33 pm** 8:33 pm
♀ ⚻ ♃ 11:48 pm

16 THURSDAY
♀ ⚻ ♃ **2:48 am**
☽ ⚹ ♄ **3:49 am** 12:49 am
☽ △ ♃ **5:48 pm** 2:48 pm
☽ □ ♀ **7:16 pm** 4:16 pm
☽ ⚺ ☿ **8:17 pm** 5:17 pm

17 FRIDAY
♂ △ ♆ **3:36 am** 12:36 am
☉ △ ♆ **9:52 am** 6:52 am
☽ △ ♅ **2:51 pm** 11:51 am
☽ ⚹ ♆ **9:52 pm** 6:52 pm
☽ ⚹ ☉ **10:49 pm** 7:49 pm
☽ ⚹ ♂ **10:51 pm** 7:51 pm
☉ ☌ ♂ 9:42 pm

18 SATURDAY
☉ ☌ ♂ **12:42 am**
☽ ☌ ♇ **3:27 am** 12:27 am
☽ ⚺ ♄ **7:38 am** 4:38 am
☽ □ ♃ **8:50 pm** 5:50 pm

19 SUNDAY
☽ △ ♀ **3:12 am** 12:12 am
☽ ⚹ ☿ **5:39 am** 2:39 am
☽ □ ♅ **5:53 pm** 2:53 pm
☽ ⚺ ♆ 9:57 pm

20 MONDAY
☽ ⚺ ♆ **12:57 am**
☽ □ ♂ **4:38 am** 1:38 am
☽ □ ☉ **5:50 am** 2:50 am
☽ ⚺ ♇ **6:34 am** 3:34 am
☽ ☌ ♄ **10:45 am** 7:45 am
☉ ⚹ ♇ **4:26 pm** 1:26 pm
☽ ⚹ ♃ **11:20 pm** 8:20 pm

21 TUESDAY
☽ ⚻ ♀ **10:32 am** 7:32 am
☽ □ ☿ **2:16 pm** 11:16 am
♂ ⚹ ♇ **8:18 pm** 5:18 pm
☽ ⚹ ♅ **8:35 pm** 5:35 pm

22 WEDNESDAY
☽ ☌ ♆ **3:45 am** 12:45 am
☽ ⚹ ♇ **9:29 am** 6:29 am
☽ △ ♂ **10:10 am** 7:10 am
☽ △ ☉ **12:35 pm** 9:35 am
☽ ⚺ ♄ **1:42 pm** 10:42 am
☽ ⚺ ♃ 10:47 pm

23 THURSDAY
☽ ⚺ ♃ **1:47 am**
☉ □ ♄ **4:47 am** 1:47 am
☽ ☍ ♀ **5:57 pm** 2:57 pm
☽ △ ☿ **10:52 pm** 7:52 pm
☽ ⚺ ♅ **11:26 pm** 8:26 pm

24 FRIDAY
☿ ⚻ ♅ **4:27 am** 1:27 am
☽ ⚺ ♆ **6:47 am** 3:47 am
☽ □ ♇ **12:40 pm** 9:40 am
☽ ⚻ ♂ **4:02 pm** 1:02 pm
☽ ⚹ ♄ **5:00 pm** 2:00 pm
☽ ⚻ ☉ **7:43 pm** 4:43 pm

25 SATURDAY
☽ ☌ ♃ **4:43 am** 1:43 am
♂ □ ♄ **11:57 am** 8:57 am
☽ ⚻ ♀ 11:19 pm

26 SUNDAY
☽ ⚻ ♀ **2:19 am**
☽ ☌ ♅ **3:03 am** 12:03 am
☽ ⚻ ☿ **8:21 am** 5:21 am
☽ ⚹ ♆ **10:42 am** 7:42 am
♀ ⚻ ♅ **10:49 am** 7:49 am
☽ △ ♇ **4:52 pm** 1:52 pm
☽ □ ♄ **9:22 pm** 6:22 pm
☽ ☍ ♂ **11:08 pm** 8:08 pm

27 MONDAY
☽ ☍ ☉ **4:16 am** 1:16 am
☿ □ ♆ **8:27 am** 5:27 am
☽ ⚺ ♃ **8:54 am** 5:54 am

28 TUESDAY
☽ ⚺ ♅ **8:22 am** 5:22 am
☽ △ ♀ **12:54 pm** 9:54 am
☽ □ ♆ **4:30 pm** 1:30 pm
☽ ☍ ☿ **8:03 pm** 5:03 pm
☽ ⚻ ♇ **11:03 pm** 8:03 pm

29 WEDNESDAY
☽ △ ♄ **3:51 am** 12:51 am
☽ ⚻ ♂ **8:43 am** 5:43 am
☉ ⚻ ♃ **12:38 pm** 9:38 am
☽ ⚹ ♃ **3:21 pm** 12:21 pm
☽ ⚻ ☉ **3:37 pm** 12:37 pm

30 THURSDAY
☿ ⚺ ♇ **3:34 am** 12:34 am
♀ ⚻ ♆ **5:13 am** 2:13 am
☽ ⚹ ♅ **4:20 pm** 1:20 pm
☽ △ ♆ 10:05 pm

Eastern time in bold type
Pacific time in medium type

NOVEMBER 2023

DATE	SID.TIME	SUN	MOON	NODE	MERCURY	VENUS	MARS	JUPITER	SATURN	URANUS	NEPTUNE	PLUTO	CERES	PALLAS	JUNO	VESTA	CHIRON
1 W	2 40 6	8♏17 51	18♊22	24♈51 R	15♏42 R	22♍05	13♏34	10♉49 R	0♓31 R	21♉35 R	25♓14 R	28♑00	19♏37	21♎55	5♏46	7♋29 R	16♈46 R
2 Th	2 44 3	9 17 51	1♋20	24 47	17 17	23 09	14 15	10 40	0 31	21 33	25 13	28 01	20 02	22 21	6 09	7 30	16 43
3 F	2 47 59	10 17 53	13 57	24 47	18 50	24 12	14 57	10 32	0 31	21 30	25 12	28 01	20 28	22 48	6 31	7 30 R	16 41
4 Sa	2 51 56	11 17 58	26 17	24 45	20 24	25 16	15 38	10 24	0 31 D	21 28	25 11	28 02	20 54	23 15	6 54	7 30	16 38
5 Su	2 55 52	12 18 04	8♌21	24 45 D	21 57	26 20	16 20	10 16	0 31	21 25	25 10	28 03	21 20	23 41	7 16	7 29	16 36
6 M	2 59 49	13 18 12	20 18	24 45	23 29	27 24	17 02	10 08	0 31	21 23	25 09	28 03	21 45	24 08	7 38	7 28	16 34
7 T	3 3 45	14 18 23	2♍19	24 46	25 01	28 29	17 44	10 00	0 32	21 20	25 08	28 04	22 11	24 34	8 00	7 27	16 31
8 W	3 7 42	15 18 35	14 00	24 47	26 33	29 34	18 25	9 52	0 32	21 18	25 07	28 05	22 37	25 01	8 21	7 25	16 29
9 Th	3 11 39	16 18 50	25 56	24 47	28 05	0♎39	19 07	9 43	0 32	21 16	25 06	28 06	23 03	25 27	8 42	7 22	16 27
10 F	3 15 35	17 19 06	8♎00	24 50	29 36	1 45	19 49	9 35	0 33	21 13	25 06	28 06	23 29	25 54	9 04	7 20	16 24
11 Sa	3 19 32	18 19 24	20 17	24 51 R	1♐06	2 51	20 31	9 27	0 33	21 11	25 05	28 07	23 54	26 20	9 25	7 16	16 22
12 Su	3 23 28	19 19 44	2♏49	24 51	2 37	3 57	21 13	9 20	0 34	21 08	25 03	28 08	24 20	26 47	9 45	7 13	16 20
13 M	3 27 25	20 20 06	15 37	24 50	4 07	5 03	21 55	9 12	0 35	21 06	25 03	28 09	24 46	27 13	10 06	7 08	16 18
14 T	3 31 21	21 20 30	28 41	24 47	5 36	6 10	22 38	9 04	0 36	21 03	25 01	28 10	25 12	27 39	10 26	7 04	16 16
15 W	3 35 18	22 20 56	12♐02	24 43	7 05	7 17	23 20	8 56	0 37	21 01	25 01	28 11	25 37	28 06	10 46	6 59	16 14
16 Th	3 39 14	23 21 23	25 36	24 38	8 34	8 24	24 02	8 48	0 38	20 58	25 00	28 12	26 03	28 32	11 06	6 53	16 12
17 F	3 43 11	24 21 51	9♑23	24 34	10 02	9 31	24 44	8 41	0 39	20 56	25 00	28 13	26 29	28 58	11 26	6 47	16 10
18 Sa	3 47 8	25 22 21	23 19	24 30	11 30	10 39	25 27	8 33	0 41	20 53	24 59	28 14	26 55	29 24	11 45	6 41	16 08
19 Su	3 51 4	26 22 52	7♒21	24 28	12 58	11 47	26 09	8 26	0 42	20 51	24 58	28 16	27 20	29 50	12 05	6 34	16 06
20 M	3 55 1	27 23 25	21 28	24 25 D	14 24	12 55	26 51	8 19	0 44	20 48	24 58	28 16	27 46	0♏16	12 24	6 27	16 04
21 T	3 58 57	28 23 58	5♓37	24 25	15 50	14 03	27 34	8 11	0 45	20 46	24 57	28 18	28 12	0 42	12 42	6 19	16 02
22 W	4 2 54	29 24 33	19 47	24 27	17 16	15 11	28 17	8 04	0 47	20 43	24 57	28 19	28 37	1 08	13 01	6 11	16 00
23 Th	4 6 50	0♐25 08	3♈56	24 28	18 41	16 20	28 59	7 57	0 49	20 41	24 56	28 20	29 03	1 34	13 19	6 02	15 58
24 F	4 10 47	1 25 45	18 02	24 29 R	20 05	17 28	29 42	7 51	0 51	20 38	24 56	28 21	29 29	2 00	13 37	5 53	15 57
25 Sa	4 14 44	2 26 23	2♉03	24 29	21 28	18 37	0♐24	7 44	0 53	20 36	24 55	28 22	29 54	2 26	13 55	5 44	15 55
26 Su	4 18 40	3 27 03	15 56	24 27	22 49	19 46	1 07	7 37	0 55	20 33	24 55	28 24	0♐20	2 51	14 12	5 34	15 53
27 M	4 22 37	4 27 43	29 37	24 23	24 10	20 55	1 50	7 31	0 58	20 31	24 55	28 25	0 46	3 17	14 30	5 24	15 52
28 T	4 26 33	5 28 26	13♊05	24 18	25 29	22 05	2 33	7 24	1 00	20 29	24 54	28 26	1 11	3 43	14 47	5 13	15 50
29 W	4 30 30	6 29 09	26 16	24 10	26 47	23 14	3 16	7 18	1 02	20 26	24 54	28 28	1 37	4 08	15 03	5 02	15 49
30 Th	4 34 26	7 29 54	9♋09	24 02	28 03	24 24	3 59	7 12	1 05	20 24	24 54	28 29	2 02	4 33	15 20	4 51	15 47

EPHEMERIS CALCULATED FOR 12 MIDNIGHT GREENWICH MEAN TIME. ALL OTHER DATA AND FACING ASPECTARIAN PAGE IN **EASTERN TIME (BOLD)** AND PACIFIC TIME (REGULAR).

DECEMBER 2023

☽ Last Aspect day	ET / hr:mn	PT	asp	☽ Ingress sign	day	ET / hr:mn	PT
1	**8:07 am**	5:07 am	☍♇	♌	1	**11:00 am**	8:00 am
3	**9:11 pm**	6:11 pm	⚹♀	♍	3	**10:50 pm**	7:50 pm
6	**8:50 am**	5:50 am	△♇	♎	6	**11:35 am**	8:35 am
8	**8:05 pm**	5:05 pm	□♇	♏	8	**10:35 pm**	7:35 pm
11	**3:57 am**	12:57 am	⚹♇	♐	11	**6:11 am**	3:11 am
12		10:48 pm	□♆	♑	13	**10:31 am**	7:31 am
13	**1:48 am**		□♆	♑	13	**10:31 am**	7:31 am
15	**11:04 am**	8:04 am	☌♇	♒	15	**12:56 pm**	9:56 am
17	**7:04 am**	4:04 am	⚹☉	♓	17	**2:58 pm**	11:58 am
19	**4:03 pm**	1:03 pm	⚹♇	♈	19	**5:47 pm**	2:47 pm
21	**9:47 pm**	6:47 pm	△☉	♉	21	**9:50 pm**	6:50 pm
23		10:40 pm	△♇	♊	24	**3:15 am**	12:15 am
24	**1:40 am**		△♇	♊	24	**3:15 am**	12:15 am
25		11:55 pm	☍☿	♋	26	**10:15 am**	7:15 am
26	**2:55 am**		☍☿	♋	26	**10:15 am**	7:15 am
28	**5:57 pm**	2:57 pm	☍♇	♌	28	**7:23 pm**	4:23 pm
30		9:18 pm	△♂	♍	31	**6:53 am**	3:53 am
31	**12:18 am**		△♂	♍	31	**6:53 am**	3:53 am

☽ Phases & Eclipses phase	day	ET / hr:mn	PT
4th Quarter	4		9:49 pm
4th Quarter	5	**12:49 am**	
New Moon	12	**6:32 pm**	3:32 pm
2nd Quarter	19	**1:39 pm**	10:39 am
Full Moon	26	**7:33 pm**	4:33 pm

Planet Ingress		day	ET / hr:mn	PT
☿	♑	1	**9:31 am**	6:31 am
♀	♏	4	**1:51 pm**	10:51 am
⚵	♊	20	**4:56 am**	1:56 am
☉	♑	21	**10:27 pm**	7:27 pm
☿	♐	22		10:18 pm
☿	♐	23	**1:18 am**	
♀	♐	29	**3:24 pm**	12:24 pm

Planetary Motion		day	ET / hr:mn	PT
♆	D	6	**8:20 am**	5:20 am
☿	℞	12		11:09 pm
☿	℞	13	**2:09 am**	
⚷	D	26	**10:10 pm**	7:10 pm
♃	D	30	**9:40 pm**	6:40 pm

1 FRIDAY
- ☽△♆ **1:05 am**
- ☽□♀ **3:09 am** 12:09 am
- ☽☍♇ **8:07 am** 5:07 am
- ☽⚻☿ **11:10 am** 8:10 am
- ☽⚻♄ **1:17 pm** 10:17 am
- ☽△♂ **9:48 pm** 6:48 pm
- ☽□♃ 9:44 pm

2 SATURDAY
- ☽□♃ **12:44 am**
- ☽△☉ **6:45 am** 3:45 am
- ☿⚹♄ **10:27 am** 7:27 am

3 SUNDAY
- ☽□♅ **3:13 am** 12:13 am
- ♀□♇ **8:29 am** 5:29 am
- ☽⚻♆ **12:31 pm** 9:31 am
- ♂⚻♃ **6:20 pm** 3:20 pm
- ☽⚻♇ **7:57 pm** 4:57 pm
- ☽⚹♀ **9:11 pm** 6:11 pm
- ☽☍♄ 10:26 pm

4 MONDAY
- ☽☍♄ **1:26 am**
- ☽△☿ **5:12 am** 2:12 am
- ☽△♃ **12:33 pm** 9:33 am
- ☽□♂ **1:52 pm** 10:52 am
- ☽□☉ 9:49 pm

5 TUESDAY
- ☽□☉ **12:49 am**
- ☽△♅ **3:45 pm** 12:45 pm
- ♀△♄ **5:51 pm** 2:51 pm
- ☽☍♆ 10:17 pm

6 WEDNESDAY
- ☽☍♆ **1:17 am**
- ☽△♇ **8:50 am** 5:50 am
- ☽⚻♄ **2:26 pm** 11:26 am
- ☽⚺♀ **4:34 pm** 1:34 pm
- ☽□☿ **11:00 pm** 8:00 pm
- ☽⚻♃ 9:42 pm

7 THURSDAY
- ☽⚻♃ **12:42 am**
- ☽⚹♂ **6:16 am** 3:16 am
- ☽⚹☉ **6:37 pm** 3:37 pm
- ☿△♃ **11:09 pm** 8:09 pm

8 FRIDAY
- ☽⚻♅ **3:24 am** 12:24 am
- ☽⚻♆ **12:45 pm** 9:45 am
- ☽□♇ **8:05 pm** 5:05 pm
- ☽△♄ 10:33 pm

9 SATURDAY
- ☽△♄ **1:33 am**
- ☽☌♀ **9:24 am** 6:24 am
- ☽☍♃ **10:41 am** 7:41 am
- ☽⚹☿ **12:46 pm** 9:46 am
- ☽⚺♂ **7:46 pm** 4:46 pm
- ♀☍♃ **10:35 pm** 7:35 pm

10 SUNDAY
- ☽⚺☉ **8:48 am** 5:48 am
- ☽☍♅ **12:03 pm** 9:03 am
- ☽△♆ **8:58 pm** 5:58 pm

11 MONDAY
- ☽⚹♇ **3:57 am** 12:57 am
- ☽□♄ **9:13 am** 6:13 am
- ☿⚹♀ **2:17 pm** 11:17 am
- ☽⚻♃ **5:15 pm** 2:15 pm
- ☽⚺☿ **9:03 pm** 6:03 pm
- ☽⚺♀ **9:35 pm** 6:35 pm
- ☉⚻♅ 10:21 pm

12 TUESDAY
- ☉⚻♅ **1:21 am**
- ☽☌♂ **5:05 am** 2:05 am
- ☽⚻♅ **5:14 pm** 2:14 pm
- ☽☌☉ **6:32 pm** 3:32 pm
- ☽□♆ 10:48 pm

13 WEDNESDAY
- ☽□♆ **1:48 am**
- ☽⚺♇ **8:31 am** 5:31 am
- ☽⚹♄ **1:39 pm** 10:39 am
- ☽△♃ **8:51 pm** 5:51 pm
- ☽☌☿ 9:47 pm

14 THURSDAY
- ☽☌☿ **12:47 am**
- ☽⚹♀ **5:55 am** 2:55 am
- ☽⚺♂ **11:09 am** 8:09 am
- ☽△♅ **8:00 pm** 5:00 pm
- ☽⚺☉ 10:15 pm

15 FRIDAY
- ☽⚺☉ **1:15 am**
- ☽⚹♆ **4:27 am** 1:27 am
- ☽☌♇ **11:04 am** 8:04 am
- ☽⚺♄ **4:13 pm** 1:13 pm
- ☽□♃ **10:52 pm** 7:52 pm
- ☽⚺☿ 10:42 pm

16 SATURDAY
- ☽⚺☿ **1:42 am**
- ☽□♀ **12:33 pm** 9:33 am
- ☽⚹♂ **3:52 pm** 12:52 pm
- ☽□♅ **9:53 pm** 6:53 pm
- ☉□♆ **10:43 pm** 7:43 pm

17 SUNDAY
- ☽⚺♆ **6:28 am** 3:28 am
- ☽⚹☉ **7:04 am** 4:04 am
- ☽⚺♇ **1:11 pm** 10:11 am
- ☽☌♄ **6:32 pm** 3:32 pm
- ☽⚹♃ 9:49 pm
- ☽⚹☿ 10:21 pm

18 MONDAY
- ☽⚹♃ **12:49 am**
- ☽⚹☿ **1:21 am**
- ☿△♃ **9:28 am** 6:28 am
- ☽△♀ **7:30 pm** 4:30 pm
- ☽□♂ **8:58 pm** 5:58 pm
- ☽⚹♅ 9:14 pm

19 TUESDAY
- ☽⚹♅ **12:14 am**
- ☽☌♆ **9:07 am** 6:07 am
- ☽□☉ **1:39 pm** 10:39 am
- ☽⚹♇ **4:03 pm** 1:03 pm
- ☽⚺♄ **9:41 pm** 6:41 pm
- ☽□☿ 9:42 pm

20 WEDNESDAY
- ☽□☿ **12:42 am**
- ☽⚺♃ **3:42 am** 12:42 am
- ♀⚺♂ **1:38 pm** 10:38 am
- ☉⚺♇ **11:39 pm** 8:39 pm
- ♀☍♅ 11:04 pm

21 THURSDAY
- ♀☍♅ **2:04 am**
- ☽△♂ **3:23 am** 12:23 am
- ☽⚺♅ **3:44 am** 12:44 am
- ☽⚻♀ **3:54 am** 12:54 am
- ☿⚹♄ **7:33 am** 4:33 am
- ♂⚻♅ **9:44 am** 6:44 am
- ☽⚺♆ **12:59 pm** 9:59 am
- ☽□♇ **8:11 pm** 5:11 pm
- ☽△☉ **9:47 pm** 6:47 pm
- ☽△☿ 9:21 pm
- ☽⚹♄ 11:08 pm

22 FRIDAY
- ☽△☿ **12:21 am**
- ☽⚹♄ **2:08 am**
- ☽☌♃ **7:53 am** 4:53 am
- ☉☌☿ **1:54 pm** 10:54 am

23 SATURDAY
- ☽☌♅ **8:33 am** 5:33 am
- ☽⚻♂ **11:22 am** 8:22 am
- ☽☍♀ **2:04 pm** 11:04 am
- ☿⚺♇ **4:51 pm** 1:51 pm
- ☽⚹♆ **6:12 pm** 3:12 pm
- ☽⚻☿ 9:50 pm
- ☽△♇ 10:40 pm

24 SUNDAY
- ☽⚻☿ **12:50 am**
- ☽△♇ **1:40 am**
- ☽⚻☉ **7:38 am** 4:38 am
- ☽□♄ **7:58 am** 4:58 am
- ☉⚹♄ **12:28 pm** 9:28 am
- ☽⚺♃ **1:28 pm** 10:28 am

25 MONDAY
- ♀△♆ **12:15 pm** 9:15 am
- ☽⚺♅ **2:51 pm** 11:51 am
- ☽☍♂ **9:08 pm** 6:08 pm
- ☽□♆ 9:57 pm
- ☽⚻♀ 11:15 pm
- ☽☍☿ 11:55 pm

26 TUESDAY
- ☽□♆ **12:57 am**
- ☽⚻♀ **2:15 am**
- ☽☍☿ **2:55 am**
- ☿⚺♀ **6:18 am** 3:18 am
- ☽⚻♇ **8:45 am** 5:45 am
- ☽△♄ **3:30 pm** 12:30 pm
- ☽☍☉ **7:33 pm** 4:33 pm
- ☽⚹♃ **8:45 pm** 5:45 pm
- ☿□♆ 11:43 pm

27 WEDNESDAY
- ☿□♆ **2:43 am**
- ☉△♃ **10:28 am** 7:28 am
- ☿☌♂ **7:31 pm** 4:31 pm
- ☽⚹♅ **11:04 pm** 8:04 pm

28 THURSDAY
- ☽⚻☿ **7:40 am** 4:40 am
- ☽⚻♂ **9:17 am** 6:17 am
- ☽△♆ **9:45 am** 6:45 am
- ☽△♀ **5:12 pm** 2:12 pm
- ♂□♆ **5:16 pm** 2:16 pm
- ☽☍♇ **5:57 pm** 2:57 pm
- ♀⚹♇ 10:01 pm
- ☽⚻♄ 10:15 pm

29 FRIDAY
- ♀⚹♇ **1:01 am**
- ☽⚻♄ **1:15 am**
- ☽□♃ **6:18 am** 3:18 am
- ☽⚻☉ **10:19 am** 7:19 am

30 SATURDAY
- ☽□♅ **9:39 am** 6:39 am
- ☽△☿ **4:00 pm** 1:00 pm
- ☽⚻♆ **8:57 pm** 5:57 pm
- ☽△♂ 9:18 pm

31 SUNDAY
- ☽△♂ **12:18 am**
- ☽⚻♇ **5:34 am** 2:34 am
- ☽□♀ **11:23 am** 8:23 am
- ☽☍♄ **1:24 pm** 10:24 am
- ☽△♃ **6:10 pm** 3:10 pm

Eastern time in bold type
Pacific time in medium type

DECEMBER 2023

DATE	SID.TIME	SUN	MOON	NODE	MERCURY	VENUS	MARS	JUPITER	SATURN	URANUS	NEPTUNE	PLUTO	CERES	PALLAS	JUNO	VESTA	CHIRON
1 F	4 38 23	8 ✗ 30 40	21 ♏ 45 R.	23 ♈ 54 R.	29 ♏ 17	25 ≏ 34	4 ✗ 42	7 ♉ 06 R.	1 ♓ 08	20 ♉ 22 R.	24 ♓ 54 R.	28 ♑ 30	2 ✗ 28	4 ♏ 59	15 ♍ 59	4 ♋ 39 R.	15 ♈ 46 R.
2 Sa	4 42 19	9 31 28	4 ♐ 05	23 48	0 ♐ 28	26 44	5 27	7 01	1 11	20 19	24 54	28 32	2 54	5 25	15 52	4 27	15 44
3 Su	4 46 16	10 32 17	16 10	23 42	1 36	27 54	6 08	6 55	1 13	20 17	24 54	28 33	3 19	5 50	16 08	4 15	15 43
4 M	4 50 13	11 33 07	28 06	23 39	2 42	29 05	6 51	6 50	1 16	20 15	24 53	28 34	3 45	6 15	16 23	4 02	15 42
5 T	4 54 9	12 33 59	9 ♑ 57	23 38 D	3 44	0 ♏ 15	7 34	6 44	1 19	20 12	24 53	28 36	4 10	6 41	16 38	3 49	15 41
6 W	4 58 6	13 34 52	21 47	23 39	4 41	1 26	8 17	6 39	1 23	20 10	24 53	28 37	4 36	7 06	16 53	3 36	15 39
7 Th	5 2 2	14 35 46	3 ≈ 42	23 39	5 34	2 36	9 01	6 34	1 26	20 08	24 53 D	28 39	5 01	7 31	17 07	3 22	15 38
8 F	5 5 59	15 36 41	15 48	23 41 R.	6 21	3 47	9 44	6 30	1 29	20 06	24 53	28 40	5 26	7 56	17 22	3 08	15 37
9 Sa	5 9 55	16 37 38	28 08	23 41	7 02	4 58	10 27	6 25	1 33	20 04	24 53	28 42	5 52	8 21	17 36	2 54	15 36
10 Su	5 13 52	17 38 36	10 ♓ 47	23 39	7 37	6 09	11 11	6 21	1 36	20 01	24 53	28 43	6 17	8 46	17 49	2 40	15 35
11 M	5 17 48	18 39 35	23 48	23 35	8 03	7 21	11 54	6 17	1 40	19 59	24 54	28 45	6 42	9 11	18 02	2 25	15 34
12 T	5 21 45	19 40 36	7 ♈ 12	23 29	8 21	8 32	12 38	6 13	1 43	19 57	24 54	28 47	7 08	9 36	18 15	2 10	15 33
13 W	5 25 42	20 41 37	20 57	23 20	8 29 R.	9 43	13 21	6 09	1 47	19 55	24 54	28 48	7 33	10 00	18 28	1 55	15 33
14 Th	5 29 38	21 42 39	4 ♉ 59	23 10	8 27	10 55	14 05	6 05	1 51	19 53	24 54	28 50	7 58	10 25	18 40	1 40	15 32
15 F	5 33 35	22 43 42	19 15	23 00	8 14	12 07	14 49	6 02	1 55	19 51	24 55	28 51	8 24	10 50	18 52	1 25	15 31
16 Sa	5 37 31	23 44 45	3 ♊ 39	22 51	7 49	13 18	15 33	5 59	1 59	19 49	24 55	28 53	8 49	11 14	19 04	1 09	15 31
17 Su	5 41 28	24 45 49	18 03	22 44	7 13	14 30	16 16	5 56	2 03	19 47	24 55	28 55	9 14	11 39	19 15	0 54	15 30
18 M	5 45 24	25 46 53	2 ♋ 24	22 39	6 25	15 42	17 00	5 53	2 07	19 45	24 56	28 56	9 39	12 03	19 26	0 38	15 29
19 T	5 49 21	26 47 57	16 38	22 36 D	5 27	16 54	17 44	5 50	2 12	19 44	24 56	28 58	10 04	12 27	19 36	0 22	15 29
20 W	5 53 17	27 49 02	0 ♌ 43	22 36	4 19	18 06	18 28	5 48	2 16	19 42	24 56	29 00	10 29	12 51	19 46	0 07	15 29
21 Th	5 57 14	28 50 07	14 38	22 37 R.	3 04	19 18	19 12	5 45	2 21	19 40	24 57	29 02	10 54	13 15	19 56	29 ♊ 51	15 28
22 F	6 1 11	29 51 12	28 23	22 37	1 44	20 30	19 56	5 43	2 25	19 38	24 57	29 03	11 19	13 39	20 06	29 35	15 28
23 Sa	6 5 7	0 ♑ 52 18	11 ♍ 59	22 35	0 22	21 43	20 40	5 42	2 30	19 37	24 58	29 05	11 44	14 03	20 15	29 19	15 28
24 Su	6 9 4	1 53 24	25 25	22 31	28 ✗ 59	22 55	21 24	5 40	2 34	19 35	24 59	29 07	12 09	14 27	20 23	29 03	15 27
25 M	6 13 0	2 54 30	8 ≏ 42	22 24	27 40	24 08	22 08	5 39	2 39	19 33	24 59	29 09	12 34	14 51	20 32	28 47	15 27
26 T	6 16 57	3 55 36	21 42	22 14	26 27	25 20	22 52	5 38	2 44	19 32	25 00	29 10	12 59	15 14	20 40	28 32	15 27
27 W	6 20 53	4 56 43	4 ♏ 40	22 01	25 20	26 33	23 37	5 37	2 49	19 30	25 01	29 12	13 23	15 38	20 47	28 16	15 27 D
28 Th	6 24 50	5 57 50	17 21	21 48	24 23	27 45	24 21	5 36	2 54	19 29	25 01	29 14	13 48	16 01	20 54	28 00	15 27
29 F	6 28 47	6 58 57	29 48	21 35	23 36	28 58	25 05	5 35	2 59	19 27	25 02	29 16	14 13	16 25	21 01	27 45	15 27
30 Sa	6 32 43	8 00 04	12 ♏ 02	21 22	22 59	0 ✗ 11	25 50	5 35	3 04	19 26	25 03	29 18	14 37	16 48	21 08	27 30	15 27
31 Su	6 36 40	9 01 12	24 05	21 12	22 33	1 24	26 34	5 35 D	3 09	19 24	25 04	29 20	15 02	17 11	21 14	27 15	15 28

EPHEMERIS CALCULATED FOR 12 MIDNIGHT GREENWICH MEAN TIME. ALL OTHER DATA AND FACING ASPECTARIAN PAGE IN **EASTERN TIME (BOLD)** AND PACIFIC TIME (REGULAR).

Notes